Globalizing Intercultural Communication

SAGE was founded in 1965 by Sara Miller McCune to support the dissemination of usable knowledge by publishing innovative and high-quality research and teaching content. Today, we publish more than 750 journals, including those of more than 300 learned societies, more than 800 new books per year, and a growing range of library products including archives, data, case studies, reports, conference highlights, and video. SAGE remains majority-owned by our founder, and after Sara's lifetime will become owned by a charitable trust that secures our continued independence.

Los Angeles | London | Washington DC | New Delhi | Singapore | Boston

Globalizing Intercultural Communication

A Reader

Kathryn Sorrells
California State University, Northridge

Sachi Sekimoto
Minnesota State University, Mankato

Editors

Los Angeles | London | New Delhi
Singapore | Washington DC | Boston

Los Angeles | London | New Delhi
Singapore | Washington DC | Boston

FOR INFORMATION:

SAGE Publications, Inc.
2455 Teller Road
Thousand Oaks, California 91320
E-mail: order@sagepub.com

SAGE Publications Ltd.
1 Oliver's Yard
55 City Road
London EC1Y 1SP
United Kingdom

SAGE Publications India Pvt. Ltd.
B 1/I 1 Mohan Cooperative Industrial Area
Mathura Road, New Delhi 110 044
India

SAGE Publications Asia-Pacific Pte. Ltd.
3 Church Street
#10-04 Samsung Hub
Singapore 049483

Acquisitions Editor: Matthew Byrnie
Editorial Assistant: Janae Masnovi
Production Editor: Laura Barrett
Copy Editor: Megan Granger
Typesetter: C&M Digitals (P) Ltd.
Proofreader: Sue Irwin
Indexer: Naomi Linzer
Cover Designer: Leonardo March
Marketing Manager: Liz Thornton

Copyright © 2016 by SAGE Publications, Inc.

Printed in the United States of America

Cataloging-in-publication data is available for this title from the Library of Congress.

ISBN 978-1-4522-9933-4

This book is printed on acid-free paper.

SFI Certified Sourcing
www.sfiprogram.org
SFI-00453

15 16 17 18 19 10 9 8 7 6 5 4 3 2 1

Brief Contents

Detailed Contents

7 Cultural Space and Intercultural Communication 122

8 Intercultural Relationships 143

9 Intercultural Communication in the Workplace 167

10 Border Crossing and Intercultural Adaptation   187

11 Popular Culture, Media, and Globalization   206

Acknowledgments

We would like to thank each of the authors who contributed to this volume. Without their innovative and critical work, we would not have this book. Their unique voices, positionalities, and histories come together to create a richly textured compilation that transverses and connects continents, cultures, topics, and research approaches. We are grateful to them for their courage, vision, and determination in tackling complex and challenging personal and theoretical issues that impact us all in our increasingly mobile, fragmented, contested, and transforming world.

We would also like to extend our gratitude to Jack (John) Condon for the direction, inspiration, and support he has provided both of us. While a generation separates us, the coeditors of this book, Jack's mentorship and friendship have had a tremendous influence on the ways we both approach the study of intercultural communication and the practice of life.

Sachi would like to thank her coeditor, Kathryn, for her guidance, trust, and spirited dialogue. This project originated in Kathryn's vision to reinvigorate intercultural communication as a transformative and empowering experience. Sachi is grateful to be a collaborative partner of this edited volume and truly enjoyed working with Kathryn. She would also like to thank her colleagues in the Department of Communication Studies at Minnesota State University, Mankato, for their invaluable support and the research grant to complete this project. She is also thankful for Gregory Husak, who provided instructional support during the course of her editorial work; Kathy Steiner, who graciously handled multiple sets of paperwork; and her students, who compelled her to cultivate more relevant ways of teaching intercultural communication. She also wants to thank her family and friends, near and far, for their continuous support and inspiration.

Kathryn is deeply grateful to Sachi for her theoretical acumen, her keen editorial skills, and her willingness to take on this project. As an undergraduate and MA student, throughout her PhD program, and now in her position as an assistant professor, Kathryn has admired Sachi's sharp mind, her facility with language, and her commitment to stay true to her embodied, lived experiences. To varying degrees, these and her other fine qualities of hard work and good humor were called on during this project. Kathryn extends her appreciation to her students for sharing their questions, their lives, and their work, which continue to inform and inspire her. She would also like to thank her friends and her families—straight and queer—for their ongoing support of her academic, personal, and spiritual work in the world.

A book such as this cannot be created without the incredible support and dedication of the editorial team. We want to thank Matthew Byrnie, our editor at SAGE, for believing in this project from the beginning; Gabrielle Piccininni and Janae Masnovi for their editorial assistance and careful attention to detail; Laura Barrett, our production editor, who brought the project to fruition; Liz Thornton and her team for their marketing expertise; and Meg Granger for her expert copyediting skills and attention to details.

Introduction

Kathryn Sorrells
Sachi Sekimoto

Over the past several decades, *globalization* has become a buzzword in common vernacular and a keyword studied, theorized, and debated in academia. Broadly speaking, globalization describes the conditions of a globally networked society deeply penetrated by the expansion of global capitalism, information technologies, and cultural interconnection. As a conceptual framework, globalization makes visible an ongoing transformation and restructuring of social relations on a global scale, characterized by "the widening, deepening and speeding up of worldwide interconnectedness in all aspects of contemporary social life, from the cultural to the criminal, the financial to the spiritual" (Held, McGrew, Goldblatt, & Perraton, 1999, p. 2). While the term *globalization* became prominent in the 1990s, the escalation and intensification of societal integration on a global scale is deeply rooted in the preceding history of capitalism, colonialism, and the development of nation-states (Winant, 2001). Thus, globalization is understood as an intensifying process that reconfigures—but does not eradicate—historically constructed structures of the world. *Structures* here refers to financial, governmental, legal, and media institutions, among others that serve to organize material and symbolic conditions and relationships of power. This reconfiguration of world structures unevenly impacts individuals, groups, and nations; yet each one of us, whether he or she chooses to be or not, is implicated in this process.

The term *globalization* cannot be used unproblematically or uncritically. Any particular view of globalization comes with implicit assumptions that shape a *version* of the world we narrate, endorse, or imagine. Appadurai (1996) focused on the social practices of imagination as a fundamental force of globalization that shapes and is shaped by the intersecting spheres (or scapes) of global connectivity. Globalization, in this case, is not a finished project dictating the course of history; rather, individuals and groups actively imagine, enact, and feed into a particular view of the world from their situated perspectives and experiences. Rather than viewing globalization as something that is happening to us or as an external force beyond our reach, then, it is important to examine globalization as deeply embedded—albeit differently and unevenly for various subjects—in our identities, lifestyles, values, and imaginations of "the world." In this sense, the world is being "globalized" not merely by the powerful transnational corporations and global political institutions but also through our everyday practices of imagining, upholding, resisting, and living in the world as such. Thus, globalization is a contested, uneven, and politicized process of arranging the world economically, geopolitically, and culturally.

From this perspective, globalization is an ideological, political, and cultural project we engage in individually and collectively, shaping the very possibilities of the world we should or could live in.

Beyond explanations and debates provided by political scientists, economists, and sociologists, the field of intercultural communication offers a unique set of practical and epistemological insights into what it means to live in a globalizing world. Rather than viewing globalization as an external and autonomous historical force beyond the reach of individuals, we approach the study and practice of intercultural communication as *an engaged praxis* of exploring, creating, and transforming our increasingly interconnected worlds. A significant shift in our perspective is needed in this process. Not only is intercultural communication happening *in the context of* globalization, but it is *an integral force* of globalization, a significant medium or space for making and remaking our worlds. Thus, we view communicative acts as an integral process of globalization, engaged and enacted by people at micro, meso, and macro levels within existing political, economic, and cultural structures.

In *Globalizing Intercultural Communication: A Reader*, we recenter intercultural communication as a process through which individuals and groups develop, critique, and enact globalized consciousness. To understand how and why our lives are inextricably connected, it is imperative to reimagine and reconceptualize "the world" we have internalized through education, media, and social interaction. At school and through media representations, many of us are taught to see the world based on names that designate boundaries of regions, nation-states, and city limits; we are taught to see "foreign" countries as locations away from home with exotic cultures and unfamiliar people; we are taught there is a divide between the West and the East, the Global North and the Global South. These real and imagined narratives of the global landscape are rapidly shifting in our current era, requiring us to develop alternative, resistive, and counterhegemonic perspectives to understand the complexity of the world at large.

In this context, intercultural communication becomes a site where we reimagine and reconceptualize the world by bringing knowledges from around the world into tension and dialogue, illuminating the linkages between the local and global, and problematizing historical and contemporary relations of power. Furthermore, intercultural communication becomes a process through which we critically examine and reflect on our status, privileges, and access to resources (or the lack thereof) within the interrelated global matrices of power, inequity, and injustice. Thus, intercultural communication becomes an area where we can exercise greater responsibility and agency toward a more socially just world, with respect to diversity, democracy, and equitable sharing and nurturing of political, economic, and cultural resources.

GLOBALIZING INTERCULTURAL COMMUNICATION: HIGHLIGHTED THEMES

The selections in this reader offer in-depth analyses and explorations of the multifaceted and nuanced themes related to intercultural communication in local and global contexts.

The case studies comprise primary, grounded, historically specific research studies addressing a range of issues from various contexts, whereas the personal narratives illuminate contextualized experiences and situated voices of living and communicating in a globalized world. In addition to illuminating concepts, theories, and issues, the chapters focus particular attention on grounding theory in everyday experience, translating theory into practice, and providing insights into personal and collective actions for social responsibility and justice. The case studies and personal narratives exemplify a range of theoretical and methodological approaches to the study of intercultural communication, with an emphasis on critical and postcolonial perspectives. More specifically, the following themes emerge through a close reading, threading among the chapters in the book: (1) the importance of historicization, (2) multidimensional analysis, (3) affective and embodied awareness, and (4) intercultural praxis and social justice. While these themes are evident throughout the book, we highlight a few examples here as an illustration.

Historicization

To historicize means to carefully analyze the processes and mechanisms of how certain social conditions and realities have come to be what they are. Exploring intercultural communication as a process that shapes and is shaped by globalization necessitates critical awareness of the kind of world we inherited from the past. The act of imagining the world remains a mere fantasy unless it is grounded in the awareness and knowledge of how social realities are historically constituted and lived in both local and global contexts.

In her personal narrative, for example, Nilanjana R. Bardhan (Chapter 3) illustrates how her postcolonial and diasporic identity is deeply rooted in the history of British colonialism in India and subsequent histories of independence and partition that dislocated her family from their cultural roots. Similarly, Eddah M. Mutua (Chapter 5), whose life journey has taken her from her home in Kenya to the United Kingdom and then to the United States, situates her evolving knowledge and intersecting identities in postcolonial histories to understand intercultural relations and intergroup dynamics today.

Focusing on issues of language, Melissa L. Curtin (Chapter 6) seeks insights into the cultural politics of language by historicizing relations and tensions among various cultural groups in the United States and Taiwan. The engaged praxis of intercultural communication entails the process of radical historicization of the relations of power and cultural formations. History is never static but always infused with hegemonic remembering and reproducing of the dominant memories. Not only should we be informed about history, but we must also be attentive to what we choose to remember (or forget) as history, and how we narrate and appropriate historical narratives in the present.

Multidimensional Analysis

To obtain a firm grasp of the impact of globalization, we must approach issues from multiple levels of analysis and understanding. We must be attentive to the ways of knowing shaped by our particular standpoints, identities, and positionalities, because our understanding of the world is always shaped by the frames through which we view it. Shome and Hegde (2002) wrote: "To globalize the study of communication is to continually produce a resistant body of knowledge about the vectors that connect and disconnect culture, space, and inevitably power" (p. 188).

In this sense, engaged intercultural communication praxis questions and resists hegemonic knowledge and foregrounds alternative ways of knowing. Faced with greater complexity and connectivity of the world, we are asked to rethink and reconceptualize the interconnectedness of our lives beyond our immediate spatial and temporal context. No matter where we live, the livelihood of local communities is impacted by globalization in one way or another. Events and conditions occurring in the world beyond our immediate sphere are tied to local experiences—however tenuous and tangled the connections may be.

For example, Yea-Wen Chen and Chie Torigoe (Chapter 8) illuminate the dynamics of interracial relationships using a micro-, meso-, and macrolevel analysis, exploring how personal identities, intergroup prejudice, and racial ideologies simultaneously shape the experiences of interracial couples. Gust A. Yep (Chapter 5) contributes to a multidimensional understanding of identities using "thick intersectionalities" as a conceptual framework beyond the mantra of race/class/gender, whereas Rubén Ramírez-Sánchez (Chapter 12) illuminates the connectivity between the local punk movement in Puerto Rico and the global network of informational capitalism.

We can no longer maintain a myopic view in addressing social issues; we must cultivate our analytical skills and interrogative mind-set to examine the interconnectedness between what is happening "here" and what is unfolding "there"—and vice versa—across and beyond physical and temporal distances.

Embodied and Affective Awareness

To effectively navigate a world that is increasingly complex and interconnected, we must focus not only on what globalization *is* but also on what globalization *does* to us. It is crucial to be aware, mindful, and self-reflexive of the impact and consequences of globalization in the way we live, feel, and relate to others. One of the recurring features of globalization is that it "amounts at its most elementary level to a transformation in the nature of our own and other people's experience of space and time" (Jones, 2010, p. 5). Claiming that globalization is a consequence of modernity, Giddens (1990) used the term *time-space distanciation* to describe emergent social conditions in which the geographical and temporal specificity of social experience (here and now) is stretched beyond or uplifted from immediate time and space. Inherent in such *intensification* of our experiences with time, space, and physical/virtual mobility is a sense of excitement and empowerment, as well as uncertainty, anxiety, and disorientation (Sekimoto, 2014). Globalization also deeply impacts our identities and sense of cultural belonging through the commodification of culture and neoliberal marketization of the individual. Thus, while theories of globalization are often armed with abstract language, the process of globalization—and its explication—is experientially grounded in deeply salient conditions of being-in-the-modern-world.

S. Lily Mendoza's case study (Chapter 3), for instance, reflects the emergent affective turn in cultural and social theorizing, where she focuses on the emotive and affective practice of falling in love with her indigenous culture and grieving its destruction as first steps to recovering our humanity, the natural world, and environmental and cultural balance. Zornitsa D. Keremidchieva (Chapter 10) also focuses on embodied experiences of migrancy as a distinct form of selfhood and subjectivity, whereas Carlo Ammatuna and Hsin-I Cheng (Chapter 9) explore how *maquiladora* workers in Mexico align their ambitions, values, and orientations toward the future within neoliberal work environments of transnational corporations. Attention to such embodied and affective dimensions of globalization is critical for developing globalized consciousness and engaged intercultural communication praxis.

Intercultural Praxis and Social Justice

Globalization provokes both tension and opportunities for critical reflection and action. Around the world, we see greater divisions, violence, and inequities while also experiencing greater proximity and possibilities of intercultural understanding and cooperation. In the context of global mobility (virtual or physical) and cultural hybridization, intercultural communication provides opportunities to engage in the process of becoming emergent, shifting, global subjects. Throughout this reader, we use the model of *intercultural praxis* (Sorrells, 2013; Sorrells & Nakagawa, 2008) as a process of critical, reflective thinking and acting (see Chapter 1). Intercultural praxis is not a predetermined set of rules or skills; rather, it offers "ports of entry" to engage intercultural communication as a transformative experience. Intercultural encounters prompt us to elucidate and problematize our lived realities and everyday practices as interconnected and interrelated with other places, worlds, people, and their imaginations.

For example, Mary Jane Collier and Karambu Ringera's personal narrative (Chapter 8) and Sara DeTurk's case study (Chapter 14) exemplify the challenges and possibilities of building intercultural alliances as sites of intervention to create a more socially equitable world. Antonieta Mercado's case study (Chapter 13) also demonstrates community-based activism to empower and educate indigenous migrants, despite the historically ingrained oppression and marginalization of indigenous peoples.

Intercultural communication is fertile ground for developing interconnected awareness and interrelated consciousness to build social relations grounded in equity and social justice. To develop interconnected consciousness—a globalized consciousness—means to constantly map out the shifting, intersecting, and competing infrastructures of connectivity and disconnectivity across global and local contexts. It is the awareness that we are all, individually and collectively, implicated in the global competition of power and influence, and we all, differently and unevenly, have the capacity to transform the world.

OVERVIEW OF CHAPTERS

Each of the 14 chapters in this reader offers both a case study and a personal narrative. We provide an abbreviated overview of the chapters here and introduce each essay individually in the chapter introductions.

Chapters 1, 2, and 3 establish the foundational concepts, issues, and contexts for studying and practicing intercultural communication. In Chapter 1, the authors use the model of intercultural praxis as a critical, metatheoretical framework of analysis and action. Kathryn Sorrells and Sachi Sekimoto historicize the field of intercultural communication and lay out the future trajectories, while Gordon Nakagawa develops an artful and self-reflective narrative on performance of racial identity. Chapter 2 examines barriers to intercultural communication, comprising a case study by Mark P. Orbe on diverse standpoints/cultural locations in a postracial society and a personal narrative by Bryant Keith Alexander on the challenges of navigating cultural, racial, and institutional dynamics. Chapter 3 centralizes the significance of history and power in studying intercultural communication. A case study by Mendoza revisits the history of colonialism and imperialism from an affective and indigenous perspective, and Bardhan provides a personal account of living in a postcolonial world as a woman from India.

Chapters 4 and 5 examine the shifting politics of identity in various contexts. In Chapter 4, Gerardo Villalobos-Romo and Sekimoto explore the impact of communication technologies, media, and migrancy on cultural practices and identities of Mexican families, while Shinsuke Eguchi shares an autoethnographic account of his embodied negotiation of gay Asian identity. In Chapter 5, the authors focus on the notions of intersectionality and positionality to politicize our knowledge and ways of knowing. Yep conceptualizes "thick intersectionalities" to complicate our ways of understanding identity, and Mutua provides a personal narrative on moving through various cultural spaces with more affectively oriented, embodied ways of knowing.

Chapters 6 and 7 focus on the shifting communicative practices of power in everyday contexts, from language (Chapter 6) to cultural space (Chapter 7). In Chapter 6, Curtin offers a historical analysis of power struggles embedded in linguistic practices, while Christopher Brown provides a compelling personal account of race, racism, and linguistic performance. In Chapter 7, Joshua F. Hoops provides an ethnographic study on the intersection of cultural space and race in a farm community, and Richie Neil Hao describes and analyzes performance of whiteness in the classroom.

Chapters 8 and 9 focus on the dynamics of relational communication in interpersonal and workplace contexts. In Chapter 8, Chen and Torigoe provide a multidimensional analysis of interracial relationships, and Collier and Ringera share their dialogue on intercultural alliance. In Chapter 9, Ammatuna and Cheng's case study illuminates the shifting meaning of work among *maquiladora* workers, and Donna M. Stringer and Andy Reynolds share an analysis of workplace conflicts in multicultural work environments.

Chapters 10, 11, and 12 foreground mobility as a salient characteristic of globalization, addressing issues of cultural adaptation (Chapter 10), globalization of popular culture (Chapter 11), and new media (Chapter 12). In Chapter 10, Keremidchieva focuses on migrancy as a distinct condition of identity and subjectivity, and Sachiko Tankei-Aminian traces her lifelong process of cultural adaptation as a sojourner and immigrant from Japan to the United States. In Chapter 11, Sheena Malhotra's longitudinal study from the early 1990s to the late 2000s shows the neoliberal influence of Western media on the imaginaries of youth in India, while Chigozirim Ifedapo Utah's personal narrative illustrates "migrant moments" of living in and between transnational and hybrid cultures as a woman from Nigeria. Chapter 12 introduces salient issues related to new media, including Nickesia S. Gordon's analysis of the global representation and consumption of Jamaican popular culture in social media and Ramírez-Sánchez's reflection on the paradox of resistive counterculture in the Puerto Rican punk scene in the context of global social media.

The remaining chapters address specific examples of intercultural conflicts that emerge as an outcome of historically rooted injustice and inequity (Chapter 13), and explore the ways various individuals and groups work toward a more socially just and equitable world (Chapter 14). In Chapter 13, Mercado shares her analysis of indigenous activism in Southern California, and Taj Suleyman shares his personal account of navigating intercultural conflicts as a man of Middle Eastern descent. Finally, in Chapter 14, DeTurk offers an analysis of strategies and practices of a multi-issue social change organization, and Amer F. Ahmed narrates his personal journey of negotiating the complexities of his multifaceted identities through hip-hop activism.

In *Globalizing Intercultural Communication: A Reader*, we invite you to join us in recentering intercultural communication as a process through which individuals and groups develop, critique, and enact globalized consciousness. The case studies and personal narratives in this book are a primer for understanding how intercultural communication is *an integral force* of globalization—a vibrant, contested, and transformative space for imagining, making, and remaking our worlds. With the unique theoretical perspectives, practical approaches, and epistemological insights offered by the field of intercultural communication, we are able to explore, create, and transform our increasingly interconnected worlds. Thus, intercultural communication becomes a site where we bring knowledges from various locations and positionalities into dialogue, highlight linkages between the local and global, problematize historical and contemporary relations of power, and exercise responsibility and agency to imagine and create a more socially just world.

CHAPTER 1

Studying and Practicing Intercultural Communication

The study and practice of intercultural communication in the context of globalization is complex, contested, and often contradictory. Thus, as students and practitioners of intercultural communication, it is important to develop conceptual models, practical skills, and effective strategies to grapple with and make sense of the multifaceted challenges and opportunities that confront us in the global age.

Understanding how cultures differ from each other in terms of values, norms, histories, and worldviews is central to the study of intercultural communication. Equally critical is an awareness of how cultural differences coexist, collide, and are contested within relationships of power. Culture, cultural differences, and the field of intercultural communication, itself, are understood and constructed within contexts of power—historical, political, economic, and social relations of power—that tend to normalize certain perspectives, histories, values, and norms, and devalue as "strange" and "other" those beliefs, practices, knowledges, and points of view that veer from or challenge dominant views.

Guided by the intercultural praxis model, the entries in this chapter illustrate the central roles power and history play in our understanding of culture, cultural differences, and the construction of knowledge. The case study by Kathryn Sorrells and Sachi Sekimoto offers a critical perspective on the history and future trajectories of the intercultural communication field, highlighting moments of contestation and rupture that challenge dominant paradigms and create alternative approaches. Gordon Nakagawa's poetic personal narrative illustrates how his experience of negotiating racial and cultural identities—the ways he has been targeted by and complicit with stereotypical representations—has led to a sense of agency and responsibility to engage everyday events and interactions as opportunities for social justice. Both entries offer insight into critical forms of analysis, reflection, and action that can create a more socially just and humane world.

Globalizing Intercultural Communication: Traces and Trajectories

Kathryn Sorrells

California State University, Northridge

Sachi Sekimoto

Minnesota State University, Mankato

People from different cultures have come in contact and communicated with one another for many millennia. The Silk Road, for example, was a cultural exchange and trade route that covered more than 4,000 miles from China to Europe and extended westward during the Han Dynasty (206 BCE–220 CE) for military and administrative purposes. Aiding political, economic, and cultural interchange, the Silk Road played a central role in the development of European, Chinese, Persian, Arabian, and Indian civilizations (Elisseeff, 2000). In another instance, from the 9th century to the 12th century, ancestors of the Pueblo and Hopi people inhabited Chaco Canyon in northwest New Mexico—a ceremonial, economic, and cultural center for indigenous peoples from distant regions who gathered periodically in the canyon. In its time, Chaco Canyon was an intercultural university and cross-cultural marketplace where ideas, technologies, beliefs, and practices were shared and exchanged (Frazier, 2005).

During the colonial period from the 16th to 20th century, intercultural exchange occurred on a worldwide scale. Sea and land routes brought people, goods, ideas, and beliefs into contact with one another in unprecedented ways. As with the Silk Road and Chaco Canyon, the exchange was not always positive. Much of the intercultural encounter during the colonial period was framed by conquest, religious decree (the Papal Bull issued in 1493), and imperial power justifying the subjugation of people, destruction of cultures, and extraction of wealth from much of the world. The contours of our current era of globalization are shaped by the worldviews and relationships of power forged during the European colonial period.

Today, we inhabit worlds that are far more complex, interconnected, and paradoxical than ever before. Thousands of Silk Roads, both real and virtual, wrap the globe; yet cultural, ethnic, racial, religious, national, and class differences segregate and isolate us. Myriad centers of intercultural exchange like Chaco Canyon bring people into proximity with one another in physical and cyberspace more rapidly and frequently than ever before; yet we tend, often, to gravitate toward what is similar, known, and familiar, minimizing or excluding those who are different. Through scientific and technological advances, we have the capacity to feed all the people of the world; yet 1 in 8 people (870 million of the 7.1 billion world population in 2012) suffer from chronic undernourishment (Food and Agriculture Organization of the United Nations, 2012). Food deserts, where nutritious food is beyond the reach or budget of average consumers, disproportionately affect low-income people and communities of color in the United States (Winn, 2008).

Communication among diverse groups—intercultural communication—has been occurring, as the examples above suggest, for many millennia. Motivated by commerce, conquest, conversion, and community, intercultural interaction can produce innovation and growth as well as exploitation and destruction. The challenges and possibilities of the complicated, increasingly interconnected and inequitable world we live in call out for intercultural communication and exchange. Any one cultural group's knowledge is partial. We need the varied approaches, alternative perspectives, and unique wisdom that all cultural groups bring—because of their differences, not in spite of them. Understanding the dynamics of intercultural communication is critical for the survival and actualization of humanity in the 21st century.

In this essay, we use the model of **intercultural praxis** (Sorrells, 2013; Sorrells & Nakagawa, 2008) to critically reflect on significant historical moments in the development of the intercultural communication field. The intercultural praxis model is used to guide our metatheoretical analysis, which reveals the politics of knowledge inherent in the production of disciplinary narratives and explicates our approach to globalizing intercultural communication. As we reflect on the history of the field, we also describe three major paradigms that characterize scholarship in intercultural communication, as well as point to recent scholarly trends. We conclude the essay by sketching out future trajectories impacting students, teachers, and practitioners of intercultural communication.

HISTORICIZING THE FIELD THROUGH INTERCULTURAL PRAXIS

As the title of this reader indicates, we—the editors and contributors of the book—are committed to "globalizing" the way we engage in intercultural communication in everyday practice and as a scholarly pursuit (Sorrells, 2010). The phrase "globalizing intercultural communication" is used here to draw attention to the opportunities and challenges of intercultural communication in an increasingly complex, interconnected, contested, and inequitable world shaped by advanced technologies, global capitalism, and neoliberal policies. Rather than normalizing hegemonic assumptions of neoliberal globalization, "globalizing intercultural communication" means we examine intercultural communication within the context of historical and contemporary relations of power, highlight linkages between the local and global, and uplift critical **social justice** approaches. To move forward toward the future, however, we must first reflect on how we, as an academic field, have come to be where we are today.

In this section, we use the model of intercultural praxis to examine key historical developments in the field of intercultural communication. The intercultural praxis model provides an analytical framework and epistemological lens that both illuminates and complicates our ways of thinking about the historical development of the academic field. The purpose is not to provide *the* overarching history of the field but to use the intercultural praxis model to reflect on the politics of knowledge inherent in the formation of an academic field. Thus, our goal is to demonstrate a process of engaging in critical praxis for global consciousness as we trace and reflect on the historical development and theoretical foundations of the field.

What Is Intercultural Praxis?

Consisting of six dimensions (**inquiry, framing, positioning, dialogue, reflection, and action**), intercultural praxis encourages us to approach intercultural communication not as an "object" of study but, rather, as a way of being, thinking, and acting (Sorrells, 2013; Sorrells & Nakagawa, 2008). Intercultural praxis entails (a) being willing to ask questions and suspend judgment (inquiry); (b) clarifying cultural frames of reference and shifting frames from micro to meso to macro levels (framing); (c) examining who/where you are in relation to others in terms of power relations (positioning); (d) engaging in open exchange of ideas (dialogue); (e) looking back and accessing your thoughts and action (reflection); and (f) taking informed and ethical actions toward a more just and equitable society. (See Figure 1.1.)

Engaging in intercultural praxis means we open ourselves to the possibility of becoming more conscious, aware, and socially responsible individuals. It also means we develop self-reflexivity and **agency** within unequal relations of power that shape intercultural interactions. It can be both exciting and frightening to think that every intercultural encounter is a moment of learning, growth, and transformation. As the world is becoming more complex and diverse, a predetermined set of skills or techniques does not guarantee effective and ethical communication. Using intercultural praxis cultivates our analytical and observational skills, develops ethical and affective orientations, and encourages responsible action as we relate with one another across cultural differences.

A central intention of the intercultural praxis model is to understand and address the intersection of cultural differences and hierarchies of power in intercultural interactions and scholarly pursuits. When people from diverse backgrounds come together, differences are there. Cultural, ethnic, and racial differences that manifest in language, dress, behaviors, attitudes, values, histories, and worldviews are real. Yet the challenge in intercultural communication is not only about differences; racial, ethnic, cultural, gender, and national differences are always and inevitably situated within relations of power. Our exploration of the confluence of cultural differences with power differences is facilitated by keeping the following questions in mind:

1. Who/what is considered different and why?

2. What/who is considered the norm?

3. Who/what is diminished or dehumanized when dominant cultural perspectives and practices are normalized?

4. What institutions, rhetoric, and discourses are used to normalize, justify, and perpetuate hierarchies of difference? Who benefits?

5. How am I personally—and the cultural groups to which I belong—advantaged/disadvantaged by maintaining hierarchies of cultural difference (race, gender, etc.)?

6. How can our individual and collective cultural resources be used to envision and enact alternative paradigms that elevate and uplift the human community?

Framing the Past

In intercultural praxis, framing is a process by which you zoom in and out through your analytical lens to evaluate a situation from micro, meso, and macro perspectives. In using intercultural praxis to review the history of the field, it is important to note that any act of remembering is always partial and incomplete (including this essay). Moreover, the frame

Figure 1.1 Intercultural Praxis Model

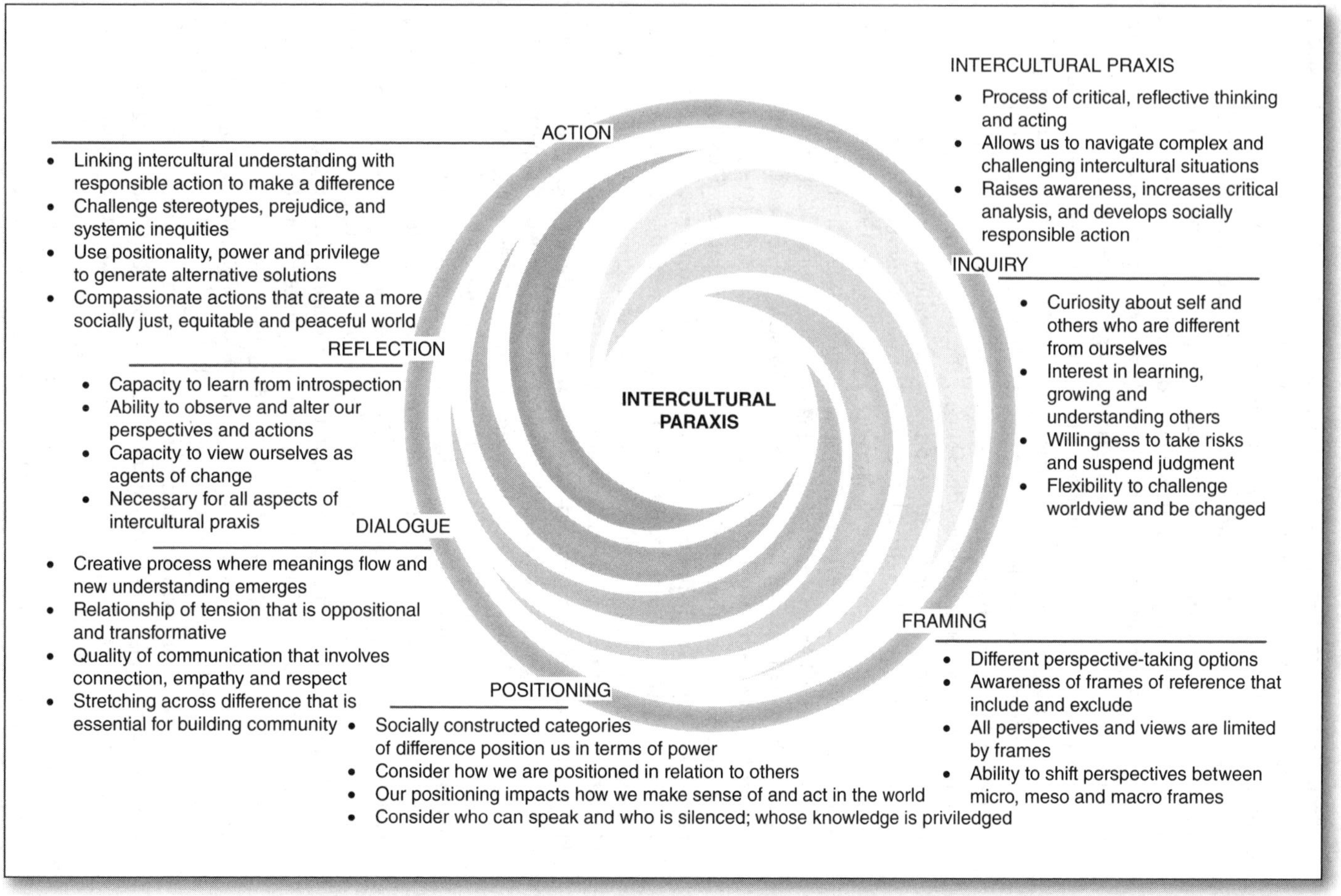

INTERCULTURAL PRAXIS
- Process of critical, reflective thinking and acting
- Allows us to navigate complex and challenging intercultural situations
- Raises awareness, increases critical analysis, and develops socially responsible action

INQUIRY
- Curiosity about self and others who are different from ourselves
- Interest in learning, growing and understanding others
- Willingness to take risks and suspend judgment
- Flexibility to challenge worldview and be changed

FRAMING
- Different perspective-taking options
- Awareness of frames of reference that include and exclude
- All perspectives and views are limited by frames
- Ability to shift perspectives between micro, meso and macro frames

POSITIONING
- Socially constructed categories of difference position us in terms of power
- Consider how we are positioned in relation to others
- Our positioning impacts how we make sense of and act in the world
- Consider who can speak and who is silenced; whose knowledge is priviledged

DIALOGUE
- Creative process where meanings flow and new understanding emerges
- Relationship of tension that is oppositional and transformative
- Quality of communication that involves connection, empathy and respect
- Stretching across difference that is essential for building community

REFLECTION
- Capacity to learn from introspection
- Ability to observe and alter our perspectives and actions
- Capacity to view ourselves as agents of change
- Necessary for all aspects of intercultural praxis

ACTION
- Linking intercultural understanding with responsible action to make a difference
- Challenge stereotypes, prejudice, and systemic inequities
- Use positionality, power and privilege to generate alternative solutions
- Compassionate actions that create a more socially just, equitable and peaceful world

INTERCULTURAL PARAXIS

5

of reference we use can radically change the nature of "history" that we accept as true. For example, if you were to write a book on your country's history, what would you include? Would you write about the major wars and histories of conquest from the victor's point of view? Would you focus on famous historical figures and powerful political leaders? Or would you focus on the lives of ordinary people who, collectively, shaped the history of your country? Shifting from a macrolevel to a microlevel framework, you see how different narratives and perspectives emerge. Thus, historicizing the field of intercultural communication requires being mindful of the frame of reference we use to define what constitutes *the* history of the field. Consider our discussion here of key moments in the development of the field as a mindful exercise in perspective taking and critical analysis to generate possibilities for greater understanding, rather than an effort to provide an exhaustive or definitive history of the field.

Like many other academic disciplines, the field of intercultural communication has undergone its own historical development and change. Various scholars have narrated and debated versions of disciplinary histories through which a commonly shared view of the field has been established (Leeds-Hurwitz, 1990; Rogers, 1999; Rogers, Hart, & Miike, 2002), as well as more recent ferment (Starosta & Chen, 2003) and historical junctures leading to critical approaches (Halualani, Mendoza, & Drzewiecka, 2009; Nakayama & Halualani, 2010). The origin of the field traces back to several key anthropologists—most notably Edward T. Hall, who worked for the Foreign Service Institute in the 1950s training U.S. diplomats to communicate effectively in foreign countries. This "genesis" of the field is significant because the political context and motivation were shaped by growing U.S. hegemony after World War II and during the Cold War. In the newly "emancipated" postwar period, it became increasingly important to use culture—instead of weapons and violence—as a medium of communication to foster international relations and spread U.S. influence. The development of intercultural communication as a field coincided with—and was necessitated by—the rise of the United States as the world superpower. Contextualizing the origin reveals how the development of the field was deeply intertwined with the cultural, social, economic, and political environment in the United States at that time. The turn to culture as a diplomatic strategy did not stop U.S. military interventions around the world (Blum, 2008; Johnson, 2010). It is perhaps more accurate to say, from a geopolitical perspective, that the emphasis on cultural diplomacy strategically appeased the political and economic tensions that accompanied the rise of the United States as the world leader.

Let's take a moment to zoom out of this U.S.-centric frame on the history of the field. It can be argued that the late awakening in the United States to the significance of global cultures points to its privileged positionality in the world as the emergent superpower. Pervasive and ethnocentric notions of "American exceptionalism" also contributed then and now to U.S.-centric global discourses (Bacevich, 2008). While the United States may have come to terms with the importance of cultural diplomacy in the post–World War II period, groups of people who were colonized by the West—indigenous peoples of the Americas, Africa, and Asia—had already been made aware of the significance of "cultural differences" marked by unequal colonial relations of power (Smith, 2005; Takaki, 2008). The Western colonizers used their "civilization" as a justification for conquest and slavery while marking indigenous ways of life as lacking in culture (Todorov, 1984; Winant, 2001).

For the colonized, culture was always already a site of contestation and survival, even without a formalized academic discipline. The increased attention to "cultural understanding" also points to a shift from colonization to globalization after World War II, whereby global bodies of governance institutionalized networks of political, economic, and cultural power (Stiglitz, 2002), often along colonial lines.

A broader look shows how the development of the field was always connected to global conditions, relations between countries, and internal intercultural dynamics. In particular, the debate over the definition of culture reflects how the United States, as a country, addressed shifting cultural relations and global landscapes in the post–World War II era. Moon (1996) noted that in the 1970s, culture was conceptualized in diverse ways. As the United States dealt with its internal cultural/racial/ethnic tensions, the impact of the civil rights movement, and the increasing population of people of color, topics such as **stereotypes**, ethnocentrism, and prejudice gained currency in the intercultural field. However, by the 1980s, the emphasis on comparative studies based on culture defined by nationality (e.g., Japanese vs. U.S. communication styles) prevailed in intercultural communication studies (Gudykunst & Nishida, 1994; Hofstede, 1983, 1991). While the definition of culture is still open to theoretical discussion and debate, the ways it has been conceptualized in the past several decades reflect the shifting historical contexts in which the question of human "differences" has become increasingly crucial in political and social life both in the United States and around the world (Ono, 1998). The following section elaborates on different paradigmatic approaches to culture.

Inquiry Into Culture

One of the key elements of intercultural praxis is one's ability to ask questions that reveal unexamined assumptions and unexplored viewpoints. One engages in the practice of curiosity and restraint by asking questions, suspending judgment, and being open to possibilities of change. Intercultural praxis provides tools to cultivate a mode of critical thinking, action, and reflection through which we come to see what may not be readily apparent or obvious to us. In many ways, the field of intercultural communication emerged and evolved as an outcome of the scholarly efforts to see what is not readily visible to our eyes: culture. As one of the founding scholars of the field, Hall (1959, 1966) carved out a distinctive area of study by focusing on the ways cultural differences manifest in subconscious, out-of-awareness behaviors in the use of space, time, and information exchange (Rogers et al., 2002). Hall focused on how cultural differences can be observed in nonverbal communicative behaviors we otherwise take for granted. In this section, we introduce three different paradigmatic approaches for studying culture and how different schools of thought attempt to make visible and understandable this elusive phenomenon called "culture."

How do communication scholars inquire about culture when it is often hidden, normalized, and unquestioned? What do communication scholars look for when they investigate the role of culture in communication? To answer these questions, we must understand philosophical assumptions that shape the researcher's approach. Figure 1.2 explains the characteristics of culture and research approaches based on three theoretical paradigms: functionalist, interpretive, and critical (see also, Martin & Nakayama, 1999). It is important to note that these perspectives are not exhaustive or mutually exclusive; theoretical perspectives

Figure 1.2 Paradigmatic Approaches to Culture in Intercultural Communication

	Functionalist	Interpretive	Critical
Constitution of Culture	Learned, Socialized, Transmitted	Emergent, Socially Constructed	Negotiated, Contested
Nature of Culture	Generalizable, Stable	Intersubjective, Processual	Fluid, Contingent
Approach to Culture	Predict, Prescribe	Describe	Critique and Deconstruct
Orientation to Context	Acontextual	Contextual, Local, Global	Contextual, Global
Orientation to History	Ahistorical	Situated, Historical	Historical, Historicized
Orientation to Power	Apolitical, Power-neutral	Apolitical, Political	Politicized, Power-laden
Object/Location of Study	Behavioral, Attitudinal, Social Regularities	Shared Patterns, Symbolic Texts/Practices, Discourses	Ideological Discourses/ Structures, Embodied Performance
Methodological Orientation	Quantitatively Measured	Qualitatively Interpreted	Qualitatively, Critically Deconstructed
Goal of Study	Prediction and Control	Understanding Patterns and Layers of Meaning	Engaged Praxis for Social Justice

often overlap and influence one another, as indicated by the dotted line separating the columns in the figure. Different assumptions, interpretations, and representations regarding the paradigms are inevitable; thus, our goal here is to invite critical and creative thinking within and beyond the paradigms rather than to limit or confine our understanding and research in intercultural communication.

Influenced by positivist and postpositivist assumptions, the first group of scholars—functionalist social scientists—approach culture as a set of variables that can be operationalized and measured quantitatively. They believe that culture manifests in one's behavioral, cognitive, or psychological traits that can be objectively observed, predicted, and generalized based on one's cultural background. For example, Oetzel and Ting-Toomey (2003) developed face negotiation theory, in which they statistically correlated individuals' cultural orientations (individualistic/collectivistic, independent/interdependent) with types of facework used in conflict (self, other, and mutual face).

The second group—interpretive scholars—approach culture as a shared system of meaning and patterns of discourse, which can be accessed through in-depth interviews, situated observations, and rhetorical/text-based analysis. Rather than measuring certain behavioral/cognitive/psychological traits of individuals, interpretive scholars believe culture can be located in symbolic practices situated in interactive contexts or text-based artifacts through which a group of people form meanings. Interpretive research encompasses studies such as Carbaugh's (1999) ethnographic study on the communicative practice of listening and its cultural significance among the members of the Blackfeet, and Collier's (2009) analysis of interview discourse of Israeli, Palestinian, and Palestinian/Israeli participants in the U.S. peace-building dialogue program from 1997 to 1998, an analysis that combines interpretive and critical approaches.

Finally, the third group—critical scholars—approach culture as a site of struggle where meanings are constantly negotiated and transformed within historical contexts. While engaging some research methods similar to those of interpretive scholars, critical intercultural scholars highlight the analysis of structures of power that manifest in textual production, discursive and institutional practices, and everyday performance, treating communication as an inherently political and ideological act. While meaningful domains—historical and political contexts and the relationship between knowledge and power—are taken for granted or not explicitly interrogated in functionalist and interpretive research, they become key objects of examination in critical approaches.

In addressing the questions of what to look for to locate culture, scholars from different paradigms approach the subject differently. This relates to the process of framing, as described in intercultural praxis, in that different answers and realities emerge through the use of different frameworks to approach the study of culture. Functionalist scholars approach culture as an objectively observable and quantifiable phenomenon, whereas interpretive scholars attend to shared patterns that are situated and contextual. Critical scholars approach culture as a process through which inequitable relations of power are ideologically and historically negotiated. In other words, the paradigmatic position and philosophical assumptions that researchers adopt shape what culture is understood to be and what, then, is studied. These points lead to our next segment, in which we explore the shifting role of the researcher in intercultural communication scholarship.

Positioning the Researcher

In intercultural praxis, the process of positioning entails a careful observation of one's social location and relationship to others within hierarchies of power. Shaped primarily by the intersection of social categories of difference—race, gender, class, sexual orientation, physical ability, nationality, citizenship status, and social/institutional roles—positionality highlights one's access/lack of access to power in relation to others. Our positionality shapes our experience and particular standpoint from which we view the world. Positioning, thus, is a process of examining relational dynamics of power and privilege between an individual and others, and among groups, based on historical and current contexts. More recently in the development of the field, intercultural communication scholars have dealt with the question of how they are positioned and how to position themselves in relation to the subject of their research. How does a researcher's social, cultural, and institutional positionality shape his or her research? Is the relationship between researchers and research participants inherently unequal? Is it possible—and necessary—for researchers to remain neutral and objective?

Through the criticism of earlier research practices in which minority cultural groups were treated as the exotic (and inferior) "other" in relation to the normative white European Americans, intercultural communication scholars have developed extensive critiques of Eurocentrism, essentialism, and whiteness ideologies embedded in how culture is theorized. Asante (1998) and Miike (2007), for example, developed alternative approaches in response to individualistic and rationalistic perspectives that dominated the Eurocentric theorizing of culture and communication. While "shifting the center" from Eurocentric approaches and relocating subject positions, these approaches may also risk reified "centrisms." Other scholars repositioned their scholarship through postcolonial perspectives and indigenous approaches to address the limitations of the Eurocentric paradigm (Mendoza, 2013).

Increasingly, intercultural communication scholars have joined hands with scholars from feminist, rhetorical, and performance studies, among others, to illuminate the complexity of culture and the academic discipline itself as a site of negotiation from critical/cultural studies perspectives. Critical approaches, committed to destabilizing any privileged center in power/knowledge formations, help us see and understand culture as processual and contingent. In recent years, the forms of academic expression have diversified from more traditional academic writing to include performative expression and autoethnographic exploration, in which the presence of a knowing subject (researcher/scholar) is implicated, articulated, and problematized in the process of knowledge construction (Gonzalez, Houston, & Chen, 2011; Holman Jones, Adams, & Ellis, 2013; Nakayama & Halualani, 2010).

Dialogue Across Contexts and Theoretical Perspectives

Dialogue offers another critical point of entry into intercultural praxis. Cognizant of differences and the tensions that emerge from these differences, the process of dialogue invites us to stretch ourselves—to reach across and exceed our grasp—to imagine, experience, and engage creatively with points of view; ways of thinking, being, and doing; and beliefs different from our own, while accepting that we may not fully understand or may not come to a common agreement or position. Academic knowledge is also a form of dialogue, where scholars engage in conversations through academic research, writing, and teaching. The field of intercultural communication continually benefits from interdisciplinary dialogues among scholars.

Since the "critical turn" in the late 1990s, there has been a significant increase in the emphasis on interdisciplinary approaches and attention to the politics of knowledge. For example, various scholars joined broader interdisciplinary conversations on the notion of whiteness as a normative center of privilege and power in a racialized society (Cooks, 2003; Nakayama & Krizek, 1995; Oh, 2012; Warren, 2001). Other scholars have contributed to the efforts to articulate the voices of historically marginalized groups by using postcolonial theories to critique the knowledge constructed by and for the West (Chawla & Rodriguez, 2011; Collier, 1998; Shome & Hegde, 2002). Furthermore, scholars have revisited foundational concepts such as cultural adaptation and cultural identity using critical perspectives (Bardhan & Orbe, 2012; Curtin, 2010; Kinefuchi, 2010). In another area, scholars incorporated queer theory to challenge the normativity of gender and sexuality from transnational perspectives (Aiello et al., 2013). The boundaries of the field and knowledge are constantly shifting and expanding, requiring us to stay informed and attentive to emergent theoretical perspectives and real-world issues.

REFLECTION AND ACTION: FUTURE TRAJECTORIES OF THE FIELD

What traces from our history guide the future study and practice of intercultural communication in the context of rapidly shifting, overlapping, and contested cultural landscapes? What trajectories contour the field of intercultural communication in the 21st century? In this final section, we make note of traces—hints or suggestions—from the history of the field that provide insight into our pathways forward and sketch out likely trajectories into the future. New exigencies will undoubtedly arise, and scholars and practitioners in our field will respond; yet here we identify three traces and future trajectories influencing the field of intercultural communication.

While still scantly researched, technologies, particularly new media technologies, are a ubiquitous trend and future trajectory shaping intercultural communication in the global context. New media technology—including cell phones; Skype; social media platforms such as Facebook, YouTube, and Twitter; and blogs—has dramatically accelerated and altered communication across cultures. Intercultural new media studies, a term recently coined by Shuter (2011), explores new media and intercultural communication theory, points to the inadequacy of knowledge and theory from the 20th century, and develops new approaches better suited for the digital age. This newly designated area of inquiry seeks to examine the impact of technologies on communication between people from different cultures, the influence of culture on the social uses of new media, and how new media affect culture (Shuter, 2012).

Increasingly, new media technologies are shaping the construction and production of intercultural identities, intercultural relationships and alliances, cultural maintenance and adaptation, intercultural pedagogy, and the formation of global semicultures. No doubt, people are tweeting and posting YouTube videos about these topics as we write! In *New Media and Intercultural Communication: Identity, Community and Politics*, editors Cheong, Martin, and Macfadyen (2012) note that research on new media challenges the field to move beyond traditional ways of viewing and theorizing culture and communication. The emergence of new media offers enormous possibilities for connection, inclusion, and grassroots intercultural alliance building, as well as challenges such as exclusion resulting from the digital divide, threats to net neutrality, and the further commodification and corporatization of public space.

Another trajectory shaping the future of the field is the increasingly explicit intention to use our intercultural knowledge and skills to improve conditions in the world and create a more equitable and just world (Alexander et al., 2014; Allen, Broome, Jones, Chen, & Collins, 2002; Broome, Carey, De la Garza, Martin, & Morris, 2005; Collier, Hegde, Lee, Nakayama, & Yep, 2001; Sorrells, 2010). This turn toward social justice in intercultural communication is grounded in, yet departs from long-standing theories and models of intercultural competence (Deardorff, 2009), which focus on developing appropriateness and effectiveness when communicating with people who are culturally different. Mindful communication also provides a foundation for a social justice approach, which emphasizes awareness of one's own and other's value systems and self-conceptions, openness to different cultural standpoints, and alertness to multiple perspectives and interpretations (Ting-Toomey, 1999).

As Broome et al. (2005) envisioned, the intercultural field *has taken* an "activist turn" that links our scholarly efforts with "action that attempts to make a positive difference in situations where people's lives are affected by oppression, domination, discrimination, racism, conflict, and other forms of cultural struggle due to differences in race, ethnicity, class, religion, sexual orientation, and other identity markers" (p. 146). What students, scholars, and practitioners do in the world to make a difference varies greatly—from engagement through pedagogy, publications, and participatory action research to intercultural alliance building, community-based work, and activism (Dempsey et al., 2011; Yep, 2008). Summarizing responses in the "Online Discussion Forum: Engaging Key Intercultural Urgencies in Today's World," Rona Halualani notes, "The real thread behind our comments is the desire for there to be meaningful change and justice for our communities around the world" (Alexander et al., 2014, p. 68).

Intercultural praxis, introduced and used here, provides a blueprint for integrating a social justice approach with intercultural communication. Intercultural praxis operates as engaged communicative action informed by an understanding of the positionalities and standpoints of the communicators. Intercultural praxis is exercised within and is responsive to particular, concrete temporal and spatial contexts that produce historical and sociopolitical as well as local and global conditions.

A final perceptible trace threaded through the history of the field is a commitment to interdisciplinary approaches. The field of intercultural communication has always been interdisciplinary. Dialogue with other disciplines, incorporation of diverse paradigms, and a willingness to grapple with multiple theoretical approaches enrich the field. Not only does this tendency resist insularity and rigidity, but it can open spaces for nondominant, counterhegemonic, subaltern, and indigenous knowledges. The increased diversity within the field—in terms of issues addressed, scholars' backgrounds, and theoretical perspectives—can translate into more literature and research grounded in various cultural traditions and localized knowledge. Dialogue with others across cultures and disciplines situates us in the dynamic "inter"—an interstitial space—a potentially scary and yet transformative place between, rather than within, familiar boundaries and accepted disciplines (Carrillo Rowe, 2010).

The emphasis on interdisciplinarity is broadly situated within the critique of modernity and the project of decolonization of knowledge. As the influence of globalization sweeps across the world, it is important that the field of intercultural communication challenge colonial legacies and cultural/academic imperialism where theories produced in the West are unquestionably applied to cultural experiences in non-Western/nonwhite contexts. Retheorizing intercultural communication from the particular perspectives and situated experiences of people locally, while being mindful and critical of global structures and relations of power, is needed. Thus, the act of globalizing intercultural communication compels us to seek out localized, marginalized viewpoints to draw more complex maps of intercultural dynamics and cultural experiences. As we theorize intercultural experiences and interactions from "below," we challenge hegemonic claims about globalization from "above." In the process, we shift the metaphor from a surficial, flat view of the *field* to a multidimensional view of the *globe*. By globalizing intercultural communication, then, knowledges from around the world are brought into conversation and tension such that linkages between the local and global are highlighted, historical and contemporary relations of power are emphasized, and critical social justice approaches are uplifted.

"Praxis What You Breach": Intercultural Praxis, Impersonation, and Stereotyping

Gordon Nakagawa
California State University, Northridge

Whaddup where you at

IC Praxis in the house

Droppin' conscious beats

Condensed into this single senryu (a 17-syllable form of Japanese poetry akin to haiku), Kathryn Sorrells' (2013) intercultural praxis offers a nuanced and liberatory process of "critical analysis, reflection, and action for effective intercultural communication in the context of globalization" (p. 251).

The value of intercultural praxis resides in its capacity to reveal and critique how culture, history, and power align with communication practices that may serve or subvert social justice in everyday events and interactions. Operating as a kind of ethical and political GPS for locating and guiding communication pathways, Sorrells' approach to intercultural praxis provides multiple access points or, in her words, "ports of entry" (pp. 16–20) for navigating local and global interactions. In this essay, I use these ports of entry—inquiry, framing, positioning, dialogue, reflection, and action—to revisit relevant life experiences that I hope will illustrate the power of Sorrells' intercultural praxis to analyze, critique, and transform relationships and communication in service of social justice.

This brings us to the story of a Japanese American boy and how he came to be born in Cleveland (aka CTown), Ohio, and how he learned to perform blackface and yellowface on an urban stage surrounded by a white racial frame—all without the necessity or benefit of makeup or costumes.

Courtesy of Gordon Nakagawa

When did he first see
A squinty Oriental
Instead of a boy

INQUIRY: This being the port of entry where we ask and are asked questions . . .

How did history
Global local contingent
Conspire in your birth

This expansive, grandiose question first appeared in far simpler form as the earliest questions I can recall being asked repeatedly as a child: What are you? Where are you from? When did you come here? When are you going back home? Even before learning my name, my childhood acquaintances, classmates, and more than one teacher would pose one or more of these questions. They have continued to recur and resonate throughout my life.

FRAMING: This being the port of entry where standpoint, history, and context intersect . . .

'My middle name is
Wayne Pilgrim' A posse of
One Nikkei cowboy

In response to any of the questions about what I was, where I was from, and when I arrived and planned to return, even at 4 years old, I declared passionately and resentfully, "I'm an American!" Typically, my interrogators laughed derisively, flatly denied that I was or could be American, and inevitably insisted, "But where are you *really* from?"

Just as early on, I knew full well what I wanted to be when I grew up: a (white) cowboy. Of course, I never uttered the word *white*, but it was undeniably implicit, as certainly as my 1950s-based cultural icons were the uber-white males John Wayne (my middle namesake, my parents told me), Roy Rogers, Hopalong Cassidy, and Gene Autry. Always already racialized as white, gendered as male, sexualized as straight, the dominant "white racial frame" (Feagin, 2010), embodied by popular culture archetypes, defined and delimited the reach and grasp of childhood dreams. Whether playing cowboys and Indians, World War II, or other imaginary role-playing games, the character masks I assumed were decidedly and decisively white, male, and U.S. American. In my world there were no cowboys (or cowgirls) of color.

Tellingly, when it was my turn to play the enemy, I would enact the "savage" or "noble" Indian or an evil Nazi, but never once a menacing "Jap" soldier. The contradiction, even for a child, was too great to bear.

This dominant framing of the U.S. cultural standpoint is characterized by Audre Lorde (1984) as

Courtesy of Gordon Nakagawa

> a *mythical norm*, which each one of us within our hearts knows "that is not me." In America, this norm is usually defined as white, thin, male, young, heterosexual, christian, and financially secure. It is with this mythical norm that the trappings of power reside within this society. (p. 116; emphasis in original)

Pervasive and taken for granted, this normative frame sets boundaries for the construction and regulation of identities and communities, always already racialized, gendered, sexualized, class based, and invested in manifold and contradictory social and cultural interests. This **mythical norm** and white racial frame have persisted into current cultural constructions of U.S. identities and communities.

> *They threw paper bombs*
> *At me shouting 'Remember*
> *Pearl Harbor you Jap'*

From first grade through my senior year of high school, I came to dread every December 7, the anniversary of the 1941 Japanese attack on Pearl Harbor. In social studies and history classes, this precipitating event that incited U.S. entry into World War II inevitably gained currency as December approached. As the only Japanese American in my all-black, inner-city elementary school, and later in all-white suburban schools, I recall feeling egregiously conspicuous, hypervisible. In their World War II coverage, our textbooks typically included pictures of Emperor Hirohito and Imperial Army General Tojo, and photos of explosions destroying U.S. ships in Pearl Harbor. Conflating Japanese nationals with U.S.-born Japanese Americans, my classmates were unable to distinguish between the enemy "Japs" and me, the homegrown version who shared the face of the enemy. On all things Japanese, Chinese, Asian, or "Oriental," I became a living visual aid and the unofficial target of other kids' having fun at my expense. By no means an every-day or chronic pattern, I was nevertheless predictably taunted and ridiculed; on one occasion, I even had paper bombs and airplanes thrown at me on Pearl Harbor Day. I learned much later that other Japanese American kids across the nation had gone through the same kind of experiences. Whenever any topic broaching Japan or Asia arose in or outside of the classroom, I learned to keep a low profile, and I discovered early on the power of words, images, and representations, and how they can carry the force of history and oppression in framing experience and positioning cultural identity. In retro-spect, what was most striking was the implicit knowledge and explicit expressiveness and performance of our respective racialized positions and the racist framing that medi-ated all our everyday interactions and relationships.

POSITIONING: This being the port of entry where power and place overdetermine perception . . .

> *In so many words*
>
> *Negroes and Orientals*
>
> *Were not welcome here*

In the aftermath of the World War II incarceration of 120,000 Japanese Americans (including 70,000 U.S. citizens), thousands of former prisoners "relocated" from con-centration and detention camps to geographic locations across the country. Although most eventually returned to the West Coast, significant numbers of Japanese Americans dispersed to cities and towns in the Midwest, the South, and East Coast regions. This internal migration dramatically changed the demographic profile of urban and rural areas. For instance, in 1940, there were only 18 Japanese Americans living in Cleveland, Ohio. By 1946, the Japanese American population had skyrocketed to 3,500. My parents were among the former camp prisoners who moved to the Cleveland area during the postwar period.

After being released from camp, my father was drafted and served in U.S. Army intelli-gence. Postwar, he attended college, graduating with a degree in accounting from the University of Michigan. Having secured his first full-time job in Cleveland, my father moved with my mother into a low-income, inner-city neighborhood on the margins of the most impoverished slums in the metro area. I was a young adult before I learned that my parents' choice of this location was circumscribed by two principal factors: housing affordability and the informal exclusionary practices and formal restrictive covenants that sharply pre-scribed and proscribed areas where people of color were permitted to reside, especially "Negroes" but also "Orientals."

Colorblindness is

Not the absence of bias

But its guarantee

The black population was predominant in my neighborhood and in the square mile that I knew as home. Within this vicinity there were perhaps one or two white families and our Japanese American extended family (mom, dad, and sister in a duplex, with my grandmother, two uncles, and an aunt living in the adjacent duplex). For all intents and purposes, from kindergarten to third grade, all my friends and classmates were black. For a CTown kid whose hospital birth records identified his race as "Yellow," residing in an all-black neighborhood, attending an all-black segregated school, and media-immersed in the dominant white racial frame, color consciousness permeated my own and others' perceptions as a simple matter of taken-for-granted common sense. The notion that being "color blind" was somehow desirable and moral was scarcely imaginable, except maybe for our white teachers, who either told us race wasn't important or never spoke of it, while demonstrating in word and action that it was one of the only things that did matter. For the rest of us, colorblindness was not only nonsensical, but believing in it and acting on it all but guaranteed you would be viewed and treated as an outcast, an incompetent, or a potential target. Framing and feigning indifference to color and positioning yourself as above or beyond color would bring loud accusations of acting "stuck up" or "uppity," which essentially translated as acting white. But while my schoolmates, teachers, and others recognized fully that I wasn't white, I discovered early on that being a "colored" Oriental was not the "same difference" as being a "colored" Negro (see Okihiro, 1994).

DIALOGUE: This being the port of entry where we conversate and keep it real . . .

Since childhood, I've struggled with a deeply embedded suspicion that I am not quite a fraud but certainly an imposter posing and posturing in a racialized character mask, a kind of mediating public persona representing particular historical and social interests, often hidden and disguised. I've felt that I was passing or covering myself as something, someone inauthentic and, more to the point, false—an imposter, a double agent from a World War II Yellow Peril propaganda film. This conflict between the fake and the real, appearance and essence, representation and identity, honesty and deception, manifested very early on, in kindergarten and elementary school. My predominant experience was hyper–self-conscious awareness as the "only." Although I have vivid and enduring memories of childhood happiness, even joy, the overwhelming affect I recall and carry into the present is shame. I wanted nothing more than to be other than what and who I was, paradoxically framing and positioning myself as an unassimilable other. For the first 9 years of my life, I tried to be (not merely become) black.

My second language

Wuz in yo face ghet-to

Until Dad got home

Despite and perhaps because of my periodic treatment as the resident foreigner, I learned over time to signify or rank with my friends, all of whom were black. I heard and repeated and even invented a few "Yo momma" jokes, often with a revealing self-deprecating if not self-loathing Orientalist slant: "Yo momma face so fat her eyes look Oriental." I could sling street slang almost as well as my black friends, although I retreated immediately to so-called standard (white) English the moment I entered the front door of our house. Code and style switching (engendering both reframing and repositioning) was a survival competency that was essential and did not come easily, but the first time I said "y'all" at the dinner table was also the last time. Dad's wrath was an arch study in effective extrinsic motivation, and I gots me some mad skills in a hurry.

> When I conversate
>
> Wid my crew how black do my
>
> Yella face become

I was never fully at home with black vernacular English. To my ear it always sounded false, as if I were masquerading or impersonating or even taunting my black friends. As deeply as I yearned to fit in, to be seen and accepted as an "honorary Negro," I felt inadequate to the task and, at times, as though I was trying too hard to talk black and to become black. And though I did not want to admit it, I also knew that the last thing in the world I wanted to be was black. The only thing I wanted more was not to be Japanese.

REFLECTION: This being the port of entry where we think before we speak . . .

> 'Why you eyes squinty'
>
> 'Because we be thinkin' hard
>
> 'We don't "Just Do It"'

I'm not sure exactly when I realized that my audition for and performance of blackness bordered on and crossed into exploitative appropriation. I was unquestionably aware of radio and television black caricatures, exemplified on television by the likes of Amos and Andy, and I was vaguely familiar with the racist tradition of blackface minstrelsy, having seen movies and cartoons depicting the stock characters, music, talk, and humor. **Blackface** can be traced back to the 19th century (some say it can be traced to the slave trade and contact with Europeans). White performers used black makeup (cork, shoe polish, greasepaint, or powder) and costuming (often involving wigs, gloves, tailcoats, or ragged clothes) exaggerating stereotypical features of blacks, thus propagating racist tropes and stereotypes. Blackface was used extensively in minstrel shows and vaudeville, and for more than 100 years it was the single most popular theatrical form of entertainment in the United States (see Chude-Sokei, 2005; Cole & Davis, 2013; Lott, 1993; Rogin, 1996). The continuing legacy of blackface has included pernicious stereotypes and racist images in the media, in

Halloween costuming, and in the recurrent incidences of blackface parties and impersonations on college campuses and in other public venues (see Daniels, 2013).

What I was utterly unprepared for as a young adult was the stark recognition that I myself had performed blackface—only without the makeup and costuming. This dumbfounding, self-reflexive moment captured for me what Fredric Jameson (1971) calls "dialectical shock," the eruption of a transformative perception at that instant when phenomena previously perceived as distinct become conjoined (p. 375). My gut response to this revelation reproduced what I had felt as a child when I was framed as a metonym for Pearl Harbor: a mix of sadness, anxiety, fear, anger, guilt, and, finally, shame. Except I was now the perpetrator, or, minimally, I was in collusion with the ethos of racist blackface minstrelsy, in complicity with systemic white supremacy.

However, as Shotwell (2011) observes, in this moment of painful reflection, "shame might enable a different optic for action. . . . The experience of shame in the face of racism—one's own or other people's—discloses both present racism and also potential for anti-racist praxis, embedded in the desire to deny the racist self" (p. 94). This "productive shame" becomes the motive force and opening for reframing and repositioning our agency as subjects engaging in a transformational antiracist praxis. Though counterintuitive, my experience of residual shame has served as a liberatory opening, a saving (g)race, an invocation to action.

ACTION: This being the port of entry where we praxis what we breach . . .

> *Yellowface peril*
>
> *Go ahead Ask me again*
>
> *Where I'm really from*

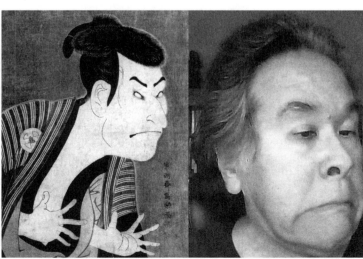

Alamy   Courtesy of Gordon Nakagawa   Universal Clips

This picture of me (I'm the one in the middle!) is an **impersonation**. It is a stereotype. It is a moment of (anti)**yellowface**. The image on the left is a classical Kabuki performer, and on the right is John Wayne appearing in yellowface as Genghis Khan. Together, these disparate representations coalesce around an Orientalist stereotype. This stereotype and its repertoire of attendant features (e.g., Asians are "forever foreign," inscrutable, suspect, diabolical) stem from the always already racialized frames that partially construct identity, irrespective of one's conscious acknowledgment and refusal or denial of their authenticity.

Recalling the questions that opened this essay (What are you? Where are you from? etc.), this senryu and visual mash-up anticipate, interpolate, and preempt the original questions by performing and impersonating the implicit stereotype carried by the questions. But this is an impersonation "that is not about performing someone else's identity but about performing into being a sense of one's own personhood" (Chen, 2005, p. 9). This subversive and resistant impersonation of stereotypic representations occurs when the stereotype is *called out as a stereotype* that has been ascribed to you, publicly, historically. As such, "impersonation is thus an act of doubled intent: it performs and challenges identity at the same time" (p. 15).

My impersonation, then, struggles toward an oppositional demonstration, admittedly awkward and inelegant, of how one might appropriate and expropriate and thereby destabilize and transmute stereotypes. In this context, **appropriate** refers to taking and (re)authorizing an image, representation, icon, and/or stereotype by recursively calling attention to reified meanings, thereby mobilizing alternate contexts, meanings, and readings. **Expropriate** conversely highlights the denial and deprivation of the stereotype's fixity by unhinging and disarticulating the representation from dominant cultural frames and privileged positionalities. Deployed together as intercultural praxis, appropriating and expropriating stereotypes becomes a performance and intervention that occupies and decolonizes the white racial frame and the white racist imaginary.

> *Impersonation*
>
> *Defaces stereotypes*
>
> *Deconstructing race*

Stereotyping is always a necessary, albeit insufficient, sense-making practice in how we frame and position ourselves in relation to others in the world. As Mitchell (2005) points out,

> We all know that stereotypes are bad, false images that prevent us from truly seeing other people. We also know that stereotypes are, at a minimum, a *necessary* evil, that we could not make sense of or recognize objects or other people without the capacity to form images that allow us to distinguish one thing from another, one person from another, one class of things from another. (p. 296; emphasis in original)

In this sense, stereotypes highlight our learned incapacities, the bounded knowledge that makes possible and contains our understandings of self and other, while coincidentally opening opportunities for us to resist, transgress, and reframe these reified self- and other representations. In any case, not only are we incapable of erasing or overcoming stereotypes, as both academic and popular perspectives have recommended, but we actually do ourselves a disservice in our futile efforts to transcend them. All interaction is always already mediated by historical, cultural, and political frames (including stereotypes) enabling us to communicate formally, informally, or intimately, or to decide not to interact at all.

Absent an understanding of how systems and practices of oppression implicate all of us, we default to either valorizing or vilifying problematic actions, representations, and experiences. We find it easier and more comforting to uncritically celebrate "positive" racial representations or discredit "negative" gender stereotypes, rather than critically examine our own accountability and complicity in sustaining systemic modes and practices of oppression. But in the end, it's not about eliminating or undoing or unlearning stereotypes; it's about *unfixing the fixity* of stereotypes. Our hope and intention must not be to disabuse people of their stereotypic frames but to engage them in critical conversation about how everyday practices sustain the regime of power and knowledge that perpetuate delimiting representations and oppressive practices.

Finally, above all else, I must ask myself every day, what have I said and done, what have I left unsaid and undone, that reproduces conditions of dominance and oppression? Equally, I must ask, what have I said and done, left unsaid and undone, that opposes and moves toward transforming conditions of dominance and oppression? This is not about "personalizing" or "individualizing" actions that undermine or advance social justice; this is about the effective human agency of Sorrells' intercultural praxis that authorizes responsible action knowing fully that we make history, though not in conditions of our own making. And regardless, we must struggle to make history through our informed choices and actions in the hope and recognition that another world is possible.

> *Learn contingency*
>
> *Bear witness that we must all*
>
> *Praxis what we breach*

KEY TERMS

agency 4	impersonation 20	mythical norm 15
appropriate 20	inquiry, framing, positioning, dialogue, reflection, and action 3	social justice 3
blackface 18		stereotypes 7
expropriate 20	intercultural praxis 13	yellowface 20

DISCUSSION QUESTIONS

1. Using the intercultural praxis model, discuss your relationship to the study and practice of intercultural communication. In other words, what questions do you have about intercultural

communication? How do your cultural frames shape how you view the world and interact with other cultures? How does your positionality impact your intercultural interactions? Through dialogue and reflection, how can you develop your efficacy as an intercultural communicator? What does it mean to use your intercultural communication skills as an agent of social change?

2. Discuss what Nakagawa means by the following statement: "I discovered early on the power of words, images, and representations, and how they can carry the force of history and oppression in framing experience and positioning cultural identity." Use examples from the author's life and from your experience to illustrate your response.

3. Nakagawa explains how "productive shame" can motivate us to reframe and reposition our agency and to take action, challenging oppressive systems and transforming the world around us. How can we address our individual and/or collective shame in the face of racism, sexism, classism, heterosexism, and other isms, and transform it for productive social change?

CHAPTER 2

Challenges and Barriers to Intercultural Communication

Today, the opportunities and venues for intercultural communication have expanded exponentially. Advances in communication and transportation technologies bring people from different cultural backgrounds together more frequently and rapidly than ever before, in face-to-face, virtual, and mediated environments. The opportunities for engagement, learning, innovation, and transformation through intercultural exchange are tremendous. Yet proximity to those who are different does not guarantee mutually beneficial and empowering intercultural interactions.

In fact, intercultural encounters, relationships, and alliances are often fraught with challenges and barriers that can be immense and daunting. These challenges include misunderstanding and conflict due to differences in cultural norms, assumptions, values, and histories, and a lack of shared language. Prejudice, discrimination, and systemic disenfranchisement, both historic and current, produce barriers to intercultural communication. **Positionality** refers to one's social location or position within intersecting webs of socially constructed hierarchical categories such as race, class, gender, sexual orientation, religion, nationality, and physical abilities, to name a few. The positionality of individuals and groups—their location within relations of power—contours vastly different lived experiences, which significantly impacts perceptions, perspectives, and communication with others.

The entries in this chapter illustrate the complex ways our positionality impacts our lived experiences, informing our perspectives and engagement with others. Using standpoint theory as a foundation, Mark P. Orbe's case study explores how individuals' descriptions of the reality of a "post-racial" society in the United States are grounded in particular racial locations/standpoints. His research provides insights into the complex ways inequitable relations of power inform perceptions and communication with others. Playing with metaphors from the children's series *The Cat in the Hat*, Bryant Keith Alexander artfully presents the possibilities of stepping out of the familiar and culturally sanctioned norms through intercultural engagement. His stories tease out deep, layered oppressions and affinities based on race, class, and culture, and how these intersect with institutional and role power to create intercultural encounters with high detonation potential. Both authors offer conceptual and creative approaches to understand and address intercultural challenges and barriers.

Diverse Understandings of a "Post-Racial" Society

Mark P. Orbe
Western Michigan University

Barack Obama's election as the 44th president of the United States in 2008 has been described as "the election of our lifetimes" (Todd & Gawiser, 2009, p. 4)—"one that transformed how race and politics intersect in our society" (Ifill, 2009, p. 1). Much of the discussion about President Obama's election has focused on what it means in terms of race, racism, and racial relations. Some U.S. Americans believed, and continue to argue, that President Obama's election would mark the beginning of a "**post-racial**" society and symbolize the end of racism; others vehemently argue that this phrase is used by those in power to ignore the saliency of race in contemporary society (Orbe, 2011). The reality is that his political accomplishments have brought existing racialized attitudes to the surface of public discourse.

According to Ono (2010), "it seems almost impossible to unlink the concepts 'postracism,' 'postrace,' or 'postracial' from Barack Obama's presidency, given how often they are associated with him" (p. 228). The logic behind a post-racial society assumes that, given Obama's journey—as a person of African descent who was not born with great societal **privilege**—racism no longer is the issue that it once was. On a logical level, most individuals recognize that President Obama's election (and/or re-election, for that matter) "did not automatically and instantaneously end racism" (p. 228). Unfortunately, much of the public discourse on the issue situates it as a debate of competing political positions.

This case study draws from a large qualitative data set to provide in-depth insight into the perspectives of diverse U.S. Americans as they understand the significance of President Obama's election in terms of race and racism (Orbe, 2011). Specifically, I draw from a large data set to highlight different U.S. perceptions on the idea that Obama's election has ushered in a post-racial era in the United States. In this regard, this research case study focuses on the intersections of power, politics, and race. Standpoint theory, as summarized next, serves as the theoretical foundation for the project.

THEORETICAL FOUNDATION

Standpoint theory (e.g., Harding, 1991; Hartsock, 1983) provides the theoretical framework for this analysis. According to standpoint theorists (e.g., Allen, 1998), life is not experienced the same by all members of any given cultural group. In explicit and implicit ways, standpoints affect how we communicate as well as how we perceive the communication of others. Although standpoint theories were established as a feminist framework (e.g., Harding, 1991; Hartsock, 1983), they can also be applied to the perspectives of those marginalized in terms of race, ethnicity, class, religion, and the like (Bell, Orbe, Drummond, & Camara, 2000; Orbe & Harris, 2008). Through the exploration of the lived experiences of persons in subordinate positions, standpoint theory focuses on the subjective social locations from which persons interact with themselves and the world around them (Wood, 2005). Moreover, standpoint theory acknowledges the specific societal structures that influence such vantage points. Recognition of the impact of a person's social group membership and field of experiences, according to this perspective, is useful in understanding how she or he perceives contemporary racial politics in the United States.

Standpoint theorists explore alternative understandings of the world that are situated in the daily experiences of both marginalized and dominant group members (Wood, 2005). When we apply these ideas to race, we understand that everyone has a **racial location**, defined primarily in terms of the racial and ethnic groups to which that person belongs (Orbe & Harris, 2008). Drawing from the work of O'Brien Hallstein (2000), we can also make an important distinction between occupying a racial location and having a racial standpoint. A **racial standpoint** is achieved/earned through critical reflections on power relations and through the creation of a political stance that exists in opposition to dominant cultural systems (Woods, 2005). Racial standpoint, then, refers to more than simply a social location or experience; it includes a critical, oppositional understanding of how one's life is shaped by larger social, cultural, and political forces. In short, everyone has a racial location, but only self-defined people of color who take a critical, oppositional understanding of how their lives are shaped by larger social and political forces maintain a racial standpoint. According to Orbe and Harris (2008), "European Americans cannot achieve a racial standpoint; however, they can develop multiple standpoints shaped by membership in traditionally marginalized groups defined by sex, sexual orientation, and socioeconomic status" (p. 12). In this regard, their perspectives on race can include a critical positionality; however, without the lived experience of being a racial co-cultural group member, a racial standpoint remains unobtainable.[1]

Incorporating the concept of **intersectionality** into studies using standpoint theories represents an important extension that reduces the likelihood of essentializing complex human beings into oversimplified categories (Bell et al., 2000; Richardson & Taylor, 2009).

METHODOLOGICAL FOUNDATION

The insight featured in this essay represents another point of reflective analysis of data collected, analyzed, and interpreted in *Communication Realities in a "Post-Racial" Society: What the U.S. Public Really Thinks About Barack Obama* (Orbe, 2011). Following the publication of this book, I embarked on a national tour promoting it. The experience of presenting highlights of the book to multiple audiences across the United States[2] and engaging (and being engaged by) individuals with diverse perspectives stimulated another layer of understanding that extended my earlier understanding. Before presenting these insights, I offer some brief descriptions of the data collection process.

Participants

For the initial study, I employed a methodological framework to fulfill one specific objective: Gain insight into diverse perspectives of President Obama's communication. To meet this objective, I worked to secure a sample that was both convenient and purposive. For a 6-month period (June–December 2010), I used site coordinators across the United States to recruit 333 participants from college classes and organizations, community groups, and social networks to take part in the study. Ultimately, this large number of participants was necessary to generate a data set that would achieve both diversity of experience and saturation of data (Wertz, 2005).

This project featured a tremendously diverse participant pool. Based on the self-report data collected, the participants featured individuals from diverse experiences based on age (57%, 30 years and younger; 30%, 31–50 years of age; 13%, 51 and over), gender (58% women, 42% men), race/ethnicity (50% European American, 27% African American, 11% Latina/o, 4% bi/multiracial, 3% Asian American, 3% Middle Easterner American, and 1% Native American), education (65% some college, 15% high school graduate, 10% bachelor's degree, 9% postgraduate degree, and 1% some high school), socioeconomic status (50% middle class, 31% lower/lower-middle/working class, 14% upper-middle/upper class), and political affiliation (39% Democrat, 31% Independent or unaffiliated, 16% Republican, 5% Libertarian or Tea Party, 1% Green Party).

Focus-Group Data

According to Patton (2002), researchers use focus groups as an efficient means to gather data in relatively structured or unstructured formats. From a qualitative research perspective, the purpose of focus groups is to gather data in a setting where participants can consider their own views in the context of the views of others (Staley, 1990). Using focus groups provides researchers the opportunity to gain insight from the unrestrained vantage point of participants—especially when facilitators use a general conversational approach whereby participants can describe their experiences with only a general focus on the phenomenon under study (Wertz, 2005). This particular use of focus groups to collect data is best characterized as flexible, probing, and synergistic, the results of which are not possible through individual interviews (Staley, 1990).

Following existing guidelines (e.g., Patton, 2002), I facilitated 42 focus-group discussions in 21 sites across 12 states in 6 different U.S. geographical regions. These sessions occurred over a 6-month period (June–December 2010). Using a general conversational approach with open-ended questions designed to elicit fairly straightforward descriptions, participants engaged in discussions about their perceptions of President Obama's communication effectiveness.[3] The responses analyzed within this particular analysis focus on times when participants discussed, directly and indirectly, the idea of a "post-racial" society. Different perspectives are explicated in the next section.

PERSPECTIVES FROM VARIOUS RACIAL LOCATIONS/STANDPOINTS

A careful analysis of focus-group transcripts produced three points that provide insight into how U.S. citizens from diverse backgrounds perceive a "post-racial" society. Within this section, I draw from a number of participant narratives to demonstrate how different perspectives about a "post-racial" United States are best understood through an understanding of racial locations/standpoints.

Young, White Racial Location: A Post-Racial United States

Among the hundreds of participants, those that were young European Americans were most likely to describe President Obama's election as demonstrative of a post-racial United States, a response that reflects a dominant racial location where white privilege does not require critical attention to race. Within this perspective is the assumption that his election was the result of a color-blind approach to politics. This point was highlighted by one young, white male graduate student from Massachusetts when he stated:

> If you talk to people 18 to 25, I don't think that we see him as the first black president. Well, he is the first black president, but I don't necessarily see him as a black president. When I watched him speak, I never really identified him as the black candidate. He wasn't Jesse Jackson, he wasn't that type of candidate. He really didn't speak like that. A lot of the buzz about him as a candidate wasn't about him being the first black president. It was more about his policies, and his issues. And a lot of people agreed with him on the issues, agreed with him personally . . . race wasn't important. (Orbe, 2011, pp. 93–94)

Within this set of comments, the person differentiates President Obama from traditional African American leaders whose politics and communicative personas were steeped in a particular racialized reality. Within this context, President Obama is regarded as reflective of a new age of transformative leadership. Other young, white women and men also discussed how the focus on a post-racial society blurs existing distinctions, including how people communicate. For instance, one young, white male undergraduate student from Illinois shared,

> I think what was even more obvious was his communication style, was what he sounded like. Unfortunately, this is based on a stereotype but white people listened to him and heard a white person talking. Obviously they saw what they saw, but they heard a white person talking. And black people identified with what he looked like, but white people heard . . . maybe they didn't "hear white," but what they heard was "presidential." He sounded like every other presidential candidate that we've had. He was an excellent public speaker. He wasn't too different. (Orbe, 2011, p. 102)

The idea that President Obama's election is evidence of a post-racial society is largely associated with the racial locations of younger generations of European Americans whose societal privilege and optimism provide a worldview where race no longer matters. Such a perspective is logical given how whiteness has been socially constructed in the United States. By definition, **whiteness** is a "social construction which produces race privilege for white people" (Rowe & Malhotra, 2006, p. 168), since they can define themselves as "unraced" and living in a world where race is irrelevant (Miller & Harris, 2005). As such, post-racial assertions are generally rooted in a decent, albeit misguided, belief that the United States has reached a moment where we are living out our lives on a level playing field in terms of race (Vavus, 2010). According to Ono (2010), colorblindness is best understood as a strategy of whiteness; it is based on the logic that if a person doesn't see race, then they cannot be racist.

In the previous excerpt, the participant acknowledged the different perspectives of African Americans in their perceptions of President Obama. In some subsequent comments, he also insightfully described how his racial location informs current-day worldviews—an important consideration, given that such sentiments were not articulated by older European Americans in the study. Specifically, he said:

> Can I jump in here? I want to clarify something that I was saying earlier. I had some more time to think about it in my head. I think that people who identify as white are more likely to say or believe that they are not racialized. People do not perceive whiteness as a race. . . . Maybe it's guilt . . . there are a lot [of] things. In society—especially those of us who are younger—we have this ideal that we are color-blind, that race doesn't matter. That's the wrong perspective to take anyway. But beyond that, we have been primed . . . we want to ignore race in a lot of ways. (Orbe, 2011, p. 188)

This participant went on to explain how when he was young, his parents would reprimand him when he asked about racial differences or described people with racial labels. Over time, he learned that noticing a person's color could lead to racism. From this perspective, the solution to eliminating racism, then, is to not notice a person's race. As illustrated in the next section, this perspective on race—informed by the racial location occupied by European Americans who were raised in the post–civil rights United States—is not one associated with the racial standpoints of many African Americans.

African American Racial Standpoints: Resisting Post-racial Claims

Almost without exception, African American participants were adamant in refuting current claims that President Obama's election was evidence of a post-racial United States. This perception, drawing from the tenets of standpoint theory, is steeped within lived experiences that have created a racial standpoint that critiques hegemonic power dimensions. As such, the passion that oftentimes accompanied comments of this nature was exceedingly more intense than for the European American participants whose comments were featured in the previous section. For instance, in a racially diverse focus group in Michigan, a young African American man responded to one white woman's description of Obama as the post-racial president by sharing the following:

> I find myself getting offended when I hear people of white descent talking about Obama like they don't see him as black. Maybe it's just me, but I do feel like every time I see Obama I feel proud because I'm black and he's black. I always see a black president. I feel like we always say that we don't—but we see color. WHY?

WHY? Even like his swag, or the way that he communicates, I feel like that is the ultimate swag of a positive black man. I see a BLACK president, not that he just happens to be black, he is a black man. (Orbe, 2011, p. 118)

Within this set of comments, this particular participant questioned the reasons why people who are white don't acknowledge seeing race; in essence, he was calling into question that woman's racial privilege, something to which he as an African American man has no access to. Comments reflecting a critical and oppositional stance to hegemonic conceptualizations of race (including arguments refuting a post-racial society) were seen across numerous focus-group discussions, especially those where the majority of participants were African American. For example, one 30-something black clergyman was clear and concise in his assertions:

There is no such thing as a post-racial society in America right now. Maybe there will be at some point. Obama is a step, or could be a step, in that direction IF it is put in the right context and geared that way. The other thing is . . . I agree with you all about the different generations viewing Obama differently. But I also think that looking at the larger issue of race, America has never dealt with the whole issue of racism. See we want to talk about race but not talk about racism. The concept of race by its very nature is racist. Race has become so ingrained into society, we often times don't even recognize how pervasive race is. I think that most people don't realize it because it has become so systemic. People don't even see it! [group talking over one another] . . . Yes, young people and all people might be interacting with one another, but in terms of the system, nothing has changed. It hasn't changed for Obama, and it [pause] won't [pause] be [pause] changing [pause] any [pause] time [pause] soon. (Orbe, 2011, p. 119)

This participant's comments were shared within a focus group of all African American men that took place in Oakland, California; the pauses between his words added emphasis to his point. Interestingly, the comments of a young African American woman attending a historically black college/university (HBCU) in Alabama also interrogated the relationship between race and racism. Within her focus group of all HBCU students, she questioned whether a post-racial goal is even desirable.

I think that living in a post-racial society shouldn't be anybody's goal. I think that a post-racist society would be the ideal. Post-racist . . . where people wouldn't make judgments that disenfranchise people based on stereotypes associated with their skin color . . . not acting on stereotypes that negatively impact people. I think that there are still racial, or cultural, differences in society that aren't all bad— that's why a post-racial society shouldn't be the goal. Race isn't the problem, racism is. (Orbe, 2011, pp. 119–120)

The racial standpoints of these three African American participants, like others throughout the study, were situated in a field of experience inclusive of various forms of racial discrimination and racism. For example, participants from the southern HBCU described several racially charged incidents that occurred around the 2008 presidential election, including the vandalism of the local Obama campaign office and local white male citizens' driving a pickup truck with a Confederate flag through campus to intimidate students from voting. The climate in this southern "red" state was so hostile that the university president reportedly sent out a mass text to students encouraging them to avoid wearing Obama paraphernalia and participating in large, loud celebrations on Election Day (see Orbe, 2011). Clearly, experiences such as these inform the students' perceptions of President Obama and claims of a post-racial United States.

Diverse Cultural Standpoints: Saliency of Race Decreasing Over Time

Participant narratives highlighted in the two previous sections appear fairly straightforward in terms of the ways specific perceptions of a post-racial society are associated with particular racial locations or standpoints. Yet it is important to acknowledge that some participants from diverse cultural backgrounds made a similar point: While President Obama's election was not evidence of a post-racial United States, it does reflect a society where racial differences are becoming less salient. Such an acknowledgement is important to make explicit, given how an individual's understanding of race relations is not uniformly produced by racial identity; instead, taking an intersectional approach to standpoint analyses reveals similarities and differences within and between groups (Warren et al., 2003).

One approach to incorporate intersectionality within standpoint theoretical analyses is to use the concept of **cultural standpoint**. Such an approach can move beyond a focus on one particular aspect of identity (e.g., feminist standpoint, racial standpoint) and advocate for a more holistic understanding based on multiple salient identity markers. This was seen in a focus group of white participants held in a rural southern Ohio community. One 30-something white man, a vocal supporter of President Obama, used the closing moments of the focus-group session to share some initial reluctance about having an African American president:

> The first thing that I thought was that the African Americans, the colored community, was going to take over. More or less, they were going to take over. And I don't know what that would mean, but I got the picture that the next time that I walk in McDonald's or something, I would hear, "White boy, you get down and wash the dishes. You go do this. We rule the country now." I don't know if that's happening. . . . Is that changing around down the South? Is what we've done to them coming back to haunt us? (Orbe, 2011, p. 133)

This participant's comments are interesting in that they acknowledge a history of racial oppression that, from his cultural standpoint (white, male, rural, lower socioeconomic status), informs concerns about changing racial dynamics within times of economic uncertainty. The concept of standpoint, consistent with existing research (e.g., Richardson & Taylor, 2009), is apropos here given the participant's rural, lower socioeconomic status. Simultaneously, his comments reflect acknowledgement of white privilege, something that he fears may be lost given the election of an African American president.

Other participants, from a variety of racial and ethnic backgrounds, described in explicit ways how President Obama's race has become less salient over time. This included some African Americans and Latino/as[4] who acknowledged that his accomplishments in office take precedence over his racial identity. This point was evident in the comments of a young male college student from Illinois whose parents were born and raised in Syria:

> I think that for me, maybe for the first year or so, he was the first black president. There were songs coming out: "My president is black!" [group laughter as he starts to rap the lyrics of the song]. Okay cool. But now in my mind, he's just the president. There was all this hype . . . but now it is what it is. It's there, but no one really cares. (Orbe, 2011, p. 106)

The idea that the saliency of race is decreasing was also seen in the comments of a number of European Americans who described their disapproval of President Obama as related more to politics than race. One 30-something man in California, for instance, shared exactly why President Obama "sucks":

> My family is all from Texas, they are all hard-core Republican. So, when Obama won I talked to my family in Texas . . . and they are a little bit racist. They were saying: "It's bullshit! He's black and that's the only reason that he won!" And all of this stuff. Then I talk to them two years later and they are like: "It's bullshit. His policies are wrong—all Democrats suck!" So, now they have moved from "black" to "Democrat." So, even a racist Republican family isn't seeing him as black anymore; now he is a Democrat. Me and my family live in California and we see it as him being a Democrat. It has nothing to do with his color; he sucks because he is a Democrat. Democrat policies suck. (Orbe, 2011, p. 136)

Throughout the study, similar comments were heard from European American participants who described Republican family members' views of President Obama. Yet others, such as one middle-aged white man (an Independent voter) who participated in a focus group in Massachusetts, also alluded to how the 2008 election marked yet another step toward a society where race holds less saliency. Reflecting on his daughter, who as a young elementary school student took part in a mock presidential election, he offered:

> I'll go back to my daughter. The first president that she knows is Obama. She is not comparing him to anybody else. Other future presidents, for her, will be compared to Obama. So, I hope . . . You know, big changes never really happen . . . change occurs in these small, everyday steps. I hope that in 100 years this will be just one of those small, everyday steps that make us a better country. (Orbe, 2011, p. 217)

DISCUSSION: THE CHALLENGES OF DIVERGENT RACIALIZED PERCEPTIONS

This research case study highlights the utility of standpoint theory in understanding different perceptions of race in contemporary U.S. culture. It also illustrates how high-quality intercultural communication can be difficult when individuals' perceptions are informed by divergent sets of lived experiences. Using exemplars from a large qualitative data set, I have presented how three different perspectives regarding a post-racial United States are situated within particular racial locations/standpoints. Standpoint theory provides an excellent theoretical foundation from which to understand how different perspectives of the same phenomenon stem from divergent social–cultural group memberships and fields of experiences. My objective here is to highlight these perspectives as a means to increase awareness and stimulate critical understanding of the source of some intercultural tensions, such as disagreement about the role that race and racism play in contemporary U.S. society.

Interestingly, this research case study demonstrates the utility of standpoint theory while simultaneously revealing one of its limitations (see Boylorn & Orbe, 2013). The first two perspectives highlighted in the previous section clearly and concisely reflect divergent racial locations/standpoints. However, at first glance, the third perspective appears grounded in a diverse field of experiences. While this initially appears incongruent with the fundamental tenets of standpoint theory, further interrogation provides the opportunity to recognize that every individual simultaneously sees the world from multiple locations, not simply those based on racial and ethnic identity. Consequently, a limitation of standpoint theory arises when scholars assume a unidimensional approach in their research. Using the concept of intersectionality (Crenshaw, 1991), while cumbersome, allows an understanding of how each perspective on a post-racial United States potentially is informed by race *and* age *and* gender *and* socioeconomic status *and* regionality *and* political affiliation (Orbe, 2011). Within this essay, I have attempted—when apparent—to highlight how intersections of identity (e.g., race and age) inform particular perspectives (e.g., a color-blind approach to politics).[5] In this regard, I use cultural standpoints as a productive vantage point to understand the similarities and differences among and between cultural groups (Cooke-Jackson, Orbe, Crosby, & Ricks, 2013; Warren et al., 2003).

This shift acknowledges a more holistic understanding of how all individuals, given the multidimensional features of identity, are situated in lived experiences that reflect both privilege and disadvantage. Given this, Martin and Nakayama's (1999) **dialectical approach** to intercultural communication offers a productive lens through which to understand the value of multiple, seemingly competing perspectives. As opposed to traditional approaches that understand human existence through binary categories (e.g., right or wrong, male or female, black or white), a dialectical approach is based on the understanding that life is best understood as a "both/and," not "either/or" phenomenon. Given this, "a dialectical approach offers . . . the possibility of 'knowing' about intercultural interaction as a dynamic and changing process" (p. 14). This framework encourages individuals to recognize how contemporary race relations are both similar to *and* different from those of historical times, static *and* dynamic, and personal *and* contextual in terms of the role situational context plays in specific interracial interactions. Accordingly, it provides a productive framework to face the challenges of intercultural communication when individual understanding is situated in overly simplistic and unproductive ways.

The ultimate value in this line of research is how it can provide insight into how different perceptions of race are best understood as extensions of particular lived experiences. An important goal for effective intercultural communicators, then, should not be trying to convince others that a particular perception is correct or incorrect; instead, the focus must be on trying to understand others' perspectives as valid given a certain set of lived experiences. This, for many, represents a tremendous challenge when communicating with others from diverse backgrounds. Striving for such an understanding is crucial if we are to gain a critical consciousness of the role of race and racism in 21st century society. This is especially true for European Americans during interactions with people of color but also relevant for individuals who strive to serve as allies in the fight against oppressions based on gender, sexuality, age, abilities, and the like (DeTurk, 2011).

So, in the end, who is right in terms of President Obama's election: those who claim that it ushered in a post-racial United States or those who insist that it did nothing to change the racial dynamics in this country? In the vein of a dialectical approach to intercultural communication, both are correct and incorrect from the particular racial location through which they were manifested. The first step toward intercultural communication competency is to recognize how one's own perceptions, as well as others', are situated within a specific set of lived experiences informed by race, gender, socioeconomic status, age, and so on. According to standpoint theory (Collins, 1986), people traditionally marginalized in society—as outsiders within—maintain a more "objective" view of societal issues. Individuals from dominant groups, in comparison, maintain perceptions that reflect more privileged views. Given this stance, it is important to note that one election (and/or even reelection) of a president of African descent[6] does not mean that the United States has moved beyond race and racism. Simultaneously, however, such a monumental event does reflect a significant development in racial attitudes that were prevalent in past decades. In short, the saliency of race continues to shape contemporary racial politics, albeit in considerably different ways compared with earlier generations. As such, a person's perception of race and racism is informed by intersections of cultural markers that require collective attention to the complex ways they influence one's thinking. In the end, this means that all individuals, regarding issues of equality, fairness, and oppression, are informed—both in productive and unproductive ways—by their multidimensional cultural standpoints.

In conclusion, the case study described within this chapter provides insight into how inequitable relations of power inform intercultural relations. I have focused specifically on perceptions of President Obama and a post-racial United States; however, countless other points of analysis exist. For instance, much debate has surrounded the role that race played in the death of Trayvon Martin, and in the ultimate acquittal of George Zimmerman. In fact, the racialization of perceptions is glaringly apparent. More than 86% of African Americans disapproved of the verdict, compared with 31% of European Americans; these perceptions coincide largely with perceptions regarding whether or not people of color get equal treatment under the law (Cohen & Balz, 2013). The opportunity to understand this reality through standpoint theories is apparent, as one *Washington Post* article concluded: "The verdict prompted renewed discussion about why black and white Americans often see events through separate prisms and whether the country can bridge the racial divisions that continue despite progress on civil rights matters over many decades" (para. 6).

These comments point to the strength of standpoint theory in that common perceptions can be understood in terms of one's social group memberships and lived experiences (Davies-Popelka & Wood, 1997). Yet some attention must also be paid to the 14% of African

Americans who supported (or were neutral about) the verdict, as well as the 31% of European Americans who disapproved. Doing so would promote understanding on how intersectionality might reveal multidimensional cultural standpoints that are not as clear-cut in terms of race alone. In this vein, this project explored both collective and individual subject positioning to offer a fruitful glimpse into the perceptions of a diverse set of individuals. By doing so, I hope that the project can serve as a model for others who are committed to capturing the vast diversity of communicative experiences that currently exist in the United States and beyond.

The Black Kat in the Hat: Tales of Cultural/ Racial Encounter and Challenge

Bryant Keith Alexander
Loyola Marymount University

On March 1, 2013, I was scheduled to read stories from *The Cat in the Hat* series to a group of second graders, in commemoration of the passing of Theodor Geisel (aka Dr. Seuss). As I entered the classroom wearing the signature red-and-white top hat of the famed mischievous cat, a little black boy exclaimed, "He's black . . . the Cat in the Hat. Yeah!" And other kids joined in the cheer. In his exclamation, he registered that I am a black man, maybe different from the series of other visitors to the after-school program. Or maybe he said, "He's back!" possibly in reference to the book *The Cat in the Hat Is Back*—not, "He's black." But I registered a conflation of the phrases and a reference to me as "the B(l)ack Cat in the Hat."

I also had a flashback to another moment of characterized identity. In 1986, while I was on the alter as part of a small church musical ensemble during a mass at St. Mary's Catholic Church in College Station, Texas, the sound of a crying cat came through an open window behind me. At the moment I leaned toward the window, a small black kitten jumped onto the windowsill to greet me. Members of the mostly student congregation began to laugh as I reached for the kitten. And the young, white, somewhat hip priest, who knew me well, interrupted his homily to say, "No worries, it is just a black kat with a black cat." And we all laughed, in that way that a sensitive awareness of intentionality can prevent a misinterpretation of **intercultural/interracial** engagement.

But the case with the children in the after-school program resonated with me in different ways. "The Black Kat in the Hat" is a construction that makes note of my being black (African American) in the recognizable cultural role of the Cat in the Hat. The construction also links the educational intentions of the books and my own professional identity as a professor/administrator, my purpose for being in that context. The moment is a reminder of the many ways the performativity of my person—how I consistently perform myself in shifting contexts—and the historical constructions of my being a black man, as it relates to stereotypes and the role I am playing at any given moment, are often conflated one in/as the other. Each of these encounters offers challenge, yet also transformative possibilities in everyday life—to recognize personal agency within inequitable relations of power and to renegotiate the potentials of meaningful intercultural and interracial encounters. In other words, these encounters offer me moments for critical **intercultural play**, moments in which I can begin *to articulate and identify hidden forces and ambiguities that operate beneath appearances* and direct attention to *critical expressions within different interpretive communities,* and do so in a way that is not punitive but has an ease of recognition that signals the effect of encounter in a way that might use a lightheartedness to avoid the painfulness of disrespect, while *providing insight and inspiring acts of justice* (Madison, 2005, p. 13). I believe such intents are core to intercultural/interracial communication. And even like the *Cat in the Hat* stories, such an approach recognizes that the role of play in the lives of children includes acts of critical decision making that also serve as a rehearsal for living.

In this personal narrative, I seek to use the above incident of the Black Kat in the Hat as a point of reference to speak to the immediacy of two intercultural/interracial encounters in aspects of my professional life. And while each of the encounters that I narrate is specific, they are both also archetypal, representative of a range of such encounters in my daily professional experiences. In short, I am asking: In what ways, after my encounter with the students in the after-school program, coupled with the church example, might I claim myself as the Black Kat in the Hat—an intervening character in a series of social contexts that seemingly disrupts the expected—and provide opportunities of exposure to and possibility for a broader commitment to intercultural and interracial dialogue?

HOME ALONE (OR "THEY LEFT YOU IN CHARGE?")

The original *Cat in the Hat* story is premised on two illustrated Caucasian children looking out a window, bemoaning that they have nothing to do on a rainy day. The children have been intentionally left home alone. Hence, the black-and-white, tuxedo-patterned Cat in the Hat enters the home under the guise of teaching the children about creative things they can do indoors on a rainy day, at the same time broadening their frame of reference to creative thinking, imagination, language use, and play—both for the children in the story and the children reading the story.

In this description I am focusing on the "home-alone" component as something that is significant to me both relative to the occasion of my storytelling and to my identity as a black professor/administrator. For you see, the black and Latino kids in the classroom are often in an after-school program designed in many ways to prevent them from actually being home alone, as their lower–working-class parents are unable to be home with them immediately after school lets out, as well as to address the safety issues for children home alone (see www.lasbest.org). The differentials between the kids in the storybook and the kids in the classroom are premised on race, class, care, and the strategies of engagement in relation to their being home alone.

The question, "They left you in charge?" is one that parallels the notion of being "left home alone" but is particular to my role as a black professor/administrator being left in charge of what is (still) assumed to be a white endeavor—that is, university teaching and higher-education administration—and the suspicion of intelligibility and competence that is still sometimes associated with black professors and administrators, based on race and not academic accomplishment. The assumption, as I have experienced it recently, is that my roles of engagement in the university are based solely on some problematically applied affirmative action that encourages workplace inclusion, sometimes at the expense of qualifications.

Each phrase—"left home alone" and "They left you in charge?"—is an insinuation of independence and an assumed responsibility, whether out of necessity or desperation. In my years as a professor/administrator in predominately white universities, I have often had unsuspecting students or parents enter my classroom or office to meet/encounter either Professor Alexander or Dean Alexander. Each position requires a particular relational orientation to the presumption of knowledge, authority, or power, and maybe class and privilege. And each of these parents, I suspect, has a sensed anticipation of the expected: What does the professor look like? What does the dean look like? What does the person in charge look like? And in a social economy of higher education, the anticipated image of authority is still white and potentially older than I currently am. And while such anticipation barters on race, it really is an issue of **cultural history**, patterns of experience that shape and preanticipate intercultural/interracial encounters. Allow me to offer this narrative:

A black male parent enters my office as the dean and, upon seeing me, says with surprise, "Oh, I didn't know that you were a brother." *Brother* in this context suggests both racial specificity (being of African/African American decent) and a particular cultural identity (meaning a community of shared practices amongst black men and black people in general). And later in the conversation—after the social and practical intentions of the encounter are laid bare and the black male parent is not getting the affirmative outcomes he had hoped to get—he says, "Now, I know that everything you have said is the politically correct thing to say as the dean. But, brother to brother, I want you to get my daughter into this university with a scholarship." In this instance, there is a bifurcation of my identity—from me as the dean to me as a black man who happens to be the dean. The black male parent is asking me to barter the nature of our academic discussion on an assumed cultural similarity, in which he might get advantaged consideration, over the particularity of me being the dean.

My role as the dean establishes a set of practices, patterns of experience, and politics as cultural necessity within the university—a set of policies and practices that actually mediate and script the potential conversation with the parent long before our encounter and the recognition of a presumed racial and cultural similarity. Though, as becomes apparent later, I believe that the black male parent would also suggest that our shared distinction as black men and potential informing experiences in black culture also establish a set of policies and practices that predate our encounter. But in this context I am, must holistically be, the dean, who is black, in which case the role of the dean is a cultural position. Such an encounter between the black male parent and me is both **intraracial** and intercultural at the same time, an encounter between two people from a shared race as well as an encounter between an academic dean and a parent, speaking through different cultural prisms—even if we share other cultural experiences outside the scope of the particular context of our encounter.

At the end of the meeting, when I cannot immediately guarantee his child a scholarship, the parent is dissatisfied with the outcome as he walks out of my office shaking his head, averting his eyes, and refusing to shake my hand. In that moment, I am not sure if that dissatisfaction is grounded only in the encounter with the dean (an administrative agent of the institution) or also in disappointment with me as a brother. Such a speculation on my part invokes a felt differentiation in power, both my authoritative or reward power as the dean to make decisions in relation to this parent's request and a form of cultural power—one potentially used by the black male parent in relation to my black male status to invoke race, historical experiences of African American people, and systems of social practices within the black community (culture), which he presumed would drive my response to his request. His shaking head, averted eyes, and refusal to shake my hand as he leaves my office feel more like his performed cultural assessment of me. And that I am feeling this way reinforces the constraints on human social relations that are the nature of power—power as a practice of authority, often negotiated and validated in relational dynamics (e.g., roles, positions, class, cultural membership), that has salient impact in the shared recognition of its importance to the social structures that one seeks to maintain or subvert in the encounter. I was feeling his practice of power over me, maybe as much as he felt my practiced power over him—but in differing ways.

Shortly after his departure from my office, and during my pained reflection on the nature of our encounter, the black male parent returns. He shakes my hand and thanks me for my time. Maybe his return signals a performed gesture of cultural civility between him and the dean, as well as him and his black brother who happens to be the dean. And while that gesture gives me some resolve, it furthers my speculation on how this is a complex intraracial/intercultural encounter. And while I believe that the black male parent and I share a commonly held set of social commitments to uplifting young black people through education, I recognize that my personal agency within this situation is in fact a recognition of inequitable relations of power—yes, my power as the dean but also his insinuated cultural power, which he sought to use as leverage in the moment.

Standing on my convictions as the dean, which necessarily set the standard for my engagement with all parents, was a political and, yes, cultural move within the confines of my job description and the university, but one that also worked to renegotiate the grounds (within a particular cultural/racial encounter) on which we were operating, thereby mediating the intercultural and interracial encounter of blackness. It is my hope that his return, and the ensuing handshake, was a validation of how such encounters can be negotiated without the residual effects of distrust. But this is only one example. Let me offer you another linked example that might seem more obvious but is never easier to encounter.

"YOU SHOULD NOT BE HERE WHEN OUR MOTHER IS NOT"

The Cat in the Hat brings a diversity of being and experience into the household as a form of exciting the imagination, but not without a sense of disarray and disorientation. The encounter between the Cat in the Hat, with his tag-a-long companions Thing 1 and Thing 2, and the children and their pet fish is intercultural in nature. It is an encounter between individuals who may not share the same cultural symbols, beliefs, attitudes, values, expectations, or norms of behavior. The nature of intercultural encounters often signals an incoherency of practiced "interpretative frames" as to how, why, and when things should be done and what they mean (Sorrells, 2013, p. 17).

The struggled attempts at communication made throughout the story by the children's pet fish—who consistently instructs the children to resist the antics of the cat by saying, "No! No! Make that cat go away! Tell that Cat in the Hat you do NOT want to play. He should not be here. He should not be about. He should not be here when your mother is out!"—are in fact consistent iterations of cultural norms that are being violated in the intercultural encounter with the Cat in the Hat. The attempts of the fish, and later of the children, are in fact evidenced attempts at intercultural communication, strivings for a recognition of expected behavior in the household in relation to the antics of the Cat in the Hat.

In the story, the cat seems nonresponsive to the pleas of the fish and the children, as they invoke rules and mother. And if *mother* is the representative of a particular form of cultural reasoning, order and control that structures the experiences of the children and the nature of the household (as is the very nature of culture itself), to what degree is the Cat in the Hat knowingly violating cultural rules to empower the imagination of the kids beyond the controls of a particular cultural socialization by presenting a series of options to/of engagement? Such a challenge, if that is an accurate assumption, in any cultural context might have good intentions but could leave a residue of resentment in the disavowal of committed practices within a particular cultural context and the lived histories of those involved in an intercultural/interracial encounter. Allow me to offer you the following narrative:

Not too long ago, when I served as an associate dean, I was required by the policies and procedures of my position and the institution to academically disqualify a student. Disqualification came after a series of stages—warnings of consistent poor academic performance, Level I probation, Level II probation, and finally disqualification. In each of the preceding steps, letters and e-mails were sent to the student, and meetings with the student were invited. It wasn't until the disqualification letter that the student decided to make an appointment. When he, a blond, white male student, entered my office, he looked at me and said, "You're the dean?!" And he said it in a way that was less a question and more a critique or assessment, as if to suggest, "They let you be the dean?" And my response, "No, I am not the dean. I am the associate dean," was a diversionary clarification to what I perceived was his actual racist intent.

I invited him to sit, and throughout our strained conversation I sensed an interracial tension that mediated the more practical issues of our concerns, with the young man consistently stating, "This is not fair. You are just picking on me because I am one of the few white kids on this campus. I get this kind of racism every day here." At the time, I was the associate dean at a predominately Hispanic-serving campus. The student kept deflecting from the reality of his poor academic performance by pointing to issues of an assumed pernicious racism on the campus, and a particular complicity in racism of the black associate dean who was engaging in his formal academic disqualification. And while I attempted to focus the student on his academic performance, he demanded to meet with the dean, whom the student knew was a white man. To assist him, I dialed the phone, oriented the dean to the situation in front of the student, and then walked the student to the dean's office, along with his academic record.

Before I departed, the dean addressed the preliminary issue by informing the student that all matters related to the academic performance of students, and particularly issues related to matriculation and retention, resided in the office of the associate dean (me). The dean then informed the student that if there was a particular claim of racism, there were formal procedures to follow, separate from the student's own academic records, which evidenced the conditions of the current circumstance. I returned to my office, and the student followed shortly. The student sheepishly apologized for the accusation of racism and admitted that he had used this method with faculty in the past and it had sometimes worked to deflect the immediacy or harshness of a decision (e.g., a failing grade, a late assignment, an alternative approach to completing an assignment) from teachers who did not want a claim of racism leveled against them.

What was important in this experience was the nature of the intercultural/interracial encounter. Certainly, this was an encounter between a white student and a black administrator within a common cultural system of the university, but with differentiated power. As in the previous example with the black parent, I held a particular power of action and decision making that had impact on the student, constraining his options for further matriculation relative to a public set of practices, expectations, and outlined consequences in the university. But in this case, the white student practiced a power to make a claim of *racism*— a powerful trope of bias in intercultural/interracial encounters that signified indifference and reduced consideration based on his particularity.

The student strategically claimed racism as an inhibiting factor to meaningful intercultural/interracial exchange in an environment in which he constructed himself as *a* minority—not only in the statistical sense of the term relative to the percentage of white students on campus but also in the manner in which the term *minority* is used as a differentiated sociological category with reduced rights or opportunities based on the determination of the majority racialized population that holds social power. And while it is possible that the white student had experienced racism at some point in his life, the invocation of that construct as a defense against his academic disqualification (with evidence of his own long-term poor academic performance), delivered to a member of a historically marginalized group, threatened to belittle the historical oppression that many have felt relative to systematic structures of racism. More so, his claim of racism actually became an embodied performance of racism.

That was part of the discussion the student and I had in my office that day—a discussion in which both the historical nature of racism in the United States was outlined and delivered by the black male associate dean, who had just been accused of racism as a defense mechanism against systematic poor academic performance on the part of the white male student. In the conversation, I needed to engage the practical infrastructure of the university (policies and procedures that govern cultural practice in this context). I also needed to engage in what was an intercultural/interracial dialogue about race, racism, and indifference as subject content of our meeting. The material fact of my black male administrator body and his white male student body became evidence in our discussion on the nature of racism and claims of racial indifference, as I strived toward building a deep understanding of his own culpability in consistently poor academic performance across his claim of racism and through our cultural differences, positionalities, and issues of power and privilege—namely, in this case, his privilege to make the claim of racism without the more palpable experiences of such oppression, and my personal offense not to the accusation of racism but to racism as a lame excuse for his consistent poor academic performance.

In the conversation, I tried to model the type of civility that intercultural/interracial communication demands to reach a shared understanding of key issues of difference and commonality. In the end, the student was still disqualified. And as pained as that conversation might have been, I believe it was the particularity of my being a black male dean carefully teasing through the variables of the issue that helped the student understand, at least in the context of that conversation, both the consequence of his academic performance and of racism as a system of oppression that had little to do with his personal academic performance across the range of courses, professors, and opportunities to receive academic assistance. I also believe that the nature of our interface forced the student to reflect on his own orientation to using racism as a defense mechanism and on ownership of his academic performance.

A CONCLUSION

> *"Oh dear!" said the cat. "You did not like our game . . .*
>
> *Oh dear.*
>
> *What a shame!"*

The preceding quote is one of my favorites from *The Cat in the Hat* series. It does not have the motivational zeal of so many other Seussian sayings, nor does it lend itself to a whimsical repetition of rhyme. The sentiment is both a question and bemoaned reality that recognizes that cultural practices, antics, play, and struggle do not always easily translate with the same level of acceptance in intercultural encounters. A challenge to intercultural communication is a commitment to listening and empathically placing oneself in the position of the other before casting judgment or critique, before acting on impulse and pressing a personal will on another.

My own expressed experiences as a black male administrator teach me every day about the potentials and problematics of intercultural/interracial encounters, as well as encounters with sameness that might still signal difference, and the effects of poor communication to negotiate cultural difference. Yet I strive to be attentive to the potentials of transformation and subversion in such encounters. I try to maintain personal and professional integrity while reflecting on each occasion to examine the positive outcomes and nurse the wounds of intercultural/interracial encounter that I sometimes inflict and suffer when communication fails to match a positive intent.

So in suggestively claiming myself as the Black Kat in the Hat, I am whimsically constructing myself as sometimes an anomalous presence in the social and political contexts of work-a-day environments, when my (un)anticipated presence as a black man provides an opportunity to disrupt the expected (e.g., politics of race and culture) and promote communication across and maybe through the politics of difference.

But when the Cat in the Hat says, "Oh dear! You did not like our game. . . . What a shame!" the exclamation also expresses a sincere not knowing—a not knowing that the games and their engagement were not seen as enjoyable in the spirit in which they were offered. The statement bespeaks the disappointment of a failed intercultural encounter that lacked the clarity of knowing and understanding and thus may have caused unknowing harm. The story of the Cat in the Hat ends as follows:

> *And the cat went away*
> *With a sad kind of look. . . .*
>
> *And THEN!*
> *Who was back in the house?*
> *Why, the cat!*
> *"Have no fear of this mess,"*
> *Said the Cat in the Hat.*
> *"I always pick up all my playthings.*
> *And so . . .*
> *I will show you another*
> *Good trick that I know!"*
>
> *Then we saw him pick up*
> *All the things that were down. . . .*
> *And he put them away.*
> *Then he said, "That is that."*
> *And then he was gone*
> *With a tip of his hat.*

It is, of course, wishful thinking to expect that the residue of all intercultural/interracial encounters can be cleaned up as easily.

KEY TERMS

cultural history 36	interracial 34	privilege 24
cultural standpoint 30	intersectionality 25	racial location 25
dialectical approach 32	intraracial 36	racial standpoint 25
intercultural 34	positionality 23	standpoint theory 24
intercultural play 35	post-racial 24	whiteness 27

DISCUSSION QUESTIONS

1. The research case study by Orbe illustrates how three different perspectives on a post-racial United States are situated within particular racial locations/racial standpoints. Using examples from the case study, discuss how sociocultural group membership, lived experiences, and racial locations/standpoints are interrelated and inform one another.

2. In what way does the analysis and discussion in Orbe's case study assist you in understanding divergent perspectives on race and racism in the United States? How might this understanding impact your intercultural interactions and relationships?

3. Define *racial standpoint* and *cultural standpoint*. What steps can you take to develop and achieve a racial and/or cultural standpoint?

4. Based on your reading of "The Black Kat in the Hat: Tales of Cultural/Racial Encounter and Challenge," what does the author mean by "intercultural play"? What examples can you find in the personal narrative of intercultural play? How can you imagine using intercultural play to facilitate intercultural communication?

5. Using an example from Alexander's personal narrative, discuss how different forms of power—cultural, racial, role, and institutional power—intersect to complicate intercultural encounters. Given these intersections, what insights can you glean from Alexander's narrative about how to navigate the complexity of intercultural experiences?

NOTES

1. The work of Warren, Orbe, and Greer-Williams (2003) on diverse understandings of conflict helps illustrate this idea. Within their research findings, they use standpoint theories to explain how some European Americans' perceptions of racialized phenomena can be informed by experiences (e.g., living in a predominantly African American neighborhood or completing a major in African American studies) that allow them to negotiate their white privilege in ways that assist in moving beyond certain unidimensional perspectives.

2. Over a 16-month period (November 2011–March 2013), I presented close to 20 public lectures/book talks to audiences in 12 states (Louisiana, Florida, Michigan, Illinois, Ohio, Massachusetts, Minnesota, Alabama, North Carolina, Texas, Missouri, Georgia).

3. To maximize the accuracy and quality of each transcript, I was committed to transcribing each audiotape verbatim within 72 hours after the focus group was completed. After all the focus groups were transcribed, the data set was 385 single-spaced pages.

4. Warren et al. (2003) offer an interesting analysis of the standpoints of Latino/as whose racial and ethnic identities simultaneously assume both privilege and disadvantage.

5. Within a more in-depth analysis of the data used for this case study, Orbe (2011) highlights how race and socioeconomic status informed some African American participants' lack of support for President Obama's politics; in several instances, their lack of support was due to Obama's proposed economic and tax policies—changes that would negatively impact their current upper-class socioeconomic status.

6. See Orbe (2011) for an in-depth discussion about how different individuals regarded the role of Obama's biracial heritage in his ability to get elected.

CHAPTER 3

History, Power, and Globalization

Intercultural communication occurs within temporal and spatial contexts that are inextricably bound to and informed by distant times and places. For example, the publicly distributed conversation between Donald Sterling, owner of the Los Angeles Clippers, and his girlfriend, V. Stiviano, occurred in April 2014 in Los Angeles during the NBA playoff games. The immediate context of time, place, and relations of power (gender, race, class, and culture, to name a few) for the conversation matters; yet the meaning, impact, and implications of the conversation are deeply rooted in the history of **colonization**, the enslavement of 9 million to 12 million Africans, Jim Crow laws, the struggle for inclusion in sports, and all white-dominated institutions since the founding of the United States, as well as historic and current representations of blacks and people of color in media and popular culture. History and relationships of power matter in intercultural interactions.

Networks of connection and global relationships of power evident today are a continuation of worldwide intercultural contact over the past 500 years. Colonization and the global expansion of the West propelled the development of capitalism, which required then and continues to require today the expansion of markets and trade, and the incorporation of labor from former colonies and what are called "developing" countries. Magnified inequity, exploitation of workers, and unearned advantages that exist today between and within nations follow racial/ethnic lines and Global North/South contours forged during the colonial period. A legacy of colonization, the insidious dichotomy between "the West and the Rest" that valorizes and elevates "the West" while dehumanizing and dismissing "the Rest," permeates our **postcolonial** realities.

Using indigenous methods of storytelling, S. Lily Mendoza poignantly calls forth a counterhegemonic narrative grounded in the knowledge and practices of indigenous peoples whose sustainable ways of being in the world contrast sharply with modernity's ("the West's") culture of exploitation, domination, and limitless expansion. She invites us to "fall in love and grieve" as first steps in recovering our humanity, our connection to the ways of the natural world, and environmental and cultural balance. In her narrative, Nilanjana R. Bardhan stitches together her post/colonial and transnational identities—scattered over countries and continents—like a tapestry made stronger through the connections and reconnections woven across time and space. She offers the notion of intercultural bridgework as a way to forge connections and relationships across difference and uneven cultural locations to enhance the work of social justice in the world today.

Out of Modernity Into Deep Ancestry: A Love Story[1]

S. Lily Mendoza
Oakland University

THEORIZING THE MOMENT

This essay maps my journey out of my romance with progress and **modernity** into the world of indigeneity and deep ancestry and the radicalizing impact that this shift in understanding has had on my theorizing of intercultural communication. Taking into account the urgent ecological and civilizational crises that form the context of virtually all global encounters in our present world, the question of constitutive rationalities is raised. Globalized modernity's linear, monocultural logic of domination and limitless expansionism is examined for its impact on what now stands as modernity's only remaining "other": the unacculturated "primitive" or "savage" (i.e., **indigenous** peoples still living on the land outside the industrial infrastructure and by an entirely different ethic of relation with the earth and with others). I argue that understanding the history of relations between the two cultures is crucial to any adequate analysis of the present moment. It makes possible the apprehending of a gestalt out of the chaos of seemingly disconnected developments all portending crises in various spheres and may well stand as imperative for global survival. Rightly reading the difference in lifestyles between these two historic subjects (modern humans and indigenous peoples) ultimately poses indigenous genius as the lone historic witness to a way of being human together that was actually sustainable. On that witness may well rest the fate of the planet. The storytelling mode is employed to perform oblique theorizing with the deliberate purpose of subverting Western dominance in the communicative exchange. And in keeping with the *affective turn* in social theory that takes subjective experience, emotive desire, bodily responses, and unconscious habituations as sites of productive reflection (cf. Brennan, 2004; Clough & Hailey, 2007; Gregg & Seigworth, 2010; Negri, 1999, among others), it weaves the fabric of its story around the twin imperatives of falling in love and grieving well as portals to transformative relations. The theoretical concerns engaged are manifold: worldview and cultural assumptions and their consequences for intercultural relations; the power of normative discourse to foreclose alternative definitions of human being; and the need to break open the limiting frame of modernity to envision other possible futures; among others. Embedding such in story form invites readers to the different pedagogy of being taught by grief and the patience of having to sit with a seemingly insoluble problem and learning deep lessons from the discipline.

* * * *

This is a story about love and grief, of interconnections across epochs, times, and spaces. It is a piece of the globalization story—in particular, of how we have come to this place in history where talks of extinction and civilizational collapse are now rife, if not (yet) in popular discourse, among the ranks of those in the know about the very real tsunami of crises threatening life as we know it on the planet and what our hope might be going into the future. As a decolonizing Filipina in the process of recovering her indigenous ways of knowing and communicating, I'm relearning the art of what postcolonial theorist Gayatri Spivak (1987) calls "worlding the world," this time through the storytelling tradition of our indigenous peoples (as the saying goes, if you ask native peoples a question, they invariably reply with a story). As a child, I used to know this narrative mode of communicating in my bones; now, many Western-educated Filipinos like myself impatiently call it "long-winded," "tiresome" ("Get to the point, please!"), having become accustomed to the deductive mode of discoursing on a subject. In this piece, I reclaim this different mode of performing cognition by doing my theorizing in a sort of roundabout way—through stories.

First story:[2] When 22-year-old Julia Butterfly Hill entered the California Redwood Forest, home to the tallest and most ancient tree species on the planet, for the first time in December of 1997, she was completely blown away. "It was like my jaw was on the ground," she says. "I just couldn't believe how beautiful. The quiet in those forests was unlike the quiet I've ever experienced anywhere. The smells . . . the air is so pure that it tasted sweet on the tongue." Falling on her knees, she cried in awe. She knew she had entered sacred ground, and she had fallen in love. Walking farther, what greeted her next was the sheer horror of a vast clear-cut. She reports: "It's like it was bombed. They clear-cut the forest on the ground and then they light it with diesel and napalm." Moments later, this grief-stricken girl who had known next to nothing about eco-activism would find herself ascending 180 feet up the redwood tree named Luna to save her from being cut down by the Pacific Lumber Company that had been clear-cutting the area. Living on two 6-by-6-foot platforms atop this ancient, giant redwood, she vowed never to let her feet touch the ground again until she knew she had done everything she could to help save the forest. She stayed on that tree a total of 738 days (2 years, 8 days) and came down only after an agreement was reached with the logging company to preserve Luna and all the trees within a 200-foot buffer zone.

I open with this story to signal that at such a time as the one we live in today, where everywhere one turns one sees signs of things falling apart—species going extinct at never-before-seen rates; our food, air, and water getting toxified by industrial pollution; mountaintops being blown off in the search for metals and minerals needed for our high-tech gadgets; dead zones spreading through the oceans from unremediated oil spills and suffocation by seas of plastic often larger than some of the islands in our (Philippine) archipelago; forests disappearing at an ever-accelerating pace; glacial ice melting and extreme weather increasing from the heating of the planet due to CO_2 gas emissions; indigenous lands being forcibly taken over in the frenzy of competition over the earth's last remaining resources; to mention only a few—at such a time as this, only two things give me courage and hope: falling in love and grieving well.

I, too, have my story of falling in love once and being changed by the experience forever. You see, like most modernized Filipinos, I, too, had been miseducated growing up (the data show that this is inevitable for anyone who goes through a modern educational system[3]). I grew up believing that Europe and the West hold the status they do in the world today because of some inherent superiority they possess and that to strive to be like them was

Photo 3.1 Tacloban, Leyte, Philippines, after being struck in early November 2013 by Typhoon Haiyan (known as Typhoon Yolanda in the Philippines), the most powerful storm on record, whose fury correlates with the rise in ocean temperatures precipitated by global warming

the only way forward for backward countries such as ours. It embarrassed me that I was never comfortable speaking English (I still am not, though no longer embarrassed by it), no matter my excellence in its written form—a response I have come to understand as my body's unconscious form of resistance to colonial imposition.[4] I was also a born-again Christian, and that meant I shunned "superstitious" beliefs and did not worship *anitos,* or spirits in nature. I recall an esteemed Christian mentor saying once that only within Christianity could science have possibly flourished, because, for the first time, people who formerly believed that there are spirit beings in nature (and were therefore afraid to explore, dissect, investigate, and experiment with impunity) now understand that spirits don't reside in trees, rocks, or animals, and that the true God is actually transcendent and his creation (gendering intended) is given to us humans to "manage," exercise dominion over, and use to his glory. No wonder Francis Bacon, the father of modern science, could boldly encourage the torture and enslavement of Nature, urging that she be put on a rack (similar to the one they used in the Middle Ages to torture so-called "witches") to make her yield her secrets.[5]

In college, I was slowly introduced to the nationalist movement at the University of the Philippines, where I began to hear a different story, one that told of the conquest of our homeland as having been accomplished through the Europeans' wielding of the sword in one hand and the Bible in the other. But it was not until a graduate course in the humanities titled "The Image of the Filipino in the Arts," taught by an ethnomusicology professor, that I would have the life-transforming experience of falling in love not unlike that of Julia Butterfly Hill in that glorious, magnificent, ancient forest.

They say that change doesn't come from willful resolution (e.g., "I resolve from now on to value what is ours, to no longer feel inferior," etc.); rather, it comes from being given a different way of seeing. This is called a **paradigm shift**. And its language is that of realization ("I used to think . . . but now I see"). This new way of seeing then rearranges you on the inside and gives you a different ground from which to interpret your reality. That moment happened for me, as I was saying, in that humanities class, where, for the first time, I encountered the amazing arts of our indigenous communities least penetrated by colonization and modern development—their intricate weaving designs, the vibrant colors of their textiles, their basketry, dances, songs, chants, and what they expressed in terms of a different way of being.

For the first time, I was introduced to the supple world of nonindividualistic interconnectedness, the delicate sensitivity of *kapwa* (shared being), the generosity of community,

Photo courtesy of Jennifer Maramba, 2013

Photo 3.2 T'nalak tapestries produced by the T'boli people of Lake Sebu, South Cotabato, Philippines, whose "Dream Weavers" report receiving the intricate patterns and designs from their ancestors in their sleep

the lack of divide between the material and the spirit world, the openness of *loob* (interiority of being), the gracious receiving of gifts of beauty and creativity from the other world through dreams, visions, and the power of ritual. I recall coming out of every class session bawling my heart out, walking back to my dorm room in tears, not knowing what it was that hit me from all the innocent descriptions of those indigenous works of art, overcome by very powerful emotion. Only later would I come to understand the meaning of those tears, that they were tears of recognition. Here at last was a different mirror held before me. The Brazilian educator Paolo Freire once remarked that when all the authoritative representations around you have nothing to do with your reality, it's like looking into a mirror and finding no one. And sitting in that class and being introduced for the first time to the unique ways of being of our indigenous peoples—talked about not in a degrading, primitivizing, and insulting way but in recognition of their true beauty, nobility, and grace—I saw myself. No longer would the intuitive world that I sensed I had always shared with the creators of those arts but had been forced to repress in favor of the purportedly superior world of the colonial masters appear in my eyes as mangled and distorted, but as compelling and starkly beautiful, calling up from within me my own beauty. (That's why I find the phrase "I see you" in the movie *Avatar* so powerful!) To have yourself reflected back to you—in all your depth and uniqueness—is to be affirmed in your innermost being. I was no longer the ugly bastard child of the West, an American wannabe. In that first-time encounter with the true beauty of our peoples, I was birthed anew, welcomed home by *Inang Bayan* (Mother Land) and told, "It is okay to be who you are": a Pinoy (colloquial for "Filipino"), a Kapampangan (native of Pampanga, site of the former U.S. Clark Air Base in the Philippines), brown-skinned, a natural groupie, with a tongue made for Kapampangan speaking and not English speaking. *Malagu ka.* You are beautiful. I have since, both in my scholarship and personal life, committed to learning all I can about indigenous ways of being and, with the help of teachers, to recovering my own indigenous soul. And the more I learn, the more deeply I fall in love.

But that was just the beginning of my journey. My sojourn to the United States (for graduate studies), not by choice but under duress, brought other realizations. One is that the much-touted **American Dream** that at one point, I must admit, also captivated my imagination is really a nightmare—built on the massacre and annihilation of an estimated 100 million to 145 million native peoples living up and down the Americas prior to Columbus's incursion into the so-called New World in 1492; the subsequent takeover of these native peoples' territories through treachery and deceit, if not outright theft; and, finally, the killing of between 30 million and 60 million Africans and the enslaving of the remaining 12 million, whose unpaid labor (estimated in today's calculus as amounting to anywhere between $1 trillion and $5 trillion) virtually produced much of the country's enormous wealth and infrastructure (cf. Stannard, 1992, p. 317). This bloody **unacknowledged history** continues to the present through the institutionalization of the interlocking ideologies of **white supremacy**, patriarchy, and capitalism that effectively secured the loot and continued the plunder. Today, the United States is 5% of the world's population but consumes anywhere from 25% to 40% of the world's resources. *Wealth*, I would find out, is never an autonomous term but a relative one. Globally, its singular condition of possibility is the violent appropriation of nature's resources as well as other people's labor and surplus product, leading inevitably to the impoverishment of the latter. The wealth creation that alone makes modern civilization possible, according to writer and indigenous teacher Martin Prechtel (2004), would not have been possible without the creation of slaves: be it the enslavement of living matter, other humans, or inert substance made over into various laboring machines.

Notice the paradigm shift from a relationship with nature as mother, as life source, sacred and holy, where you take nothing from her without giving something back, to modern culture's view of nature as nothing more than "resource," dead matter to do with as we please. Prechtel (in Jensen, 2001) tells of the case of the Tzutujil Mayans, whose spiritual economy of the village requires that you give a gift to that which gives you life. He writes:

> A knife, for instance, is a very minimal, almost primitive tool to people in a modern industrial society. But for the Mayan people, the spiritual debt that must be paid for the creation of such a tool is great. To start with, the person who is going to make the knife has to build a fire hot enough to produce coals. To pay for that, he's got to give a sacrificial gift to the fuel, to the fire. . . . Once the fire is hot enough, the knife maker must smelt the iron ore out of the rock. . . . A ritual gift equal to the amount that was removed from the other world has to be put back to make up for the wound caused to the divine. . . . When the knife is finished, it is called the "tooth of earth." It will cut wood, meat, and plants. But if the necessary sacrifices have been ignored in the name of rationalism, literalism, and human superiority, it will cut humans instead.

He concludes:

> All of those ritual gifts make the knife enormously "expensive," and make the process quite involved and time-consuming. The need for ritual makes some things too spiritually expensive to bother with. That's why the Mayans didn't invent space shuttles or shopping malls or backhoes [not because they couldn't]. They live as they do not because it's a romantic way to live—it's not; it's enormously hard—but because it works.

And indeed, this premodern paradigm (for lack of a better word) has been working so well for our ancestors for hundreds of thousands of years that they have not seen the need to change it fundamentally. Theirs is a circular loop of reciprocal gift giving and generosity that has effectively preserved the balance of life and honored the holy in nature. (What we call "waste" is also nonexistent in such cultures, in that one's "waste" invariably becomes food for another.) Death itself is simply part of that cycle of giving and receiving, of feeding and becoming food for others. The Goddess of Decay, the Composter of Failure, is the most revered of the deities because although she cannot have children of her own, she causes everything else to sprout. As expressed beautifully by Prechtel (2004) in describing the ways of the Tzutujil Mayans in Guatemala (before the U.S.-sponsored death squads decimated their village during the civil war):

> The Tzutujil were not trying to build a nonsuffering world. The world they were part of was not run by humans, and it had only live things residing in it. There were no dead things. Instead of eradicating all the misery of the world, the Tzutujil were trying to suffer together creatively in a beautiful way to keep their world of delicately balanced live things more vital by feeding it the grief of their human failures and stupidity. These failures were made beautiful by the ornate and graceful way the people dedicated their suffering to the earth and to that which made life live, in a proven ritual attitude of great antiquity. (p. 198)

With the linear invention of time and its concomitant logic of progress, unbridled taking without giving back, and unrelenting competition for more and more and more, the new imperative of conquest, hierarchy, and domination began to spread and take root and has now become the default condition of all us modern humans. A new definition of human *being* began to be concocted in service of the conquering syndrome. Enshrined in the language of **liberalism**, the new qualifying standards for being human required that for anyone to be considered fully human, he or she needed to exhibit a certain form of rationality that excluded feelings, passions, and intuition; a natural desire to accumulate wealth, enjoy a life of material comfort, and master nature; an individualistic orientation that's not beholden to relationships of mutual interdependency with others; and, finally, a possessive, acquisitive nature that issues in a belief in private ownership (cf. Mendoza, 2013b, for a fuller treatment of this thematic). And since indigenous peoples lived by an entirely different ethic than these, they did not qualify as human beings and therefore could be dispossessed of their land, territories, and resources with impunity.

The arbitrary naturalization and universalization of this liberal understanding of what it means to be a human being took a very long time to accomplish, with roots in the 10,000-year-old invention of the logic of domestication and (agricultural) settlement, emerging as a global project in the past 500 years of colonial conquest and reaching its zenith only in the past 200 years of industrial civilization, not without resistance from indigenous peoples around the globe. Still and all, relative to the 2 million to 3 million years of the known human species' existence on the planet (depending on how a "human being" is defined, whether or not it includes hominid prototypes such as *Homo habilis*, *Homo erectus*, etc.), modernity's career is but a blip on the screen. Prechtel (2011) nonetheless remarks on the success of this modern propaganda thusly: "Modernity is not something that people can take or leave, for, uninvited, it invades us insidiously in a million nerve-jangling ways for which most humans have no resistance" (p. 436).

Today, in our global technoculture, we have become utterly dependent on the industrial machine to feed, clothe, educate, and entertain us. We are unaware of where our food comes from, how the clothes on our backs got to be produced and under what conditions. We revel in the wonder of our latest tech gadgets, not curious to know what mountaintop was blown off or what forest was clear-cut or what indigenous people's land was mined or what sweatshop labor was used for their production. We spend the majority of our time with our bodies encased in living-matter–devouring machines called buildings, traversing long distances in automobiles, planes, or water vessels run on the blood of our ancestors (which is what fossil fuel is). No longer do we sit leisurely with our neighbors and tell stories but, instead, spend most of our time plopped in front of our television screens or computers, reinventing the notion of friendship with the click of a button.

It is no secret that to power the industrial machine that sustains our synthetic comforts, we will need to find more and more places to dig, mine, drill, log, and harvest, and more and more ways to genetically modify crops to create bigger, sturdier, higher-yielding varieties that can withstand travel across thousands of miles in our super-globalized food system. And in our corporate, profit-driven world, our modern industrial culture cannot but find more and more ways to dupe, cover over, and justify why growth for the already obscenely wealthy 1% of the world is ultimately good for the rest of us.

Today, the only remaining places in the world where there are "resources" still left untapped and unexploited are under the feet of indigenous peoples—unsurprisingly so given their very different ethic of relation with their ecology. Having lived mostly on the generosity of their healthy ecosystems, they have had no use or need for what our modern industrial machine has to offer, nor do they want anything to do with our consumption-driven economy. I'm referring of course to those indigenous cultures that are still intact, that still retain much of their cultural integrity. The few still intact cultures, such as the Kogi of the Sierra Nevada mountains in Colombia, the Kung in the Kalahari Desert, the Hoarani tribe in Ecuador, or the previously uncontacted tribes in Peru, want and need absolutely nothing from our modern culture but only to be left alone to continue living as they have always done. That many of our own tribes in the Philippines have been reduced to needing dire help is no indication of their inherent poverty, weakness, helplessness, or fragility; rather, it is an indictment of how far our modern industrial culture has impoverished them and taken advantage of their lack of guns, immunity to disease, and steel (to cite Jared Diamond's [1999] famous account of Europe's remarkable takeoff beginning in the 15th century from being a small backwater at the edge of a great Islamic civilization to a global superpower), as well as their lack of paper land titles and literacy in our modern culture's convoluted legal doctrines, to steal their land and turn them into pitiful beggars in their own territories. The genocidal impulse in our modern culture—now globalized—is evident in the way it cannot stand to have any group, any tribe, standing as testament or witness to the fact that there are other, more life-giving ways to be in the world and, thus, its insistence on the adoption of a uniform monocultural vision by all the peoples of the world. Dare to defy it, and you are dealt with accordingly, like the Zapatistas in Mexico, who have had to take up arms if only to be left alone and not be coerced into joining the global economy either as producers or consumers.

This realization of what our modern civilization has meant for indigenous peoples around the world came to me in a very stark way while I was staying at my sister and brother-in-law's place inside what used to be the U.S. Clark Air Base in our home province of Pampanga, after I attended a Philippine conference in 2008. Walking around the beautiful parade grounds one morning, I found this iron-etched memorial at the entryway that read (as translated from the Filipino original):

> Former home of the Aeta. Became Camp Stotsenburg in remembrance of Col. John Miller Stotsenburg of the first Nebraska Regiment, 1902. Land designated for the U.S. Army, 1 September 1903. Airstrip built and named Clark Field in memory of

Maj. Harold Melville Clark, pilot, 1919. . . . Remained under the administration of the U.S. according to the RP-US Base Military agreement of 1947, Clark Air Force Base, 1949. Terminated, 1991. Converted to Clark Special Economic Zone, 1992.

I have no words to describe the impact of that moment for me. Here was one of the choicest, richest lands of my home province Pampanga, grudgingly acknowledged as the original home of a group of thriving hunting-and-gathering tribes called the Aeta, prior to any modern development. Yet, without any tinge of regret or apology, it was summarily taken over, first by the U.S. colonial government and then by the Philippine state at the termination of the RP-US treaty. Now it comprises a bustling zone of commerce, call centers, and trade, providing employment for thousands of modernized Pinoys and pulling in revenue for the Philippine government and its foreign private investors. "Converted to Clark Special Economic Zone since 1992" was the concluding tribute. Period. No more mention was made of the place's original inhabitants. Whatever happened to them? How were they driven away? Did they resist, and like the millions of Native Americans who were slaughtered by the European colonizers, were they also massacred, forced to flee deeper into the mountains, or confined to reservations? Where are they now? What became of the hundreds of thousands of them?

Photo courtesy of Perry Paz, 2012

Photo 3.3 Clark Field memorial at the entrance of the former U.S. Clark Air Base parade grounds in Angeles City, Pampanga, Philippines

Come to think of it, I'd seen some of them here and there during my visit at Clark—dark, kinky-haired kids and women, often barefoot and in tattered clothes, peddling their root crop harvest of *camote* and *saging saba,* and/or their crafts of musical instruments made of bamboo. One of them, "the singing Aeta boy," has made it to YouTube through the well-meaning efforts of one tourist who wanted to help, hoping he would be discovered and perhaps given a future in the entertainment industry. Standing before that memorial plaque, I began to cry, experiencing a grief not unlike Julia Butterfly Hill's in coming upon her first clear-cut. The realization that washed over me was that I wasn't innocent, that perhaps my acculturated lowland-settler ancestors were also party to the scheme that drove away my Aeta brothers and sisters. After all, the Aeta looked different from them—my mestizo ancestors with their straight hair and fairer skin who no longer lived by hunting and gathering or by a subsistence form of economy but by settled monocrop agriculture committed to growth, progress, and development. The Aeta, once a thriving, proud, and self-sufficient people, bearers of encyclopedic knowledge about their ecology, no longer roam these massive spaces of Clark freely as they once did in the olden days; and if ever now, they walk hunched over, feeling small and ashamed, reduced to mendicancy, producing and performing for tourists, having become nothing more than targets for missionary largesse in exchange for their souls and for charitable "helping and development projects" from the very government that allowed the theft of their lands in the first place.

What would real justice look like in such a case as this? What would it mean to really do justice by our indigenous brothers and sisters whose lands have been mined, clear-cut, dam inundated, taken over, and settled by beneficiaries (this writer included) of this now globalized system of hierarchy and theft?

I said at the beginning that what we need, if we are ever to have the courage to face the truth of our time, is two things: We need to fall in love, and we need to learn to grieve well. I do not know if I would've known to respond in grief before that bitter memorial at Clark had I not first fallen in love with the different way of being of my indigenous ancestors. And to see that way of being unceremoniously dismissed, done away with, and now patronizingly recuperated in helping projects by the likes of us on the other side of the development divide while we continue to hold the stolen goods, brings a sharp pain to my heart that I have yet to learn how to ease. And the deep grief comes from a place of love, having caught a glimpse of our indigenous tribes' beauty and having seen them for who they really are: strong, autonomous, proud, fiercely independent, diverse in their ways of being, and bearers of ancient memory who still know how to honor the Agreement with the Wild (what Quinn [1996] calls the "the law of limited competition," which states, "You may compete to the full extent of your capabilities, but you may not hunt down your competitors, or destroy their food, or deny them access to food" [p. 118]).

At the last international conference on indigenous knowledge held in my country in 2012, I had the rare opportunity for an intercultural encounter with a delegation from the various Philippine tribes who were among the invited participants. Presenting a version of this essay, I was moved to end with an apology addressed to the indigenous delegates sitting in the audience in their diverse, colorful garb, resplendent in their beauty and quiet dignity. With quivering voice, I spoke the following words:

To our indigenous brothers and sisters in this conference, I want to say, I see you, and I—we, the rest of us who no longer live by the Agreement with the Wild—owe you a debt, a debt we can never hope to repay for the destruction of your cultures and your beautiful ways of being. And now you stand here among us gracing and honoring us with your presence without anger or recrimination, which would have been just given the history of our relations—and for that we are humbled even more. Our culture, this modern civilization, has reached the end of its logic; the (postmodern) future belongs to you—you who still know how to live gently on the planet and without the enslaving of others. With your sufferance, I would like nothing more than to sit at your feet and learn from you. And I want to say, forgive me, forgive us, for having trashed your world. We live the way we do—full-bellied, in high-tech comfort and convenience—because you live the way you do—impoverished, your lands taken over by corporations that serve the likes of us consumers. For now, I have nothing to offer but my tears, and the baby steps toward relearning the old ways again (planting corn; listening to the land; restoring kinship not only with the two-legged but also the four-legged, the seed peoples, the winged, the crawlers, and the finned; greeting Grandfather Sun in the morning; and other small gestures of remembrance). My hope is that someday, I and my people may no longer live the way we do today—by this monstrous industrial machine that turns all living into dead—but in recognition once more that we, even we amnesiac modern humans, live and breathe and move and have our being ultimately only by the generosity of Earth Mother, the Holy in Nature, and the ungrudging exuberance of all that is wild, free, and beautiful. *Siyanawa*. May it be. *Maraming salamat po*. Thank you.

There was not a dry eye in the audience, certainly not mine. I was approached later by a colleague who said she was "stunned." She said she had always known that stuff came from somewhere and that "development" had a price but that she had never, until now, "connected the dots."

Recently, I had the privilege of attending the Detroit premier of *American Revolutionary: The Evolution of Grace Lee Boggs,* a film on the life of the 98-year old Asian American long-time activist, philosopher, and elder. The film opens with Grace saying matter-of-factly, "I feel so sorry for people who are not living in Detroit," while surveying the devastation of a once grand city, home to the great industrial revolution. She continues, "People always striving for size, to be a giant . . . and this is a symbol of how giants fall." Indeed, nowhere is the track record of the project of modernity and globalization more truthfully told than in a city such as Detroit—with its racial coloration (deciding the disposition of wealth and power), the free-for-all looting by banks and corporate vultures, and the testing—in a very major way—of neoliberal austerity measures in a U.S. city. But amidst the grim reality, a quiet hope remains alive for those of us able to get over our romance with scales of grandeur and technologized culture. As I wrote elsewhere (Mendoza, 2013a):

I see [Detroit] as a place of fruitful gestation. The first post-industrial city in America that some analysts say is the likely future of most cities around the world a decade or so from now, it appears to be birthing a whole other culture, this time no longer the color of rust, steel and iron, but green. Organic life is slowly returning to the city, with its residents knowing the bitterness of betrayal by the false promise of development, unlimited growth, wealth, and prosperity. The miracle is that neighbors now are speaking to each other, forming communities, growing gardens and taking care of their poor and homeless. (p. 255)

I now live in this city of stark contradictions, with a memory constantly hailed by this other world of much older ancestry—a world of love, grief, and longing, auguring death but also the promise of a resurrection, albeit of a different kind. I do not know for sure if, as a globalized culture, we will get there and survive the dying, but for now, love for that which is possible—as testified by the silent witness of the last standing unconquered ("uncivilized") devotees to the ways of exquisite beauty, subtlety, and complexity—is my sole beacon.

Building Bridges Along the Edges of Culture

Nilanjana R. Bardhan
Southern Illinois University–Carbondale

We live in a world that is increasingly global as well as post/colonial. European colonialism since the 15th century and the more recent Euro/American **hegemony** continue to shape intercultural relations and perceptions about cultural differences (Sorrells, 2013). The pressing question, then, becomes: What kinds of intercultural praxis do we need to engage in so these perceptions and hegemonic relations can be ruptured and altered for the sake of more equity and social justice?

In this essay, I explore the notion of **intercultural bridgework** and how it can teach us to forge connections across difference and uneven cultural locations. I narrate my identity journey through the vicissitudes of post/colonial globality, history, and power. I describe how, as a **post/colonial** and **transnational subject**, I vacillate between marginalization and privilege in various cultural locations. I specifically focus on intercultural communication encounters that demonstrate how the search for voice, self-determination, and **agency** from shifting cultural locations can take unexpected turns, resulting in disruptions and connections one may not have imagined before. I conclude that intercultural bridgework can teach us to lean toward those who are different from us and help us build connections, however tenuous, with cultural others, to navigate humanely through an uneven world full of cultural pitfalls (Sobré-Denton & Bardhan, 2013).

PERFORMING INTERCULTURAL BRIDGEWORK

Intercultural bridgework requires us to be comfortable with the ambiguous space of difference between cultures (Bhabha, 1994). Living and traveling along the edges of cultures as a post/colonial subject has taught me that the space of the "inter" in intercultural communication, while full of ambiguity, is also the productive site for intercultural bridgework (Bardhan, 2012). According to Carrillo Rowe (2010),

> the inter of intercultural communication is a capacious site of unfolding interactions across lines of difference. . . . The space of the inter into which we must insert ourselves in order to engage an/other is fraught, frightening, even as it brims with transformative possibilities. (pp. 216, 224)

Intercultural bridgework entails taking creative risks in how we communicate across cultural differences. With cultural and power differences in full view, intercultural bridgework aims to **decolonize** the marginalized self and spark self-reflexivity to problematize dominant cultural positions in relation to marginalized others. Bridges can be moments; they may or may not be long-lasting relationships. Connections sparked through bridgework can slowly or radically transform us and reconfigure oppressive power relations and hierarchies. They can also help build intercultural alliances.

Chicana scholar Gloria Anzaldúa (2002), to whom much of the notion of bridgework can be attributed, wrote:

> To bridge means to loosen our borders, not closing off to others. Bridging is the work of opening the gate to the stranger, within and without. . . . Effective bridging comes from knowing when to close ranks to those outside our home, group, community, nation, and when to keep the gates open. (p. 3)

Bridgework is especially necessary as cultures are increasingly intertwined in globalization. While we are more aware of the world as a single place today (Robertson, 1992), profound inequities continue from the past into the present. In fact, to steer globalization in more humane directions, it is imperative to perform bridgework through which we imagine the possibilities of agency and reconfigure hegemonic cultural relations.

CULTURAL ROOTS AND ROUTES: ON BEING DOUBLY DIASPORIC

I have always traveled along the edges of culture, and I have never experienced feeling firmly rooted in any particular culture. I absorb a little from here and a little from there to cobble together a sense of self as I make my way through this world. In this ongoing embodied performance of cultural cobbling and interstitial selfhood, the power configurations of how I relate with cultural others and how they relate with me keep shifting according to place, space, and context (Shome, 2003).

To contextualize my narratives of how I discovered the value of intercultural bridgework, I need to start from the position that cultural roots cannot always be taken for granted. Cultures have always traveled (Clifford, 1992), and identities have been tossed around in the play of roots and routes for ages, especially through colonial encounters. Post/colonial scholars highlight how difficult it is to constrain identities geographically, particularly within the borders of the nation-state (Shome & Hedge, 2002). Therefore, post/colonial approaches to intercultural communication help shape vocabulary for those who are unable to easily speak the language of roots.

Colonization strikes at the roots of cultures and their identities. Colonial ideology exhorts the colonized to reform their "backward" identities and emulate the "progressive" colonizer. This, however, is never fully accomplished since the colonized mingle their pre-colonial identities with those imposed on them. This results in **hybridity**. Once hybridity sets in after the colonial encounter, it is impossible to return to pristine precolonial identities (Loomba, 2005). As a post/colonial and transnational subject, to me culture and identity have always been more about difference, hybridity, and ambiguity than about sameness, purity, and certainty (Bhabha, 1994; Hall, 1990).

The global and post/colonial forces that have shaped my hybrid sense of self were set in motion long before my birth. I was born **diasporic** in the nation-state of India (formerly a British colony for about 300 years). The term *diaspora* is derived from a Greek term that means "to scatter from an origin." People in diaspora live physically away from their "homeland" and constantly dwell in the tension of being between "here" and "there" (Clifford, 1994). There was no distinct nation-state called India when my parents were born. Before my birth and around the time of formal independence from colonial rule in 1947, my parents and their families were dislocated from the country known today as Bangladesh to the country known today as India. Growing up, I heard numerous tales of the Partition (the violent splitting of the subcontinent into India, Pakistan, and eventually Bangladesh) and the refugee experience. I still hear these stories today as retired relatives spend their time creating and sharing family trees that crisscross national boundaries in attempts to find a sense of cultural roots. These trees have many proliferating branches, but the roots always remain ambiguous and open-ended.

To add another layer to cultural displacement, I was born in a place within India (Delhi) that is a good distance away from the region where people of my ethnicity (Bengali) mainly reside (Kolkata). I was a *probashi* (a Bengali term for someone who is from but lives outside the culture). We traveled every year during my summer holidays to Kolkata, met with relatives and did the work of connecting with "our culture." But during all this, I never felt as though I completely belonged. I was always the *probashi* cousin, granddaughter, or niece who was from Delhi and would leave soon. While in Delhi, I was the Bengali (an ethnic minority) whose family came from somewhere else.

Years later, I moved across continents and gradually built another home in the United States. For the past 20-some years I have been doubly diasporic in my transnational existence. My parents moved back to Kolkata after 40 years of living in Delhi, and our Delhi home was razed to the ground by developers. An apartment building has gone up in its place, and there is no physical evidence anymore of the house where I grew up. Within the United States, I will always be someone who came from somewhere else. Home, for me, is scattered across multiple cultural spaces and has no sense of geographic permanence about it. I'm always from somewhere else, and this now feels natural to me.

According to Hall (1990), the diasporic consciousness is defined "not by essence or purity, but . . . by a conception of 'identity' which lives with and through, not despite, difference; by *hybridity*" (p. 235; emphasis in original). How does one think of cultural identity and belonging when the forces of colonization and globalization have made routes, rather than roots, more prominent in one's life? Should I search for a cultural center in my identity when I have never experienced being culturally rooted? Do I put myself in an impossible position when I do that? Despite these persisting questions, the one thing that has become clearer to me over the years is the value of spaces *between* cultures, spaces that seem closer to those moving along the edges. I have come to mark and treasure those moments when hybrid embodied performances of my culturally decentered self help disrupt stereotypes and build bridges between different cultural locations (Anzaldúa, 2002; Malhotra & Pérez, 2005). I now share some moments in my post/colonial identity journey that have guided me toward intercultural bridgework.

"ALL YOU INTERNATIONAL STUDENTS—SO UNRELIABLE!"

More than 20 years have passed since this encounter, but I still tell the story—especially in the classroom, since it illustrates how certain ascriptions and labels can deeply alter our sense of self and how bodies are positioned and racialized within the cultural politics of a post/colonial world. It was an encounter that brought home to me, in a visceral way, the experience of being overtly labeled as the racial other. I had experienced otherness before, but none of those times had felt so harsh, oppositional, and distancing.

As a brand new "international student" (a label I hadn't quite internalized yet) in the United States, I was looking for work to cover my living expenses. I was hired for a part-time dining hall job, but in a matter of days I also received a full assistantship. I felt torn since I did not want to disappoint the woman who had hired me, nor did I want to give up the much-needed assistantship. My naïve solution was to find another graduate colleague who was looking for a job. I assumed she could replace me, that I would save face and also spare the supervisor the trouble of looking for someone else. When I explained the situation to the supervisor (an older, white, U.S. American woman), the immediate words out of her mouth were: "All you international students—so unreliable!"

I was speechless, with no response to her outburst. Her words made me realize, in one fell swoop, that I was without a doubt the lesser other. While race was not brought up explicitly, I was acutely aware of its power in this moment. After all, most international students come to the United States from majority nonwhite societies. I was now a member of this sweeping category of "all you international students"—collectively responsible, with all these students who arrive from so many different cultures around the world, for being inadequate and generally unreliable. For the first time in my life, I experienced what it feels like to be dismissed and disparaged as an alien brown body in a majority white context. I was shaken to the core by this translation of my identity. My graduate colleague, a white, U.S. American woman, simply kept quiet. She later expressed to me that I had been treated unfairly, but when I asked if she would help me follow up on this matter, she quickly shied away.

This encounter was my first overt experience of being positioned as a body of color in a transnational context marked by European colonial constructions of racial hierarchy (Young, 1990). Up to this point in my life, while I had not experienced cultural rootedness, I had lived in a country where most people looked like me. I had also enjoyed class privilege.

Scarred by 300 years of British colonialism, the postindependence India I grew up in was preoccupied with the need to construct a positive national identity. Stepping outside that environment and into a majority white context inevitably had consequences for my identity.

Said (1978) has eloquently made the case that the construction of "the Rest" (or the non-West) during colonial times put firmly into place a hierarchy of how bodies of color (the colonized other) are coded discursively and imagined in white colonizing societies. They are the negative or binary opposite of the desired identity of the white body (Loomba, 2005). If the white body is rational and advanced, then the colonized body of color is overly emotional, primitive, and childlike. If the white body is reliable, then the colonized body of color is not. In the specific context of race history/relations and perceptions of foreigners (especially foreign labor) in the United States, my post/colonial body had been positioned within this Euro/U.S. hegemonic racial hierarchy. While I recognized this, I could not allow it to damage me.

SPEAKING BACK THROUGH EMBODIED HYBRIDITY

Hoffman (1998) wrote that "if [cultural] translation [of the self] doesn't break you, it can enrich you very much" (p. 23). Post/colonial scholars such as Homi Bhabha and Stuart Hall also emphasized that identities and meanings associated with colonizers and the colonized can be fixed and unfixed. The cultural spaces we travel through inevitably translate our identities. In this process of translation lies the possibility for disrupting negative stereotypes, challenging dominant identities, and building connections across differences. This is something I learned eventually.

About a year later, I was in queue at the bursar's office. When my turn came, and before I even opened my mouth, the woman (white, U.S. American) behind the counter began to speak very slowly and loudly, obviously assuming I would have trouble comprehending her English. While she did not say anything overtly discriminatory, I once again experienced being automatically positioned as the lesser other, and my mind immediately flashed back to the encounter narrated above. The presence of my "international" body of color had triggered for her certain assumptions regarding my linguistic abilities.

I had two clear options: I could let my previous encounter color my judgment and perform difference in a way that would widen the gap between us, or I could let this slide and nurse the wound of another assault on my identity. In those few moments I wondered if there was another way, a way to push/speak back against this particular translation of my identity and challenge hers as well. In so doing, could I also perform my hybrid self in a way that would accomplish a moment of connection across uneven cultural locations? Just pushing back would serve the purpose of rescuing my own sense of self, but would it bring about any transformation or spark self-reflexivity in my interlocutor?

The process of colonization includes colonizing language. English is the dominant language of globalization not because it is naturally superior to other languages. The languages of European colonizers, specifically English, have colonized other languages for centuries, to the extent that most of the post/colonial writers and scholars today write in the very language of the colonizer. But communicating in the colonizer's language does not mean one has to buy into the colonizer's ideologies. It is possible to talk back in that very language (hooks, 1989; Rushdie, 1982) for the purpose of disrupting hegemonic constructions of difference. In fact, using the colonizer's language could be seen as a subversive move that allows post/colonial subjects to perform the linguistic politics of disrupting the constructed superiority of the colonizer's language (Weedon, 2004).

I could clearly see that my interlocutor had a limited sense of the relations between diverse post/colonial bodies of color and the English language. One cannot blame her entirely, since she is part of a larger system that promotes this ignorance. Students from former colonies who grow up with English as one of their primary languages and wish to study in the United States are required to take tests to prove their English proficiency before they are admitted. The assumption is clear—English does not belong to these post/colonial bodies. I have lost count of the number of times I have heard people born and bred in the United States exclaim with surprise, "Oh, you speak such good English." Why shouldn't I? Was it not thrust upon me long before I entered this world? English is a simultaneous rather than a second language for me. However, it is not the only language that defines me; I am fluent in two Indian languages as well. Audre Lorde (1984/2007) has written how the master's tools cannot dismantle the master's house as long as we believe that the master's house is our only means of support. As a post/colonial and transnational subject, I see myself as a gestalt of more than the master's tools, and I chose to channel this gestalt to disrupt my interlocutor's perception of me and of herself.

I responded to her in fluent English, at a regular tempo and volume, in a deliberate effort to position her way of speaking as absurd. The stark contrast between her speech and mine produced the effect I was hoping for. I saw a moment of what seemed like a combination of dissonance and embarrassment flicker across her face. My response had sparked a pause—a moment of self-reflexivity, I hoped. She then smiled slightly (which I returned), looked down, and resumed her interaction with me in a normal tone and rhythm. We had a smooth transaction, and I left feeling I had spoken back and yet not alienated this person. I know that I changed a little in that moment. I will never know if and how this encounter changed her, but I left feeling hopeful for both of us.

I walked away realizing that it is possible to talk back against stereotypes through how we perform difference in everyday encounters, even if one is ostensibly in a position of less power in a particular cultural space. I realized that such performances require that we position ourselves in ways that say: "I don't fit your stereotype, nor am I glued to any particular cultural identity. I am like you, and yet I am not" (for a similar narrative, see Chawla & Rodriguez, 2011, pp. 113–123). I was like my interlocutor in that I fluently shared her language; I was unlike her, for starters, in my obviously marked brown "international" body. I realized that the performative power of cultural maneuvering can unsettle hierarchies and stereotypes, possibly spark self-reflexivity in the dominant other, and create connection, albeit tenuous, rather than ill feelings. I realized that power does not have to be a zero-sum game. This experience of speaking back instead of feeling speechless, and disrupting without attacking, felt empowering.

Here, I am reminded of the words of Sandoval (2000), who writes that marginalized and historically oppressed people perform "differential consciousness," which entails being able to maneuver between different ideologies and identity positions with a politics that strives to "ensure that ethical commitment to egalitarian social relations be enacted in the everyday, political sphere of culture" (p. 61). According to her, differential praxis is a performative (re)coding of the self in context and in relation to cultural others, and is driven by hope and the desire to decolonize the self.

THE VALUE OF BRIDGEWORK

From where I stand today (and the ground keeps shifting), it is in these spaces between cultures where I find hope and a sense of agency, home, and belonging. I no longer carry the label of "international student," and my power locations have shifted over the years I have lived in the United States. I am now a tenured professor, and I vacillate between privilege and marginalization depending on cultural location and context (Martin & Nakayama, 1999). In the classroom in the United States, I have privilege as a teacher, but I am also still an immigrant and woman of color. I use my privilege when I can to disrupt colonial viewpoints and be an ally to those who are marginalized. When I find myself in positions of obvious cultural disadvantage, I look for opportunities to perform myself in ways that disrupt the hegemonic perceptions of those in positions of power, and welcome them as allies. Marginalization and privilege seem so arbitrary and yet so very real, with real consequences. Hope seems to lie in the space of the "inter."

The "inter" is a space we must pay careful attention to. It is a space where, as Warren (2008) argues, we understand how we "do" difference and choose to engage in alternative performances of difference so we can "increase our ability to be agents of interruption, critique, and change" (p. 300). Thus, bridgework entails performing difference in creative ways to break stereotypes, reconfigure hegemonic relations, and create connections across differences. It also entails a specific approach to belonging that is not about clinging to cultural centers but about leaning toward the "edge of one's self"—it is a "movement in the direction of the other" (Carrillo Rowe, 2005, pp. 17, 27). To lean toward others we have to learn to deessentialize our identities and recognize that we are all a mix of roots and routes. For the marginalized and for those who are used to moving along the edges of culture, the arbitrary nature of identities may be more obvious. But what about those who feel firmly rooted in their cultural identities and positions of privilege?

My final point is that *bridgework is the responsibility of all bodies*—not just bodies of color in positions of less power and those who live through hybridity. Bridgework requires those who see themselves as more culturally rooted or in obvious positions of power to lean toward the cultural other with the desire to connect across differences. It requires them to cultivate the ability to recognize invitations to bridgework and work as allies for the sake of social justice. The ability to enter the "inter" requires a form of reflexive intercultural praxis and ability to realize that our identities and locations of cultural power, however stable they may seem, are always open to reconfiguration. One airplane ride across national boundaries or even a visit to a different neighborhood across town can change how we are perceived and positioned.

My post/colonial life journey has taught me that privilege and marginalization can be experienced by the same body. No one is completely privileged or completely marginalized, and the cultural other is not always someone who is different from us—we may be the other in a particular cultural location. Difference is not a deficiency but a fact of human diversity. Wherever we may stand, we need to realize that the ground can shift. Therefore, intercultural bridgework requires that we engage with the other and resist closure of the self. It requires that we accept that identities and cultures are not set in stone and recognize that the way we choose to perform difference can both aid and hinder the work of social justice for a more humane world. Our conscious, reflective performance of intercultural bridgework can make the difference.

KEY TERMS

agency 55

American Dream 48

colonization 43

decolonize 56

diasporic 57

hegemony 55

hybridity 57

indigenous 44

intercultural bridgework 55

liberalism 50

modernity 44

paradigm shift 47

postcolonial 43

post/colonial subject 55

transnational subject 55

unacknowledged
history 48

white supremacy 48

DISCUSSION QUESTIONS

1. Throughout her narrative, Mendoza juxtaposes indigenous and modern cultural values and ways of being. Discuss the differences between the two worldviews. Why is an understanding of the history of relations between the two cultures crucial to an analysis of the present global condition?

2. Both entries in this chapter draw on postcolonial theory and perspectives. What are the central themes of postcolonial theory, and why are these perspectives important for the study and practice of intercultural communication today? Using examples from both entries, discuss the impact of colonization on cultures, identities, worldviews, and the environment.

3. What does Mendoza mean when she argues that modern education is a type of miseducation? How is this realization connected to her paradigm shift and the process of decolonizing?

4. Discuss intercultural bridgework as explicated by Bardhan. What is entailed in engaging in intercultural bridgework? Develop a real or imagined scenario where performing intercultural bridgework is central. How might falling in love and grieving as discussed in Mendoza's narrative relate to intercultural bridgework as articulated by Bardhan?

NOTES

1. A version of this essay was delivered at the International Conference on "Indigenous Knowledge in the Academe: Bridging Local and Global Paradigms," June 25 to August 1, 2012, University of the Philippines Baguio City, Philippines.

2. Quotes were culled from Julia Butterfly Hill's recounting of her story in various YouTube videos (cf. YouTube: Julia Butterfly Hill).

3. For a telling account of how this process happens, see the film Schooling the World: The White Man's Last Burden (schoolingtheworld.org).

4. In a bid to join the race to superpowerdom, the United States invaded the Philippines at the turn of the 20th century, killing from half a million to a million Filipinos in the process. For a longer account of my experience of U.S. colonization growing up, see the autobiographical essay in Mendoza (2006).

5. See the direct quote from Francis Bacon in *New Atlantis and the Great Instauration*, as cited at http://sentientpotential.com/acceptance-vs-questioning-kurzweil-jobs-and-francis-bacon/ (retrieved June 30, 2013).

CHAPTER 4

Identities in the Global Context

Theorizing identity provides many insights into our understanding of intercultural communication. To examine and reflect on one's identity means to understand the self as a historical and social being. Critical exploration into one's identity illuminates the processes by which one becomes a cultural, social, and historical subject through interactions in discursive, ideological, and material worlds. We cannot become effective or competent communicators without understanding the particular social and historical location from which we communicate with others. Moreover, from a social justice perspective, we cannot take ethical or socially just actions without understanding the implications of our privileges or the lack thereof within dynamic relations of power.

Globalization has significant implications for the way identities are formed and experienced. In the context of globalization, the concept of identity formation expands beyond our immediate circle of family and friends, and is often removed from our familiar geographical locations. Identities are no longer fixed in one location or ethnic group; an increased level of mobility and connection allows individuals to form relationships and interact with people outside of their immediate contexts. At the same time, our identities are shaped and informed by the global circulation of images, representations, and desires underscored by the greater interconnectivity and inequity across the world.

The entries in this chapter broadly address the complexity of identity construction and negotiation in global contexts. In the case study from the Mexican city of Aguascalientes, Gerardo Villalobos-Romo and Sachi Sekimoto challenge U.S.-centric understanding of transnational migration by focusing on the experiences of Mexican families who remain in Mexico after their family members and relatives have migrated to the United States. Based on the interviews with local residents, the case study reveals how their transnational familial identities and relational dynamics are mediated through media and communication technologies. Shinsuke Eguchi provides an account of his transnationally mediated identity as a gay Asian man from Japan. His experience of coming to terms with what it means to be gay in the United States is constantly shaped by the global binary discourses of Asia/West, femininity/masculinity, and subordination/domination. His embodied performance of gay identity becomes a contested site of identity negotiation and resistance against hetero/homonormative ideologies and the global imaginations of Asian bodies.

A View From the Other Side: Technology, Media, and Transnational Families in Mexico–U.S. Migration

Gerardo Villalobos-Romo

University of Illinois, Urbana-Champaign

Sachi Sekimoto

Minnesota State University, Mankato

In the United States, the immigration debate remains largely U.S.-centric. Whether people support immigration in the name of human rights or oppose it in the name of economic protectionism and xenophobia, public and **media** discourses are primarily consumed by the economic, political, and cultural implications of immigration on the United States as the recipient nation of transnational migrants. What remains largely unexplored is the impact of transnational **migration** on the families who remain in their home countries while their relatives migrate to and live in the United States (Benítez, 2012). How are those families impacted by transnational migration, and how do they deal with the separation of families across national borders? This case study explores the experiences of familial relationships and hybridized cultural practices of those who remain in Mexico by focusing on the intersections among transnational migration, media, and communication technology. Transnational migration dislocates not only those who leave home but also family members who are left behind and keep in contact with their migrant relatives as they wait for their return home. Migrants and families create cross-border networks of intercultural exchange and evolving notions of the transnational family, supported by the expanding technological infrastructure of our global information society (Wilding, 2006).

In this case study, we focus on the reciprocal, yet uneven impact of transnational migration, paying particular attention to how the experiences of families who remain in Mexico are mediated by communication technologies and media representations that bring them in contact with their relatives in the United States and with images of U.S. culture. Using face-to-face interviews and ethnographic observation, the first author, Gerardo, interviewed five individuals—four women and one man between the ages of 35 and 61—who are the heads of their households in the city of Aguascalientes, Mexico.[1] These adults come from impoverished communities and in some cases migrated from rural areas to the city. Gerardo conducted in-depth individual interviews with the participants in their homes, asking them to share their thoughts, experiences, and feelings on three main topics: technology, mass media, and relatives' emigration. The following questions guide our analysis of interview responses: How does the increased presence of communication technology in Mexican households reconfigure the relational dynamics and communicative interactions among family members both locally and across the border? In what ways are cultural practices and familial identities of those who remain in Mexico transformed and contested in the context of global media consumption and transnational migration?

Our analysis reveals how the cultural space of "home" is transformed and reconfigured through media, communication technology, and migration; how mediated intercultural contact with relatives in the United States and with U.S. culture evokes desire, ambivalence, and a sense of resistance; and how migrant relatives' return home makes visible the asymmetrical power relations between the two countries and the growing cultural and economic distance between those who stay and those who emigrate to the United States. Taken together, these themes point to the disruption and dislocation of familial and cultural identities in the context of transnational migration.

In the following sections, we first provide a brief discussion of relevant social and historical contexts, including the intersection between communication technology and the formation of **transnational families**; the historical context of the impact of the Mexican diaspora on Mexican national identity; and a description of the city of Aguascalientes, Mexico, where the interviews were conducted. We then discuss the three main themes that emerged from our analysis and conclude by briefly addressing the insight gained from this case study.

MIGRATION, COMMUNICATION TECHNOLOGY, AND TRANSNATIONAL FAMILY

Transnational migration brings significant relational changes to families in the context of ever-growing **information and communication technologies** (ICTs) (Bacigalupe & Cámara, 2012; Bernhard, Landolt, & Goldring, 2009; Hiller & Franz, 2004). In the past, families were separated upon migrants' departure abroad, and communication between migrants and family members back home was highly limited. The spread of new technologies, particularly mobile phones and the Internet, enables migrants and family members to maintain frequent contact with each other. In this sense, migrants with access to ICTs never completely leave their "home." If transnational migration deterritorializes migrants' sense of belonging, ICTs help both migrants and families reterritorialize their familial contact zone in telecommunication or virtual space. Thus, ICTs impact the nature of the transnational family and the relational dynamics within, altering the experiences of sharing time and space as a family. According to Benítez (2012), *transnational family* implies "everyday practices and a feeling of collective identity and social reproduction that take place in plurilocal transnational social spaces" (p. 1441). Benítez uses the term **e-families** to describe how transnational families construct, imagine, and enact their identities as a family using ICTs. In this sense, ICTs mediate and contextualize the evolving nature of long-distance family relationships in transnational migration.

E-families, connected through ICTs beyond physical distance, also experience challenges and conflicts. The intensified connectivity between migrants and family members can make visible the inequalities and disparities in terms of their economic status, lifestyles, and cultural values that evolve and change when migrants settle down and gain economic viability relative to families who remain back home (Benítez, 2012). Transnational migration can also cause a widening generational gap when children of migrants assimilate into the host culture and lose contact with their native culture and language (Phinney, Ong, & Madden, 2000; Vargas, 2008). Furthermore, the "imagined proximity" or "virtual intimacy" enabled by ICTs cannot completely overcome physical distance, reminding families of the reality of separation, especially at the time of crisis or tragedy (Wilding, 2006). Thus, the impact of ICTs is not always positive, or ICTs cannot always resolve issues that arise from migration and familial separation.

MEXICAN IDENTITY IN DIASPORIC TRANSNATIONALISM

The impact of Mexican migration is not limited to political, economic, and cultural changes in the United States as a host country; rather, the formation of diasporic communities through transnational migration deeply impacts the home country, Mexico, particularly in relation to "the construction and reconstruction of homeland national identity" (Shain, 1999, p. 662). Ever since the annexation of Mexico's territory in the 1840s, the Mexican government and its citizens have held ambivalent views toward those who have crossed the border and joined U.S. society. Prior to the 1970s, "both official Mexico and many Mexicans have long considered Mexican Americans as deserters who have 'forsaken their impoverished homeland for capitalistic U.S. comforts'" (p. 669). While conservative groups viewed Mexican Americans' assimilation into U.S. culture as cultural betrayal, the mistreatment of Mexican Americans in the United States also enraged Mexico's national pride.

The genesis of Mexican national identity has an extremely complex history. In the 1930s, under the support of the Mexican government, Mexican intellectuals attempted to frame Mexican identity as a unified, homogeneous group, which generated a considerable cultural clash due to the presence of multicultural society in Mexico. Since then, capitalist policies, tension between tradition and modernity, demands of modernization, and the Western paradigm of civilization have shaped Mexican nationalism and the national identity (Lomnitz, 2001). In the 1970s, growing empowerment and social mobility of Mexican American communities in the United States drove the Mexican government to develop strong ties with Mexican Americans to gain access to their political and economic resources. Efforts toward rapprochement between Mexicans and Mexican Americans as a national policy were solidified in the context of accelerated economic integration marked by the North American Free Trade Agreement in the mid-1990s (Shain, 1999). Moreover, due to the economic decline in Mexico over the past few decades, the basic economic survival of its citizens is sustained by remittances from their migrant relatives, which constitutes the third-largest source of foreign income behind oil and tourism. In this context, Mexican officials transnationalize Mexican culture and citizenship by conferring Mexican Americans with greater rights and privileges as members of Mexican society, supporting "a pluralistic sense of belonging to the Mexican nation" (González Gutiérrez, 1999, p. 559).

The ambivalent relationships between Mexico and Mexican American communities reflect the tension between Mexico and the United States in larger political, economic, and cultural contexts (Shain, 1999). For Mexico, Mexican Americans represent both the promise of Western modernity and the destruction of traditional Mexican values due to Americanization and U.S. economic domination. In an attempt to modernize (yet not Americanize) the nation, the preservation of tradition becomes a contested site of identity struggle for those who remain in Mexico (García Canclini, 1995). The presence of Mexican American communities across the border, and their Mexican ethnic pride and growing economic prosperity, is a significant economic and ideological resource for Mexico to rein-vent and reimagine its national identity. In this sense, Mexican national identity is transna-tionally mediated and negotiated through ongoing contact with Mexican Americans in the United States. It is within these complex historical roots, political contexts, and economic conditions that Mexican families maintain and negotiate their transnational familyhood with their relatives in the United States.

LOCAL CONTEXTS OF AGUASCALIENTES, MEXICO

Situated at the country's core, the city of Aguascalientes has about 800,000 residents as of 2010 (INEGI, n.d.). In the past, Aguascalientes, like many other very productive agricultural cities, was strangled by both Mexican government agricultural policies and national eco-nomic reconversion strategies. Now, about 30% of the economic activity comes from the manufacturing industry (mainly operations of transnational corporations, such as Nissan's assembly plant), and around 16% is from small businesses called *comercios*, restaurants, and hotels (INEGI, 2011). During 2013, unemployment reached almost 5% (INEGI, 2014), and in 2012 the average salary was about $18 a day. Although it is not considered a zone of expulsion or a zone of considerable migration to the United States, Aguascalientes is part of the traditional region of immigration—a region that has historically and constantly expelled people—which includes the states of Durango, Guanajuato, Jalisco, Michoacán, San Luis Potosí, Zacatecas, Aguascalientes, Colima, and Nayarit. Because of its strategic geographical location, the city is an obligatory stop on one of the immigration paths to the North; national and international immigrants cross through and sometimes settle permanently in the city.

Every family who was interviewed for this study has been affected by the ups and downs of the economy. Some of the families are running their own businesses; self-employment is a consequence of lack of job opportunities, government policies, and the economic crisis. The interview participants live in the socioeconomic conditions characterized by daily struggles, deprivation, and hope. These and many Mexican families wake up facing many challenges, particularly those related to economic subsistence. Their economic lives were and are still directly or indirectly sustained by foreign remittances from their relatives in the United States. As in the rest of the country, the city is a space of unresolved economic disparity and cultural gaps deepened by globalization. Based on the broader historical and local contexts provided here, we now discuss three themes that emerged from the inter-views and observations.

COMMUNICATION TECHNOLOGY AND THE RECONFIGURATION OF DOMESTIC CULTURAL SPACE

Despite the influx of new communication technologies such as the Internet and cell phones, traditional media such as radio and television still bring Mexican families and neighbors together and create communal spaces. The neighborhood in Aguascalientes mimics the dynamic of a small city where people know one another and family remains one of the most important values (Lomnitz, 2001; Paz, 1985). The streets are busy during the day, and at night adults take chairs outside and chat while children play and gather in the streets. Music from radio stations provides the background for this daily routine and these moments of connection. This time of intimacy represents a traditional value of interpersonal connection and a cultural practice acknowledging others as family. These practices shape children's cultural identity, firmly grounding their childhood memories for the rest of their lives. After these moments of collective solace, family members retreat into their houses. Some watch television, while others, particularly children, text their friends or navigate the Internet—isolating themselves from the rest of the family but connecting with representations of the world beyond their community. In the Mexican households observed, communication technologies create a space of familial connection as well as isolation; family members spend time conversing and listening to music on the radio or gathering around the television, while the younger generation is increasingly involved with new technologies that connect them to cyber realities and virtual communities.

Communication technologies shape family dynamics beyond the local streets and familiar space of home in Aguascalientes. For the families interviewed, the absence of family members who migrated north and work in the United States has a life-changing impact. They attempt to maintain virtual relationships with their relatives in the United States. Families and migrants creatively use technological resources to preserve ties with home, culture, and family between the United States and Mexico. Separated by distance and borders, technology is a way of integrating and bringing families closer. Communication technologies create a contact zone in the household where traditional and new technologies merge, shaping the communication experiences of these families.

Gloria, who moved from Guadalajara to Aguascalientes a couple of years ago, narrated her view on how technology helps her feel connected with her relatives in the United States. She and her husband started a business, but they are struggling economically because sales are low. They have two daughters and one son. The family rents a small apartment, and they do not own a car. There are two television sets in the house, but only one is connected to cable service. A computer and cell phones are also among their household gadgets. At least once a week, Gloria uses her cell phone to talk with her brother and parents living in the United States. While Gloria is taking care of both their business and house chores, her daughter is more involved and competent with technology. Occasionally, she chats with her uncle (Gloria's brother) while she is navigating the Internet; sometimes she talks to him through video chat. While Gloria sees technology as a means of communication, her daughter is appropriating technology and transforming its meaning. For Gloria's daughter, technology is not just a means to connect with the global world but also a commodity to gain social status. Gloria recognizes that watching her brother through the computer screen is a wonderful experience, although it is not the same as having him physically in the same place. Gloria explains how being able to see her relatives on the screen helps her connect with them emotionally:

> On the screen you are seeing your relatives. It is not the same as having them here, but you feel the emotion. Yes, there is more technology now. And through the phone you just can hear their voices; it is very different. (Personal interview, July 20, 2013)

Although Gloria values the computer and the Internet as "a good thing," especially to stay in touch with her relatives, she is reluctant to learn how to use it. The rapid shift in technological devices in Mexican households creates an intergenerational gap in terms of who uses what type of technology. The digital assemblage of voice, image, and text might help strengthen transnational familial ties, but technology itself is often experienced as a barrier for some adults.

For example, Magdalena does not own a computer and refuses to speak to her son on a computer. Magdalena is a widow who is financially dependent on her son, a U.S. resident. Every weekend Magdalena anxiously awaits her son's phone call from the United States. His migration to the United States has been a difficult experience for her. After a long period of depression and not having a job, he decided to go to the United States. His relatives helped by giving him money to cross the border. As with many immigrant workers, at the beginning, circumstances were extremely difficult. He saved every penny to repay the money he borrowed from his relatives, but now he financially supports his mother, who lives alone. Magdalena and her son stay in touch by telephone. She feels that computer-mediated communication intensifies the sense of separation and physical distance from her son in the United States. She says her son "does not want to video chat; [he] just [makes] phone calls" (personal interview, July 22, 2013).

Occasionally, when Magdalena is in her daughter's house, her granddaughter is online video chatting with Magdalena's son. Magdalena refuses to see him through the computer screen. "I do not want to see him, and he does not want to see me either," says Magdalena (personal interview, July 22, 2013). Seeing him reminds her of the traumatic experience of his leaving the country, which triggers all kinds of sentiments. The emotional toll of seeing each other on the screen is unbearable for her son as well, she says: "I feel that he will have more anguish and nostalgia. Probably he is imagining how we are" (personal interview, July 22, 2013). For Magdalena and her son, seeing each other on the computer screen makes the physical distance more real and reminds them of the painful reality of separation. Even though they talk to each other only on the phone, Magdalena says that her son "feels so close to us that it has been his motivation; it is his engine to continue his new life" (personal interview, July 22, 2013).

Another interviewee, Clara, is economically stable because of her husband's transportation business. The material details of their house reveal their economic success; she and her husband each have a good car, and the whole family wears good-quality, fashionable clothing brands. Clara's brothers migrated to the United States a couple of year ago, and then her youngest brother, desperate because of the lack of job opportunities, decided to migrate as well. Clara has a similar view of communication technology as Magdalena when it comes to communicating with her youngest brother, whom she adores:

> When my youngest brother migrated to the U.S., I was worried. I went to the U.S. and I saw my three brothers, and when I got back to Mexico I felt that I left almost my entire heart, but after a couple of years, now my [youngest] brother, thanks God, he is staying with a family and it is a big family. My brother doesn't want to use a computer to be in contact with us. I mean, my older brother told me that now he has a computer with a video camera and we can have a video chat with our youngest brother, but he doesn't want that. He prefers cell phone; he doesn't

want to see us, he doesn't want to video chat with any of us. All this time it was pain, anguish. My [youngest] brother and I are very close, and when he called us, I hear his voice and I said, "He is not well!" Now, now I can hear his voice and I can tell that he is OK. (Personal interview, July 24, 2013)

In their familial relationships, technological devices are not just instruments; they are also places of imagination, spaces to re-create a sense of family, and vehicles for creating new linkages between U.S. and Mexican cultures.

Though they do so differently, Gloria, Magdalena, and Clara are using communication technologies to create familial spaces where experiences of both closeness and distance are intensified. Communication technologies not only increase the amount of information consumed in the domestic space; they fundamentally reconfigure communicative interactions and relational dynamics in the Mexican families who participated in the study. Home, now wired to the world through cable television and the Internet, is a critical site for constructing identity. In these households, daily activities are tied to and shaped by the use of traditional or new media. Home, seen as a hub of mediation, is an intercultural space (Morley, 2000) where cultural borders are blurred, transgressed, and transformed.

DESIRE, AMBIVALENCE, AND RESISTANCE IN MEDIATED INTERCULTURAL CONTACT

In Mexico, communication technologies are more than just instruments of information exchange; they represent the promise of modernity. While technology facilitates communication and the flow of information, the families interviewed perceive technological devices as commodities that confer social status and an embodiment of social aspirations and elevation toward modernization. Despite economic hardships, they make economic sacrifices to participate in practices that signify their inclusion in a culture of globalization. The commercial dimension of technology within the culture of globalization redefines people's values and their relation with the world. While access to the latest technologies and consumer products symbolizes status and success for these individuals, the participants share both desire for and ambivalence toward the promise of modern technological life.

For example, Gloria's daughter is very involved in the world of Hollywood cartoons, teen TV programs, and movies. She wants to go to Disneyland, and Gloria has had the same desire ever since she was 9 years old, when her father migrated to the United States. Both Gloria's and her daughter's generation have grown up with idealized images of U.S. culture through media representations. However, Gloria is not completely persuaded by glorified images of the United States. While her daughter wants to move to the United States and live there, Gloria opposes this idea based on what she knows from her relatives about life in the United States:

Here in Mexico you have time to play and do whatever you want. There, in the U.S., you are going to work and work, and there is no time to be with your friends, go to the movies, or play. Here you have your family, and you have the opportunity to enjoy and share so many moments with your relatives; there, you will be alone. (Personal interview, July 23, 2013)

Gloria's idea of a difficult and solitary life in the United States contrasts with a happy, carefree life in Mexico. Gloria's assessment reflects the contradictions between media images of the United States and her family's personal experiences as migrants. Her daughter, who does not have any experience of migration, on the other hand, perceives the United States as a wonderful place to live. Gloria holds ambivalent feelings toward the United States:

I would like to know [the United States], but to live there no. Actually we are hoping to have them [tourist visas] now that we have our own business, because the children want to go there [to the United States], but moving there, no. I imagine . . . I imagined it as a beautiful place, but then I see all these things, on television. . . . Are all those things happening? . . . And you are like . . . then you think, well then it is not such a beautiful place. (Personal interview, July 23, 2013)

Similar to Gloria, Eréndira has a mixed view of the United States. She owns a grocery store, but she has a difficult time feeding her family because of her limited income from sales. She does not have a landline telephone or a computer. She is the only one of the interviewees who has visited the United States, and when she was there, she viewed the orderliness of U.S. society positively: "There, in the U.S., the law system works, the cities are clean, everybody respects the law, and a comfortable life is possible" (personal interview, July 20, 2013). However, she incisively points out that "one thing is to be a tourist, and other is to live there." For Eréndira, the social life in the United States lacks the communal experience she finds important in her upbringing in Mexican culture:

There are so many differences [between Latin American and U.S. values], a lot . . . because here you can sit outside your house, outside the store, you have the small grocery store in the corners of the street, so you can walk to get your groceries. There [in the United States] you can't do that; you need a car. You don't know your neighbors. There, the human relations are bad. Well, that was the impression that I had. (Personal interview, July 20, 2013)

While in the United States, Eréndira also observed the plight of young Mexican migrants who struggled with the lack of economic opportunities and, in some cases, drug addiction or drug trafficking:

I was fortunate to visit Los Angeles, and I went to this place where there are poor people living in terrible conditions. . . . They are from different Mexican cities. . . . I asked them, "Why you are here, why you are living like this?" Oh no, it was horrible. They were young boys who arrived with no addictions, no vices, with nothing [money], and they got their wickedness there [in the United States], because all of them migrated with the dream of a better life for them, their brothers, and their parents, to buy a house for dad and mom. There they got those addictions. At some point, they get involved in drug trafficking. (Personal interview, July 20, 2013)

Both Gloria and Eréndira hold some positive views of U.S. culture and society at the superficial level, but they clearly separate what they perceive as idealized images and reality. Their ambivalent views are negotiated through media representations as well as their interpersonal contact with migrants in the United States.

In contrast with Gloria and Eréndira, Rodrigo has an oppositional view on and resistant relationship with technology. Rodrigo runs his business from his house. His garage is full of tools, with a worktable at the center; raw materials and unfinished products complement the scene. On a weekend morning, Rodrigo is working on one of his projects. His young-adult children, grandchildren, and wife are constantly moving throughout the house, making it feel like a honeycomb. Every night from 8 to 10 the family "religiously" (as a ritual) takes their homemade grill onto the street to cook and sell quesadillas. Afterward, family and friends go in the garage and sit around the worktable, where animated conversations begin. As if part of the family, popular music plays. When asked about cell phones, computers, and the Internet, Rodrigo ponders before responding: "I do not know so much about all those devices, and I do not use a computer. I work the whole day, and I just watch television news at night" (personal interview, July 21, 2013). There is a television in the living room, occupying the core of the house.

Rodrigo separates himself from using communication and information technology. He defines himself as a traditional man, taking care of his family because it is the most important thing. He repeats again and again in the conversation that we have to maintain our solid family relationship. With confidence, he says that he does not care too much about having an expensive cell phone or a computer. Limited by their economic realities, the rest of his family adapts to using outdated technology and paying through finance plans. Rodrigo is very critical of the proclivity toward consumption:

How many people have a cell phone? Parents do not have money to buy school supplies, but they have the money to buy a good cell phone. Instead, I would like to have the money to buy school supplies and not a computer. (Personal interview, July 21, 2013)

Rodrigo's statement captures the dilemma of being part of the global technological culture and yet not able to participate fully in it due to economic constraints. In his view, basic necessities are sacrificed for luxury items. His opinion points to the social pressures pushing children and families toward conspicuous consumption of technology. Rodrigo also has strong views on migration:

Definitely I do not know borders. I am happy this way. I am happy because I never wanted to leave my town. To be realistic, I can support myself here in a similar way as I can do it on the other side [in the United States]. (Personal interview, July 21, 2013)

Rodrigo also has a critical view of the materialistic emphasis in U.S. lifestyles:

> A house, cars, bank accounts, and retirement plan are the motivation and life priority for migrants. . . . Why do you [the migrants] spend your entire life working day and night to have all those things? At the end you waste opportunities to enjoy life. (Personal interview, July 21, 2013)

MIGRANTS' HOMECOMING: NEGOTIATION OF CULTURAL VALUES

As shown above, families who remain in Mexico are constantly influenced by the increased presence of communication technology, media representations, and their communication with migrant relatives in the United States. Furthermore, their domestic cultural dynamic changes when migrant relatives return home from the United States for holidays and special occasions. Typically, every year or two, migrants return home, especially for Christmas celebrations. The entire family gathers to welcome *the visitors*. Migrants' homecomings are both joyous and potentially contentious. Family members' migration to the United States creates hierarchical relationships between migrants and family members who remain in Mexico. Families in Mexico are financially dependent on their migrant relatives for expenses, from children's school tuition and housing to basic daily necessities. Sometimes the migrant relatives pay all expenses for the family members to visit the United States. When migrant relatives visit home in Mexico, the families organize big parties to welcome them. Extended families and friends participate in these celebrations. The increased and uneven relations of dependence, contextualized within the shifting cultural practices and Americanization, create points of contention and negotiation over traditional cultural values and norms.

In narrating their experiences, families manifest a conciliatory, although ambivalent, attitude toward their relatives' cultural expressions. Eréndira describes her brother's homecoming, which is mixed with a sense of joyous reunion and culture shock with her brother's Americanized children:

> It is a party. It is a pleasure because when he [my brother] comes [home], the "sacred" family is together. . . . And to see . . . to hear my nieces and nephews speaking only in English . . . and I tell them, "Speak Spanish because Spanish is your language.'" (Personal interview, July 20, 2013)

After a couple of days, when everyone returns to their daily routines, migrant relatives become strangers in their own homes. Families start experiencing cultural differences because the migrants' cultural practices have been altered. The following quote is representative of how families perceive and live the intercultural influence of their relatives. In this interchange with her niece, Eréndira expresses some cultural concerns:

Eréndira: For instance, here the tradition is that a man has to ask for his parents' permission to date a woman, and when visiting his girlfriend the man has to stay outside the house. . . . Here [in Mexico] in the past, a man would come to the house but stay outside, and there [in the United States] . . .

Niece: C'mon, aunt, how is that? The boyfriend has to go inside the house to talk.

Eréndira: No, my sweetie, it is outside.

Niece: No, aunt, there [in the United States] it is not part of the culture.

Eréndira: What I mean is that Latinos change their values when they arrive in the United States. Rather, Latinos adapt to the U.S. way of being and thinking. (Personal interview, July 20, 2013)

Second-generation migrants' relational norms, language, display of material possessions, or even the simple acts of hugging, kissing, or joking are different from the traditions of their relatives in Mexico. For Eréndira, the cultural contact with migrant relatives changes families in Mexico. Despite her sense of cultural loss, she nonetheless associates such changes with progress and improvement: "From there [contact with relatives] is where cultural change is coming to all of us that stay in Mexico, the poor, a desire for self-improvement, of progress, with the idea that we can live better, by studying, obviously" (personal interview, July 20, 2013).

Migrant relatives' homecoming evokes mixed feelings of joy and loss for Rodrigo. Every time Rodrigo's sisters come from the United States, the taste and smell of Mexican food permeates the house. Family and food are strong elements of Mexican cultural identity. Home is an evocation of memories and meanings. Rodrigo expresses his sense of loss when describing the lack of familiarity and personal connection with his nieces who grew up in the United States:

My sister, the one that has more time living in the U.S. . . . her children are from there [U.S. citizens]. When they came to visit us, you know, they [his nieces] see me like a stranger and with indifference . . . and I said, "Hi, I am your uncle," and they just told me, "Ah, OK, you are my uncle!" There is no empathy; there is no sentiment; there is nothing . . . because there is no contact over the year. They come to see you [their Mexican relatives] because their mother tells them that we are relatives . . . but they never have experienced familial contact with us, like taking care of them when they were babies. (Personal interview, July 21, 2013)

The distance Rodrigo feels from his sisters and nieces is not merely because of the lack of everyday contact. Rather, he finds it difficult to relate to his migrant relatives' emphasis on materialistic aspects of life:

My other sister, she took her family from Mexico to the U.S., they are different. Different because my sister changed a lot regarding our relationship because sometimes she . . . she doesn't know what she wants. She has one thing and she wants more, and they, you become greedy, you lost ground. (Personal interview, July 21, 2013)

The homecoming of Rodrigo's sisters creates both a moment of celebration and a sense of disruption caused by the differences in lifestyles embedded in uneven economic status between migrants and family members:

> When my sisters came to visit us it is a party. My mother, my mother is like, "My daughters are coming!" And my brothers are with great expectations; they are always guessing the time they are arriving, and my brothers are always there, in my mother's house, waiting for my U.S. relatives. It is totally different. I have to struggle to get the money to survive . . . but it is difficult for us to see how they came with . . . uh! They came with these big trucks! (Personal interview, July 21, 2013)

This familial dynamic reflects not only the pronounced economic gap between Rodrigo's migrant relatives and his family but also his ambivalence toward economic success achieved at the expense of traditional Mexican family values. In this case, his sisters' Americanized lifestyle, which he equates with materialism, is at odds with his traditional sense of family and familial unity. Despite all those changes, says Rodrigo, "we have to adapt to those circumstances! It is normal! People change! After all, we are family!" (personal interview, July 21, 2013).

CONCLUSION

Communication technology has dramatically changed the connectivity and accessibility of daily familial contact for migrant families who are geographically separated from one another. The analysis provided in this case study revealed how the increased presence of ICTs in Mexican households reconfigures the domestic cultural space and relational dynamics locally and transnationally. Intercultural contact with relatives in the United States and mediated representations of U.S. culture evoke desire, ambivalence, and a sense of resistance. Those who remain in Mexico have access to information about U.S. culture, migration, and notions of a "good life" that shape their worldviews. However, the narrative accounts of these five individuals also point to how the tensions and negotiations that emerge from familial separation are still deeply relevant even in a highly networked society. For some individuals, ICTs made the physical separation more pronounced and real; others viewed materialistic success as undermining family tradition and happiness; and some cherished their Mexican tradition while also admiring American lifestyles.

Despite ongoing connection through technology, when migrant relatives return to Mexico, families still experience a sense of cultural loss and culture shock. Migrant relatives' return home makes visible the asymmetrical power relations between Mexico and the United States, accentuating an awareness of the growing cultural and economic distance between those who stay and those who immigrate to the United States. While transnational migration brings financial support and cultural aspirations for families who stay in Mexico, their sense of family—the sense of being a "Mexican" family—is fundamentally contested and changed through this process. In a global information society, transnational families' lives are full of contradictions. Insights into how families and migrants live, manage, and negotiate these contradictions of family, home, and identity are central to understanding the implications of transnational migration in both host and home countries. In the context of globalization, ICTs, media, and migration are conduits of intercultural communication. Above all, migrants' transnational familial interactions and connections are key elements in understanding the contested and evolving identities of those who migrate and those who remain home.

"But, I Ain't Your Geisha!": (Re)Framing the "Femme" Gay Asian Male Body in the Global Context

Shinsuke Eguchi
University of New Mexico

In May 2001, I moved from Japan to the United States to attend college in Orange County, California. Before my first semester in August 2001, I took my first trip to San Francisco to see what a globally known gay mecca was like, as I had been dreaming of going there. While in Japan, I had been exposed to the U.S.-based queer (nonheteronormative) media information that presents San Francisco as a "utopia" where gay men embrace a way of gay American life. During my trip, I opened the door of a gay Asian bar called N'Touch. As soon as I entered the racialized fetish bar, I began to feel shocked by what I was witnessing. As an 18-year-old, I could not believe that a large number of "skinny little Asian boy[s]" (Han, 2010, p. 83) were chasing after a small number of muscular white men who looked older. This culture shock triggered my struggle in negotiating discursive and ideological meanings embedded in the material realities of my "femme" Asian body.

The binary between the West as *normal* and *superior* and the East as *foreign* and *inferior* has produced the historical feminization and subordination of Asian men. For example, the notion of **Orientalism** explicates how multiple constructions of Eastern cultural traits and differences have been essentialized in a homogenized manner. Said (1979) maintained:

> "The Orient" is itself a constituted entity and that the notion that there are geographical spaces with indigenous, radically "different" inhabitants who can be defined on the basis of some religion, culture, or racial essence proper to that geographical space is equally a highly debatable idea. (p. 322)

To separate the East from the West, "Asians were [deemed] inferior to and deformations of Europeans, and Orientalism's purpose was to stir an inert people, raise them to their former greatness, shape them and give them an identity, and subdue and domesticate them" (Okihiro, 1994, p. 11). Because of Orientalism, the U.S. media have framed Asian male bodies as *feminine* and white male bodies as *masculine* (Nakayama, 2002; Okihiro, 1994). Asian men have been represented as emasculated in contrast to "sexualized" white men (Hamamoto, 1994; Nakayama, 2002). The binary continues to reinforce the image of Asian men as *weaker* and white men as *stronger* in the multiple contexts of intercultural encounters.

The feminization and subordination of Asian men was also translated into queer communities. Like Asian women, gay Asian men are framed as *feminine, subordinate, and passive others*. For example, the Western cultural system of **heteronormativity**—the idea of heterosexuality as a norm—reinforces the gender binary of Asian femininity and white masculinity. This heteronormativity coconstructs and coshapes white gay masculinity as (homo)normative behaviors and beliefs embedded in the material realities of queers (Muñoz, 1999). Specifically, white, affluent men function as the standard of gay American life (e.g., Fung, 2005; Han, 2006, 2008, 2009, 2010; Phua, 2002, 2007; Poon, 2006; Poon & Ho, 2008). This racialized, gendered, and class relation of **homonormativity** reproduces the stereotype that a skinny, "femme" Asian man is waiting to be chosen by a "macho" white man who is older and wealthier (e.g., Han 2008; Phua, 2007). Asian men are perceived as desperately looking for **whiteness** in their partner choices. Han (2009) reinforced this idea: "The social context of gay racial stigma toward gay Asian men includes the feminization of gay Asian men as a contrast to hypermasculine White men" (p. 119). This construction is metaphorically called "geisha of a different kind" (Han, 2006).

At the same time, globalization dynamically changes inter/cultural spaces in which gay Asian men are positioned (Eguchi, 2011a, 2011b). Poon (2006) argued, "Global capitalism has transformed this [gay Asian] identity from being stigmatized to being celebrated, turning it into a commodity—an Asian 'lifestyle'" (p. 47). While globalization cultivates new representations of gay and Asian, younger and educated gay Asians are increasingly participating in industries such as fashion, lifestyle, culture, education, and politics (Nguyen, 2002; Poon, 2006). Accordingly, gay Asian men become equipped to actively perform multiple resistances against their racialized, gendered, and class marginalization (Poon, 2006; Poon & Ho, 2008). As Sorrells (2010) stated, "globalization is a complicated and contested concept with multiple and layered meanings, which is understood and experienced in a broad array of ways by individuals and groups with different interests, positionalities and points of view" (p. 171). Thus, (re)articulating knowledge(s) embedded in the material realities of gay Asian men requires attention.

In this essay, I write my **performance (auto)ethnography** of being gay and Asian. Alexander (2005) maintained, "Performance ethnography is and can be a strategic method of inciting culture" (p. 411). Through this method, a researcher analyzes his or her lived experience as performance that illuminates cultural, sociopolitical, and historical elements for his or her scholarly engagement (Hamera, 2011; Madison, 2012). Specifically, I unpack the simultaneous (dis)connections between my embodied performance and the sociocultural practices of gay Asian identity construction. Sekimoto (2012) reinforced, "Culture is a negotiated and contested space through which one embodies a possible self" (p. 236). By explicating my bodily knowing, I aim to complicate the multifaceted realities of gay Asian men.

MY "FEMME" GAY ASIAN PERFORMATIVITY AS RESISTANCE

My partner choices have been a space in which I struggle with white colonization of my Asian body. Based on gay Asian stereotypes, others perceived me as a *geisha of a different kind*. Others' ascriptions of my body were reproduced as my verbal and nonverbal performance (i.e., fashion, hairstyle, vocalism, and kinetics), expressed on my 5-foot-7, 125-pound body, conformed to the pop-cultural stereotypes associated with flamboyant and effeminate gay men from fashion industries (see Eguchi, 2011b).

For example, when I went out to a gay bar called Cobalt in Washington, D.C., in 2008, one taller and bigger white male stranger, "Jeremy," in his late 30s initiated a conversation with me. Jeremy was shocked to learn that I was attending a historically black university to pursue my PhD. He said, "You do not look like an academic. You look like someone who works in fashion." As he was sipping a cocktail, he continued: "You must like big black guys, don't you? I thought Asian men are desperate for white men. You want a white man deep down, though." I responded, snapping my fingers, "But, I ain't your geisha!" Johnson (1995) explained that "the 'SNAP' is onomatopoetic in form, in that the word sounds like the behavior. It consists of placing the thumb and the middle finger together to make a snapping sound" (p. 123). The nonverbal form of snapping emerged from African American cultural performance mostly practiced by women and gay men; non-African Americans began to adopt an art of snapping due to the contemporary pop-cultural commodification of African American identity performance (Johnson, 1995). Coming from Japan, I adapted the nonverbal art of snapping to engage in an *Americanized* performance. After my snapping, I left the conversation with Jeremy while I illustrated another form of exaggerated flamboyant performance, the twirl. Kenya Moore, an African American female cast member of *Real Housewives of Atlanta,* repeats "Now twirl!" in her song "Gone with the Wind Fabulous" (2012).

While Jeremy exercised his power to subordinate my body, I resisted his colonizer's act by illustrating my queer critical race consciousness. Poon and Ho (2008) offer support, stating that "negative stereotypes have imposed certain meaning onto gay Asians' bodies but they [gay Asian men] do not simply accept these meanings" (p. 260). The aforementioned casual encounter indicates that my development of queer critical race consciousness has been necessary for me to navigate white, hetero/homonormative spaces. My (dis) identifications with whiteness in my partner choices are a negotiated product of my intercultural encounters that (re)produce the hetero/homonormative hierarchy that has emerged from Western imperialist racialized ideology. Muñoz (1999) argues, "Disidentification resists the interpellating call of ideology that fixes a subject within the state power apparatus" (p. 97). In this space of Western imperialist power relations, I have embodied a "bitchy" persona to prevent my "colorful" body from being colonized by the white male gaze.

The Western imagination of (gay) geisha has also been reinforced in my *color-to-color* relationships. Jackson and Moshin (2010) argued that "we bear witness to marginalized racial Others whose identities remain seemingly inescapably constituted, defined, and dominated by the perennial White subject" (p. 358). For example, I lived with my previous partner "Jesse" for three months in Washington, D.C., in 2011. Jesse identifies himself as a black bisexual man and is about 5 foot 10 and 205 pounds, and 1 year older than me. What was troubling in this relationship was that he expected me to perform gay Asian stereotypes. As a member of the U.S. Navy, Jesse had lived in Japan for 4 years. There he performed his colonial superiority, as the U.S. military continues to maintain a number of bases in Japan. The U.S. soldiers are "protectors" of the Japanese territory. In this sociopolitical and historical context, Jesse internalized hegemonic constructions of Western imperialist masculinity. He developed and negotiated his Western imagination of Asia as feminine/submissive/passive to engage in his embodied performance of gender, sexuality, and race in the transnational context. His black body became a contradictory site of reinforcing the white/Western production of U.S. Americanism.

Based on West/East binary thinking, Jesse thought I should be the one who took care of the household, including cooking and cleaning, because he is the U.S. American (or *masculine*) and I am the Japanese (or *feminine*). Whenever I expressed my opinion that he should be helping me, he would say, "The Japanese I knew were not opinionated. You must be Korean or something." With this statement, he not only avoided addressing the various binary constructions but simultaneously challenged my Japanese cultural identity performance that did not conform to his "Western" imagination. His sarcasm was meant to irritate me, because he knew the historical complexity of Japan–Korea relations. Furthermore, he often (re)produced the binary between himself as an *American* and me as a *foreigner* when we disagreed on relational issues. He would say, "You think that because you are FOB (fresh off the boat)."

To resist Jesse's internalization of the Western imagination of (gay) geisha, I again engaged in the exaggerated performance of femininity. When Jesse suggested I should cook and clean, I replied, "Well, I will do so as long as you will promise to take me out to an expensive dinner date this weekend," paired with my snapping. He heard me, as he took me out for the dinner. As our relationship further deepened, however, Jesse did not positively interpret my resistive performances. When I expressed my resistance against Jesse, he judged me as being too dramatic. He said, "Why do you have to make everything complicated? You are dramatic. I am getting tired." Soon after, he began to dismiss my resistive voice and performances, and my relationship with Jesse ended. I wonder whether our relationship would have survived if I were able to successfully perform passive, domestic, and caretaking acts.

Given the effects of global imperial politics, I feel as though it is impossible for me to escape from the Western imagination of (gay) geisha in my intraqueer/intercultural encounters. However, I continue to prefer to position myself in queer color-to-color relationships because queers of color share multiple racialized, gendered, and class experiences in a larger white, hetero/homonormative world. Simultaneously, queer color-to-color relationships occur within the historical continuum of globalization where the West remains hegemonic. Queers of color are also subjected to internalize power dynamics of Western imperialist racialized ideology. I acknowledge that the localized space in which I engage in my embodied performance is paradoxical.

PARADOXES OF MY INTERSECTIONAL IDENTITIES

Upon becoming a college professor, I began to negotiate my advantage in the context of my disadvantaged positionality as a "femme" gay Asian man. Martin and Nakayama (2010) argued, "Individuals may be simultaneously privileged and disadvantaged, or privileged in some contexts and disadvantaged in others" (p. 68). As viewed from outside the Ivory Tower, I acknowledge that I have a certain advantage due to my degree and occupation. My higher educational status reproduces the *model minority* stereotype, as Asian Americans "are believed to enjoy success in education, rising income, a strong work ethic, and freedom from problems in mental health and crime" (Sun & Starosta, 2006, p. 120). However, my "femme" Asian body, which does not conform to the hegemonic representation of being a college professor, complicates my supposedly advantaged positionality. My body signifies the racialized and gendered images of being younger and immature in the white-majority Ivory Tower because I am not a *typical* white, heterosexual male professor who is above the age of 40.

For example, on the first day of the fall 2012 semester, in my class of 30 students, I introduced the syllabus and asked, "Do you have any questions?" One white female student in her early 20s asked, "How old are you?" I responded, "Why does it matter?" She replied, "You look so young for a PhD." In this moment, she reinforced how my body is not the hegemonic signifier of being a PhD faculty member. I responded, "You will get to know me as the course goes on," to avoid a potential intercultural clash on the first day. At the same time, I questioned if she would have asked the same question of an older, more "mature" faculty member (or of a young, white male professor). My "femme" Asian body potentially allowed her to feel comfortable asking the question in the classroom setting.

Additionally, I was sitting with a couple of other faculty members, talking about tenure and promotion at a communication conference in April 2013. Another faculty member's graduate student, a tall white man in his late 20s, joined the conversation. I introduced myself and handed him my business card. The conversation about tenure and promotion continued for 5 to 10 minutes, and then the student asked me, "Where and what are you studying?" Suddenly, everyone went quiet. I resisted his ascription of my body by saying, "I am actually a faculty member, although I look like a student." In this scenario, the student could not process the (dis)connection between my status and body even when he heard our conversation. He could not associate my body with what he envisioned as an "authentic" faculty member.

While I provided two instances here, I frequently encounter similar situations in which I am mistaken for a student. Alexander (2012) argued, "The university and the classroom as a specific cultural site is a powerful location of cultural conflict and potential transformation" (p. 88). The moment others challenge my professional identity, it is clear how "my body is a text complete with codes and signifiers, meanings, and messages" standardized by the white/Western imperialist racialized ideology (p. 95). To prevent others' ascriptions on my gay Asian body, I often disclose what I do at the beginning of conversations with new acquaintances. However, I question why I feel pressured to brag about my occupation. Why do I need to justify what I do?

My resistive performance to others' ascription becomes another paradoxical aspect of who I am. My Japanese nationality further complicates the meanings of my body in the white-majority Ivory Tower. As I have embodied my Asian American racial category to make sense of my gender, sexuality, and body, my authentic "Japaneseness" has become paradoxical in my intercultural encounters. Calafell and Moreman (2010) argued, "As we repetitively answer the discursive call, our racial identity becomes naturalized for ourselves and for others" (p. 403).

For example, I was invited to guest lecture for a gender and Japanese popular-culture course at my current institution in April 2013. After the lecture, the students asked me about queers in Japan. One white female student asked, "What is it like to be gay in Japan today?" This question put me on the spot because I actually do not know how to be gay in

Japan. Since 2001, I have been in the United States. I have developed my way of gay life in the United States. As I began to feel like *a foreign other* in this conversational moment about queers in Japan, the instructor asked me, "Do you know if there is a gay pride and parade in Japan? Is it big like in New York?" I know that a parade and pride event occur in Tokyo; however, I have never attended the event. Feeling that my authentic "Japaneseness" was questionable, I reflected on my transnational processes of becoming gay and Asian.

A couple of years after I moved to the United States, I deeply wanted to escape from others' view of me as an FOB gay Asian. I was insecure about my accent when I spoke English. In my hope of compensating for my accent, I tried to imitate the way I thought gay Asian Americans nonverbally perform, because the label *Asian American* signifies the authenticity of U.S. American membership with "Asian" bodies. I wanted to be an (Asian) American to escape from the historical foreignization of my body. However, the domination of whiteness is everywhere. Whether American-born or foreign-born, gay Asians/Asian Americans are marginalized in queer spaces. In this context of marginalization, I cultivated my racialized identification as a gay man of color to resist white normativity. Simultaneously, I began to view African Americans as the "authentic" racial minority because I internalized the notion that "'race' means, quintessentially, African American" (Delgado & Stefanic, 2012, p. 75). I admired, desired, and/or adapted forms of African American cultural identity performance to perform my identity as a gay man of color. Consequently, I "forgot" to renew my authentic "Japaneseness" in (queer) Japan.

My reflection reminded me of how I felt about my reentries to queer Japanese spaces. Anytime I went back "home," I visited *Shinjuku Nichoume* (新宿二丁目) in Tokyo, where the queer district is located. I have been to gay bars such as Advocates, Arty Farty, and Dragon. As soon as I reentered those spaces, I observed the circulation of U.S. pop-cultural imperialism. They played U.S. songs by artists such as Beyoncé, Chris Brown, Ne-Yo, and Nicki Minaj. The bars were designed very similarly to gay bars in the United States. Chávez (2013) maintains that the white/Western normative ways of gay life are constantly exported to non-Western countries. This phenomenon is called "gay imperialism" (Haritaworn, Tauqir, & Erdem, 2008). In this space, I felt temporarily "at home" because I felt as if I was in one of the gay bars in the United States. Soon after I entered the space, however, I began to feel like a *foreign other*.

For example, I was drinking a cocktail with my Japanese female friend at a gay bar in Tokyo in January 2013. One guy around my age said to me, "Hey, what's up! Where are you from?" Just like younger, cool American men, he engaged in the nonverbal performance of a head nod, as Hollywood movies globally circulate the normative American ways of interaction. However, his accent hinted to me that he spoke Japanese. So I responded in Japanese, "I am Japanese. You can speak Japanese with me." He code-switched to Japanese and answered, "Really? I thought you were Asian American or maybe from Singapore. You do not look Japanese."

In this moment, I faced what Goodman (2012) called *henna-nihonjin* (変な日本人), meaning that Japanese returning from abroad are perceived as *strange* because of their "foreign-like" identity presentation. On the one hand, I should take this man's ascription as a compliment; since I left Japan in 2001, I have wanted to express the performative illusion of "Americanness" to fit into (queer) America. On the other hand, I feel strange that I am otherized in (queer)

Japan. I was born and raised in Japan. Chen (2010) reinforced, "As context shifts, one's identity takes on new dimensions and different meanings" (p. 488). So *who am I?* Answering this question is part of my ongoing journey of living globally and locally.

(RE)FRAMING MY PERFORMATIVITY

I hope that I have offered my readers an alternative perspective on the contested and contradictory nature of intercultural communication through my performance (auto) ethnography. I want to emphasize that I am not angry being trapped in my body; however, I feel it is my academic responsibility to voice my vulnerability and emotion in my research to promote social justice. Challenging, negotiating, and resisting my embodiment of culture through communication is a way for me to transform legacies of colonization that (re)produce the feminization and subordination of Asians. To further unpack hetero/homonormative power relations in the historical continuum of globalization, I am actively (re)articulating the global imperialist imaginations of binaries such as Asia/West, femininity/masculinity, and subordination/domination embedded in the material realities of my "femme" Asian body. Through my exaggerated performance of femininity, I am also disrupting the global politics of racialized, gendered, and class hierarchy. At the same time, my resistive performance (re)produces contested and complex paradoxes of assimilation as resistance and visibility (in the United States) and as alienation (in Japan). For that reason, I will continue speaking about my bodily knowing as a paradoxical form of assimilation/resistance.

In closing my narrative, I invite my readers to reflect on their everyday identity performances. How do you identify with and contribute to hegemonic relations of power? How do you engage in resistive and counterhegemonic performances to disidentify with hegemonic relations of power? Do you adapt particular forms of performances to resist hegemony? If so, why and how? I suggest that all readers engage in unpacking their embodied performances to articulate how hegemonic relations of power (re)produce their experiences. In so doing, readers will take a step of critical transformation to (re) frame their intercultural encounters.

KEY TERMS

diasporic
   transnationalism   67

e-families   66

heteronormativity   78

homonormativity   78

information and
   communication
   technologies   66

media   65

migration   65

Orientalism   77

performance (auto)
   ethnography   78

performativity   78

transnational families   66

whiteness   78

DISCUSSION QUESTIONS

1. In Villalobos-Romo and Sekimoto's case study, how does transnational migration impact families in Mexico? How is the definition of "family" changing in the context of transnational migration and through the use of communication technology?

2. In what ways do Villalobos-Romo and Sekimoto argue that media and technology reconfigure the domestic cultural space of Mexican families' homes? How do communication technologies shape the way you and your family use private space and interact with one another in your home?

3. In Villalobos-Romo and Sekimoto's case study, what kind of insight do you gain by looking at "the other side" of Mexico–U.S. migration? How can we challenge the U.S.-centric views of immigration and understand the interconnected nature of transnational migration?

4. Eguchi critiques how the feminization of gay Asian men as "geisha of a different kind" feeds into white hypermasculinity within lesbian, gay, bisexual, transgender, and queer (LGBTQ) communities. How can we challenge the stereotypes of feminized Asian masculinity without perpetuating the sexist stereotypes of Asian women as docile and submissive? How is Eguchi's struggle as a gay man different from and/or similar to that of heterosexual Asian women?

5. In Eguchi's personal narrative, how do both heteronormativity and homonormativity shape his identity struggle? How are normative ideologies of race and gender in heterosexual contexts translated into, and reproduced within, LGBTQ relationships?

6. Eguchi uses the term *gay imperialism* to describe the spread of a Western gay lifestyle in the form of commodities in non-Western countries. In what ways are LGBTQ cultures commodified, and what are the political implications of the commodification of their identities on a global scale?

NOTE

1. Gerardo translated the interviews from Spanish to English.

CHAPTER 5

Intersectionality, Identity, and Positionality

Engaging in intercultural communication can be a transformative experience, not only because we learn about different cultures but also because it pushes us to learn about ourselves. When we encounter "differences," we are compelled to examine how our perspectives are informed by particular experiences and situated social locations. Engaging in intercultural communication requires self-reflexivity to understand how we have become who we are as a result of historical and social forces and how we enact and perform our identities within shifting historical contexts and geographical locations. This chapter provides analytical perspectives and concrete examples of how we can understand, analyze, and transform communicative practices in intercultural contexts by focusing primarily on intersectionality and positionality. Intersectionality is a concept that illustrates the multiplicity of social forces that shape our situated experiences and identities, whereas positionality points to the fact that our identities are always relationally shaped within hierarchies of power.

Gust A. Yep problematizes "the race/class/gender/sexuality mantra" that underscores the way intersectionality is used as a theoretical concept. Yep cautions against a formulaic and superficial treatment of identities as a set of intersecting categories and instead proposes "thick intersectionalities" as an alternative approach that accounts for the lived nuances and embodied specificities of situated subjectivities that resist a neatly organized conceptual modeling. In her personal narrative, Eddah M. Mutua provides autobiographical vignettes to illustrate her shifting intersectional identities and ways of knowing as she moved from her home country, Kenya, to the United Kingdom and, finally, to the United States. In each cultural location, she encounters various ways in which post/colonial histories shape intercultural relations and intergroup dynamics. She takes a critical, self-reflexive approach as a way of decolonizing and cultivating ways of knowing that are at once historically informed, culturally situated, and transformative.

Toward Thick(er) Intersectionalities: Theorizing, Researching, and Activating the Complexities of Communication and Identities

Gust A. Yep[1]

San Francisco State University

The concept of intersectionality is in a strange transitional phase between emergence and ubiquity. The former commands attention but risks suspicion; the latter confers a legitimacy but risks loss of specificity. It both explodes into a proliferation of identity categories and implodes into a distillation of such categories into a simplistic model.

—Levine-Rasky (2011, p. 239)

Since its emergence in black feminist thought several decades ago (Combahee River Collective, 1977/2003), **intersectionality** has become a critical concept and analytical tool for the examination and understanding of identities in the sociocultural domain in an era of neoliberal globalization (Anthias, 2005; Brah & Phoenix, 2004; Levine-Rasky, 2011; McCall, 2005). Facilitated by policies of massive government deregulation, privatization, and economic advantages given to private enterprise at the expense of social services, community development, and the public good, neoliberal globalization refers to the rapid increase of uneven cultural flow, including ideas, connectivities, and products, from one nation-state to another, mostly fueled by large transnational corporations driven by market expansion and profit (Elia & Yep, 2012). Intersectionality, according to McCall (2005), refers to "the relationships among multiple dimensions and modalities of social relations and subject formations" (p. 1771). Put more simply, intersectionality refers to how race, class, gender, sexuality, the body, and nation, among other vectors of difference, come together simultaneously to produce social identities and experiences in the social world, from privilege to oppression.

Recognizing the importance of intersectionality, communication scholars—particularly those in critical intercultural communication, feminism and womanism, and performance studies—have incorporated it in their work in recent years (e.g., Chávez, 2009; Fisher, 2003; Houston, 2012; Johnson, 2001, 2013; Lee, 2003; Yep, Olzman, & Conkle, 2012). However, as intersectional research continues to proliferate in communication and elsewhere, a number of theoretical and methodological issues have emerged (Levine-Rasky, 2011; Yep, 2010, 2013b). In this essay, I explore some of these issues by elaborating on my earlier conceptualization of "**thick intersectionalities**" (Yep, 2010, p. 173). To do so, the essay is divided into three sections. First, I discuss some of my concerns with current work on intersectionality in communication. Next, I explore ways, by using the notion of "thick(er) intersectionalities,"[2] to produce more nuanced and complex examinations of identity in communication in an era of neoliberal globalization. I conclude by discussing some of the methodological and political implications of using thick intersectionalities in our work.

SOME (OF MY) CONCERNS WITH CURRENT INTERSECTIONALITY WORK

Since intersectionality focuses on the simultaneous interplay and collision of major social categories, such as race, class, gender, sexuality, the body, and nation, among others, in the production and constitution of who people are and how they experience the social world, it is not surprising that social identity is a key site of intersectional work. As a social construction, identity gives people a sense of "being" (i.e., who they are in a group or community), a lens through which they perceive and experience the social world (i.e., what they see and feel in their daily interactions), and a prescription for ways of "acting" (i.e., how they are expected to behave in a group or community) (Yep, 2002).

Identity, from an intersectional perspective, can be characterized as political, historical, fluid, subjective, and nonsummative (Brah & Phoenix, 2004; Levine-Rasky, 2011; Yep, 2002). First, social identity is political because it is contingent on power and ideology. Second, social identity is historical—that is, influenced by social, economic, and political conditions at a particular time. Third, social identity is fluid, which suggests that it is ever changing and in an ongoing process of becoming. Fourth, social identity is subjective—that is, dependent on people's experiences and interactions. Finally, social identity is nonsummative—a gestalt that cannot be reduced to discrete parts, such as simply race or simply gender, without understanding how such parts interact to form a whole that is greater than its individual components. In short, social identity is full of complexities and contradictions. For example, how people navigate the demands and expectations of being a student, a relational partner, a coworker, a family member, and so on, in San Francisco, California, or San Miguel de Allende, Mexico, in the 21st century neoliberal global world is riddled with intricate negotiations. In an attempt to make sense of such complexities and contradictions, much of current intersectional work, in my view, tends to adhere to what José Esteban Muñoz (1999, p. 166) calls "the race, class, and gender mantra," which, in more recent years, might have expanded to race, class, gender, and sexuality. This mantra raises a number of issues, which I discuss next.

The **race/class/gender/sexuality mantra** produces a flat, formulaic, superficial, and "roster-like approach" to intersectionality by simply listing such categories as components of an individual's identity (Yep, 2010, p. 173). In the process, it tends to homogenize people inhabiting similar intersections. For example, working-class, heterosexually identified, able-bodied people from India participating in the global neoliberal economy are imbued with similarities based on seemingly identical identity categories, irrespective of their own life experiences, journeys and personal trajectories, and individual and collective politics. Such homogenization contributes to the erasure of their subjectivities and experiences. In addition, it ignores and hides how power is intricately involved in the production of social categories and identities; as Muñoz (1999) reminds us, the mantra "smoothly positions minority identity designations within a syntax of equivocations that defer the work of theorizing relations of power" (p. 167). In other words, it does not examine the "how" (i.e., the ways nodes of difference, such as race, class, gender, sexuality, the body, nation, and others, relate to—in fact, constitute—one another to produce a specific identity) and the "now" (i.e., the ways such identities are created in time and space, such as the identity of a "terrorist" in a post-9/11 United States and global world, for particular political and ideological reasons; Muñoz, 1999).

The mantra tends to focus more on marked (e.g., poor, U.S. African American trans women who are lesbian identified) rather than unmarked identities (e.g., white, middle- to upper-class, heterosexually identified, able-bodied men who are U.S. citizens). In the process, whiteness, middle- to upper-classness, heterosexuality, ability, and U.S. citizenship, among other characteristics, are reinforced as normal—that is, the invisible standard against which "other" identities are measured and from which they are declared to deviate (Yep, 2002). Although this is partly connected to the genealogy of intersectionality, which was conceived as a perspective to focus on the structures of inequality and oppression and the experiences of individuals who have been marginalized and oppressed in society, such tendency ends up ignoring the coexisting relationship between domination and oppression (Levine-Rasky, 2011). To put it differently, domination and oppression are two sides of the same coin; for example, no border exists without a center, and no oppression exists without privilege (Yep, 2013a). Focusing on the "'other side' of power relations," Levine-Rasky (2011) urges us to examine "the intersections of whiteness and middle-classness (and the complications arising from ethnicity)" to explore "power in relation to the enduring inequities between groups" (p. 239). In sum, there is a need to examine both marked and unmarked intersections so more nuanced operations of power in society can be revealed.

The mantra leaves out certain significant aspects of identity—nation and the body, for example—in the current global neoliberal social world. As "an imagined political community," a nation provides people with a sense of affiliation, belonging, and comradeship (Anderson, 1991, p. 6). Such a sense of belonging is so powerful that individuals are willing to sacrifice, fight, and even die in the name of community and national identity (e.g., fighting in a war to defend one's nation). As a "text," the body is a site of complex signifiers that are rendered legible and meaningful in a sociocultural domain (Chávez, 2009, p. 23). Signifiers such as body type (e.g., endomorph, ectomorph), body size (e.g., thin, fat), bodily functionality (e.g., able body), and bodily productivity (e.g., disabled body that can work) are all significant aspects of identity in a neoliberal world economy. For example, the marketing of different products and services for different types of bodies and the imperative for bodies to be economically productive so they are not considered a "drain" on a society suggest that the body is an important vector of identity. To the extent that nation and the body are not fully incorporated into intersectional work, we risk reinforcing U.S.-centrism and a host of body normativities, respectively (Shome, 2010; Yep, 2013b). For example, thin, U.S. bodies—intersecting with whiteness, femaleness, middle-classness, and heterosexuality—might continue to be perpetuated as the standard for "beautiful women" in the neoliberal global world.

Finally, the mantra tends to ignore the role of space in the production and constitution of identity (Sekimoto, 2012; Shome, 2003). Space involves more than physical attributes, such as topographical characteristics of a nation-state. Indeed, space involves multiple relations, such as political and economic relationships between nation-states, operating along with the temporal, such as historical relationships between nation-states (Chávez, 2010). In short, space and time mutually influence each other in the production of identity. For example, a brown, able, adult male body is perceived and read differently, at this historical moment, on the U.S.–Mexico border—where his ascribed identity might be of an "illegal" border crosser, regardless of citizenship—and on the streets of a white, affluent, gay male neighborhood in Sydney, Australia—where his ascribed identity might be of an "exotic" sexual being, regardless of his sexual orientation. In other words, by simply focusing on vectors of difference, such as race, class, gender, and so forth, without attention to "spatial relations of power" (Shome, 2003, p. 44) in a neoliberal global world, our understandings of identity might be incomplete, inaccurate, and misleading.

TOWARD THICK(ER) INTERSECTIONALITIES

Inspired by the work of Clifford Geertz (1973) about the importance of contextual and cultural specificities of our descriptions, I use the concept of "thick intersectionalities" (henceforth TI) to highlight more complex and embodied ways of thinking about intersectionality (Yep, 2010, p. 173). Recognizing that power is always already in all social relations, this concept refers to a deeper

> exploration of the complex particularities of individuals' lives and identities associated with their race, class, gender, sexuality, and national locations by understanding their history and personhood in concrete time and space, and the interplay between individual subjectivity, personal agency, systemic arrangements, and structural forces. (p. 173)

As such, this concept suggests that we need to attend to the lived experiences and biographies of the persons occupying a particular intersection, including how they inhabit and make sense of their own bodies and relate to the social world (Yep, 2013b).

TI features four defining characteristics associated with social identity in a neoliberal global world. First, it struggles against coherence and premature closure of identity. Second, it embraces the messiness of everyday experiences in the social world. Third, it focuses on the affective investments that people make in their identity performances. Fourth, it attempts to understand identities as embodied and lived by people within specific geopolitical and historical contexts.

To highlight and illustrate these features, I draw on a critical ethnography of Filipina trans women in San Francisco (Magat, 2013).[3] As is the case with any population, it is important to note that there is no singular or monolithic Filipina/o trans community in the San Francisco Bay Area. Indeed, there are multiple intersecting communities based on immigration status, social class, body type, gender performance, and sexual expression, among others. For example, Manalansan (2003) explores these complexities based on ethnographic work with Filipino gay men in New York City. Magat's (2013) study focuses on the racialization, gendering, and sexualization of the bodies of Filipina trans women who work as hostesses, servers, and cabaret-style entertainers at Asia SF, a famous San Francisco restaurant/bar with an international clientele. Such processes produce spectacular, desirable, and commodifiable Filipina trans bodies (e.g., exotic, beautiful, and hypersexualized) in the space while rendering "other" trans bodies invisible, undesirable, and abject (e.g., trans women who do not or cannot conform to the rules of exotic beauty and their accompanying hypersexualization). The study focuses on the performances of identity, among other things, of several women: Jasmine, who has worked at the restaurant since its opening; Aliyah, Darna, and Amber, three of the restaurant's servers/performers; and Tita Aida, an Asia SF host and transgender activist. In this essay, however, I mostly highlight the identity performances of Jasmine and Tita Aida, which simultaneously defy a number of U.S. cultural binaries, such as man/woman and heterosexual/homosexual, and reify a range of U.S. cultural normativities, such as physical beauty and femininity. In other words, their identity performances are complex and "thick."

Struggling Against Coherence and Premature Identity Closure

TI struggles against coherence and premature closure of identity through the exploration of consistencies, contradictions, and tensions in context-specific ways. This feature of TI emphasizes that identity is an ongoing process, one that is more about "becoming" than "being" (Yep, 2002). Given the processual, fluid, and ever-changing nature of becoming, identity, in this sense, is always already incomplete and full of possibilities. Acknowledging the incompleteness of identity, TI attempts to narrate these possibilities by understanding the microcontexts (e.g., communication setting and interpersonal dynamics) and macrocontexts (e.g., larger social and structural forces) in a neoliberal global world.

In his ethnography, Magat (2013) focuses on how the trans women enact their identities as racialized, gendered, and sexualized individuals at three key moments: in the dressing room when they transform themselves into "the ladies of Asia SF" by putting on makeup, wigs, clothes, and accessories, and shifting their energies to start work for the evening; in the restaurant when they serve and interact with patrons and, of course, perform various musical numbers and acts; and in their everyday lives when they navigate the social world outside of Asia SF and fulfill the duties and obligations of their "day jobs." In the process, their identities shift and change and cannot be prematurely closed and fixed as they navigate the microcontexts of interactions and relationships (e.g., employer, coworkers, patrons) that are always already infused with larger structural forces and cultural discourses (e.g., legal, political, and employment discrimination against trans bodies; cultural prejudice; racial and gender exotification; sexual objectification). Although such identities appear to be local, they are already infused with global meanings. For example, how we read and relate to Filipina trans women in San Francisco is influenced by global meanings of the "Third World woman" as a powerless victim of her own native culture (Mohanty, 2003, p. 19).

Embracing the Messiness of Everyday Lived Experiences

TI embraces the messiness of everyday experiences and interactions by narrating the emerging, fragmented, contradictory, improvisational, and creative ways identities are constituted, expressed, and deployed in a neoliberal global world. In this sense, TI calls attention to the performative and creative aspects of identity that include a mixture of socially scripted behaviors, and creativity and improvisation through the process of enactment. In other words, how an individual inhabits an identity—say, that of a poor, educated, U.S. Latina domestic worker—is a complex interplay between social scripts (e.g., a docile, agreeable, and subservient woman who performs various duties as demanded by her employer with gratitude and without hesitation or complaint) and creative enactment (e.g., a unique woman who demonstrates her intelligence and educational levels and displays greater emotional sensitivity to the children than perhaps their own parents do). Such interplay of the messiness of everyday experiences and interactions is recognized and embraced rather than ignored and discarded in explorations of identity using TI.

Tita Aida serves as an illustration in Magat's (2013) study. She inhabits many identities—a service provider for trans-identified people at a local health services and HIV/AIDS nonprofit organization (her "day job"), a host at Asia SF (her "night job"), and a local public figure and community activist (one of her "everyday" personas), among others—that play with and against one another as she navigates her social world. For example, she notes that "Tita Aida"—the identity she embodies in the local San Francisco social scene—is a mixture of script and improvisation. As a loving, caring, and humorous "aunt," imagined and modeled as an amalgamation of the campy Filipina character Doña Buding and the advice-giving U.S. columnist Dear Abby, Tita Aida adheres to the script of the health counselor provided by the HIV/AIDS medical establishment while creating the simultaneously funny and concerned woman that many San Franciscans, particularly those in queer communities, have come to know.

Focusing on the Affective Investments of Identity Performances

TI focuses on the affective investments individuals make in their identity performances. As such, TI calls attention to the affective charges and intensities of identity, including processes of identification, counteridentification, and disidentification (Muñoz, 1999). Identification refers to the process of adherence and subscription to the dominant discursive and ideological (e.g., racism, xenophobia, heteropatriarchy) forms and structures in a culture, a process that produces "good subjects" (e.g., a docile and conforming cultural citizen who maintains and perpetuates dominant cultural discourses and ideologies). Counteridentification refers to the process of rejection of and rebellion against dominant cultural ideologies and structures, a process that produces "bad subjects" (e.g., a resistant and rebellious cultural citizen who refuses to participate in racist, xenophobic, and heteropatriarchal practices of a given society). Disidentification refers to the process that neither completely assimilates nor strictly opposes dominant cultural ideology. Muñoz (1999) further explains, "This 'working on and against' is a strategy that tries to transform a cultural logic from within, always laboring to enact permanent structural change while at the same time valuing the importance of local or everyday struggles of resistance" (pp. 11–12). Disidentification produces a politically conscious subject that recycles and reworks dominant cultural meanings to include, and potentially empower, marginalized identities in a cultural system. The performance of identity by a disidentifying subject carries many affective investments (e.g., rage, delight, fear, equanimity), which TI attempts to articulate in their fragmented and contradictory ways.

In Magat's (2013) ethnography, Jasmine, who has worked at Asia SF from the beginning, describes her own affective journey—one full of sadness and excitement, fear and strength, rejection and popularity—as she transitioned to become a beautiful trans woman who has a "proper" education (e.g., she went to nursing school), holds "proper" jobs (e.g., she is a server and entertainer at Asia SF and an HIV counselor and health educator at a community health care agency), and lives a "proper" life (e.g., she is a productive cultural citizen in a neoliberal world economy) in spite of U.S. cultural hostilities toward and limited life chances available to trans people, particularly trans women of color. Jasmine's joy and pride associated with her own life successes are examples of the affective investments she makes in her daily identity performances as a trans woman whose circulation in the social world is a powerful political statement about surviving—in fact, thriving—in a cultural climate that denies trans people the right to exist. In addition, her performances of femininity and womanhood, for example, seem to give Jasmine a powerful affective charge of satisfaction, pride, and empowerment.

Understanding Identities as Embodied

Finally, TI attempts to understand identities as embodied and lived by people within particular geopolitical and historical contexts. In other words, identities cannot be understood simply as abstract social categories (e.g., race, class, gender, sexuality, nation, and the body; Sekimoto, 2012). Rather, TI focuses on the complex interaction between such abstractions and how individuals make sense of, enact, and contest these categories as they are simultaneously enabled and constrained by them in various ways and to different degrees (e.g., how a trans woman of color might be objectified and hypersexualized by her beauty within the perimeters of Asia SF, which simultaneously enables her to earn a living and limits her as a gendered person with many aspirations, talents, wishes, and dreams). In addition, TI recognizes that this process of embodiment takes place within spatial and historical relations of power.

To illustrate such relations, let me return to Magat's (2013) ethnography—and, more specifically, Jasmine—one more time. After the ladies of Asia SF conclude their staged performances, they return with a tray carrying a single shot glass containing Bailey's Irish cream and Amaretto almond liqueur topped with whipped cream, known as the "blow job." Jasmine, who had just performed a popular musical number for her audience, was now the central character of the "blow job," an act that invited a restaurant patron to drink the contents of the shot glass, placed in Jasmine's crotch, without the use of hands. The act resulted in a series of bodily contortions as the patron—a straight, older, white male tourist from Texas, in this case—attempted to consume the messy drink between Jasmine's legs. As he wiped the whipped cream from his face, the embodiment of his identity was thrown into a state of temporary crisis: He was infantilized and forced to twist his body and imitate a "gay" sex act under the direction and supervision of Filipina trans women. Through the process of embodiment, TI provides a lens to understand such a crisis within spatial (e.g., the restaurant, the larger social spaces that privilege straight white men) and historical relations of power (e.g., the colonial and imperial relations between the United States and the Philippines). For Jasmine, on the other hand, her embodiment enables new relational possibilities (e.g., opening up different ways of relating to U.S. American, straight, white men) as well as limits articulations of her identity (e.g., perpetuating the accessibility of trans bodies for voyeuristic gaze and public consumption).

SUMMARY, IMPLICATIONS, AND CONCLUDING THOUGHTS

In this essay, I noted the increasing scholarly attention to intersectionality in communication and related disciplines. Although it represents an important move in current research, a number of concerns have, in my view, emerged. Such concerns are associated with how the race/class/gender/sexuality mantra is conceived and treated in this research. More specifically, the mantra produces a flat and superficial treatment of intersectionality, focuses primarily on marked identities, leaves out nation and the body as significant aspects of social identity, and tends to ignore spatial relations in the production and constitution of identity in a neoliberal global world. To remedy some of these concerns and to produce deeper and more nuanced understandings of identity, I proposed the concept of thick intersectionalities. TI has four major features: struggle against coherence and premature closure of identity; incorporation of ways to understand identity through its messiness, fragmentation, contradictions, improvisation, and creativity; focus on the affective charges and investments associated with identity performances; and exploration of identity as embodied and inhabited by people in particular geopolitical and historical contexts. I used Magat's (2013) critical ethnography to illustrate how these features can be put into motion in research. I conclude by discussing some of the methodological and political implications of TI.

As McCall (2005) accurately reminds us, "there has been little discussion of *how* to study intersectionality, that is, of its methodology" (p. 1771; emphasis in original). She goes on to identify three broad methodological approaches—anticategorical, intercategorical, and intracategorical—to the examination of intersectionality. Anticategorical complexity is a methodological perspective that deconstructs social categories (e.g., how and why certain intersectional identities, such as whiteness, middle-classness, maleness, heterosexuality, U.S. citizenship, and so on, are unmarked in U.S. culture and appear unremarkable while other intersections are marked and regularly scrutinized). Intercategorical complexity is a methodological approach that is used to examine relations of power and inequality among groups by provisionally affirming existing social categories (e.g., how and why economic disparities and political power exist between various groups—say, Native American working-class women and their European American counterparts in the United States). Intracategorical complexity is a methodological perspective that attempts to reveal the intricacies of lived experiences of individuals in a social group by simultaneously holding a critical stance toward categories and provisionally maintaining them to analyze relations of power in a social system (e.g., how individuals within a social group—say, middle-class, able-bodied, Jewish Americans—inhabit their identities in Beijing, China, in the 21st century). Research using TI is more concordant with methodologies that highlight anticategorical and intracategorical complexities. In Magat's (2013) ethnography, for example, the focus is on intracategorical complexity as he examines the nuances and intricacies of the lives of Filipina trans women in his study.

A starting point for methodological choices in TI work might begin with the person initiating this exploration asking a seemingly simple question—"How do I inhabit my own intersectional identity?"—before proceeding to study the intersectional identities of others. Such a question encourages what Jones and Calafell (2012, p. 963) call "intersectional reflexivity," which refers to the acknowledgment of and reflection on one's own intersectional identity (whether marked or unmarked in a particular space and time) and one's own self-implication in systems of privilege and marginalization. To put it more simply, before rushing to understand someone else's identity, TI encourages people to reflect on, and deeply understand, their own intersectionalities and to see how they are implicated in maintaining systems of privilege and oppression in society. For example, men in the United States are generally unaware of their own male privilege (Deutsch, 2010; Woods, 2013). By becoming more aware of such privilege, U.S. men can become more conscious of how their gender privilege is complicated by race, class, sexuality, and the body to produce their own intersectional identities and subjectivities. Although this reflexive practice is not necessarily comfortable, it can be enlightening—and ultimately empowering—to examine relations of power in the flesh through understanding Muñoz's (1999) "how" and "now" of intersectional identities, discussed earlier.

Finally, TI has several political implications. First, with its emphasis on how people live and interact with social categories in the flesh, TI avoids the erasure of individual subjectivities and experiences. Second, with its emphasis on fragmentation, contradiction, and improvisation of identities, TI provides a more complete view of how individuals negotiate meanings and operate in the social world. Third, with its emphasis on the affective investments associated with identity performances, TI recognizes and can potentially deploy affect, such as anger, rage, and devotion, for political change. Last, with its emphasis on spatial and historical relations of power, TI effectively reminds us, in Levine-Rasky's (2011) words, "power is 'always already' involved in intersectionality" (p. 244). The exploration of the complexities of the identities of Jasmine and Tita Aida in Magat's (2013) ethnography can hopefully help people, from those who are completely unfamiliar to those who are deeply familiar with the lives of Filipina trans women in San Francisco, increase their understanding of the everyday experiences of individuals who are deemed unintelligible in U.S. culture. Such understanding can also increase people's awareness of the daily violence perpetrated against trans people in society and illuminate the processes of commodification of certain trans bodies for consumption and profit in a neoliberal global economy. Awareness of the symbolic and material violence against trans individuals can encourage people to use disidentification as a strategy to promote social change, such as normatively gendered people's subverting gender norms and combating gender violence. With understanding, people can develop more empathy and sensitivity in their everyday encounters with difference. With empathy, other affective changes and intensities, such as deep appreciation of the courage and resilience of trans people as well as anger and rage against individuals and systems that perpetuate and normalize transgender violence in society, can become more salient and can be deployed instrumentally to transform culture by changing hearts, minds, laws, and other unjust social structures.

How I Came to Know: Moving Through Spaces of Post/Colonial Encounters

Eddah M. Mutua

St. Cloud State University

In 2007, I began to reflect on my lived experiences after many years of living outside of my country of birth, Kenya. The impulse to critically examine my being—past, present, and future—was to help me better understand my personal growth in different locations and, notably, in the place I currently reside, the United States of America. I bear multiple identities based on my culture, history, geographical origin, nationality, ethnicity, race, and gender. I am African, Kenyan, Kamba by ethnic group, female, educated, born after Kenyan independence from British colonial rule, and an American citizen by naturalization. Some of the labels that identify me are sources of my marginalization and liberation. I have been subjected to prejudice in the West based on my geographical/national identity and race. My education has served as a tool to understand my own marginalization and seek ways to reach out into new spaces and experiences. It has given me the privilege to travel the world and interact with different people who have stirred me to raise questions and gain knowledge about identities in global contexts. As such, writing this narrative allows me to learn more about myself in the context of these multiple factors shaping my identity and embodied experiences.

The value of theorizing my experiences lies in contributing to knowledge about intercultural engagement in global contexts. This understanding is relevant in the global context characterized by an increasingly dynamic, mobile world facilitated by communication and transportation technologies, intensified interactions, and exchange among people from different cultures across geographical, cultural, and national boundaries (Sorrells, 2013). My narrative interrogates the complexity of identity and brings into conversation factors that draw attention to critical awareness about difficult historical experiences, diverse cultural values, intercultural alliances, and decolonization efforts. These factors reveal ways that "identity is variously construed, claimed, and contested" (Nyamnjoh, 2007, p. 73).

In this personal narrative, I reflect on my embodied experience of movement across and within geographical, cultural, and racial boundaries, using autobiographical vignettes that include growing up in Kenya, schooling in the United Kingdom, and living and working in the United States. In different ways, each location reveals factors that ease and/or complicate my interactions with those I come into contact with. I explore themes illustrating lessons learned from experiences of moving through spaces of post/colonial encounters. Such themes include cultural traditions of community, resistance against acts that reproduce the hegemony of **neo/colonialism,** and using insider–outsider/outsider–insider **positionality** as an epistemological tool for self-decolonization and education.

In addressing each of the themes, I discuss experiences that enable me to assume a critical interrogative positionality to engage with others different from me. I go back and forth recalling, connecting, and disconnecting what I have come to learn, relearn, and unlearn from my experiences in diverse locations. These experiences define my journey to self-discovery and the reasons that impel me to yearn for more than having my body bounded by history, geography, and birthplace. My critical engagement with myself and the world is to make sense of my body, birthplace, and the politics of identity, culture, and knowledge (Mutua, 2012). Overall, this narrative demonstrates enactment of intercultural praxis and the possibilities of intercultural alliance building.

Theoretical framing of the themes discussed draws from vast literature in postcolonial theory, transnational studies, critical intercultural communication, global feminism, and black feminist theory to make meaning of my experiences in a global context. Specifically, I draw from epistemological concerns raised about knowledge production, representation, and circulation (Mutua & Swadener, 2004; Smith, 1999; wa Thiong'o, 1993, 1994; Wane, Kempf, & Simmonds, 2011). Questions about what I know, how I know, and why, and about what I do not know and why allow me to deconstruct the way difference has been positioned through colonial processes. As such, my actions are geared toward reeducating myself and finding possibilities of building solidarity and humanizing the other.

POSITIONALITY AND EPISTEMIC CONCERNS

In relating my experiences, I begin by showing how my cultural upbringing problematizes my lived experiences and calls for a critical reflective response to diverse intercultural encounters. Sorrells (2013) observes that "different experiences, understanding, and knowledge of oneself and the world are gained, accessed, and produced based on one's positionality" (12). My positionality/positionalities are formed by the limits of cultural and historical contexts that define, undefine, and redefine me. By mapping how this has happened over the years, I am then able to make sense of my interactions in global contexts.

Patricia Hill Collins's (1986) notion of dual vision of marginalized people situates how I enter this conversation. First, my "alienated positionality" (Murillo, 2004, as cited in Alvarez, 2013, p. 51) positions me as an outsider/the other. Second, I am an "**outsider-within**" (Collins, 1986), as well as an **insider–outsider**. The multiple positionalities become the vantage point of constructing resistance, allowing me to consciously make decisions about how I respond to critical questions about who I am and also about how my identity and belonging in different spaces are constructed, construed, or misconstrued. Tensions about identity and what I know/do not know allow me to critique power relations and political, economic, cultural, and educational systems that produce hegemonic worldviews impacting my interactions in global contexts. In keeping up with changes in my being, I am constantly making sense of my journey from one point to the next.

My experiences vary as I am culturally and geographically placed and removed from inside and outside of the culture of my birthplace. Thus, subjectivities that influence my identity have been challenged by the urge to interrogate what I know, how I know, what I do not know, and what I seek to know about myself and others. Diverse cultural contexts and new experiences mean I desist from the "That's what we do (or do not do) where I come from" attitude. Instead, I choose to question colonial naming and representation of the other. My goal is to gain knowledge about different ways of knowing that "promote modes of being that lessen the threat of our differences by pushing us to understand and embody the world from new and different positions" (Rodriguez & Chawla, 2010, p. xiii). Writing this narrative is an act of resistance and courage to ask critical reflective questions about "what it means to be particular kinds of people, in particular places and at particular times" (Adams & Jones, 2013, pp. 2–3).

Kenya: Cultural Traditions and Start of Decolonizing Journey

Growing up in rural Kenya, I was socialized into cultural traditions of collectivism that shaped the performance of my everyday life. This pattern of cultural life prioritized values about community, friendships, responsibility, visiting, hospitality, interactions, unity, patience, problem solving, gender roles, religious obligations, and, in general, attributes that ensure maintenance of social order and sense of community. In addition, communication forms such as proverbs, folktales, and songs served as important sources of cultural knowledge. The socialization of shared cultural interpretations from my childhood continued into my adult life. My grandfather often cited a Swahili proverb as I prepared to travel to different parts of Kenya and the world—"*Milima haikutani, bali binadamu hukutana*" ("Mountains do not meet, but people meet"). The application of this proverb defines ways Africans view interactions, friendships, personal relationships, and hospitality toward whomever they come into contact with. It is also a warning against bad deeds to others. It speaks to African people's investment in human interactions. In essence, my grandfather's intention paralleled "excessive attention to traditions" (Gyekye, 1996, p. 165) that helped me learn standards of well-intended interactions with people different from me. My decolonizing journey has been enriched by these community values instilled in me and by what I have learned about the possibilities of building solidarity among people of African descent.

Schooling in different regions in Kenya enabled me to interact with students from diverse ethnic groups (including non-African Kenyans), religious affiliations (Christians, Muslims, Buddhists), and social statuses. The multicultural setting that my secondary education provided was instrumental toward my intercultural growth beyond the limits of my ethnic identity. However, as Shome (2012) opines, this multicultural setting is not to be understood through the conceptual logic and framework of Western engagement with multiculturalism in scholarship or discourse. In Kenya, as in other former British colonies, multiculturalism is "a kind of negotiated **accommodationism** that is part of the neighborliness and hospitality of many postcolonial societies" (Bhabha, 2002, as cited in Shome, 2012, p. 159). The history of British colonialism and ethnicity in Kenya explains the complexity of identity and belonging. The tensions between ethnic identify vis-à-vis multicultural/national identity popularized after Kenya's independence in 1963 point to contested notions about Kenyan identities. In an effort to reconcile internal ethnic and racial divisions, the postcolonial state had to negotiate ways to "accommodate" Kenyans of all racial and class backgrounds. Examples include deracialization of residential areas and schools, and officialization of Kiswahili as the national language. In hindsight, these efforts can be viewed as fostering, in the words of Shome (2012), "officialized" diversity and serving as accommodations needed to counter ethnic and racial divisions.

My efforts to understand identity and belonging continued at the University of Nairobi (UoN), where I learned about **Pan-Africanism** as resistance. Nairobi is a modern urban city where people from all over Kenya and other parts of the world reside. In describing my experiences at the university, I use *we* several times to acknowledge that what I learned and unlearned was based on collective experiences that were not all about *I/me* but often about *us/we*.

The faculty and student body at the university comprised diverse Kenyans (including Kenyans of British and Asian descent) and exchange students from Ghana, Japan, the United States, and Europe. Studying African literature, religious studies, and sociology deconstructed my assumptive views about identity of self and the other. This academic experience introduced me to scholarly works of renowned postcolonial theorists, including Ngũgĩ wa Thiong'o, Chinua Achebe, Taban Lo Liyong, and Walter Rodney, among others. I joined the UoN Free Traveling Theatre, where I was introduced to political activism through performance of African plays, dances, and poetry. Our activities drew inspiration from the Kamirithu theatre project started by wa Thiong'o in the 1970s, which had become a voice of protest against the status quo. We engaged our bodies in political discourses of justice, freedom, and knowledge. We learned to relearn our knowledge, reclaim our solidarity, and value borderlessness of our identities. In particular, Rodney's (1984) *How Europe Underdeveloped Africa* was instrumental in revealing effects of African colonial and neocolonial history resulting in destruction of African social solidarity and responsibility.

Getting to know refugee students from South Africa, Rwanda, and Uganda who were defined by the political narrative of the day as "foreigners" (a term used to refer to non-Kenyans) helped me gain a better understanding of Pan-Africanism. The National Theatre located across the UoN main campus provided space for Pan-Africanism renaissance. South African performers who generously shared their artistic talents and experiences in apartheid South Africa were not foreigners but a valuable source of knowledge about resistance to apartheid. Many cross-national interactions and transnational experiences evoked the spirit of Pan-Africanism among us. Popular music by Bob Marley and Miriam Makeba and the lasting memory of Angela Davis's visit to UoN during the 1985 UN Women's Conference energized us to continue with postcolonial struggles. We chose to identify with transnational experiences, for example, by wearing our hair in Afros and dreadlocks, in support of the global struggles of women and people of African descent all over the world. For me, the experiences at UoN raised critical awareness about self, history, culture, and solidarity, and enabled me to continue with discourses of resistance inside and outside of Kenya.

United Kingdom: Resisting Hegemony of Neo/Colonialism

My experience living in London defined how I developed a global identity beyond my ethnic, national, African, and Pan-African identities. The experience expanded my views about resistance against acts that reproduce the hegemony of neo/colonialism. I interacted mainly with transnational communities from Africa, Asia, Brazil, and the Caribbean. Our interactions were eased by the fact that we shared a common historical identity of colonization. This identity allowed us to engage with the "politics of **postcoloniality**" (Shome & Hegde, 2002). Occasionally, I would engage in conversations at The Africa Centre and Bush House (former home of the BBC World Service) about British **neo/colonialism** and decolonization efforts. These conversations strongly resisted colonial imposition and sought strategies to decolonize structures altered by imperialism. In particular, concerns were expressed about institutionalized economic structures that created dependency of the colonized on the colonizer through institutions such as the World Bank, International Monetary Fund, and Department of International Development, formerly known as the Overseas Development Agency. Revisiting colonial relations in the colonial capital, London, begot solidarity among colonized people to denounce common neo/colonial experiences and imagine freedom at "home."

My friendship with international students in my graduate program was transformative in educating me about global identity and social justice. This group of students from Kenya, Israel, Greece, Nigeria, Zambia, Tanzania, Brazil, Pakistan, Palestine, and Saudi Arabia was united by its diversity and quest for a peaceful world. We shared diverse experiences that solidified the desire to maintain valuable intercultural relationships and alliances amongst us. Lessons learned from our interactions became the basis of a commitment to have one another's "backs" and build "intercultural bridges" (Sorrells, 2013) to carry us across painful and difficult encounters. Sorrells observes that engaging in "**intercultural bridgework**" means developing sensitivity, understanding, and empathy, and extending vulnerability to transverse multiple positions, creating points of contact, negotiation, and pathways of connection (p. 168).

I recall the day my two classmates from Israel and Palestine responded to a bomb attack in Tel Aviv and an air strike in the Gaza Strip in a manner atypical of what we were used to as far as media coverage of the intractable conflict was concerned. Media images and rhetoric of the conflict often suggest the impossibility of cordial conversation; however, my classmates, in pain from a conflict endured throughout their lifetimes, were still able to find possibilities of peace by educating us about their lived experiences with honor and integrity.

We used our intercultural friendships to build a safe community for ourselves. Sharing our best and worst experiences with compassion helped me learn about the value of intercultural relationships in global contexts. I felt comfortable and safe with my classmates. The time we spent together cooking and eating, enjoying cultural music and dance, and working in study groups not only expanded my worldview but also shielded me from prejudice. I did not feel exposed to prejudiced and racist encounters so long as I was with my friends. In hindsight, this "exclusion" might have been a naïve practice, but it was necessary at the time. Looking back, I can now understand why I was petrified when a white man demanded that my Kenyan friend vacate a seat for him on a train from Birmingham to Aberystwyth. I did not know how to respond to such an act of blunt disrespect. However, my friend's refusal to concede to bigotry stands out as a brave act of resistance against colonial encounters. At the time, we did not know about Rosa Park's story, but I believe we were driven by her quest for justice to resist injustice. In retrospect, I can no longer assume it is possible to be "shielded" from the intrusiveness of racism and prejudice as a person of color in the West.

United States: Critical Self-Education and Possibilities of Solidarity

My experiences in the United States reveal struggles to claim knowledge about self and the other in a racialized and transnationalized location. Questions about **epistemology**, identity, and belonging burgeoned within me. The intent was to deconstruct the basis of epistemic structures that had barred me from knowing the U.S. and African Americans with whom I share a common ancestry. For example, why was I educated about geographical features such as the Great Plains, the Prairies, the Great Lakes, the Bay Bridge, and the coal mines in Pittsburgh? Why did I read John Steinbeck's *Grapes of Wrath* in my high school literature class and not, say, Frederick Douglass's *My Bondage and My Freedom*? Why in the 21st century are African Americans still treated in condescending ways? The need to address these epistemic concerns, coupled with a personal commitment to Pan-Africanism, enabled me to seek connection with the history of African Americans.

An anticolonial approach to knowing was crucial in enhancing my understanding of self and my relationship to the place I now call "home"—the United States. Additionally, I wanted to understand the hegemony and greed that "forced material seizure and confiscation of indigenous lands and resultant displacement that entailed a total reconfiguration of the social systems, of relations between land and its people and among people" (Catungal, 2011, p. 27).

Linda Smith's (1999) concept of "researching back" was relevant in reclaiming knowledge about the marginalized history of African Americans. Hence, my priority in my new "home" was to acquire African American historical and cultural knowledge, rather than focus solely on the process of acculturation/assimilation expected of new immigrants. For me, resisting this norm was an epistemological tool to seek knowledge that transcends differences and acknowledges interconnectedness among people (Kim, 2015).

Critical self-education was my avenue to get to the "center" of discourses about difference, silenced voices, and history. It became a "remedy for survival" (Outerbridge, 2011, p. 116) powered by stories of people's struggles and triumphs. These are stories not told in vain. Wa Thiong'o (1993) opines that they are voices coming from the center to free culture and knowledge from Eurocentrism.

My journey began in Sacramento, California, the first place I called "home" in the United States. Living in a transnational community of African immigrants gave me comfort and familiarity but not answers to my epistemic concerns. Visits to Oakland and Berkeley educated me about the civil rights movement and Vietnam antiwar protests. Learning about Stokely Carmichael's political and social justice activism with his wife Miriam Makeba and University of California, Berkeley's history of activism offered possibilities of connections to the history of antiracism that I yearned to learn about. I felt the same sense of connection after attending talks by renowned African Americans and Africans such as Spike Lee, Ed Gordon, Angela Davis, Cornel West, and the Reverend Archbishop Desmond Tutu. Attending an African American church allowed me to experience those "voices from the center" speaking about struggle for freedom, dignity, faith, and justice. The church gave meaning to key historical events that symbolize the sweat, tears, and blood of African Americans as the price paid for my freedom. This consciousness validated my position as an ally of the antiracist struggle in the African American community.

Uncovering the painful history that has pitted Africans and African Americans against each other was troubling. The claim that Africans sold African Americans into slavery, resentment, lack of knowledge, and stereotypes about each other remain problematic and polarizing. In learning more about the conditions of this estrangement, it became clear to me the inaccuracy of grouping all "black" people together without paying attention to specific historical experiences. African immigrants are Africans who are also identifiable by their country of origin and not as African Americans or black. This is a historical fact many African Americans are aware of and are ready to let Africans know: "You are not us." For example, in early 2000 to 2005, racial tensions in my community in Minnesota between African American and Somali students were caused by contestations over the complexity of identities of people of African descent. Somali students' efforts to "fit in" with their African American peers did not work. Nonetheless, the tension evoked in me a need to revisit efforts by Marcus Garvey, Walter Rodney, and Kwame Nkrumah to promote solidarity and alliances among all people of African descent. Hope for reconnection is evident in the work of transnational groups such as TransAfrica, a Washington, D.C.–based group working to free Africa from HIV/AIDS, poverty, genocide, and apartheid. Additionally, the National Communication Association's Black Caucus and African American Culture and Communication Division provide space to engage in conversations about the possibilities for connection among people of African descent who have been fragmented by history and racism.

CONCLUSION

In this narrative, I have addressed issues of identity/belonging; diversity and solidarity; colonization and decolonization; intercultural friendship, community, and prejudice; epistemic concerns; and intercultural praxis. In different cultural contexts, I tried to capture the essence of critical self-reflection and education in understanding the complexities of my epistemic journey and intercultural growth. Even though my epistemic journey is not over, I believe that what I have shared will motivate readers to consider their own epistemic journeys. As bell hooks (1989) observed, longing for self-recovery is not simply about the description of one's woundedness, one's victimization, or repeated discussion of problems but also about experiencing a new and different relationship to the world that was lacking. The journey of self-recovery fosters a sense of dignity and respect for people marginalized by history, culture, and geography. I have come to know that my identity and what I know reflects a convergence of multiple factors. I now have a better awareness about how my understanding of self continues to shift and expand as I uncover, reclaim, and resonate with my own and others' experiences.

KEY TERMS

accommodationism   97

epistemology   99

insider–outsider   96

intercultural
   bridgework   99

intersectionality   86

neo/colonialism   95

outsider-within   96

Pan-Africanism   97

positionality   89

postcoloniality   98

race/class/gender/sexuality
   mantra   87

thick intersectionalities   86

DISCUSSION QUESTIONS

1. The notion of intersectionality became popular because it allows researchers to account for multiple dimensions of identities—specifically, race, gender, class, and sexuality—without privileging or diminishing one or the other. In what ways could this approach be problematic? Are there situations where intersectional analysis can end up neutralizing or diluting identity politics?

2. According to Yep, what is intersectionality, and what are its conceptual strengths and limitations? What are the major differences between the traditional use of intersectionality and Yep's conceptualization of "thick intersectionalities"? What insights are gained by applying Yep's concept of thick intersectionalities to analyze your own identities?

3. In Mutua's personal narrative, how does the condition of postcoloniality inform her intercultural encounters in three different countries? How does her critical interrogative positionality of "insider–outsider" help her navigate across, and connect with, various issues underscored by histories of colonialism?

4. Discuss how Mutua's personal narrative demonstrates enactment of intercultural praxis (see Chapter 1) and the possibilities of intercultural alliance building.

NOTES

1. Portions of this essay were presented at the panel "Celebrating Three Decades of Community: Pioneers and Emerging Scholars of Identity Theory—Past, Present, and Future" at the 98th Annual Meeting of the National Communication Association, Orlando, FL, November 2012. I dedicate this essay to my canine friends Yogi ("the Yogster"), a sweet and faithful Pomeranian who keeps me company while I work; Sparky ("Sweet Face"), a smart miniature schnauzer who could do demonstrations on the obedience ring; Ace ("Fresh Face"), an active springer spaniel who enjoys vigorous play; and Rocky ("Fat Mosca"), an exuberant Pomeranian/sheltie mix who knows ways to resist our city walks. Together, we demonstrate intersectional affinity and bonding across species.

2. I am using the term in the plural to denote the multiplicity and complexities of identity as they are produced, constituted, and inhabited in the context of historical and spatial relations of power. I thank Dr. Wenshu Lee and Dr. John Elia for our ongoing discussions about intersectionality in our research and pedagogy. The chapter is, in many ways, a product of those conversations.

3. Jonathan Magat is a former student of mine. His project reflects a thoughtful engagement with thick intersectionalities in research.

CHAPTER 6

Language and Power

Language is central to intercultural communication. While language may seem "natural" and "neutral" as part of our everyday communication, it is a medium through which our deeply held values, beliefs, and ideologies are produced and maintained. For example, public response was mixed when Coca-Cola aired its 2014 Super Bowl commercial featuring a multilingual rendition of "America the Beautiful." The controversy surrounding this commercial—and whether languages other than English should be used in this quintessentially American song—reveals the complex relationships among language, the politics of belonging, and cultural/national identity.

Questions regarding the nature of language have provided ongoing philosophical debate: Does language merely reflect or mirror the external reality? To what degree does language shape our perception? Is language a set of neutral vocabularies and expressions that anyone can use freely to articulate their thoughts? How is our identity shaped by the very language or languages we use? These questions hold important implications when communicating across cultures. In intercultural communication, linguistic differences are not simply a question of translation but, rather, are differential ways of being-in-the-world grounded in cultural acts of communication.

The entries in this chapter address how language and power influence each other in intercultural contexts. In the case study, Melissa L. Curtin considers various examples from the United States and Taiwan to examine how linguistic practices and policies in increasingly multilingual and globalized societies reveal complex identity politics. Linguistic practices are always shaped by particular sociohistorical contexts and are sites of negotiations regarding citizenship, nationalism, and hybridized cultural performance. In the personal narrative, Christopher Brown recounts his memories of racialized encounters as an African American man navigating the institution of higher education. His narrative exemplifies the relationship between language and race, and how "speaking" as a racialized subject is never a neutral act. Both entries shed light on the political and constitutive nature of language and its significance in understanding the dynamics of intercultural/international/interracial relations.

Language and Identity in the United States and Taiwan: Negotiating Power and Differential Belonging in a Globalized World

Melissa L. Curtin
University of California, Santa Barbara

Language is never a simple conduit for communication and is rarely, if ever, a neutral medium. Whenever we use language, we engage in "a form of social action" by which we create contexts that often involve power relations between individuals or social groups (Ahearn, 2012, p. 8). Our language practices are especially important as we navigate "contexts of **differential belonging**"—that is, social and geographic spaces wherein certain people are granted a legitimized presence but others are marginalized or delegitimized. This phenomenon can take place at all levels of social interaction—from a short-lived, small-scale event between two people to a decades-long, large-scale struggle regarding linguistic rights for populations within a nation or transnational region.

In this essay, I first present examples from the United States that are likely to be familiar to readers. In doing so, I introduce several key concepts for understanding how language practices are important when negotiating sociocultural identities, particularly in relation to existing social hierarchies. I then present several examples regarding language policies and practices that have been important in negotiating identity and belonging in Taiwan. Taken as a whole, this material demonstrates that we must pay close attention to specific contexts—historical, sociocultural, geopolitical, economic—to understand how linguistic practices can be sites of struggle in negotiating a politics of identity and belonging. This discussion also demonstrates that various processes of globalization—such as transnational migration and the increasing influence of cultural and economic globalization—shape both language attitudes and actual language practices.

NEGOTIATING LANGUAGE AND IDENTITY IN THE UNITED STATES

Attitudes toward linguistic practices and national belonging are readily apparent in the public **discourse** of the United States today. In fact, throughout U.S. history, there has been a shifting tension between an **ideology** of **pluralism**, which envisions a national identity based on being "together-in-difference," and one of **assimilationism**, which prescriptively asserts that national identity be based on a condition of homogeneity, including **linguistic homogeneity** (i.e., English **monolingualism**; Leeman, 2004).

A Brief History of Immigration and Language Policies in the United States

An example of forced assimilation occurred between the late 1800s and mid-1900s when many Native Americans were forced to shift from speaking their indigenous languages to English only. This largely involuntary language shift was due to government policies to "civilize and Christianize" Native Americans, particularly via the forced relocation of thousands of children to distant boarding schools with strict English-only rules. Federal policies were very explicit in calling for the destruction of "barbarous dialects" and the imposition of English monolingualism; this approach was believed to be central to Native Americans' "assimilation of thought and behavior" to dominant Anglo-Saxon culture (Battistella, 2009, p. 127).

During this same period, sign language among the Deaf was also considered a dangerous practice because it supposedly isolated users of "manualism" and threatened national unity. Consequently, sign language was actively suppressed in schools and "oralism" was promoted for decades; in time, more than 80 % of schools for the Deaf promoted spoken language over sign. By the mid-1960s, however, Deaf education based on oralism was proclaimed to be a dismal failure for most nonhearing students; consequently, educational policies have since embraced sign language (Battistella, 2009).

The history of language policies in the United States also involved restrictions on so-called foreign language education. As early as 1751, Benjamin Franklin argued against the "Palatine Boors" (German immigrants) turning Pennsylvania into a "Colony of Aliens" by establishing their "Language and Manners, to the Exclusion of ours" (Crawford, 2000, p. 23). However, English monolingualism did not become central to the public discourse on national identity and "legitimate belonging" in the United States until the late 1800s. One key factor was the large wave of immigrants during this time of rapid industrialization and urbanization; between 1880 and 1920, more than 20 million immigrants entered the United States (comprising 15 % of the total population, the highest percentage to date; Pew Research Center, 2013).

Concerns about the assimilation of newcomers into an imagined, uniform national community became especially strong at this time. A number of states passed laws restricting or even prohibiting the teaching of foreign languages in schools; laws also restricted the use of "foreign" languages in public spaces. In general, "foreign languages were seen as promoting a heterogeneity at odds with good citizenship" (Battistella, 2009, p. 130). Pressures of cultural and linguistic assimilation were mostly directed toward Native Americans, the Deaf, and European immigrants—people who were viewed as potentially "assimilable" to Anglo-Saxon cultural practices (albeit at low socioeconomic status; Pavlenko, 2002). In contrast, the children of Chinese and Japanese immigrants were not considered suitable candidates for citizenship and were segregated into nonmainstream schools. These policies toward Asian immigrants allowed them to maintain their language and cultural practices, but they also marginalized the Chinese and Japanese immigrants and their children. On the whole, then, any consideration of a national identity model allowing for both bilingualism/biculturalism *and* integration into U.S. American society was largely lacking in the public discourse at that time.

The 1965 Immigration and Naturalization Act dropped the quota system that favored Northern European immigrants, thereby allowing for much larger percentages of Latin American (50 %), Asian (27 %), and African (4 %) immigrants to enter the United States (Pew Research Center, 2013). In response to this new wave of immigration, the country is once again witnessing heated public debates about language and national identity. Although English is solidly positioned as the dominant language throughout the country, many people nevertheless view bi- or multilingualism as a willful rejection of U.S. American identity and as a threat to national unity (Leeman, 2004). This ideology is evidenced in state propositions that severely restrict access to bilingual education (e.g., in Arizona and California), as well as in the fact that nearly 30 states have passed laws declaring English to be an official language.

Overall, then, understanding historical contexts can help us carefully analyze today's discourse that discourages U.S. residents from accommodating linguistic others, whether such efforts involve curtailing bilingual education or even restricting the use of non-English signage—a point to which we will now turn.

Negotiating Everyday Linguistic Practices in the United States Today

In addition to some official language policies, everyday linguistic practices can also create spaces of differential belonging. One common domain concerns the display of language scripts in the public **linguistic landscape** (LL) of a school, neighborhood, city, or even nation (e.g., language used on signage, advertising, posters, brochures, and so on). For example, in 2007, a controversy arose in Merrimack, New Hampshire, when the police department asked the town council for permission to hang Spanish-language signage to post rules against alcohol consumption, smoking, and other activities at the local beach. However, some townspeople felt that all signage should be restricted to English. As one councilor stated, "I am in the United States of America, and I am not going to spend my tax dollars to put up foreign-language signs" (Lovett, 2007). After months of debate, the police proposal was rejected. Instead, the council decided to *restrict beach access* to residents and their guests only (Lovett, 2008). This incident exemplifies how a controversy purportedly about language is often a proxy for other social issues—in this case, the exclusion of "ethnic newcomers" to a locale. It is also an example of **"racialization of language"** wherein speakers of non-English languages are constructed as "essentially different and threatening U.S. cultural and national identity" (Leeman, 2004, p. 507).

Moreover, this incident is evidence of a **linguistic hierarchy** in the region. As one online commentator wryly noted, some townspeople of Merrimack had apparently "forgotten" that signs at New Hampshire's state borders have long welcomed arrivals with the semi-bilingual greeting, *"Welcome-Bienvenue to New Hampshire."* In this case, French is understood as signaling an inclusive, cosmopolitan attitude toward visitors. The different assessment of French and Spanish on public signage indicates a regional linguistic hierarchy in which English and French are both valued above Spanish. Moreover, *speakers* of these languages are differently valued. Such language attitudes clearly contribute to a hierarchy of differential belonging in the area.

French has not always been valorized in New England, however. In the late 1800s and early 1900s, nearly a million French Canadians immigrated to the region to meet the burgeoning labor demands of textile and shoe mills (Kelly, 2013). Many New Englanders of Anglo-descent were alarmed by the swift demographic change in their cities and towns. A *New York Times* editorial proclaimed that the French language "perpetuated French ideas and aspirations" and was a severe obstacle to "the assimilation of these people to our American life and thought"; it furthermore argued that all education in the United States should be conducted in English only ("French Canadians in New-England," 1892). This example illustrates that language ideologies shift over time; thus, they are culturally constructed in response to particular economic, historical, and political contexts. Importantly, they are *not* based on any linguistic attributes of the language itself.

Another recent controversy over public signage arose in a very different setting—the Flushing neighborhood of Queens, described as one of New York City's "most polyglot immigrant neighborhoods," where about 120 different languages are spoken (Bilefsky, 2011). In this case, some locals complained to city representatives that they felt marginalized "in their own country" because they couldn't read shop signs such as the Chinese-language signs posted on food stores (see Photo 6.1). Council member Peter Koo, a Chinese American originally from Hong Kong, proposed a measure that would require all storefront signs to be at least 60% English. Koo believed that "diminishing the [so-called] proper role of English on signs threatened to alienate non-Asian customers and residents" (Bilefsky, 2011).

Reactions were varied. Some residents claimed that the majority of signage did in fact use English. Others felt that a regulation requiring English to be predominant on signage would undermine ethnic diversity in the neighborhood and would actually run *against* U.S. American values. One Chinese immigrant resident summed the situation up well when stating in fluent English that, although he was sorry that some people felt alienated by Chinese-only signs, these signs were very meaningful for the cultural identity of Flushing; in Mr. Sun's apt words, "We all need a place to call home" (Bilefsky, 2011). For some, the public display of non-English scripts was seen as exclusionary; for others, these same displays were interpreted as inclusionary and emblematic of U.S. democratic freedoms.

Photo 6.1 The display of non-English signage in the Flushing neighborhood of New York City has been controversial for some residents.

Residents of Merrimack and Flushing have interpreted the use of non-English scripts in the LL as creating spaces of differential belonging on *both* local and national levels of identity. These examples illustrate that members of a community interpret language practices differently, whether that "community" is a neighborhood, a small town, or an entire nation. They also reveal a common belief that monolingualism should be the social norm, and that multilingualism necessarily contributes to intergroup conflict and/or lack of national cohesion; monolingualist ideologies thus tend to position speakers of "minority languages" as inherently unpatriotic (Leeman, 2012; Woolard, 2004).

However, there are about 6,000 to 7,000 languages in the world, but only about 198 countries. Consequently, although nations have varying degrees of linguistic diversity, virtually all countries are multilingual. Furthermore, more than half the world's population is believed to be bi- or multilingual (Romaine, 2001). Therefore, bi- or multilingualism—at both the individual and societal level—is the *global norm*. The United States is a case in point. The territory of what is now the United States has been multilingual since time immemorial; before the arrival of the Europeans, there were about 250 Native American languages (Mithun, 1999). The arrival of the European colonizers brought a number of colonial languages, primarily Dutch, English, French, German, and Spanish. The forced migration of African slaves also brought about 100 languages and dialects, although these soon disappeared due to harsh conditions of slavery (Parrillo, 2009). Currently, there are nearly 300 languages spoken in the United States (MLA Language Map Data Center, 2010), with Spanish and Chinese being the top non-English languages spoken. Despite this linguistic diversity, most of the U.S. population is proficient in English, and English is predominantly used in most domains, including business, education, and government (U.S. Census Bureau, 2013).

In sum, monolingualist ideologies do not match the everyday reality of multilingualism in the United States or elsewhere in the world; rather, they serve to exclude—socially, politically, geographically, and/or economically—those who are perceived as "linguistic others." Moreover, with today's accelerated globalization, we see an increase in the movement of populations, resulting in an increase in multilingual environments. This social condition of cultural and linguistic "superdiversity" underscores that we must learn to accommodate linguistic others in our language policies as well as in our everyday interactions (Blommaert & Rampton, 2011).

While the examples above involve quite explicit language ideologies, we are not always aware of our language attitudes and ideologies. For example, Hill (2008) argues that "Mock Spanish" used by some Anglos in the United States reveals an attitude that ranks "orderly English" over "disorderly Spanish." This hierarchy also maps onto racial/ethnic biases— white over Latino/a—based on presumed social qualities such as intelligence, morals, diligence, cleanliness, and so on. One tactic of Mock Spanish involves the **misappropriation** (inappropriate borrowing) of positive or neutral Spanish expressions that are then used to convey negative qualities (a process called **semantic pejoration**). Neutral terms such as *nada* ("nothing"), *pesos* (monetary unit), *adiós* ("good-bye"), *hasta la vista* ("see you later"), and *mañana* ("tomorrow") are used to convey negative qualities such as worthlessness, cheapness, disloyalty, violence, or laziness.

At one level, Mock Spanish is simply language play, a common and enjoyable human activity in most, if not all, cultures. However, Hill's (2008) analysis reveals a **covert racism**.

She employs the concept of **social indexicality**—the use of language to point to (index) certain social identities and qualities—in analyzing Mock Spanish, noting that it actually involves a **dual indexicality**. On the one hand, these expressions convey a positive view of the Anglo speaker (or author) as a person who is laid-back, creative, funny, and somewhat cosmopolitan by knowing a little Spanish. On the other hand, the expressions carry an implied negative indexicality for members of Spanish-language cultures—especially Mexicans and Mexican Americans.

Those who appreciate the humor of Mock Spanish are aware of its positive indexicality. However, to really "get" the humor, one has to implicitly discern the tensions between the direct, positive indexicality and the less direct, negative indexicality. For example, *adiós* is often used in a pejorative manner; rather than "good-bye," it is used to convey "good riddance" or as a jocular insult of "disloyalty." Hill (2008) describes a greeting card featuring a small man with a sombrero and a serape and the word *adiós*. Inside, the card "defines" this term: "That's Spanish, for sure, go ahead and leave your friends . . . just take off!" Mock Spanish in printed form frequently reinforces the negative indexicality with negative images, such as an ugly, flea-infested dog ("Fleas Navidad") or a man, wearing a large sombrero and serape, jumping over a bean ("Mexican Jumping Bean"). (For these and other examples, see language-culture.binghamton.edu/symposia/2/part1/index.html.)

By Hill's (2008) definition, Mock Spanish is largely pejorative and involves the misappropriation of Spanish by members of an outgroup—Anglos who are not proficient in Spanish. (Also, linguistically, it is not a true language variety but, rather, a concocted version of how some outgroup members think Spanish sounds.) Hill's main concern is that the "humor" behind Mock Spanish creates a "White public space"; that is, it contributes to spaces of differential belonging—socially and geographically—which legitimate the presence of Anglos but hold suspect that of people with Spanish-language heritage.

This is not to say that language mixing is inherently racist. In fact, many varieties of U.S. Spanish creatively employ **code-mixing** (most often with English, sometimes called "Spanglish"; Mar-Molinero, 2010). In fact, language mixing can be an effective tool in *resisting* overly simplified categories of race and ethnicity. For example, Bailey (2000) observed the linguistic creativity of Dominican American high school students who simultaneously identify as Latino/Hispanic, of African descent, and as American. These students are proficient in Standard American English (SAE). To assert their nonwhite identities, though, they include features of African American Vernacular English (AAVE) in their speech. However, they don't identify as "African American"; so to highlight their Dominican heritage, they also use Spanish language expressions, pronunciation, and word order. In sum, they creatively use their **linguistic repertoire** to enact their complex identities and resist simple U.S.-based categorizations of ethnic/racial and linguistic identities, such as Spanish = Latino, SAE = white, or AAVE = African American.

Overall, we should consider how linguistic practices are locally and regionally contextualized, as well as ideologically informed. Nevertheless, these general phenomena—language ideologies, linguistic hierarchies, social indexicality of language, and (ethno)linguistic identities—are common to humans around the world. Understanding these concepts can help us better understand how linguistic practices often involve power relations and thereby create spaces of differential belonging. With this information in mind, let us now consider some issues of language, identity, and belonging in another part of the world—Taipei, Taiwan.

NEGOTIATING LANGUAGE AND IDENTITY IN TAIWAN

Taiwan is an island nation of more than 23 million people that lies just 110 miles off the southeast coast of Mainland China. Slightly larger than the state of Maryland, Taiwan is much smaller than the United States and has a very different **ethnolinguistic** population and history. Nevertheless, the two regions share some similar patterns regarding language histories and successive waves of immigration/colonization. Both are home to diverse indigenous languages and have long been multilingual. Both also experienced colonization in the 16th and 17th centuries, which placed great pressure on the native populations. Additionally, both have had periods when a dominant group forced its language on others, in an effort to assimilate them into an imagined, homogeneous national identity.

To understand Taiwan's current-day dynamics of language, identity, and power, it's important to know a few details about the island's history (Simpson, 2007). The original inhabitants were Aboriginals who spoke about 20 diverse Austronesian languages (14 groups remain). In the mid-1600s, Chinese migrants began moving to the island. These early settlers came from two very different groups—the Hakka Chinese from Canton province (now called Guangdong) and the Southern Min–speaking Chinese from Fujian province. Both groups have distinctive cultures and languages (i.e., Hakka and Southern Min are not mutually intelligible). By the mid-1800s, ethnic Han Chinese comprised about half the island's population.

In 1895, Taiwan was ceded to Japan when the Qing dynasty of China lost a war with Japan. For 50 years, Taiwan was a Japanese colony, during which time Japan tried to compel the islanders to shift to identifying as Japanese. One strategy was to make the Japanese language predominant in education, media, and the government. Although many islanders learned Japanese, most retained their native languages (Aboriginal, Hakka, Southern Min) and did *not* come to identify as Japanese. Rather, they began to collectively identify as *Taiwanese* in opposition to the occupying Japanese.

At the end of World War II, Japan was forced to give up Taiwan. To secure control of the island, the Chinese nationalists (the *Kuomingtang* or KMT) sent representatives and troops from China. At that time, though, a civil war was raging on the mainland between the KMT and the Chinese Communist Party. In 1949, the KMT lost the war and retreated to Taiwan, bringing about 2.5 million "Mainlanders" with them who spoke Mandarin as their common language. (Mandarin, Hakka, and Southern Min are three different Chinese languages; this is a bit like Portuguese, French, and Italian being different languages but belonging to one language group, the romance languages.)

When relations between the Taiwanese and the newly arrived Mainlanders deteriorated, the Taiwanese rebelled and the KMT declared martial law (1949–1987). During this time, the KMT imposed strict linguistic measures to "re-Sinicize" the Taiwanese. Mandarin Chinese was vigorously promoted as *guoyu* ("national language"). Japanese was banned from use in public and local languages (Southern Min, Hakka, and indigenous) were suppressed. Soon Southern Min, the language spoken by the vast majority, was banned from public places and from the media; at school, students were punished for using any non-Mandarin language. These language policies put the Taiwanese at great disadvantage—politically, economically, and educationally—as most did *not* know the newly imposed national language, Mandarin Chinese. However, due to the KMT's aggressive national language movement, nearly everyone became proficient in both spoken and written Mandarin within just 40 years (1945–1986).

This history documents that both the Japanese colonizers and the KMT imposed harsh language policies promoting a nonlocal language (Japanese, Mandarin) in all public domains. This linguistic suppression was based on an ideology of **assimilative monolingualism**—the belief that national unity can and should be promoted by forcing people to shift from their heritage languages to a single national language. This history is somewhat similar to that of the United States where many people (Native Americans and certain immigrant groups) were pressured to shift to English monolingualism.

Today, however, Taiwan has a vibrant, democratic government and its residents are issued passports from the Republic of China (ROC). And while Mandarin continues as the official language and serves as the **lingua franca** of the island, both the government and society explicitly embrace the pluralistic, multilingual diversity of Taiwan. Elementary school students take classes in at least one non-Mandarin language that is natively spoken in Taiwan (i.e., Hakka, Southern Min, Austronesian). Some television news programs and other shows also use native languages. And the rapid transit system in the capital city, Taipei, makes public announcements in Mandarin, Southern Min, Hakka, and English.

Nevertheless, tensions about language and identity still arise. Some worry about the dominance of Mandarin, particularly as the younger generation is (gradually) losing the ability to communicate well (if at all) in their heritage languages. Ironically, however, the ability to speak and read Mandarin has economically benefited the Taiwanese, because Mainland China (where most people also speak Mandarin) has now emerged as a global economic powerhouse. For example, more than 2 million mainland tourists visited Taiwan in 2013, representing about 25% of Taiwan's total number of tourists for the year ("Record Number Travel," 2014). Furthermore, China is now Taiwan's largest trading partner, comprising a whopping 40% of its export trade in 2012 (Executive Yuan Office of Information Services, 2013).

Many Taiwanese, however, are concerned that their economy has become *too* integrated with that of Mainland China, thus making Taiwan economically and politically vulnerable. This concern stems in part from the fact that the People's Republic of China (PRC, or Communist China) claims Taiwan as one of its 23 provinces and has an explicit policy of (eventual) "reunification" of Taiwan with China—by military force if necessary. However, most people of the island identify as Taiwanese and as citizens of the ROC (i.e., Taiwan), *not* as part of the PRC.

Concerns about Taiwan's identity in relation to China are sometimes reflected in the island's LL. For example, let's consider the predominant use of Mandarin in signage throughout Taiwan (see Photo 6.2). Given that the vast majority of Taiwanese are of Chinese descent and speak/read Mandarin, the prevalence of characters seems to quite

Photo 6.2 The majority of Taipei's LL is in Mandarin Chinese, using traditional characters.

naturally index their Chinese culture, language, and ethnicity. Yet Taiwan uses *traditional* Chinese characters, whereas China uses a system with *simplified* characters. For example, when mainland tourists visit Taipei, they readily observe that signage for Longshan Temple Station is 龍山寺站 (cf: 龙山寺站) and Zhongxiao Fuxing Station is 忠孝復興站 (cf: 忠孝复兴站) (compare the first and fourth characters, respectively). Thus, traditional characters visually index Taiwan, the ROC, as a distinct cultural and political entity from Mainland China (PRC).

The Taiwanese government vigorously promotes traditional characters as an important cultural asset of Taiwan. Taipei holds an annual New Year's Day "Chinese Character Festival," where thousands of residents come together to practice their calligraphy and celebrate the beauty of traditional Chinese characters. President Ma Ying-jeou has directed all government agencies to stop using simplified characters, even on material for mainland tourists (Sui, 2011); he has even stated that business signs and advertisements should not use simplified characters ("Traditional Characters Embody Beauty," 2014). Taiwan has also requested that the United Nations Educational, Scientific and Cultural Organization (UNESCO) grant "world heritage status" to traditional Chinese characters (Ko, 2009). These strategies are, in part, an effort to distinguish Taiwan from Mainland China, which itself has been vigorously promoting Mandarin—with simplified characters—as a global language (Seng & Lai, 2010).

Another example concerning the indexing of language and identity in Taipei's LL has centered on which Romanization system to use in official signage (Curtin, 2009). (Romanization, or *pinyin*, is the transcribing of Chinese characters into the Roman alphabet; e.g., "Taipei" is the common Romanization for the characters 臺北.) For years, signage for Taipei's streets and other public places displayed widely varying Romanization. This was, in part, because there are many different systems and because Romanization is not taught in Taiwan. For example, in 2000, the street name 忠孝東路 was variously transliterated as "JungShiau E. Rd," "Chung Hsiao E. Rd.," and "Zhongsiao E. Rd." Not surprisingly, businesspeople and other visitors not literate in Mandarin found it difficult to travel about the city.

At last, officials agreed to standardize signage using one Romanization system, but they couldn't agree on which system to use, *hanyu* or *tongyong*. One group supported *hanyu* because it is now commonly used throughout the world. However, *hanyu* was developed in Communist China and is widely used there. Some Taiwanese thus felt that using *hanyu* would index too close a relationship with China. Instead, they wanted to use *tongyong,* developed by Taiwanese linguists and described as 85% similar to *hanyu* (some describe the difference between them as similar to that between British and U.S. American English spelling). Importantly, *tongyong* would index Taiwan as a political and cultural entity distinct from China (much as traditional characters do; Lin, 2002). Two camps emerged, more or less aligned with the two main political parties of Taiwan: The KMT supported *hanyu* and the Democratic Progressive Party supported

Photo 6.3 Official signage in Taipei is now consistently rendered in one system of Romanization, *hanyu pinyin.*

tongyong. From 1996 to 2008, there was an "orthographic tug-of-war" where *both* systems could be seen on signage throughout Taipei city and county, at times even on the same sign (e.g., in the metro).

Today, most official signage in Taipei is standardized using *hanyu.* For example, the street name 忠孝東路 is now consistently transliterated as "ZhongXiao East Rd." (see Photo 6.3). Consequently, those not literate in Mandarin can now navigate the city relatively easily. And, as time passes, *hanyu* is becoming more naturalized in the city's LL. For many, however, the visual prevalence of *hanyu* now gives Taipei a strong "mainland flavor"; it can also reinforce mainland tourists' perception that Taiwan is integrally connected to China. This example underscores that debates over writing systems are often *ideological debates* about different ethnic, political, and (trans)national identities.

Fifteen years ago, it was quite challenging for people not literate in Mandarin to make their way about Taipei. Today, however, Taipei's LL features consistent Romanization as well as several "international languages." For example, English is used on signage in the airport, in metro stations and at bus stops, as well as on street signs (see Photo 6.4).

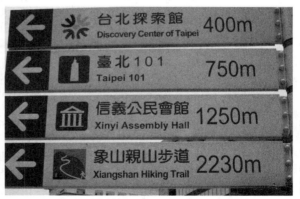

Photo 6.4 Much official signage in Taipei now includes English as an international language, attesting to an increasing degree of **cosmopolitan accommodation** in Taiwan.

This increased use of English as an international language contributes to Taipei's "sense of place" as a modern, global city.

We should note, however, that the use of English as an international language involves a global linguistic hierarchy in which English, as the "hypercentral" world language, holds a privileged position over all other languages (Ammon, 2010). The use of English to accommodate international visitors is highly naturalized as an appropriate LL practice in Taipei as it transitions to being "a globalized city." In Curtin (2014), I term this attitude **presumptive cosmopolitanism**, whereby locals are expected to linguistically accommodate visitors or newcomers. Interestingly, even though Spanish and Chinese are also major world languages (Ammon, 2010), presumptive cosmopolitanism did *not* seem to hold sway for Spanish signage in Merrimack, New Hampshire, or even for Chinese signage in the Flushing neighborhood in Queens, New York City. Moreover, for Taipei, the use of English and other international languages decreases opportunities to promote Taiwan's non-Mandarin languages (e.g., Aboriginal, Southern Min, or Hakka), which are mostly absent from the capital city's LL. Thus, in our highly globalized world, LL practices that accommodate presumptive cosmopolitanism can themselves be plagued with diminishing both the local and national.

CONCLUSION

We have only touched on the complexities of language and identity in the United States and Taiwan. Nevertheless, from this discussion, we can see that both societies have, at times, promoted cultural and linguistic homogeneity. At other times, both have developed more inclusive cultural models that embrace a pluralistic, multilingual society. These case studies also demonstrate that language ideologies are often invoked to create spaces of differential belonging—socially, geographically, and even politically. And they show how processes of globalization, including transnational migration as well as cultural and economic integration, shape the sociolinguistic contexts in which we interact with others.

We should remember that issues of language, identity, and belonging always occur within specific sociocultural, historical, political, and economic contexts—as these are positioned from the local to the global. One useful strategy is to develop **indexical competence**, an understanding of how particular language practices involve *multiple* interpretations that can reinforce or contest hierarchies. Moreover, by developing **indexical empathy**, an empathic understanding of *why* others feel the way they do about specific linguistic practices, we can adjust our language attitudes and practices to be as inclusive as possible. Also, on a more structural level, we can actively promote socially inclusive language ideologies, policies, and practices that *value* linguistic diversity (Piller & Takahashi, 2011). In doing so, we can further refine our intercultural praxis (Sorrells, 2013, p. 31) as we find our way in this highly interconnected—and interdependent—world.

Black Like Me, Black Like I Am! The Language and Memories of Race in Higher Education

Christopher Brown
Minnesota State University, Mankato

I hear *it,* and then I feel *it.* I either challenge or dodge *it*! But I always stand before *it.* Nowhere to run! Nowhere to hide! Sometimes *it* is metaphorically quite humorous; other times, *it* literally pisses me off! *It* is often delivered through nonverbal behaviors. *It* could be made rather innocently. *It* can be actualized and internalized. Nameless! Invisible! Whiteness! These are the theoretical euphemisms that posit how *it* harbors something more dangerous and damaging, only to divulge and discover its disguised meanings. But scholarship only helps me talk about *it* in more intricate ways. Intuition is what helps me see *it* coming before *it* rears its ugly head. And experience is what helps me manage *it.* I know when to laugh at *it.* I know when to give *it* an unsettling smirk. I know when to withstand and withdraw from *it.*

Most believe it best to altogether turn a blind eye to *it.* Color-blind! That's the term they use to respond to *it,* always stating that all-too-familiar color-coded mantra—"I don't care if you are red, blue, green, or yellow!" Leaving out the colors of black and white is fundamental to this phrase, a testament to being blind to skin hue. They prefer to believe rather that President Lincoln freed us from *it*; President Obama's presence proved that *it* doesn't matter! Or the one friend of a different skin tone excuses them from *it.* But admittedly so, there were times when I was surprised by *it.* I even missed *it*! I got caught sleepin'! But *it* was so cleverly crafted—language sweetened with sympathy and a sly smile—only to be deciphered moments later. Even after, it persists as part of my memory. I can neither erase nor eliminate *it,* constantly engrossed by the burden of total recall.

You may be wondering, what is this *it*? As if you don't already know! But I hesitate to talk about *it.* Many would rather *it* were kept concealed, lamenting that *it* had a history! *It* has been dismantled; *it* has been devoured by other more pressing *it*(s). In fact, some have tried to convince me that the *it* that impacts me should take a backseat to the *it* affecting them, without considering how much the *it* that acts on me is implicated in the *it* acting on them. Many believe that those most harmed by *it* are those who hype *it* the most—those so vindicated by playing *its* card! Still, *it* has been benched for other more prominent starters, past its prime, unable to mount a new offensive to counter the more enduring defenses on the **postracial** playing field. Stop *it*! This game of *it* is child's play!

But *it* still has a history; perhaps *it* is timeless. Despite calls for "moving past *it,*" or illusions of the *post, it* persists because of the pain inflicted from the poundings of the past. Rather than persist on this pretense of ignorance, *it* is—wait, "drumroll please!" As if you don't already know! It is *race*! Race surrounds us; we take it with us and see it everywhere we go! We wear it on our skin and rely on it to describe those unfamiliar and foreign to us. We create oversimplified expectations of others with regard to race. We even see it in those who look like us. Much like language, race shapes our experiences and assists in the way we assign meaning to others. It is encoded in our interactions—not in our DNA—albeit stored and effortlessly retrieved from and returned to consciousness. But *it* is always etched in memory.

In his critically acclaimed memoir, *Black Like Me*, John Howard Griffin (1961) documented his experiences as a White man who underwent medical treatments to deliberately darken his skin so he could travel the racially segregated southern United States as a Black man. Griffin's racial impersonation invited White personal experience in recalling stories of racism, using this historically reprehensible performance as evidence of enlightenment. But to speak of memory is to highlight the presence of the past in stories of the present. Yet, it is inevitable to tame memories, to smooth out the roughest edges by forsaking remnants of the past. Hence, the past irreconcilably ruptures the present and mars the future. In a postracial society, then, it is more desirable to imagine a time and place without racism than to conjure memories of its shameful past. But forgetting the past seems to pervade postracial thinking even in those instances of racial division where reflecting on *it* would be most beneficial.

NEVER FORGETTING!

From the time when I was an 8-year-old kid, overcome with emotion and providing emphasis, forcefully, to the word *nigger* while delivering a speech to an all-White audience; the time when I was a young college student in a foreign country, staring into the eyes of a White man who yelled "little ni___" (I didn't let him finish!); the time a 4-year-old Latina expressed that I was not smart because of the color of my skin—I have come to understand that human beings are so enthralled with physical differences, only to explain intelligence, personality, and mannerisms. But these racialized experiences offered opportunities to revisit narratives that often are neglected in a so-called postracial society.

I am Black. Yes, Black with a capital *B*! I am an African American heterosexual male born and raised in the inner city of Chicago, Illinois. Like many African Americans of my generation, I was raised by a single mother and enjoyed the rap lyrics of KRS-One, NWA, and Public Enemy. I, too, was captivated by sermons of the church pastor. As a child, I witnessed struggles in my community that most people only read about in books or see in movies. I grew up in an all-Black neighborhood where co-op leaders took away the basketball hoops on the concrete court and turned the football field into a parking lot. Oh yes, I cannot forget the large chain-link fence that restricted entrance into a churchyard where my friends and I played baseball, after the fatal shooting death of a childhood friend. I also cannot forget playing in the nondescript playground that was eventually reduced to rubble! These all-too-familiar circumstances left a slew of African American children with nothing to do but relish the prospect of wearing gold chains, sporting designer jeans, and holding *fat wads* like the neighborhood nonparental role models—dope dealers and gangbangers. But it was also in these circumstances that I started to register the nature of experiences of being *Black like I already am*—experiences that included putting up with stop-and-frisk practices, enduring the suspicious stares of storeowners as I *shopped while Black*, wrestling with stereotypes about intelligence and work ethic, and negotiating multiple racial selves while still kickin' it in a way that is familiarly Black. Needless to say, it was not until I left my community and was thrust into the White-dominated culture of college campuses that I learned that ideas of race are much more muddled than the White/Black binary would suggest.

Currently, I am an assistant professor, but it was as a college student that I started to trouble my own assumptions of race and racism. My experiences as a student underscored the meaning of being the "only spade in the deck!" At certain points, I have been the *only* Black person someone has ever spoken with; the *only* Black person in the classroom; the *only* Black friend; the *only* Black person a professor has worked with; the *only* Black male to graduate with honors; the *only* Black face at an academic conference, job interview, or social affair; the *only* Black person someone felt comfortable talking about race with, or even repeating racist jokes to—like the one about the hanging, shining red apple and lynched Black men—for austerity purposes. That one received the unsettled smirk and a sarcastic rebuke for austerity purposes! Through these instances, I realized that I would rarely find other empathetic voices on issues of race relations. Then again, I felt a great responsibility and sometimes burden of being part of something bigger than me. Being thrust into the position of the *only* eventually led to my experiencing a series of *firsts*—a position that forced me to fit in while standing out!

For instance, I have been the *first* Black male to work in an organization, to lead a student organization, to receive a PhD from a department. I also have been the *first* Black teaching assistant and faculty member in a department, and the *first* or *only* Black professor for many of my students. These series of *firsts* aren't celebrated, but they also permit those who exploit my presence to attest to satisfying a diversity requirement, or to verify my contributions as part of prescripts of the postracial society. I am sure many Black students and professors could develop similar lists where their **blackness** has been turned inside out, where they pulled together an array of identities to overcome feelings of isolation within the Ivory Tower. Drawing on these insights, I highlight racialized experiences that make me *Black like I already am.*

In this essay, I provide a few brief anecdotes from an emic (insider's) view, where the roles of researcher and subject are intertwined, while illustrating memories of personal and professional understanding of the role of language in shaping race and racism in academia. For example, I will never forget when I informed my White female graduate colleague that I was invited to speak on a panel on diversity training in Chicago, to which she replied, "Don't you hate it when people ask you to speak because you are Black?" I wonder if she thought that I would otherwise have nothing to offer. I will never forget when I helped a White male professor open a jammed door. After pulling open the door, he jokingly responded, "Your people are good at getting into locked doors, ha, ha, ha"—a dorky laugh followed by a sharp blow with his open hand on my back. I wonder how he felt when I didn't laugh. I will never forget when I told a seemingly interested White female professor that I have research interests in philosophy and critical race theory. To which she responded, "Critical race theory, yeah, I should have known!" I wonder if it would have been better to say that I studied chemistry! While these circumstances should act like gamma radiation, triggering the rage that would transform me into the Incredible *Nigg_* with an "a" ending, I channel the series of onlys and firsts and tame the beast within, controlling the metamorphous into the stereotypical creature of their expectations—the angry Black *nigg__* with an "er" ending. But I cannot tame the memories of racial experiences that are permanently tattooed on my consciousness.

IT'S NIGGA, NOT N____!

It was my freshman year of college, and I was talking to a White male college administrator about race after an event sponsored by the Black Student Association. I informed him that in one of my classes, a White student stated that "calling a Black person a nigger was the same as calling a White person a honky or cracker." I expressed how I understood this student's point of view because words such as these could equally cause harm. But the man disagreed and stated, "Chris! It is much worse to use the N-word." I immediately replied, "Aren't these words equally derogatory?" He answered, "No! As a White person I have much more social capital so calling me a honky or cracker would be almost laughable, but the N-word has had negative consequences." I then asked, "So how would you feel if I called you a honky?" He responded, "I would laugh like I did when George Jefferson called Tom Willis a honky." After our conversation, I assumed that this man believed that the absurdity of this comparison is underscored by the idea that social capital provides many Whites with considerable influence in social matters. I also considered that this comparison diminished the racist historical folklore in expressions of the N-word as a harbinger of violence, power, and hate. But years later, I realized that ideologies of equality were so influential to my view on humanity that I believed that all concepts could be treated in the same way. At this point, I started to see equality as more than the metaphor of "balance" inferred in the Black/White binary and instead against the backdrop of promises of freedom that have been historically denied—the bad check that came back with insufficient funds to which Dr. Martin Luther King Jr. referred.

In my academic career, I was surprised to see how much the N-word would follow me. For example, an African male graduate-teaching colleague once yelled, "What is wrong with these niggers?" while discussing the perceived antipathy of two African American students in his class. I also recalled an African American female professor and friend who became angry with a White male senior colleague who, oddly enough, criticized her for using the N-word as an example in her presentation. I mean, really! Besides the obvious power differences in gender and job status, I found it ironic that this White male professor would view the use of the N-word by a Black female as an expression of personal disrespect, since this term historically signed off on his own status and privilege. On another occasion, I was sitting in a computer lab with other students when my Indian colleague walked toward me. While extending his hand to greet me, he stated loudly, "Nigger-nigger-nigger, what's up, my nigger, my boy. We talked about hip-hop in class today!" The students in the computer lab became quiet, waiting to see if I would transform into the Incredible Nigga. But I looked at him without saying a word. I stared at his hand as it hung in the air, and then stared intensely into his eyes. Despite what he might have learned in class, I wanted him to understand that using the N-word was unacceptable. He apologized, but I walked away in silence without acknowledging it.

In classroom discussions, the N-word generates much reaction as some students police perceptions of racism while others refuse to be inhibited by the language police. But language is a place of struggle (hooks, 1989), and the discussion of the N-word is corrupted by the primacy of equality and freedom of expression. This was obvious on separate occasions when a White American and an Eastern European colleague informed me that Black students walked out of their respective classes after White students complained that it was unfair they couldn't use the N-word. After some conversation, they asked me to talk to their classes. After denying their request, I stated that "they can't ask a Black person to clean up the racial mess they created." I then suggested that talking about the N-word without placing it within a historical context leads to trivial discussions on who has the right to say it.

WHATCHU BE SPEAKIN'!

Michael Eric Dyson once wrote that many Black people "bend to the tongue it tumbles from at any given moment in time" (as cited in Touré, 2011, p. xiv). He uses Obama and Oprah as examples of how many Black people can take on an array of identities within any given context. But such performances are not only reserved for the most powerful among us. As a young kid, I always crashed into the bulwark of an authentic blackness. This includes expressions of blackness created in the struggles of generations before me. In academia, I learned to appreciate the fluidity of blackness as constructed around a series of axes beyond narrow notions of authenticity. I realized early on that the way I am heard impacts how I am perceived, as language is a source for (re)constituting identity. This is to say that language is as explicit to geography as it is complicit in racial politics. So regardless of how many degrees I receive, books I read, words I enunciate, manuscripts I publish, classes I teach, or acts of **code-switching** I perform, the accent of Black speech is an inescapable fact of my Black body.

Racial linguistic profiling is a common practice in academia. This largely involves measuring how closely speech patterns mirror the American Standard English (ASE) way of speaking. For example, some Black students and professors support using only ASE because they see Black English Vernacular (BEV) through racial ideologies of intelligence and nihilism. Even in my intercultural class, some students admitted to avoiding professors with perceptibly Asian names, believing in the likelihood that they would not speak ASE. While on a job interview, I even witnessed a White male professor perform the stereotypical head rotations and hand gestures, mimicking the voice of a Black female while saying, "Y'all betta recognize," snapping his fingers and rotating his arms in a circular motion.

But in academia, I have received frequent reminders of *talking while Black,* whether it is being corrected for the absence of a copula ("We straight") or use of an intensified continuative ("He *steady* trippin'") in my daily speech, or hearing someone playfully, yet flippantly mimic these expressions immediately after they gush from my mouth. In these instances, I have found that my body shapes and mediates others' expectations of my own voice. This means there are predetermined expectations that I will speak in a high-pitched or loud tone, mispronounce a few words, and not enunciate my endings. As my White student once stated, "When interacting with a Black person, I know that I am going to have to listen really carefully." So, to the delight of the class, I responded by speaking very slowly and explaining that the different rules for *language use* can be a source of interracial communication conflict. The presumption of a "standard" or "academic" language signifies power in particular language norms that are readily accepted. Despite this, I refuse to be stuck in neutral, instead always using my verbal stick shift and language-operated clutch to maneuver between streetwise vernacular and academic prose.

For example, in the first week of class, I usually inform students that I will use code-switching tactics in class discussions. In doing so, I demonstrate how I alternate between BEV and ASE; most students laugh and some applaud in appreciation. One day, a White female professor came to my class to evaluate my teaching. During my lecture, I repeatedly used the word "ax" rather than "ask," along with other Black idiomatic syntax. For instance, a student overstated a response to a question, and I responded, "Why you trippin'!" The student, along with the rest of the class, burst out in laughter as we further evaluated his answer. After class, the professor complemented my class management skills but stated, "You know, Chris, you cannot speak 'Ebonics' in the classroom." I replied, "I know that teaching requires a . . ." She interrupted, "You will lose credibility with your students!" I stared in silence for a moment. But she continued anyway: "Okay, alright now, repeat after me—ask!" I purposefully replied, "Ax!" She repeated, "No, ask! You have to get it right. Now say, ask!" I walked away without responding with other words that came to mind. I know that as a professor I am measured largely by my ability to carry the banner of ASE. But apart from the pretty bizarre exercise of purging the word "ax" from my vocabulary, I was most troubled with the underlying assumption in the phrase "losing credibility," which bolsters racial ideologies of Black intellectual inferiority.

CONCLUSION

I hear *it* again. As always, I pause! Suddenly memories of *it* emerge in my mind. As my brain synapses fire, I must instantly choose how to respond to *it*. Should I do what my right brain tells me and creatively slap *it* in the face? Or should I do what my left brain tells me and respond with reason that gently rubs the rough exterior of *its* face? And yet logical reasoning doesn't always apply, while emotional outbursts provide only a momentary spark. At this point, my mind remains a bit foggy. I try to see through the mist of *it*. I know what to say; I just don't know how to say it. Even more ironically, I am not angry, because I expect *it*. I have been raised to expect *it*. And yet I haven't been trained to endure *it*. But *it* is a real game with real consequences to my sheer existence! As a Black man, I expect to emerge from this game like the Mikes—Jordan, Jackson, Tyson, and Dyson, that is—champions of their craft! Too bad my name isn't Mike; it's Chris! I have neither the natural ability nor the talent to *be like Mike*! These anecdotes attend to a sense of remembering how I came to understand *it*, and yet constant reminders of *it* subtly eat at me. Indeed, White professorial policing of my voice, misinterpretations of the N-word, and my own performance of ASE show that through language I became an object and subject of others' perceptions of blackness. These reminders bring about memories that continue to haunt my subconscious. I can neither erase the impact of *it* nor forget *it*. But I don't want to forget *it*! Because, like others that came before me, as my body arrives at a particular place, language mediates these moments of racialized meanings that make *it* even more unforgettable.

KEY TERMS

assimilationism   104

assimilative monolingualism   111

blackness   117

code-mixing   109

code-switching   119

cosmopolitan accommodation   113

covert racism   108

differential belonging   104

discourse   104

dual indexicality   109

ethnolinguistic   110

ideology   104

indexical competence   114

indexical empathy   114

lingua franca   111

linguistic hierarchy   106

linguistic homogeneity/ monolingualism   104

linguistic landscape   106

linguistic repertoire   109

misappropriation   108

pluralism   104

postracial   115

presumptive cosmopolitanism   115

racialization of language   106

semantic pejoration   108

social indexicality   109

DISCUSSION QUESTIONS

1. According to Curtin, U.S. language policies historically played a crucial role in assimilating Native Americans, the Deaf, and European migrants into the United States, often against their will or to the detriment of their cultural and social well-being. What do you think the consequences are of these official policies? How do these historical language policies and their implications shape intercultural communication today?

2. Based on Curtin's and Brown's discussions, address how and why monolingualism becomes problematic in intercultural contexts. How does globalization contribute to monolingualism? How does the dominance/hegemony of the English language relate to cultural imperialism?

3. What does Curtin mean when she writes that our language practices shape "contexts of differential belonging"? How does it relate to the "code-switching" discussed by Brown? Use specific examples from their discussions.

4. Brown's personal narrative illustrates how race is more than physical appearance or categorization; rather, race is performed through one's linguistic practice. In what ways do you perform your race through language?

CHAPTER 7

Cultural Space and Intercultural Communication

Cultural space refers to the communicative practices that construct meanings in, through, and about particular places. Consider how particular architectural features, artifacts, and nonverbal practices, as well as people and languages create the cultural space of, for example, a sports bar, a country-western club, a synagogue, or a university. These are all cultural spaces that are constructed through communicative practices developed and engaged in by people in particular places. Communicative practices include the languages, slang, dress, artifacts, behaviors, and patterns of interaction, as well as the stories, discourses, and histories that are told in and about places. Cultural spaces, constructed in particular locations, give rise to collective and individual cultural identities.

Globalization has dramatically accelerated the displacement and replacement of people, cultures, and cultural spaces since the early 1990s. As people and cultural forms move more frequently and rapidly around the globe, overlapping and intersecting cultural spaces are increasingly the norm rather than the exception today. Penetration, disruption, and mixing of cultural spaces have occurred since the European colonial era. **Segregated, contested**, and **hybrid cultural spaces** experienced today often sustain and reproduce historically forged relations of unequal power.

Joshua F. Hoops's ethnographic case study of a farm community in Washington State explores the intersection of cultural space, race, identity, and belonging within inequitable relations of power. In a community that relies on migrant workers from Mexico and other parts of Latin America, discourses of whiteness produce unique experiences of the town's topography, stores, and neighborhoods, and very different (and contested) understanding of these spaces. Richie Neil Hao's personal narrative examines the challenges and complexities of the classroom as a cultural space where the politics of identity are always negotiated—especially for faculty of color. His focus on students' performances of whiteness, their reluctance to acknowledge their complicity, and how this affects intercultural communication is particularly informing. Both entries point to the ways whiteness is embodied and performed in and through cultural spaces.

The Intersections of Race and Space: A Case Study of a Washington State Farm Community

Joshua F. Hoops
William Jewell College

Most of us go about our daily tasks without a single thought about how we've set up and arranged our space. And even fewer of us spend time thinking about how these spaces—material, physical, and concrete—impact our identities, inform our cultural activities, and influence race relations. Yet the spaces where we live, work, worship, and play are not independent of cultural construction. We may associate the creation of space with the work of city planners, interior designers, and architects, but places are also fluid constructions, experienced and engaged by those who pass through (or are denied access to) those locations. Spaces, although they may appear to be static to us, are always contested, in that individuals and groups do not experience them in the same way. This contestation reflects the "cultural" dynamic of cultural space, which refers to the communicative practices that define what a place means, who gets to occupy it, and how it is to be used (Martin & Nakayama, 2004).

To research the relationships between culture, space, race, and identity, I conducted an ethnography in a rural farm community in central Washington that relies on the contributions of (im)migrant workers from Mexico. In fact, the Hispanic population is the demographic majority within the town's city limits. Throughout the rest of this case study, I will distinguish between white and Hispanic participants. It is important to note that using the term *Hispanic* to describe the diversity of Latin American heritages is problematic. As a classification that was originally imposed on individuals with Spanish-speaking roots by the U.S. government in the '70s, the label effectively erases the heterogeneity of Hispanics living and working in the United States. I have chosen to use this term, however, because it is employed by both white and Hispanic residents of the town where I conducted my research.

During the months of January through April 2011, I observed the interaction in Farmville (pseudonym) and I interviewed members of both the white and Hispanic populations. My observations took me to various locations throughout the town, including churches, schools, social clubs, restaurants, stores, town meetings, and recreational events. Space plays an integral role in fostering collective identity, and Farmville is no exception. The town is surrounded by more than 200,000 acres of farmland and located 10 miles from the nearest freeway, creating a quasi-isolated community with a "shared" identity. Today, Farmville produces more than $2 billion in crops, which include alfalfa, fruit, wheat, beans, wine grapes, and potatoes (Murray, 2010).

SPACE, IDENTITY, AND RACE

The traditional understanding of space as fixed and unchanging was challenged by the work of Henri Lefebvre. Lefebvre (1991) argued that space is defined through human interaction, representation, and social production. Hence, space does not simply exist independent of our engagement with it. Discourses of space are usually constructed in ways that give communities meaning, legitimacy, and value (Antoine, 2007). Many scholars have explored the implications of Lefebvre's work for how we understand identity, which includes attachment to certain spaces that may be local, regional, national, and international. Van Maanen and Barley (1985) argued that territoriality is a primary catalyst for groups' collective identities. Movement in and between spaces and the conscious and subconscious decisions to reside, work, and play in certain spaces while avoiding other spaces foster connections with some and create an "us" versus "them" binary with others (Hetherington, 1998). For example, individuals and groups located peripherally and having less connection (e.g., lineage) to an in-group's spatial epicenter are often evaluated negatively, constituting both dominant and marginalized identities (Relph, 1976). Narratives of space are thus evoked to authenticate certain identities and not others (Dickinson, 1997). Consequently, the act of crossing boundaries can invoke tension regarding identity for both (im)migrants and established residents of a town.

The relationship between space and identity is continuously being (re)arranged by the flow of transnational capital, which highlights the fluidity of identity (Shome, 2003). For example, to a great extent, the autonomous farmer—owner of a small, private, family-run farm—has been replaced by the corporation (Molnar & Wu, 1989). In this "brave new world," reliance on (im)migrant workers has become essential to U.S.-based farmers' survival, while also prompting farmers to renegotiate what it means to be a resident of their communities. For white farmers, how they understand their identities and their communities is (re)animated in relation to (im)migrant workers.

What is underappreciated in Lefebvre's work is the role that race plays in the creation, maintenance, and embodiment of space. As racial actors, we orient ourselves in reference to our perceptions of space and subsequently make decisions about our behavior in those spaces—for example, whether even to enter or avoid a location. Social spaces have racial histories, in which concrete spatial characteristics lend to, but don't determine, those histories. While space is produced through communication, the specific geographical, physical, and material dimensions of space matter. For example, living within a gated community, as opposed to a diverse cityscape, prods particular ideological perspectives. One such ideological perspective, **whiteness**, intersects with spatial control in myriad ways.

Whiteness has been examined within many different disciplines. Frankenberg (1993) articulates three aspects to connect this vast scholarship: (a) Whiteness is a location of structural advantage (e.g., better police treatment, judicial process, housing, education, jobs, health care, etc.); (b) it is a lens through which white people examine themselves, others, and society; and (c) it refers to a set of unmarked cultural practices, often considered "acultural" by white Americans, which effectively asserts whiteness as the norm. One of the sources of its pervasive power in U.S. society is that it is unacknowledged, and therefore unscrutinized, such that many whites are not aware of the profound effect that being white has on their lives or the lives of cultural others.

Communication research has contributed a lot to our knowledge of this concept, such as how whiteness shapes the way we discuss and think about race. The meaning of white skin is constructed through communication in diverse contexts, regardless of whatever biological characteristics engender white skin (Johnson, 1999). Silence on whiteness, however, preserves its material advantages by making the denial of **white privilege** and systemic racism plausible (Crenshaw, 1997). Promoting the ideologies of colorblindness and meritocracy, the language of whiteness renders the status quo as "natural," enables white people not to "see" race, and disregards racial positionality (Moon, 1999; Nakayama & Krizek, 1995). While some people are labeled "white," everyone within the United States has been influenced by whiteness, and thus whiteness is not limited to white people, who also experience, benefit from, and/or challenge whiteness in different ways.

In addition to its rhetorical, social, cultural, and ideological characteristics, I seek to understand some of the ways whiteness is also spatial. In the past 50 years, whiteness has perhaps been predominant in shaping suburban realities. According to Dickinson (2006), "suburbs are marked by the presence of whiteness" (p. 220). In this specific article, the author looked at film portrayals of suburbs (*The Truman Show, American Beauty, Pleasantville*) as homes for white people. Yet suburbanization constructs the identities not only of those who live in suburbs but of outsiders as well, shaping race, class, and social relations (Antoine, 2007). The inclusion of space in conceptualizations of whiteness moves beyond the symbolic constructions emphasized by communication scholarship, for whiteness is not just symbolic but embodied in material spaces. These spaces are not static, however, as they both produce and are produced by what it means to be white in those locations. There is no absolute expression of whiteness, and a focus on space illuminates its particularities.

Spaces are invariably changed by the discourses, including those of race, that are circulated within their "boundaries," informing behavior, shaping experiences, legitimating cultural expressions, and creating subject positions. While the physical properties of spaces are ascribed with meaning by inhabitants, those properties are also instrumental in forming collective identity. Representations of space often obfuscate its political dimensions and contested nature (Davis, 2003). By demystifying constructions of space, we can identify spatial organization simultaneously as a site of social empowerment. As Massey (2005) exclaims, "the hope is to contribute to a process of liberating space from its old chain of meaning and to associate it with a different one in which it might have, in particular, more political potential" (p. 55). In terms of praxis, social justice movements that affect change in spatial practices transform cultural relationships as well (Johnson, Chambers, Raghuram, & Tincknell, 2004). However, these transgressive practices do not automatically achieve a more egalitarian society, as hybrid cultural spaces enable dominant groups to respond to challenges to their power by normalizing exclusion and segregation as natural and necessary (Durrheim & Dixon, 2001). The objective of approaching whiteness from a spatial perspective is to propose alternatives for how space can be experienced, distributed, and negotiated more equitably.

MEXICAN (IM)MIGRATION

Despite legal restrictions, global economic realities have solidified the consistent flow of immigration. For example, U.S. agricultural imports since the passing of the North American

Free Trade Agreement in 1993 have led to the displacement of Mexican farmers, previously protected by tariffs, who could no longer compete with subsidized U.S. prices. To fill the need for agricultural labor, Farmville actively recruited these farmers (Murray, 2010). Unlike other crops that can be harvested by machine, much of Washington's harvest must be picked by hand, and Mexican (im)migrant workers' low wages enable Washington growers to be competitive internationally.

Yet migrants' presence often challenges farmers' perceptions of "their" communities. They may express sentiments that their town is just not the same (Tuan, 1977). Both migrants and members of receiving communities negotiate their cultural identities, as "border-crossing is not in one direction only, but includes cultural Mexicanisation of Anglos as well, within a political economic context still dominated by Anglo-Americans" (Campbell, 2005, p. 25). Farm communities' interactions (and requisite renegotiation of white identity) with Mexican (im)migrants have been multifaceted and contested. Lemanski and Saff (2010) analyzed long-term residents' perceptions of the influence migrants had had on their communities. The participants reported increased crime (despite statistics that pointed to the contrary), overcrowding, destruction of residential space (material and social), exploitation of public services (schools, health care, etc.) and property value depreciation. These constructions stand in stark contrast to newspaper reports of immigrant laborers who have to sleep in cars, woods, irrigation ditches, and riverbanks. Tensions in Washington farm communities have fermented over matters such as bilingual programs in schools and churches (Mapes, 2000).

Migrant farmworkers negotiate their marginalized role in farm communities, avoiding deportation and/or removal from spaces in which they are subordinate and dependent. They must be both visible and invisible: visible to be hired by local farmers but also invisible to avoid "spooking" (prejudiced) residents. Both extremes are risky endeavors for Mexican farmworkers, who are well aware of existing community opposition (Cleaveland & Kelly, 2009). Within a political environment seeking to define who belongs, who is a citizen, and who is "legal," material and discursive practices render the immigrant as spatially out of place (Shome, 2003). It is apparent that whiteness in spatial organization has material effects on how immigrants negotiate their presence in rural farm communities.

White residents often construct migrant workers as threatening outsiders—fear that is consequently drawn on to justify exclusionary practices (Lemanski & Saff, 2010). Thus, while white and Hispanic residents may occupy the same physical environment, they simultaneously reside in very different social spaces. For example, many Washington farm communities fail to include Mexican residents in their historic murals, despite the fact that the overwhelming majority of residents are of Mexican descent. White residents' descriptions of migrant workers as "a community apart" (Lemanski & Saff, 2010, p. 533) imply a multiplicity of spatial experiences, which intersect, align, and contradict, as dictated by the processes of identity construction within power-laden contexts (Hise, 2004). In the rest of this case study, I explore further the relationships between contested spatial experiences, identity constructions, and race relations in the town of Farmville.

INTERSECTIONS OF RACE AND SPACE IN FARMVILLE

In this community, discourses of whiteness produce unique experiences with the town's space. Spatial constructions are significant in that they inflect the interracial relationships that occur there. Representation of the spatial environments we find ourselves in, such as natural, rural/urban, commercial, and residential, influence our perceptions of the world, and consequently our racial realities.

"Natural Spaces" and an Agricultural *Ethos*

In Farmville, the modes of production (Harvey, 1990; Lefebvre, 1991) enabled by the soil and the climate are integral to residents' communal identification and their articulations of an agricultural *ethos*. It is not surprising that residents, both white and Hispanic, conceive of the town as an agricultural community, with the "typical" Farmvilleite being involved in agricultural production: growing, harvesting, supplying, processing, and so forth. As one long-time resident explained, "All we knew was farming." This agricultural *ethos*, therefore, is not merely a statement of the area's leading industry but a central facet of how residents have constructed their identities.

Illustrating one manifestation of whiteness discursively and spatially, white residents' citation of an agricultural *ethos* is a component of a much broader discourse of multiculturalism, in which residents position the town as racially progressive. For example, a 15 + white resident, who had moved to Farmville later in life, said,

> [Farmville] is pretty accepting. They tend to accept people for who they are, and not what they look like, and not what their cultural background is. People are willing to give everyone the benefit of the doubt when they meet them and be respectful to each other. There's a lot of that here that I haven't seen in other places.

This racial progress is often linked to the perceived agricultural opportunities. The spatial ideology is codified in the town's motto: "Opportunities unlimited." A sign highlighting the town's spatial construction greets drivers as they enter Farmville. Putting a new slant on the American Dream mobility myth, the town's motto asserts that the fertility of the land, augmented by the climate, enables residents to cultivate a diversity of crops, signifying the unlimited opportunities and potential for prosperity in Farmville *for all*. A (20 +) white resident who had recently graduated from college cited the minimizing effect of agriculture on racial difference: "Almost everybody's in the agriculture industry, you know, so I guess you [*sic*] racially it doesn't matter." What this participant is conveying is that because farming theoretically requires everyone to be involved one way or another in the cultivation of the soil and to be dependent on its fertility, agricultural spaces consequently perform an egalitarian function. As a contested cultural space, what is ignored in this construction is the importance of means and property for fulfilling this ideal.

Photo 7.1 This sign greets individuals as they drive into Farmville.

Amidst these so-called infinite possibilities, the townspeople, according to one white resident, are just "happy with being here. They're just not here necessarily to make it big or rich. Just common people, just carrying on a simple life." The effect of this sentiment is to naturalize the town's economic inequality (U.S. Census Bureau, 2010) as merely an unintentional, nonstrategic development, for white residents are deemed to be living simple, nonmaterialistic lives. As understood through the lens of a community that purportedly does not seek an extravagant lifestyle, if inequality does exist, it is not the result of a mapped-out system of domination but instead can be attributed to the "culture" of Hispanic members of the population.

White residents rationalize economic inequality through attribution of cultural differences in fiscal responsibility. One resident stated, "Poverty level, a little bit lower than what you would expect. It doesn't have to be that way. . . . They choose to be this way. I don't drive an Escalade, they do. I don't have fancy wheels, they do." This discursive delineation proffers "cultural differences" (i.e., irresponsible budgeting/exorbitant spending/skewed priorities) in lieu of acknowledging economic inequalities, thus normalizing labor subordination (Maldonado, 2009) and preserving the Farmville hierarchical status quo.

In contrast to white residents, many Hispanic participants challenge the notion of Farmville's identity being one of "unlimited opportunity." Said one resident, "[Farmville] *es pobre en todo. . . . No hay más oportunidades* [Farmville is completely poor. . . . There aren't more opportunities]." Hispanic residents also perceive very different white reactions to their presence along the lines of type of crop. For example, orchardists, who have a higher need for low-paid workers, are believed to be more "welcoming" of Hispanics. White residents' citation of an agricultural *ethos* distinguishes whiteness discourses from those that are circulated in urban (Harvey, 1972) and suburban (Antoine, 2007) spaces. The "natural" spaces (i.e., farmland) of Farmville play a unique role in the discourses of whiteness in this community, as they are constituted so as to reconfigure the American Dream myth and promote the town as "multicultural" while simultaneously normalizing economic inequality.

Rural Spaces: "An Oasis in a Desert"

White residents dichotomize urban and rural spaces. As one resident described Farmville, "It's kind of an oasis in a desert." The metaphor in this passage signifies not only a geographic location but a social one: a close-knit community surrounded by fragmented and disjointed cityscapes. As Foucault (1986) attested, space is impregnated with our desires and ideologies, evoking feelings of belonging and identity. The farm community is constructed as a safe, clean, friendly, neighborly, generous, and not "super-cliquish" place to raise a family, and is thus positioned in contradistinction to the urban city. Invoking the agricultural *ethos*, a second resident linked the "small-town" personality of the town to its agricultural roots:

> I think there's a lot of community pride in the townspeople and the surrounding area, maybe a little more laid-back than say metropolitan areas, part of that I think is the nature of the businesses and with an agricultural base I think you tend to be a little more laid-back.

This resident identifies the modes of production, the "agricultural base," as a central factor in the creation of the town's identity, explicitly distinguishing the town from "metropolitan" or urban spaces. Made more possible by a population of less than 6,800, white residents signify Farmville as a place where everyone knows everyone else, people watch out for one another, and people are willing to help others who are in need, fostering a sense of belonging, safety, and comfort. Residents avow this social support as a unique facet of small towns, set apart from larger communities.

As a hybrid cultural space, however, white residents simultaneously lament that the community is no longer as chummy as it used to be, becoming more like the "west side" (west side of Washington State; i.e., Seattle), as a perceived result of growth. One white resident said,

> I don't like the big-city problems we're starting to have here. . . . Drugs, gangs, like if my kids have to walk home from town, I worry they'll get hassled [by Hispanic youth]. I shouldn't have to feel that way living in [Farmville]. I didn't feel that way as a teenager.

Relying on a spatial binary of big city = danger and small town = safe, this resident expresses no longer feeling sheltered in his (white) community, noting the presence of drugs and gangs. Imbedded in his statement is a pervasive notion that the town is distinct and should be immune to the issues faced by larger communities. In opposition to Farmville, the symbols "big city" and "Seattle" become code words for "diverse" and "undesirable." In the dominant whiteness narrative, "new" (i.e., Hispanic) settlers have threatened the idyllic, simple paradise. Although the residents quoted in this section do not explicitly identify race, which is a rhetorical strategy of whiteness itself (Crenshaw, 1997), whiteness is evident in how Farmvilleites have constructed their rural town in relation to urban (i.e., diverse) cities and how Hispanic newcomers are described.

Segregated Commercial Spaces: "Catering" to Hispanics

In Farmville, specific stores, restaurants, and bars, located mostly downtown, are constructed as "Hispanic," *catering* to Hispanic townspeople, with few white residents frequenting those locations. On one level, this oft-repeated term (*catering*) connotes availability of certain goods purchased more regularly by Hispanics, bilingualism of sales staff, the establishment's decor, and how welcoming the climate is to members of the Hispanic community. But on another level, there is an underlying implication that the space is not

Courtesy of Joshua F. Hoops

Photo 7.2 This grocery store, used primarily by white residents, is not framed in terms of ethnicity.

"for" white members of the town and thus white residents must do their shopping elsewhere, either oblivious to or ignoring the ways the majority of the town's commercial businesses "cater" to the town's statistical minority, white Farmvilleites. These spaces, although not represented as "white," are enjoyed almost exclusively by white residents. For example, a coffee shop in town serves as a meeting place for white farmers to share stories and make various arrangements amongst themselves. "White" businesses are not identified according to race but, rather, with labels such as "traditional" and "mainstream."

The descriptions of businesses "catering" and "targeting" are framed in either/or classifications. The establishment either caters to Hispanics or it is shared space for everyone. One resident explained, "Basically, right now we have just one larger grocery store. Several smaller groceries that cater to the Hispanic population." These classifications (nonracialized grocery stores vs. grocery stores catering to Hispanic residents), as adopted by this resident, are not problematized, reinforcing the white assumption that no space exists that caters to white residents. These perceptions create feelings of nostalgia and a sense of loss toward their community's space. The same resident expressed,

> Right now, it's so migrant, so many Spanish [*sic*] moving in . . . it's really, really a Spanish town. We have more Mexican restaurants than ever before. We have to dine out of town. We have no business that we can shop at for clothing. The Spanish people, the Mexican people do. They have two or three shops. We have none. And so it's kind of deteriorated because we're so heavily populated by with Spanish [*sic*].

Communicated quite clearly in this passage is the feeling that the town no longer belongs to the white residents, who now must grapple with what it means to be the ethnic "minority," albeit still the economic majority. This transformation is not considered merely a change but a change for the worse, a "deterioration," which compels white residents in town to travel elsewhere to meet their shopping and dining needs.

Whiteness discourses normalize this shopping exodus, rationalized by white residents who claim victimhood as the result of being pushed out of their hometown. "There's so few stores now, so many people are treated as outsiders that they don't want to shop here." As a result of feeling mistreated, white residents normalize shopping elsewhere as their only option. While whiteness has often meant "fleeing" from a town when "too many" people of color have moved in (Kruse, 2005), in this particular community, whiteness has also come to signify shopping outside of the city, taking not only their resources out of Farmville but their time as well. While some white residents have moved as a result of demographic changes, the performance of whiteness is not limited to this particular movement. White residents emphasize the microdecisions

Photo 7.3 Whereas some businesses are labeled "Hispanic," "white" businesses are not labeled as such.

Courtesy of Joshua F. Hoops

businesses made to close shop, creating fewer (more expensive) options. These economic shifts, it should be noted, coincide with Hispanic population growth. Yet white residents make sense of the shopping exodus in relation to the unpredictability of farming. According to one resident,

> With farming, it's such a roller coaster. You know, one year you could be just doing really well and the next year you're almost bankrupt . . . and so you have to shop around and when you shop around you know it hurts businesses in town. You'd like to do business in town but we have very few of 'em left.

In this passage, the resident constitutes space, and the ascribed unpredictability of that space for Farmville industry, to normalize the outflow of white capital from a town that has become "more Hispanic." In contrast, Hispanic participants point to racial discrimination, for if a Hispanic resident is maltreated, word spreads and members of the Hispanic community will boycott that establishment, making it difficult for the store to remain in business.

Even when residents affirm the diversification of a town previously "controlled by Anglos," they lament segregated businesses, critical of Hispanic newcomers "who just want to turn [Farmville] into Mexico. Why'd you leave Mexico then? That's where the white population has a problem." This resident, like in the previous two passages, provides justification for the shopping exodus, defensive of the perceived ways "Hispanicness" is squeezing white individuals out of "their" town. And yet the spatial mobility intrinsic to the shopping exodus suggests white residents' privilege, not only to freely move between spaces at will (Tuan, 1977) but also to detach from the Farmville community when it suits them.

Segregated Residential Spaces: Spatializing Race in Farmville

The creation of segregated cities and homogenous suburbs has been instrumental in formations of whiteness (Kruse, 2005). As a result, many white Americans "came to see their isolation as natural and innocuous. . . . The ultimate success of white flight was the way in which it led whites away from responsibility for the problems they had done much to create" (p. 258). In Farmville, this disconnect began with the first residents of Farmville living near the railroad tracks. There were economic benefits to living within close proximity to the train tracks, with more immediate access to goods and information. Over time, however, those (white) residents moved away from the tracks as migrants made Farmville their home. The tracks' physical location on the fringes of Farmville has consequently marked its marginal status (Krause, 2008). While some white participants opt to identify the area only according to income level, others (both white and Hispanic) note its racialization, known to Farmvilleites by its unofficial moniker "Tortilla Flats." In contrast, the white section of town is simply known by its geographical location (i.e., "the southwest") rather than as a racial counterpart to the north end's Tortilla Flats, a manifestation of whiteness both discursively and spatially.

The north end, or "the other side of the tracks," became segmented in terms not only of ethnicity but of desirability, as ascribed by both white and Hispanic residents. This spatial displeasure was initially associated with the environmental conditions of living adjacent to the train tracks, which meant increased exposure to smoke permeating the northeast section of town. The train tracks thus came to symbolize both a material and symbolic marker of racial difference. According to one white resident, "The north of the tracks would be regarded as more of the crime area. . . . Typically the southwest is not as many problems." The marginality created by a racialized town is not solely a material phenomenon but a symbolic one (Hetherington, 1998). In Farmville, for example, Hispanic residents explain that where one lives in town becomes a marker for his or her identity and whether he or she is ascribed as being from the "problem" or "upscale" part of town, positioning Hispanic residents both spatially and socially (Giddens, 1984). Hispanic residents are also much more explicit about the spatial hierarchy:

> The southwest is the white population. This is where you want to be. This is where the streets are calmer, where the white-picket fence [*sic*]. This is where you want to be. All the good areas where you want to raise your kids will be in the southwest.

This resident paints an idyllic picture of the southwest part of town, one with stereotypical "white"-picket fences and calm streets.

Historically, suburbs and rural communities were just as (if not more so) segregated as urban cities. However, discourses of class stratification naturalize this segregation, enabling residents to view it as a natural occurrence rather than the result of intentionally racist decisions or structures (Kruse, 2005). For example, as Hispanic residents started, and were able, to relocate into other sections of town, many members of the white population decided to move outside of the city limits. As one Hispanic resident commented, "They're not enjoying the mix of people as much, so they moved out, some of them." Amidst anecdotes of racial segregation, white residents collectively dismiss the racialization of the northeast section of town, opting for the language of "affordability." Hispanic residents, however, contest this narrative. As one resident explained, "Nobody [Hispanic residents] would live on that side [southwest], because they [white owners] would not sell or rent to them [Hispanics]. Over there [Tortilla Flats], they [white owners] did." As a result of discriminatory practices, the majority of Hispanic residents either lived in a housing complex nicknamed the "cockroach apartments," due to its dilapidated condition, or out of town because they had difficulty finding a landlord who would rent to them. In Farmville, the spatial/discursive manifestations of whiteness can be evidenced in how the different residential neighborhoods are represented, how segregation is rationalized, and how social exclusion is subsequently justified.

THE IMPLICATIONS OF CONTESTED SPACE

Spatial discourses unify and divide, producing contested representations of physical, geographical, and material sites. Hispanic Farmvilleites challenge the dominant whiteness narratives that (a) position Farmville as a town of "unlimited opportunity"; (b) point to the unpredictability of farming, rather than racial discrimination, to explain faltering businesses in town; and (c) naturalize racialized sections, instead of elucidating the role of previous racist practices. The constructed nature of white residents' experience of Farmville as an "everyone-knows-everyone" community becomes apparent in contrast to Hispanic residents' accounts of the alienation they have encountered living in Farmville. White and Hispanic residents may occupy the same physical space but live in very different social spaces.

As students of intercultural communication, it is important that we critically examine our spaces: how they are created, how they are arranged, and, perhaps even more important, the meanings we give them. No space is inherently multicultural, close-knit, desirable, or catering but is constructed in ways that serve particular ideological interests and identities. Especially within a post-Obama political environment, where the dominant message is that race no longer matters, whiteness, albeit in often convoluted and contradicting discourses, intervenes in these representations to obscure the role of history, political economy, and, yes, race in social productions of space, including where people live, work, shop, worship, spend their free time, and even attend school. The effects of these relationships between space, race, and communication are not insignificant, as they often intersect to justify segregation and naturalize labor subordination. Thinking critically about spatial representations, how might we seek to understand diverse narratives of space and re-create and rearrange our spaces accordingly?

Space does not exist independently of discourse but is internalized and reified through language, cementing insider/outsider binaries (Harvey, 1996). Whiteness must be understood in relationship to the spaces where it is produced, as there is no singular, monolithic expression of whiteness. In this case study, I've specifically examined natural, rural, commercial, and residential spaces; however, these classifications are far from exhaustive. Educational, recreational, and religious could be added, to name a few. Whiteness produces particular experiences of Farmville space, intersecting with spatial control to exacerbate continued racial division. As Sorrells (2013) points out, "segregated, contested, and hybrid cultural spaces . . . sustain historically forged relations of unequal power" (p. 76). While whiteness is symbolic, constructed, social, rhetorical, and discursive, it is also profoundly spatial.

Whiteness as Pedagogical Performance: A Critical Reflection on Race and Pedagogy

Richie Neil Hao
University of Denver

O n a cold winter day, I start the new year teaching my first graduate seminar, Critical Intercultural Communication, for an MA program outside of my department. I am excited and anxious at the same time. While my academic training in intercultural communication prepares me to teach this course, I am teaching students from another department that does not study intercultural communication from a critical perspective. I enter a classroom right outside of my department office. As I put my class materials down on a table, I smile at the students and start to scan the 21 bodies right before me. Along with four students of color, my Chinese Filipino body is a minority in this predominantly white classroom.

Reflecting on my journal entries over the 10-week seminar, I will share and analyze some of the conversations I had with my students inside and outside of the classroom (e.g., during office hours) that situate and recenter whiteness as a privileged ideology. According to Moon (1999), whiteness is "a system of domination" (p. 178) perpetuated through performances of white identity (Warren, 2001). Even though whiteness is often discussed as marked on the white body, it can also be performed by people of color (Carrillo Rowe & Malhotra, 2006). Whiteness is also part of the everyday ideological performance, such as what occurs in the classroom, and through these performances, it gets constituted, reproduced, and socially constructed (Hytten & Warren, 2003). Therefore, "whiteness is not just about bodies and skin color, but rather more about the discursive practices that, because of colonialism and neocolonialism, privilege and sustain the global dominance of white imperial subjects and Eurocentric worldviews" (Shome, 1999, p. 108).

Because U.S. academic institutions have been historically segregated (Sorrells, 2013), the spatial aspect of the performance of whiteness in the classroom is significant to examine. As a cultural space, meanings are constructed "in, through, and about" (p. 77) the classroom where hegemonic white ideologies and bodies are privileged. In fact, according to Orfield and Yun (as cited in Sorrells, 2013), schools in the United States "are resegregated to the same level as in 1970s" (p. 89); "White students attend schools that are approximately 80% White" (p. 89), which is representative of the academic institution where I currently teach. In a series of pedagogical interactions and interventions as **intercultural praxis**, I examine and question how my students' performances of whiteness affect intercultural communication, especially when confronting and problematizing their privileged white bodies and voices in a contested classroom space where "oppositional and confrontational strategies of resistance" (p. 91) are performed. I also examine how different pedagogical events in my graduate seminar have provided insight for my understanding of the classroom as a contested cultural space and my teaching of intercultural communication.

WHITENESS, RACE, AND PEDAGOGY

Intersectionality and Whiteness

As my students and I discuss the **intersectionality** of race, gender, and sexuality in popular culture, I begin with Collins's (1990) "matrix of domination," which addresses different forms of domination (e.g., race, class, gender) that "most heavily affect African-American women" (p. 225) and other marginalized groups. As I start the discussion on power and privilege, some white women in the class shake their heads to show disagreement that their race and class are significant identity markers that privilege their bodies over others. Even though they acknowledge that their gender is disadvantaged compared with men, they feel defensive when I bring up that affluent or educated white women have certain advantages over other women, especially women of color. I feel the environment growing tense, with some white female students looking at me with anger in their eyes, as if I have offended them. It is apparent to me then that whiteness is invading the classroom space where the physical marker of my white students has become named and visible. As Nakayama and Krizek (1995) note, whiteness is a rhetorical construction in an "uninterrogated space" (p. 293). As a result, naming my students' whiteness creates a mechanism to defend their white bodies and the classroom space from becoming privileged. I wish I could do more in that pedagogical moment of reflection as we discuss the intersectionality of identities, but I believe that engaging my white female students in dialogue about their privileged identities provides opportunities to at least reframe their worldview, especially related to their whiteness.

As we transition to another article, a white female student leads a discussion on Nakayama's (1994) piece on the representation of Asian American masculinity in a U.S. film. After summarizing the article, she proceeds to say that Nakayama, a Japanese American, is biased because of his Japanese American identity. I decide to enter the conversation as a form of intercultural praxis, which is to "practice a way of being, thinking, analyzing, reflecting, and acting" (Sorrells, 2013, p. 15). Intercultural praxis has

> interrelated points of entry into the process: (1) inquiry, (2) framing, (3) positioning, (4) dialogue, (5) reflection, and (6) action. The purpose of engaging

in intercultural praxis is to raise our awareness, increase our critical analysis, and develop our socially responsible action in regard to our intercultural interactions in the context of globalization. These six points or ports of entry into the process direct us toward ways of thinking, reflecting, and acting in relation to our intercultural experiences, allowing us to attend to the complex, relational, interconnected, and often ambiguous nature of our experiences. (p. 16)

To engage my student in intercultural praxis, I say to her that if she does not agree with Nakayama, it does not mean his reality does not exist. After all, our framing or "our perspectives and our views on ourselves, others and the world around us are always and inevitably limited" (Sorrells, 2013, p. 17). For instance, cultural constructions of Asian American male bodies as asexual, effeminate, threatening, and undesirable continue to dominate U.S. popular culture, while white men are often depicted as rugged and sexually linked with Asian women (Nakayama, 1994). I also emphasize to my class why we need to be self-reflexive in critiquing another person's work. According to Nakayama and Krizek (1995), **reflexivity** encourages us to consider what has been silenced or invisible in academic discussions (such as whiteness). Reflexivity also urges us to consider the presentation of research and articulation of the researcher's position. My student's facial expression suggests that she does not agree with what I am saying. She pouts but carries on with her presentation. Based on her nonverbal communication, my student is upset about my pointing out her lack of **self-reflexivity**. I am not bothered about my student being upset, but I am disappointed that she does not seem to be open to criticism about not acknowledging another voice that is different from her own.

The same white female student who presented Nakayama's article comes to see me during my office hours. She says she feels that I "silenced" her by calling her out on her critique of Nakayama's "biasness." Then she becomes emotional and starts to tear up. I begin to feel discomfort. I do not understand how asking her to be self-reflexive results in her crying in front of me. I pause and give her a moment to say whatever else she wants to express. The moment of silence signals my turn to speak. I tell her that I apologize if I offended her, but we do not have to agree; she must understand that Nakayama's positionality matters in how he interpreted the film. Her disappointment is still visible on her face. In some ways, I argue that my student's opposition to my calling her out is an example of "civil talk" (Patton, 2004, p. 65) in the classroom, which is to "play nice" so that her white body is not read as racist and to situate my Asian American body to conform to the model minority myth. According to Chang (2001), the model minority myth also categorizes Asian Americans as apolitical and lacking vocal leadership. I feel that my student's performance as a "white victim" necessitates that I engage in civil talk. As a "white victim," she also erases the possibility of her privileged status as a white woman. Consequently, she also performs whiteness by continuing to contain my body not only in the classroom but also in my office. Her strategic performance as a "white victim" also prevents me from handling the situation any differently, considering I am put in an uncomfortable position as a teacher.

Laughing About Whiteness: Making Whiteness Invisible

A white American woman presents an article on the discourse of whiteness in the classroom (Johnson, Rich, & Cargile, 2008). This student is someone I consider to be the "joker" of the class. She engages in "playful" interactions with me, such as giving me a funny, confused look if she does not understand something, and likes to comment in class with sarcasm. My student begins describing Johnson et al.'s interpretation of how students engage in performances of whiteness. As she summarizes the article, she squints her eyes and makes a point that "apparently every white person is a white supremacist!" Laughter erupts in the classroom. I do not know if her peers are laughing with her because they find her funny or if they agree with her point. Because "white supremacy" is often associated with white supremacist groups such as the Ku Klux Klan, my student does not believe that white supremacy should be associated with white people who do not engage in extreme performances of racism. However, hooks (in July, 1997) refers to "white supremacist capitalist patriarchy" as interlocking **systems of domination** (e.g., race, class, and gender). Thus, white supremacy should not be understood simply as overt racism; instead, everyday performances of domination, such as whiteness, are tied to historical, structural, institutional, political, and social contexts. Underneath my student's particular remark, I argue it is not only a form of exaggeration and sarcasm but also a truth: It makes people laugh because they are all implicated through their participation in white supremacy. They laugh not only because it sounds sarcastic but also because they are uncomfortable. Laughing is a way of erasing one's own complicity in the history of dehumanization. Therefore, my student's sarcastic comment gets her and her white peers off the hook for their performances of whiteness. Even though I did not laugh with my students, I realize that I, too, participated in their classroom performance of whiteness through civil talk by not questioning their "jokes."

INTERCULTURAL PRAXIS: CONFRONTING AND CHALLENGING WHITENESS

An Arab American woman leads the discussion on whiteness. Looking somewhat nervous, she shares a narrative about her mother's dining experience when she was seated in the back of the restaurant, even though there were plenty of seats in front. Her eyes begin to tear up as she talks about how her mother chose to ignore the discrimination. Even after the narrative has ended, everyone in class sits still and a few students wipe tears from their eyes. This student's narrative is a good example of reflection as intercultural praxis (Sorrells, 2013) because it is so powerful and impactful that it drives everyone to listen carefully and to want more after experiencing "the capacity to learn from introspection, to observe oneself in relation to others" (p. 19). By engaging her peers and me in the dialogue of how whiteness works to privilege certain bodies over others, she helps us reflect on her narrative to disrupt the space of whiteness, even if just for a moment—not only how it is performed in everyday life but also how it is currently present in the classroom.

In her discussion of Carrillo Rowe and Malhotra's (2006) "(Un)hinging Whiteness," a white student who identifies as lesbian asks the class to answer the following questions/prompts written on six pieces of butcher paper and taped to the classroom walls:

- "Why do I choose to engage in whiteness?"

- "I engage in whiteness in the following ways . . ."

- "How do you see whiteness play out in America?"

- "I am impacted by whiteness in the following ways . . ."

- "What does it mean to take whiteness out of the body?"

- "I can work to disrupt whiteness by . . ."

She instructs her peers to write their responses on sticky notes and place them on the corresponding pieces of paper. Students are receptive to the activity, and they eagerly write their responses and move around the room to place the sticky notes where appropriate.

In the student responses, some white students express that they feel as though they are being "attacked" for being white:

"Not all white people are evil."

"I am white, so people assume they know me or my background."

"People place me in the box of 'whiteness' in which I can't escape."

"Whiteness, more so than anything, confuses my own identity. Its pervasiveness makes it hard to detach from. I don't like it."

"Not to be judged by the actions of 'white' past."

These responses illustrate how many white people do not want to be thought of as bad or evil; therefore, they feel that collective memories of the past, such as slavery and colonization, are no longer relevant to discussions in current times (Madison, 1999), which is a strategic rhetoric of whiteness that erases white bodies from their privileges (Nakayama & Krizek, 1995).

Moreover, many students argue that whiteness has great influence in different aspects of our lives. In particular, students talk about how whiteness is a form of power that grants one access to material, political, and social privileges. "White men own/influence everything!" is a common statement, expressed in different words but always with a similar sentiment, which I find intriguing in part because there is no statement that mentions specifically white women as having the power to dominate Others. Reflecting on this activity, I wish I had asked my students why they referred only to white men as those who have the power to "own/influence everything." While I understand the privileges of white men, I should have also asked my students about white women's privileges, which would allow other pedagogical opportunities to emphasize the intersectionality of identities.

Another classroom activity that challenges whiteness is demonstrated through my Filipina American student's presentation on "civility" and how this can erase critical voices when talking about race and racism (Patton, 2004). Patton considers hegemonic civility as inferential racism in higher education, which operates as a

> normalized or naturalized behavior—appropriate behavior—even as the action can be incivil or even silencing in order to uphold the hegemonic order . . . an organized process which results in suppressing or silencing any opposition, in favor of the status quo. (p. 65)

My student passes out note cards to everyone, as well as printouts of McIntosh's (2010) list of implications of her white privilege. She instructs everyone to read the printout they have received and write down what McIntosh's statement means to them. Everyone in class does what they have been asked to do.

As I listen to different student responses, I start to think about their implications. In particular, how are they reinforcing and recentering whiteness? For instance, one of McIntosh's (2010) statements is read: "I can be pretty sure that if I ask to talk to 'the person in charge,' I will be facing a person of my race" (p. 101). A white student responds in a commanding voice: "I am the norm, standard, hegemonic, dominating, although I am a woman." This response is telling of how some white women in class perform their whiteness by being open to critiquing issues of gender and class inequalities but reluctant to acknowledge their whiteness. In this sense, they feel that they are as marginalized as women of color. However, as Collins (1990) points out, the intersectionality of race, class, and gender must be taken into account since each person's experience is different, and we can be simultaneously advantaged and disadvantaged based on our identities.

After all the students have shared their responses to McIntosh's statements, the student presenter unexpectedly proceeds with a bold statement that we have been performing the **guise of civility** in the classroom. What she has said shocks me, but I am not surprised, because I am beginning to see how I can engage in the guise of civility to let some white students contain me and other students of color on different occasions. My student's concern is an example of how dialogue functions as intercultural praxis (Sorrells, 2013) to disrupt the space of whiteness where my students and I

> stretch ourselves—to reach across—to imagine, experience, and creatively engage with points of view, ways of thinking and being, and beliefs different from our own while accepting that we may not fully understand or come to a common agreement or position. (p. 19)

While I have called out students on lack of self-reflexivity, there have been moments when I have let them off the hook. I enacted an understanding of civility in the classroom as a performance of teacher professionalism by engaging my students in "safe" classroom discussions. Thus, engaging in the guise of civility is a performance of whiteness because I did not problematize some of the classroom discourses that supported dominant perspectives. Nobody dares to respond to my student's claim that we have been engaging in the guise of civility. Not even me. I, too, have taken part in it.

DISCUSSION: WHITENESS, CULTURAL SPACE, AND INTERCULTURAL COMMUNICATION

It has been a tough 10 weeks. I have never experienced a classroom environment so tense and uncomfortable, especially when we discussed readings related to whiteness, which proves that the classroom is a contested space where "oppositional and confrontational strategies of resistance" (Sorrells, 2013, p. 91) are performed. As a teacher of color, engaging my white students in confronting and challenging their whiteness was difficult. However, the overall outcome of the course was still good because many students expressed that they learned about perspectives different from their own. I gained insight to identify whiteness as pedagogical performance, understand the classroom as a cultural space, and teach intercultural communication from a critical perspective.

In my classroom, many white female students framed whiteness as "symbolic racism" (Madison, 1999, p. 404); they admitted that they do not like overt racism, but they still upheld their white privilege, especially when we discussed intersectionality of identities and the matrix of domination (Collins, 1990). In this regard, my white female students understood their white bodies as natural rather than cultural (Nakayama & Krizek, 1995), which prevented their whiteness from being connected to power relations embedded in their daily lives. Consequently, white bodies are framed simply in terms of color and should not have cultural implications to race and racism. However, whiteness is about so much more than bodies; it is also performative and ideological.

Furthermore, many of my white students framed historical events related to whiteness, such as slavery and colonization, as collective memories of the past. According to Nakayama and Krizek (1995), white students tend to associate negative definitions with white bodies because they "see white as meaning that they lacked any other racial or ethnic features; hence, they must be white by default" (p. 299). Nakayama and Krizek add: "This negative definition may be related to the invisibility of whiteness as a category or a position from which one speaks" (p. 299). Therefore, many white students are defensive when past atrocities are brought up in classroom discussions. While it is true that most white people today were not involved in these past atrocities, denying their white privilege only reinforces the notion that racism and performances of whiteness no longer exist in the so-called "postracial" U.S. society.

As a teacher of color, I often struggle with how to present myself in the contested classroom space. When I walk into the classroom, my Chinese Filipino body is already and always marked with different cultural assumptions that categorize me as Other. Therefore, it is sometimes necessary for me to perform whiteness by acting "professional" through civil talk when I discuss whiteness, race, and racism. Otherwise, I am likely going to be painted as another angry teacher of color who has an agenda to accuse my white students of racism.

Despite the contested classroom space, there were pedagogical moments that allowed me and my students to engage in intercultural praxis. For example, my Filipina American student talked about classroom civility and how that transpired in the classroom. Also, my Arab American student shared her mother's experience of discrimination. Finally, my white lesbian student challenged us to think about whiteness in our daily lives. As a critical intercultural communication teacher-scholar, I strive to engage my students in dialogue to question and challenge dominant assumptions about culture and identity. Even if my students disagree with me, I want them to engage in intercultural praxis by becoming self-reflexive, acknowledging other voices and perspectives, and examining how whiteness operates in their lives.

Teaching critical intercultural communication reaffirmed my understanding of how complex the classroom space is, where the politics of identity and culture are always being negotiated. Teaching intercultural communication is never easy, but approaching it from a critical perspective adds other pedagogical challenges, especially when I engage my students in dialogue about issues of power and privilege. Despite these challenges, it is fundamental for students to understand the micro and macro performances of culture, such as whiteness, that shape our identities in different contexts.

KEY TERMS

contested cultural space 122	intercultural praxis 135	self-reflexivity 136
cultural space 122	intersectionality 135	systems of domination 137
guise of civility 139	pedagogy 134	white privilege 125
hybrid cultural space 122	reflexivity 136	whiteness 124
	segregated cultural space 122	

DISCUSSION QUESTIONS

1. Using Hoops's case study, discuss the complex relationships among cultural space, race, identity, and power. Now, engage in a similar discussion using examples from cultural spaces (e.g., classroom, gym, university, neighborhood, or city), racial/cultural identities, and power dynamics you are familiar with.

2. Based on your reading of the personal narrative by Hao and the case study by Hoops, define and discuss whiteness. Give examples from the essays and from your experience of how whiteness is symbolic, embodied, performative, and ideological.

3. Both essays illustrate how people who are white often are unwilling to see and name their complicity with and benefit from dominant-group membership. Why is this? How is this accomplished (identify specific strategies that obfuscate or deflect from being implicated)?

4. Both entries provide ample examples of how the construction of cultural spaces intersects with race and power to reinforce and embody historical and hegemonic relations of power. As a coperformer and cocommunicator within cultural spaces, what actions could you take to negotiate more equitable spaces, for example, in the classroom, your university, home, or city?

CHAPTER 8

Intercultural Relationships

Social hierarchies of difference are historically marked and maintained by politically sanctioned segregation or prohibition of certain types of intergroup relationships. In the United States, for example, **antimiscegenation laws**, the segregation of public schools, and the Defense of Marriage Act all shaped and regulated interpersonal relationships as a form of social control. Relationships do not always form as neutral or purely voluntary practices; rather, the question of whom we build relationships with and under what conditions is always intertwined with and has implications for our access to resources, our social status, and our identities. At the same time, interpersonal relationships are one of the most significant and transformative sites for intercultural communication.

Relating across cultural differences is fundamental to developing cultural self-awareness, intercultural alliances, and a sense of community in a multicultural world. Rather than reducing the complexity of intercultural relationships to a celebratory discourse on multiculturalism or individualism, it is crucial for students and practitioners of intercultural communication to attend to how historical contexts, ideologies, power, and privilege manifest in relationships, and how intercultural relationships can be sites of transformation across differences.

The entries in this chapter address the challenges and possibilities of forming intercultural relationships. In the case study, Yea-Wen Chen and Chie Torigoe analyze how interracial couples in New Mexico talk about issues related to their avowed/ascribed identities, intergroup stereotypes and prejudices, as well as whiteness and color-blind ideologies. In the personal narrative, Mary Jane Collier and Karambu Ringera discuss their experiences of working with each other as intercultural allies for International Peace Initiatives in Kenya. In their dialogic exchange, they share the insights they gained through negotiating differential power relations as a scholar/practitioner from the United States and scholar/practitioner from Kenya. Both entries in this chapter point to the complexity of intercultural communication as a relational practice.

"We Get Bad Looks, All the Time": Ideologies and Identities in the Discourses of Interracial Romantic Couples

Yea-Wen Chen

Ohio University

Chie Torigoe

Seinan Gakuin University

The number of interracial, heterosexual couples in the United States has increased dramatically in the past few decades, growing from 1% in 1970 to 9.5% in 2010. The percentage of interracial unmarried households was as high as 18% in 2010 (U.S. Census Bureau, 2012). Two primary factors contribute to the growth of interracial romantic relationships: first, changing demographics due to the rapidly increasing immigrant populations from Latin America and Asia (e.g., Qian & Lichter, 2011) and, second, changing attitudes toward interracial marriages (Jordan, 2012; Troy, Lewis-Smith, & Laurenceau, 2006). Interracial marriages were prohibited in more than 40 states until the Supreme Court declared antimiscegenation laws unconstitutional in *Loving v. Virginia* in 1967. In contrast to survey data in 1986 that revealed only 30% of U.S. Americans considered interracial marriages acceptable, 63% of Americans today find such marriages acceptable (Wang, 2012). Nevertheless, the "growing" acceptance does not mean that interracial romantic relationships are now celebrated or embraced, and communication research on interracial romantic relationships remains scarce.

On the surface, interracial romantic relationships seem to have become "normal" or "less unusual" over the past 50 years. Discourses around statements such as "Race does not matter anymore" or "We do not see color anymore" might further facilitate interracial couplehood. However, this does not mean that interracial romantic partners no longer have to deal with racial and cultural differences. Childs (2005) suggests that interracial relationships, especially black–white couples, represent "racial transgressions" (p. 4) and expose racial borders, which can reveal problems of race that are otherwise hidden. In response, we investigate in this case study discourses of interracial romantic couples across three levels: the micro (individual) level, the meso (cultural group) level, and the macro (social, institutional, and ideological) levels (Sorrells, 2013). Specifically, we explore how partners in interracial, heterosexual romantic relationships negotiate their divergent racial and cultural identities, how race-based stereotypes/prejudices affect the couples, and what kinds of race-related ideologies emerge in interracial, heterosexual couples' interview discourses.

We conducted this case study based on our beliefs that interracial/intercultural romantic relationships can be critical sites of **intercultural praxis** (Sorrells, 2013). Intercultural praxis is a relational practice: Throughout their relationships, partners in interracial relationships have opportunities to understand and critically reflect on their own and their partner's cultures, positionalities, and challenging intercultural contexts. Such relational learning leads to the awareness of their responsibilities and capabilities for working toward social justice.

PAST RESEARCH ON INTERRACIAL, HETEROSEXUAL ROMANTIC RELATIONSHIPS

Interracial, heterosexual romantic relationships are considered sites where intersecting cultural identities, privileges, racial group marginalization, and power dynamics are constantly created and negotiated (Childs, 2005; Thompson & Collier, 2006). However, most research on interracial relationships in the field of communication, sociology, and social psychology is grounded in social scientific perspectives that tend to ignore the existence of power dynamics among different racial groups, and how ideologies enable and constrain relational partners' agency (Chuang, 2003). Also, the majority of research that relies on more traditional perspectives usually takes a micro frame to analyze interracial romantic relationships. Therefore, these studies focus on, for instance, how educational attainment predicts the likelihood of interracial marriages (Qian & Lichter, 2011), gender differences in interracial marriage (Wang, 2012), or how interracial and intraracial couples differ in conflict and/or attachment styles (Troy et al., 2006). It is problematic to regard partners' racial identities as static and single entities, like a "check box" of racial categories, and to treat them as variables that predict partners' behaviors.

Given these issues in academic discourses on interracial romantic relationships, some researchers call for unraveling ideological aspects of interracial romantic relationships from a critical perspective. Killian (2002) found that homogamy, hypersensitivity of partners of color, and ignorance of history were the three dominant racial discourses reflected and reproduced in black–white interracial couples' interview discourses. Similarly, Thompson and Collier's (2006) study with 12 black–white interracial, heterosexual couples found that color-blind and whiteness ideologies were reflected and re-created in their interpersonal discourses. As these studies suggest, analyzing interracial couples' discourses from micro, meso, and macro levels expands our understanding of interracial, heterosexual romantic relationships and unravels unequal social systems of race relations that are hidden under the dominant **color-blind ideology**.

STUDY BACKGROUND

In this case study, we examined interracial, heterosexual romantic partners' discourses in conflict situations within two spheres: private interpersonal relationships and public/professional settings. We believe that analyzing such conflict situations—where partners negotiate their salient cultural identities challenged or threatened by others and social structures, including various "isms" (Collier, 2005; LeBaron, 2003)—helps bridge the micro, meso, and macro contexts. Nine interracial, heterosexual couples identified through our personal networks participated in this case study. All the participants were between 19 and 26 years of age, their length of dating or marriage ranged from 9 months to 3 years, and they were residing in New Mexico during this research (see Table 8.1). Between October and December 2006, we conducted semistructured face-to-face interviews with each couple. To explore the processes of negotiating identities between partners, we interviewed both partners in each other's presence and also encouraged them to talk to each other. After asking them to share their relationship history, we invited them to speak about conflict situations they had faced both in private and public settings. Conflict situations in private settings include conflicts with each other, family members, or friends, whereas those in public settings refer to conflicts that one or both of them faced in their workplace, at restaurants, or on public transportation.

Table 8.1 details the participants' chosen racial/ethnic labels to better contextualize racial/ethnic positionalities as relational. In particular, some racial/ethnic labels that the

Table 8.1   Participants' Chosen Racial/Ethnic Labels

Name	Sex	Age	Race/Ethnicity	Status	Length
Walter	M	19–26	Black, African American	Dating	2 years
Amanda	F	19–26	Hispanic, Spanish		
Daniel	M	19–26	Hispanic/Spanish/Mexican	Dating	1 year, 7 months
Cindy	F	19–26	White		
Michael	M	19–26	Asian American	Dating	2 years
Mary	F	19–26	White/European American		
Matthew	M	19–26	African American	Married	2.5 years
Tina	F	19–26	Black/Spanish/Hispanic		
David	M	19–26	Hispanic/British	Dating	1 year, 4 months
Jen	F	19–26	White/European American		
James	M	19–26	Hispanic	Dating	1 year, 5 months
Jeanne	F	19–26	White/European American		
Gilbert	M	19–26	African American	Dating	9 months
Cassie	F	19–26	White/European American		
Doug	M	19–26	Spanish American	Dating	1 year, 7 months
Katy	F	19–26	Hispanic American		
Ed	M	19–26	Native American	Dating	3 years
Alicia	F	19–26	Spanish/Hispanic American		

Source: U.S. Census Bureau (2012).

participants chose are unique to New Mexico. To contextualize the participants' discourses and our analysis, we provide below a brief overview and history of race relations in New Mexico.

According to the 2010 Census, New Mexico's population is 47% Hispanic/Latino, 39.8% white, 10% Native American, and 2.4% black/African American. Although the Census uses the label "Hispanic/Latino," many in New Mexico identify as "Spanish" or "Spanish American." The use of these labels dates back to the 1850s, when New Mexicans were striving for self-government (Nieto-Phillips, 2004). At that time, Spanish-speaking people were perceived as nonwhite and deemed unqualified for either full citizenship or self-government. Thus, New Mexicans and Anglo newcomers tried to convince lawmakers in Washington, D.C., that they were capable of self-government by arguing that the Spanish-speaking people were actually racially "white," with their roots in Spain. The collective Spanish (American) identity, thus, was a rhetorical tool to fight against racism and to accommodate white **body politics**. To this date, these labels are pervasive among New Mexicans.

In extracting analytical frames from the participants' discourses, we carefully went through the transcripts and collaboratively interpreted emerging themes. We attended to three themes corresponding to the interrelated micro, meso, and macro frames, respectively: (1) negotiating cultural identities in conflict situations; (2) how partners cope with responses from families, friends, and communities; and (3) emergent dominant ideologies rooted in racism.

ANALYSIS AND INTERPRETATIONS

Negotiating Identities: Microlevel Analysis

Interracial partners' discourses in this case study demonstrate that their relationships are sites where they enact and negotiate their racial differences at the individual (micro) level. One of the prominent topics is the tension caused by the gap between the participants' avowed and ascribed racial identities. **Avowed identities** are the perceived identities that an individual subjectively enacts within a certain context, whereas **ascribed identities** are cultural identities that are attributed, assigned, or labeled by others (Collier, 2005). Here is an example from Matthew, an African American male, and his wife, Tina, a black/Spanish/Hispanic female.

Matthew: Honestly, I really don't look at her being a half. I know she is Hispanic, but a lot of times . . . I don't ignore it but I don't see it sometimes. I always forget she's half Hispanic, because she doesn't look like it. . . . I think if she looked that way, maybe it would be an issue sometimes.

Tina: I just like to be counted more than just Hispanic. I don't want to be counted as [just] Spanish. But then, again, I don't want to be counted as black, either.

Another example is Michael, a quarter-Chinese/Asian American man, negotiating the discrepancy between his avowed and ascribed racial identities.

Michael: I mean, I'm Asian, but nobody, nobody treats me like it.

Mary: Well, I thought you were Hispanic when I first met you. I thought he was Hispanic because he is so dark, not fair.

Michael: I mean, people don't come right out and say it, but when I tell them I'm Chinese, it's like, "Oh . . ."

Michael said being treated as Hispanic was "something I'm used to" in New Mexico, but he also explained that he was not treated as Asian American when he visited Hawaii with one of his Japanese friends. He stated, "Every single one of his friends is Japanese. So, I'm Asian as well, but to them, I don't look [Asian] at all. So I was 'the white guy' there."

These participants' discourses illustrate that the process of identity avowal and ascription is always political. The level of agency differs depending on which cultural group an individual belongs to in the local and global contexts, and it constrains the choice of how she or he claims who she or he is or is not (Collier, 2005, 2009). People of color are more likely to experience conflicts between their avowed and ascribed identities inside and outside of their relationships. In this case study, participants who are white, or who "look" white, also expressed their frustration. One example is Amanda, a Hispanic/Spanish female dating a black man, Walter. Amanda has fair skin that leads people to assume she is white, and she talked about how her own racial group constantly challenged her racial and relational identities:

I'm sure that people look at me, they think I'm Anglo, because I don't look like a Spanish person. . . . We automatically get the whole "black guy with a white girl" [look]. . . . Ever since I was little, I've been called, "Oh, white girl," "Oh, you're not Spanish." I'm constantly having to prove myself to my own [race].

She also mentioned that being with Walter, a black football player, constructed her as a white woman, "'Cause there's a stereotype that white girls chase after athletes." Amanda's quotes show that race is constructed as relational, and her interracial relationship with a black man subjects her to complex race relations.

Similarly, Doug, a Spanish American male who also "looks" white, strongly resists being treated as white by his Hispanic American girlfriend, Katy.

Katy: Every time I call him, "You are so white boy, a small-town white boy," and he is always like, "No, I am not." . . . To me it is a joke, but I know it bothers him.

Doug: I don't really see myself as in a white category, blonde-hair/blue-eyes white category. I always see myself more like a Spanish Caucasian. I don't know, so that is kind of weird to be boxed in that particular stereotype.

Additionally, participants' discourses indicate that identity management is a relational practice: Both partners negotiate not only their own individual racial identities with each other but also their positionalities as an interracial couple in the local and national contexts of race relations. For example, Matthew, an African American male, and his wife, Tina, a black/Spanish/Hispanic female, explained how their interracialness became salient because of Tina's half-Hispanic appearance.

Matthew: Our neighborhood [back in Mississippi] is predominantly one race, and then, if you see someone out of the race, they are all known as an outsider.

Tina: If we go back to Mississippi, I don't quite fit in, because I'm not all the way black or all the way one color.

All these interracial couples' discourses indicate that an individual's appearance, or body, is the site where racial categories and memberships are constructed, as well as where power relations are marked and negotiated. The participants' struggles with their avowed and ascribed identities as well as their relational identity as an interracial couple in private and public settings thus can be considered a practice of "body politics" (Sorrells, 2013, p. 52). Also, the participants' discourses highlight an important aspect of race: It is not something inherent in individuals, but it is constructed and enacted in their relationships, which relates to complex race relations in the United States.

Interracial Couplehood as Different, Deviant, or Dangerous: Mesolevel Analysis

At the cultural group (meso) level, interracial couples' discourses in this case study indicate that both partners wrestle with approval/disapproval of their cross-race bonds in the eyes of family, friends, and/or communities. Since the 1967 landmark decision in *Loving v. Virginia*, interracial marriage, though no longer illegal, has still been viewed as challenging, disrupting, or transgressing social norms. Not all couples in our study encountered outright disapproval from family and friends, but the issue of approval/disapproval was a concern. Mary, a white female, explained, "I think the whole approval thing. You're scared of what they [partner's family] think of you." Amanda, a Hispanic/Spanish female, echoed this concern: "My dad's side of the family does not approve of me being with black people." Some couples (e.g., black–Hispanic/Spanish and black–white couples) further experienced racial looks, stares, or profiling in public settings. Overall, discourses about interracial romantic relationships become contested spaces where racial and cultural stereotypes, prejudices, and discriminations slip through and collide.

The invisible normalcy of same-race relationships becomes visible when deconstructing family members' and friends' responses. Family, in particular, "is the source of greatest hostility toward interracial relationships" (Childs, 2005, p. 109). In this case study, couples' discourses suggest that interracial relationships between Hispanics, whites, and Native Americans are more common in New Mexico and receive less familial hostility than do other relationships. For example, Alicia, a white female dating a Native American male, stated: "It is not weird. Especially in Gallup, lots of people date out of their race." Jen, a white female dating a Hispanic/British male, commented: "My parents don't care that David is Hispanic." By no coincidence, Daniel remarked that all the Hispanic guys in his family had white wives.

Instead, familial hostility is expressed via cultural frames. Some friends and family members indirectly construct the interracial romantic relationships as more challenging to develop and maintain on the basis of "cultural" differences. Cindy, a European American female, explained her mother's objection: "She was like, 'Maybe you would have an easier time with someone from your own race. . . . Well, it's maybe a cultural thing.'" Bonilla-Silva (2006) coined the term *cultural racism* to describe relying on culturally based arguments to justify, naturalize, or mask the reality of racism. In this case study, couples' deemphasizing race suggests that some friends and family members recode race into culture to strategically justify their disapproving of interracial relationships (Sorrells, 2013). The rhetorical move of conflating race and culture underscores an apolitical understanding of culture in that cultural differences are perceived as only "natural."

Other family members and friends confronted and disapproved of their loved ones—especially women—dating interracially. Amanda, a Hispanic/Spanish female dating Walter, a black/African American male, experienced both explicit and implicit racial opposition. Amanda's father disapproved of her "dating black people," whereas some of Amanda's friends voiced their objections indirectly, stating: "I don't know how you date a black guy. . . . Oh, I would never do it." Both Amanda's family and friends clearly expressed their disapproval in racial terms (e.g., "being with black people"). Similarly, Cindy, a white female, commented on her friend's lighthearted challenge to her dating a Hispanic man:

> My friend Sophie, like once I told her his last name and she said, "Oh, so you're dating a Hispanic guy?" and I was like, "Yeah." Then she said, "Good job!" I don't know what she meant by that. I don't know.

In juxtaposition, black–Hispanic/Spanish couples such as Amanda and Walter experienced more hostile racial objections from family and friends than did white–Hispanic/Spanish couples such as Cindy and Daniel. Further, such hostile objections render black–Hispanic/Spanish interracial relationships not only as different but as deviant and problematic. This supports Childs's (2005) argument that "black–white intermarriages represent far greater racial transgressions than those between other" racial groups (p. 4).

While most white–Hispanic/Spanish couples remarked on how common interracial dating in New Mexico was, relationships between blacks and Hispanics or whites stood out and were marked as deviant in the public eye. Discourses from these interracial couples depict frequently being watched, followed, and even picked on, which demarcates a forbidden color line of blacks dating nonblacks. Walter, a black/African American male, and Amanda, a Hispanic/Spanish female, expressed that they got "bad" looks all the time, mostly from African Americans and Hispanics.

Amanda: We get looks, and . . .

Walter: That's how America, I mean, that's how society is.

Amanda: We get bad looks, all the time.

Walter: When we go to Spanish restaurants, and the Spanish guys, they don't give me dirty looks, 'cause how I look, but . . . you can tell that someone's watching her, you could tell how different they act if she's by herself or with her girls, or with a Spanish guy, than dating me.

Ed, a Native American male, and Alicia, a white/European American female, didn't experience "getting looks from strangers" until they ventured outside of New Mexico, where they became aware of public stares. They had an experience in Kansas, where Alicia said that they were perceived as "a white and black couple in Kansas." Getting bad looks from strangers can be understood as an act of public surveillance, where the "gaze" exercises power and control over interracial couples. That is, "getting looks" and the discourses surrounding these acts imply that being in an interracial relationship—especially with a perceived black person—is suspicious and abnormal.

Some strangers did not just look but further subjected interracial couples to racial profiling, which most white partners had not experienced before. When considering race as relational, white partners in interracial relationships can experience "the browning" of their racial identity vis-à-vis being seen with partners of color. Cassie, a European American female dating Gilbert, an African American male, shared an encounter of being followed at a bookstore:

One time, we were being followed at Barnes & Noble. Usually we may get a glance from strangers, and that's about it. That time at Barnes & Noble was the only time we had ever been followed. It was quite weird.

Being racially profiled in public was a surprising experience for Cassie. Similarly, Jeanne, a white/European American female, described protesting when her partner, James, a Hispanic male, was selected for a bag check at Wal-Mart.

Jeanne: One time we were at Wal-Mart. One of the ladies there, she stopped us and she asked to check our bags. He was carrying juice or something. She was like, "I need to check it." I was like, "What?" I was mad.

James: That has happened to me more than one time.

Jeanne: Oh my god, I can't believe this happened. I thought she would check both of our bags, but she only checked his bag.

Public acts of following and/or profiling interracial couples further render them as "suspicious criminals." For the white (female) partners, they experience "secondhand racism" through being with their nonwhite partners. Taken together, objection, disapproval, or surveillance from friends, family, and strangers construct interracial relationships as contested spaces where racial stereotypes/prejudices leak through—whether in cultural, racial, or relational terms.

Whiteness Ideologies in Couples' Discourses: Macrolevel Analysis

At the ideological (macro) level, interracial couples' discourses in this case study evidence how whiteness ideologies function in today's society, where groups of people hold competing beliefs about race. In essence, **whiteness** is a socially constructed *location* of racial privilege—a *standpoint* from which whites experience themselves, others, and the social world—and "a set of *cultural practices* that are usually unmarked and unnamed" (Frankenburg, 1993, p. 1). Depending on identity positions and race consciousness, whiteness enables and constrains how individuals and couples experience, enact, and negotiate their relationships in ways that reinforce colorblindness or differential racialization.

Colorblindness

Omi and Winant (1994) refer to U.S. society from the 1960s onward as a color-blind society. Contrary to popular belief, colorblindness works against racial justice. Erasing the notion of "race" makes people ignore individual racial identities and histories of racial injustice; it also rationalizes systems of exploitation and domination that sustain and reproduce racial stratifications, maintaining "unnamed" white privileges (Bonilla-Silva, 2006). The function of color-blind ideology is to promote a pseudo-egalitarian society by evading race, masking racism, and reinforcing the postracial belief that "racism is a thing of the past" (Omi & Winant, 1994). As an illustration of this mind-set, Cassie attributed her grandmother's opposition to her dating a black man to her upbringing:

> It was because of the way she was brought up. She lives in a very segregated area, and she never really interacts much with other ethnic or racial groups. . . . Later she realized that she was being ridiculous.

In this case study, white and Hispanic/Spanish Americans tended to evade, deny, or discredit the relevance of race. As an example of discrediting race based on social acceptance of white–Hispanic/Spanish relationships in New Mexico, David commented: "Hispanics aren't the minority here. . . . It [Hispanics dating whites] is accepted. It is not really seen, and people don't really see it." That Hispanic/Spanish Americans deny racial identities as people of color may result from (a) their positionality as the dominant racial group in New Mexico, (b) the history of claiming racially white identity to earn statehood (Nieto-Phillips, 2004), or (c) deemphasizing race to maintain a positive relational identity as an interracial couple (Childs, 2005). The following exchange between Jeanne, a white European American female, and James, a Hispanic male, exemplifies such racial denial:

Jeanne: I don't really realize that I am in an interracial relationship until someone asks. I don't think of him as someone from a different background. He is just my boyfriend . . .

James: I don't really label myself anything. I am just my own person. I don't really pay attention to race or anything like that.

Similarly, Alicia, a Spanish/Hispanic American dating Native American Ed, remarked: "We don't have a problem with race or that word. Both of our families are very receptive of both sides." Doug echoed: "My family or friends don't really think it is a big deal that I am dating a Hispanic American since all my friends dated around, so that has never been a big deal." These examples correspond to Thompson and Collier's (2006) finding that interracial partners dissociate themselves from the label of "interracial relationship," preferring to emphasize individuality and diminish the racial differences between them.

While interracial couples might buy into a color-blind ideology for the sake of their relationships, enacting colorblindness serves different functions for whites and Hispanic/Spanish Americans in the system of whiteness. For white participants, colorblindness can reproduce a position of racial privilege that shelters them from seeing raced bodies vis-à-vis their interracial partners, discourages challenging disapproval of interracial relationships, and maintains white dominance as the standard. For Spanish/Hispanic American participants, colorblindness reproduces their in-between racial position, promotes assimilation to white cultural practices, and maintains the status quo. By doing so, certain bodies of light-skinned Hispanic/Spanish Americans can pass as or be elevated as members of the white group. However, colorblindness ultimately denies racism and cultural differences, thus limiting the potential of interracial relationships to challenge racial inequality and promote racial justice.

Differential Racialization

The racial structure stratifies groups based on arbitrary racial categories, pits groups against one another, and (re)produces differentially raced bodies. That is, not all bodies are equally raced to serve the interests of different races in a racialized social system (Bonilla-Silva, 1996). In our case study, discourses from participants who occupy marginalized racial positions (e.g., blacks, African Americans, or mixed-race individuals) emphasize **differential racialization** where their races are named, marked, and stigmatized (e.g., getting "bad looks" in public). Also, as discussed earlier, partners in certain interracial relationships can experience the "browning" or "lightening" of their bodies vis-à-vis their relationships. However, interracial relationships between partners located at the opposite ends of the racial spectrum (i.e., black–white couples) are considered most deviant, dangerous, and transgressive, which evidences differential racialization of interracial relationships (Childs, 2005; Thompson & Collier, 2006).

Several couples described and pointed to a racial hierarchy, with black–white identified couples having the lowest status and being marked as "odd":

Daniel (Hispanic/Spanish/ Mexican male):	[As a couple] I think being white and Hispanic is a lot easier, because especially if you are Hispanic and if you are white, there's a lot of different shades, you know. But if you are black and white . . . [or] black and Hispanic or Asian, then it's more difficult. . . . If you see someone walking down the street, I see black woman and white guy, you know, the first thing that pops in my head is not "That's cool" or "That's right," but "That's odd."

Daniel's comment illustrates that interracial couples are not just raced but also gendered. Whereas black–white couples are considered more transgressive than other interracial couples, a black woman dating a white man is viewed as even more transgressive than the reverse. Michael, an Asian American male dating a white American female, also considered his relationship as less challenging than those of black–white couples. When he met Mary's parents for the first time, he did not have to "worry about whether they are going to care that I'm quarter Chinese." Michael continued: "If it was, you know, a major interracial relationship where I was going home to meet my African American girlfriend's parents, that would be one thing that [is] racing in your mind." As a member of racially/ethnically underrepresented groups, Michael demonstrates in his explanation that people of color also internalize racism against blacks and black–white couples.

Walter and Amanda, a black male and Hispanic/Spanish female, described the same racial hierarchy. Interestingly, both of them had faced hostile behaviors, comments, or disapproval from people of their own races. Walter said that some black women tried to get his attention by making a sigh sound or rolling their eyes when he was with Amanda; he interpreted that behavior as the black women being mad at his betrayal in choosing a white woman. This evidences Childs's (2005) contention that black families discourage black–white unions to "maintain the strength and solidarity of black communities" (p. 129). On the other hand, Amanda said, "Spanish guys have even called me an N-lover." Objections from Hispanic/Spanish communities to black–Hispanic/Spanish unions might stem from the fear of further "browning" the group, which could result in being cast further down the racial hierarchy. Although the processes of differential racialization enable certain interracial couples to remain raceless while racially marking others, understanding how differential racialization emerges can also open up critical spaces for interrupting and transforming the racialized system (Bonilla-Silva, 1996).

CONCLUSIONS

We investigate in this case study how partners in interracial, heterosexual romantic relationships negotiate gaps of avowed and ascribed identity positions, and we also examine dominant ideologies governing discourses about interracial couplehood. Interracial couples' discourses showcase that the intersections of identities are the locations where individuals' agency is constrained and enabled; that interracial relationships are sites where couples negotiate their cultural differences between themselves and with friends, family, and communities; and that whiteness ideologies reinforce competing views about race and racialization. Our analysis finds that connections across micro (negotiating identity positions), meso (norms of romantic relationships), and macro (whiteness ideologies) contexts influence couples' experiences, and that cultural identity (e.g., race and ethnicity) is a relational construct and cannot be treated as a static entity.

Also, this case evidences that interracial/intercultural couples' experiences with gaze, stereotype, and discrimination (re)affirm whiteness ideologies, which are the normative standard for making sense of romantic relationships in private and public settings. However, the severity of perceived deviance or hostility—public or private—toward interracial couples differs along racial lines. For instance, three of the couples with black male partners recounted experiencing more public gaze and familial objections than did the other couples. Hence, the similarities and differences across the couples' discourses demonstrate a hegemonic system of race that puts whites on top and people of color on bottom. The couples' discourses also illustrate that both whites and people of color participate in perpetuating the racialized system. At the same time, discourses from interracial couples that represent greater racial transgression (e.g., black–Hispanic/Spanish couples) suggest that interracial relationships are sites for challenging hegemonic race structure and promoting racial justice. Further, this study demonstrates that the ways whiteness ideologies manifest are contingent on racial politics in New Mexico as a "tricultural state" where Hispanic, Spanish, and Native American are salient and prominent identity positions.

Implications

In considering how the findings in this case study can have practical implications for promoting more just, equitable, and inclusive romantic partnerships, we build on Sorrells' (2013) intercultural praxis as a critically relational practice. Grounded in the site of interracial romantic relationships, we stress attending to the central sphere of the practices, processes, and norms regarding *relating* (i.e., how partners relate to each other across intimate, private, and public spaces) as multifaceted entry points for enacting intercultural praxis for social justice. For example, being in an interracial relationship, whether with racial minorities or partners of color with lighter skin, can affect one's experiences with one's own race and body (e.g., the browning of one's body). As a result, whites and partners of color with lighter skin can develop a heightened sense of awareness about race, racism, and social justice (Childs, 2005). Finally, we urge more systematic attention to interracial/ intercultural relationships so as to reimagine new possibilities for more equitable and inclusive relational standards, norms, and ideals.

Intercultural Allies Dancing With Difference: International Peace Initiatives, Kenya

Mary Jane Collier
University of New Mexico

Karambu Ringera
International Peace Initiatives

W elcome to a conversation with two intercultural allies who have worked together for 13 years. Our alliance is dedicated to inspiring, encouraging, expanding, and enhancing peace building and advocacy for women and vulnerable children through our work with International Peace Initiatives (IPI). We think of our **intercultural alliance** as dancing with difference; each ally must learn many dances, lead and follow, and move apart and together. In this narrative we show how we apply intercultural praxis tools of inquiry, framing, positioning, dialogue, reflection, and action (Sorrells, 2013) in many ally relationships to enrich IPI work for equity, inclusion, and justice in Kenya and beyond. We build on Collier's (2002) previous research on alliances to describe how our allyhood is constructed of various commitments; commitments to better understand how different contexts structure our relationship, to work through conflict related to our multiple cultural differences, and to enhance the sustainability of our relationship, which enables our work to continue. First we turn to how it all began.

HOW OUR ALLIANCE AND IPI DEVELOPED

Dr. K:[1]   I was at the Iliff School of Theology in Denver, working on a second MA degree, when I found the PhD program in culture and communication at the University of Denver. After being accepted into the program, I thrived in the seminar mode of engaged learning. When MJ agreed to direct my dissertation, I was thrilled. Hence, our dance of mentor/advisor/ally/friend began.

Prof. MJ: Upon meeting Karambu, I was immediately inspired by her insights, knowledge, and passion for community-based social change. I visited Kenya in 2003, visited with women's groups, met kids made vulnerable by HIV/AIDs, stayed with families, and collaborated with Karambu to offer intercultural communication workshops. I felt called to this collaboration.

Dr. K: I realized that one could make a big difference applying what is learned in class to actual situations, with a goal of transforming these situations. Forming an international nonprofit, nongovernmental organization (NGO) was the key to more resources. I have never looked back. I registered IPI as a 501(c)(3) entity in the USA (MJ was a founding board member) and as an international NGO in Kenya.

As of 2013, IPI has sent 1,000 kids to school, impacted 2,500 families, and touched the lives of 15,000 people in Kenya, Africa, India, USA, United Kingdom, Austria, and Australia. IPI has numerous programs: Institute of Nonviolence and Peace, Orphans and Vulnerable Children's Education Fund, Community Support Initiatives, Amani Children's Homes, and IPI College Scholar's Program. All these programs support women and children to overcome vulnerabilities brought about by poverty, disease, and violence. We have built a space that contains an environmentally friendly home for vulnerable children (Kithoka Amani Community Children's Home, or KACH), including a dining hall used for community meetings; an organic farm with an irrigation system; an ecolodge for visitors; a workshop for enterprises such as weaving and making jewelry, detergent, and other products; a council/prayer building; and a nearby house for the IPI office. More and more, IPI has become an organization that models the possibility for people to respond to their challenges using resources available locally, hence demonstrating that the power for change can be found within each person and every community.

This work is built on the collaboration of people and relationships moving with and through difference. This kind of work is essential in Kenya given our history as a colonized country, our commitment to democracy, and our current economic, environmental, and political struggle.

CONTEXTUAL CHALLENGES

Kenya's history is characterized by colonization, a struggle for independence, patriarchy, and a commitment to **democratization**. Education is highly valued. While political corruption is also a challenge, poverty and social inequality undermine the lives of marginalized groups of people such as orphans, poor youth, women, and people living with HIV/AIDS; without economic, human, and social rights, they are unable to have a say in wider decisions affecting their lives.

International development interventions in Kenya are often based on outsider-driven, reactive, short-term approaches that create dependency and lack sustainability. They also deny marginalized groups' agency to voice their needs and fail to inspire innovative, relevant, homegrown solutions. They fail to produce independence for disenfranchised groups of people, as they exclude them from decision making on matters that impact their lives.

Prof. MJ: Another aspect of context is that our dance occurs in the "between spaces" of difference (see Ringera & Collier, 2014). Our abilities to connect are affected by living in different places with different contexts. How we live, what we can buy, where we can travel, how safe we feel, and our access to reliable technology—these are sometimes worlds apart.

Dr. K: The in-between space of our difference that we negotiate is a very critical aspect to understand, as is the context of being long-distance allies. Internet access is a 20-minute drive to town from where I live, and it's often down. Rolling power blackouts are common. The context of having things happen as planned is very relative in Kenya; hence, certain things are never on time the way they can be in the USA. These varied contexts drive the community-based, ground-up work of IPI and set the stage for our alliance dance.

OUR ORIENTATION TO INTERCULTURAL ALLYHOOD

Prof. MJ: Our alliance is built on several common commitments. A key commitment for our alliance is that we share a political itinerary; we share some fundamental orientations to peace building and conflict transformation. One important orientation includes recognizing the role of multiple levels of context, including macro, meso, and micro frames. For example, we attend to structures and institutions, which are macrolevel factors, with an eye toward enhancing equity, inclusion, and justice. The programs of IPI are evidence of this. In national, international, and transnational community engagement, I think we both hold that community members must drive change, which is attending to meso-, group-level factors such as community-based participant action approaches. Finally, we see the importance of micro, interpersonal, and individual factors such as knowledge, experience with conflict, and desire for collaboration. What do you think?

Dr. K: We do share a political itinerary that is based on being present to how the macrolevel issues impact what we do at the meso and micro levels of IPI work. Matters of justice in peace building are critical in the work we do, as well as recognizing that unless these processes are people driven, there is no ownership. We recognize that when there is no ownership, the projects die as soon as the facilitators leave. We both agree that for holistic change to take place, people on the ground must be given the opportunity to learn, understand, and craft solutions for the problems they wish to end in their communities.

Prof. MJ: As allies, other commitments we share are that we are both unwavering feminists and we both criticize colonialism and power relations that historically and currently create inequity; we also ask questions about international "aid" and "development." In new projects, we both ask questions such as, Who controls resources and access? Who is speaking? For whom? Who benefits? Who is included/excluded? We each have a personal drive to reflexively "walk our talk."

Dr. K: I agree. IPI focuses on modeling a different kind of "development" that is "transforming spaces that do not serve us well." Our alliance and IPI work for transformation by uncovering and challenging metanarratives (for example, about what development is said to be, for whom it is said to be done, and by whom). Transformation requires that many alliances intervene at the meso, micro, and macro levels.

Prof. MJ: Yes! Finally, I'd say as allies, we are both committed to maintaining our relationship; we each value the other's knowledge, intellect, passion for the work, heart, and spirit. We both honor a form of transcendent spirituality that emerges in our alliance; this becomes a foundational calling and a reminder to slow down, to carefully listen to each other and our higher selves. It is in this space where we connect. A specific difference is that I am more critical of institutional forms of religion, including Christianity, and you are comfortable working inside as well as outside of the large number of Christian churches in Kenya. Respect for this difference and nurturing our own spiritual connection are important.

Need for Reflexivity

Prof. MJ: As a U.S. citizen, European American, middle-class, heterosexual, able-bodied, well-educated professor with lots of unearned advantages, it is important for me to engage in reflexive dialogue with you about how these overlapping and sometimes contradictory identifications impact my work with IPI and my relationship with you. It is challenging to talk about how our own positionalities may be driving the dance in the wrong direction, or driving us to opposite sides of the floor.

Dr. K: As a Kenyan, a feminist, an international peace builder and activist, and a woman with a doctorate from the United States, my positioning changes depending on what country I am in and what group I am meeting with—the space of conflict, problem solving, or policy development. My international networks, who I can talk to on policy-level issues nationally versus my relationships with the local women I work with at the grassroots level, provide an interesting space to explore my changing positioning. The relations that are affected by culture, politics, governments, religions, and so forth affect the relationships we can construct together. All these factors affect our allyhood, too.

Dancing Through Conflict

Prof. MJ: Sometimes the topic and tone for a conversation, like the music in a dance, can feel discordant to one of us. For instance, I may end up stepping on your toes by using my dominant U.S. board voice to demand late reports about funding allocations, or you may leave the dance floor to work with other groups in Kenya and leave me without an ally.

Because the U.S. board provides some funding, we expect IPI Kenya to be accountable and provide us with records of costs and expenditures. This can sound like we are setting up IPI Kenya as dependent and can strain our relationship. As a U.S. board member, I tend to emphasize macroeconomic, governmental, and legal frames in requiring accountability and records of expenditures. But this is also a move that can be read as a bid for domination; we "require" you to provide regular reports due to our needs to answer donors' questions about how their money was spent. We are also dominated by institutional requirements such as tax laws and policies to keep our nonprofit status. When you speak for IPI Kenya by talking about the basic needs of the kids, safety of KACH, and sustainability of the program/projects, these are micro and meso frames. We are looking at the work through different lenses and see different pictures, and this invites continuing conflict.

Because I also offer monetary support to IPI and am a U.S. American socialized to view my money as hard earned and personal, I am a donor, like most, who wants to know where my money goes. All of us know of many international nonprofit organizations where individuals have taken funding and "cooked the books," lining their own pockets with the funds. But there has *never, not once,* been an instance where the U.S. board has questioned your ethics or found that you took donors' money for your personal purposes. You don't own a car; you live in a modest rental house that you share with the IPI office. Donors' wanting to tell you how to do your work and demanding reports of every penny spent must feel reminiscent of colonialism, surveillance, and internationals telling you what is best for Kenyan kids at KACH. These kinds of relationships are not inclusive, equitable, or just, and they are not sustainable.

Dr. K: My relationship with the IPI Board is based on many contextual issues (what other international NGOs go through, for example) and the way I am seen by them (as a Kenyan, can I really make a program like IPI succeed?). It is also based on many contextual aspects on their side (what their media say about Africa, what their experience with other organizations has been like, their expectations of our relationship, their needing to be needed, etc.). An important strength of our allyhood has been working on this board relationship dance over time, which has helped to keep the relationship alive.

As for our allyhood and dealing with our other differences, an ally in my view is one who is courageous enough to hold the mirror for the other as well as brave enough to see herself or himself in the mirror held out by the other. For me, being in this alliance is not about "you" and "me"; rather, it is about endeavoring to "be what neither of us can be on our own," always present to both of our contextual positionalities, including board membership, cultural identifications, and privileges.

Prof. MJ: Absolutely. I will add that in our dance with difference, we also are allies who must manage conflict with others. We both speak up and problematize our cultural identities and the ways we are positioned by others as complex, multilayered, and contextual. For example, both of us avoid categorizing individuals as having only one cultural identity. I try not to "speak for" the kids at KACH or generalize about Kenyan males as sexist. These kinds of stereotypes are overgeneralizations and discount other identifications. For example, the kids at KACH have varied abilities and "vulnerabilities," ethnic and religious affiliations, and diverse stories, and male IPI staff often enact feminist positions and advocate for women's rights.

Dr. K: Remember how one guest at KACH from the West said the IPI male staff are sexist because they tried to stop her from going to an unsafe region of Kenya? It had nothing to do with thinking she cannot take care of herself; we wanted her to be safe. Also, if anything happened to her, IPI would be in trouble with her government. In such instances, your voice is important in influencing the way such a person will listen to me and my staff and hear us.

Prof. MJ: I am grateful that I can ask you, "What am I missing here? What am I assuming that you are not? What am I taking for granted?" That's when the alliance teaches me extremely important information about how I am to others. In our ally dance, I am trying to move from the observer and the "judge," a positioning that sounds as if it is from "out there" or "above," to walk alongside you. I can't ever "walk in your shoes" completely, but I can walk alongside and see/hear/feel with you.

Dr. K: Your connection with me and my work is special. You "see" and "understand" deeper than others because of your "sense of call to this work" and your intercultural awareness or consciousness. You also align with a spiritual depth that resonates with mine at many points. I value that because this understanding has enabled you to be a bridge for the "in-betweenness" of the IPI U.S. Board and IPI in Kenya. This helps keep IPI U.S. linked with us in Kenya in a good way. You point out power and privilege issues that most U.S. Americans are not aware they have. So to me, your presence on the board has been a gift and a blessing for the board members, for us in Kenya, and for me personally; you have been our teacher. I confront my own biases and judgments and shortcomings in relating to the board, but when we talk, I get back to being reminded that, yes, we are all in this together, for the kids and the women. I'm reminded that many kinds of alliances benefit our work as praxis.

KITHOKA COMMUNITY PEACE FORUM: A CASE STUDY OF PRAXIS

Prof MJ: During my 2012 visit, I got to witness your working to create community alliances through the Kithoka Community Peace Forum. The day-long event was held at KACH, and 44 women and 4 men met to discuss community challenges. You shared the leadership/choreographer role and walked alongside community members, inviting them to choose the dance and steps. You created a space for a community-level alliance to take transformational action! You modeled how to be an ally to the community and how to protect the community's space and agency to problem solve without input from "international visitors," and you offered a problem-solving structure that enabled them to develop their own alliances with each other.

Inquiry

Dr. K: We meet once a month. We gather and people talk about their situations. I might begin with what I am seeing and why it is not working for me. I will ask people what they are seeing and what is not working for them. From there the talk is rich. Then we will start to ask, "Why is this happening? What can we do about this? What resources do we need? What do we have that can start us off?" The people ask themselves these questions, and I listen. These are the same moves we also make in our own alliance when there are issues that are bothering us.

Framing

Prof. MJ: As the group reviewed a summary of issues that youth shared at a previous forum, I noticed that three contextual levels were covered. Macro frames of economics (political corruption, widespread poverty, and lack of jobs for the unskilled and educated), meso frames (community norms reinforcing patriarchy and sexism for males, and feminism among females), and micro frames (individual youth stories about peer pressure and family climate) all emerged. Problems were identified and discussed, including joblessness, drug abuse, availability of alcohol (some of the privately distributed alcohol is laced with drugs that cause blindness and sexual proclivity), poverty, financial instability, peer pressure, and lack of guidance from parents.

Positioning

Dr. K: Our work has grown organically from listening to the people on the ground and partnering with them to implement the change they want. In programs such as the peace forums, my positioning is to facilitate the capacity of the women and children so they can transform their circumstances and create self-resilience. Community participants are important drivers of the issues they need to articulate, share, and make decisions on as a group, to work on together. Your positioning as an ally here was that of invited observer, with the group's permission to be present.

Dialogue

Dr. K: Our ways of engaging the community enable all of us to be heard and valued, and thus feel we have made a contribution. This is the dialogue part of praxis. I listen from the premise that I have some knowledge and exposure that enable me to ask certain questions and be listened to. I have certain resources that can add value to what the people say they already have. We talk about how we can add value to what they already know and have. They also add value to what I know and have. I dance among positions of facilitator, teacher, learner, and community member, engaging their positions as community members, males and females, family providers, Christians, and critics. We all step in and out of different voices and positionalities.

Reflection and Action

Dr. K: Praxis includes reflection and action, and we do both. We talk about what we will do, who we will involve, and where we will go for what we need. We meet every so often to catch up and to evaluate where we are and what we are achieving. In between, everyone reflects on what this process means to them. People then talk about the changes at personal, family, and community levels, and see how they are agents of change. Throughout this process I am an ally for and with them, and they are becoming strong allies for one another and the community.

   The next steps are about taking action in their daily lives. When an issue occurs, people will meet by themselves, do the inquiry part, and figure out solutions through framing, reflection, and dialogue. Once they have the resources, they will go ahead and take action. This for me is *real* transformation—when people who thought of themselves as hopeless and helpless take their fate into their hands and take action in their community. They have stepped into the dance of intercultural allies because they bring different identity positions into the community peace-building work.

Prof. MJ: To answer any questions about what was accomplished, one action agreed on was that fathers, mothers, and guardians in the coming weeks would discuss with their older children alcohol use and other issues suggested by the youth. As well, a demonstration was planned and held a few days later. Community members marched to the home of an individual illegally distributing tainted alcohol. A representative of the local school read a letter demanding that the distributor stop selling the alcohol. Additionally, the community volunteered to pay an unfair fine levied against the assistant chief for her recent arrest of another alcohol distributor, because the community had asked her to take this action. This demonstration resulted in the district officer attending the event and promising support, and the liquor distributor later being arrested. Justice prevailed!

ALLIANCE DANCES: NEGOTIATING WHEN TO STEP BACK AND STEP UP

Prof. MJ: During my first visit to Kenya in 2003, I learned a valuable lesson about positioning. I was determined not to be an "ugly American" or a "Lady Bountiful" with U.S. resources to give to "needy" Kenyans. I deferred to you in our workshop at the University of Nairobi and didn't step in to present material; I insisted you take the lead role. I learned later that, as your teacher and a supposedly internationally recognized intercultural trainer, I had stepped back too far.

   In my recent trip to Kenya in 2012, I felt better about when to follow your lead in focus groups we led, when to solicit stories from others and let them construct their positions through their stories, when to advance my credentials, and when to share my experiences and suggestions. I also saw that you trusted me to interject and step into leading; sometimes you called on me to speak, and other times you reframed my comments so others could better understand them.

Dr. K: Your last visit to Kenya was very interesting to me. I knew the IPI U.S. Board had sent you with questions to ask; yet you seemed to have come more to learn than to ask questions. That is hard for you (I think) because you are a researcher, a teacher, and a person with curiosity about these alliance dances we have done over time. I felt you had "slowed" down and had not come with the researcher "cap" on your head. There was a settledness that made me think, "We have time to talk." That was very settling for me, too, because there was no sense of "Oh my gosh! MJ is here and we need to do this and that and the other," or that you had come to "investigate" me. I felt you were here to *be* with me/us. I felt supported and known. We could talk from a genuine place as allies. Your sense of "I am here to learn and observe" helped me/us uncover some important aspects of the work we do. I was deeply touched by your "here I *am*."

Prof. MJ: Thank you for sharing that. This slowing down would be helpful at other moments when I have overstepped. For instance, when questions came up about payment for our visits, I told an international visitor and potential funder, "Just like all international visitors, certainly I am paying KACH for room and board out of my own pocket! Aren't you? KACH doesn't have extra money to pay for our food, water, and electricity!" I presumed that funder was speaking from a position of privilege and entitlement. This was like stepping out onto the dance floor and demonstrating how her dance should proceed. I could have paused and inquired further about a previous agreement with you.

It is also important to remember that our particular allyhood is absolutely driven by our work and that our relationship is related to so many past, present, and future relationships in Kenya and beyond. The quality of who we are and how we are with each other is what enables and constrains the work both of us are called to do. And we have accomplished a lot!

THE WORK OF ALLIES ENABLES THE WORK OF IPI

We value our allyhood and our dance with difference. Sometimes we step into a line dance with others, sometimes work from afar on solo performances, sometimes revisit traditional music and dance steps, and sometimes take the role of audience members. The dances we do—sometimes in person, sometimes virtually—occur as a global performance in a dynamic context. We continually negotiate where and how we engage, and who we are in shifting spaces and places.

Kenya is a place rich with its own music. We invite you to come and see and hear international, intercultural alliances in action! As volunteers, interns, researchers, or practitioners, you will develop your abilities to use intercultural praxis and will see and hear about Kenya from Kenyans. You will be able to compare international "development" agendas and local community projects run by Kenyans, where we determine our priorities, needs, concerns, resources, and vision. You will also be able to see, hear, and step into a rich space of diverse alliances and cultivate your own ways of dancing with difference. Get more information from the IPI website (www.ipeacei.org) or Dr. Karambu's Facebook page. This is an opportunity to move into new dances and experience alliances in ways that will forever change and enrich all your intercultural relationships.

KEY TERMS

antimiscegenation laws   143

ascribed identities   147

avowed identities   147

body politics   147

color-blind ideology   145

democratization   157

differential racialization   153

intercultural alliance   155

intercultural praxis   144

reflexivity   159

whiteness   152

DISCUSSION QUESTIONS

1. Chen and Torigoe's case study shows how the racial demographics and tricultural histories of New Mexico uniquely shape the experiences and perceptions of interracial couples. Can you observe similar dynamics in your local context? What are the specific racial relations and historical narratives that inform the way people perceive interracial relationships in your region?

2. What do Chen and Torigoe mean by "differential racialization," and how does it impact interracial relationships? How does this notion relate to whiteness ideologies?

3. In your reading of Collier and Ringera's dialogue, what makes their intercultural allyhood effective and strong? How does the notion of "dancing with difference" apply to the way they negotiate differences and deal with conflict?

4. Both entries in this chapter problematize and highlight the issues of privilege that shape intercultural relationships and alliances. Discuss why it is important to be attentive to the issues of

privilege in intercultural relationships. How, using intercultural praxis (see Chapter 1), can we address power differences in relationships?

NOTE

1. We choose to use our professional titles when designating who is speaking to remind young women readers in Kenya, as well as many others, of their potential to earn similar positions. We also want to illustrate the importance of researchers' and practitioners' asking each other for and understanding the context and implications of using titles and names in intercultural relationships and community engagement work.

CHAPTER 9

Intercultural Communication in the Workplace

Economic globalization has brought many drastic changes to the way people interact with others in the workplace. As a result of the rise of transnational corporations, global migration, and advanced communication and transportation technologies, the workplace has become increasingly diverse and multicultural. Furthermore, communication technologies enable virtually mediated business communication, bringing both opportunities and challenges for businesses. Today, college graduates are more likely to work with those who come from different countries or cultures, navigating across different cultural norms, values, and languages. Thus, it is important to understand how neoliberal globalization shapes cultural dynamics of the workplace, and how individuals make sense of the shifting global workforce. This chapter presents a case study and a personal narrative that highlight the impact of globalization on the workplace from intercultural communication perspectives.

Carlo Ammatuna and Hsin-I Cheng's case study focuses on how *maquiladora* workers in Mexico negotiate and make sense of their shifting life goals and values in relation to neoliberal policies and practices catalyzed by the North American Free Trade Agreement. In pursuit of better economic opportunities, the workers adjust their lifestyles, ambitions, and communication practices to the ethos of individualism, self-efficiency, future orientation, and a vision similar to the American Dream. These changes often collide with or take a toll on traditional values and practices that define their family and community. In their personal narrative, Donna M. Stringer and Andy Reynolds share examples of working through cultural differences in the workplace, based on their lifelong careers as diversity consultants. Their illustrations and analyses show how cultural differences manifest in communicative practices—such as individualism/collectivism and power distances—and can complicate workplace communication. They point to the importance of paying attention to the historical contexts and intergroup dynamics that make these seemingly benign cultural differences problematic sources of conflict and misunderstanding.

"A Person Who Covers a Post": An Exploration of Mexican *Maquiladora* Workers' Neoliberal Identity Negotiations

Carlo Ammatuna
Santa Clara University

Hsin-I Cheng
Santa Clara University

INTRODUCTION: A GLOBALIZED WORLD AND A BACKGROUND ON *MAQUILADORAS*

The world is more intertwined and interconnected today than ever before. What were once specifically regional economies and cultures have become integrated through a network that now spans just about our entire globe. Big companies are not just national players anymore; rather, they are global powers that operate and exist in myriad different cultural contexts and settings (Harvey, 2005; Hickel, 2012). *Maquiladoras,* or *maquilas*—factories and assembly plants that exist in Mexico and Latin America—present a significant example of interrelated business, as foreign-owned, multinational companies have established a presence in a cultural context that is not their own.

In 1964, the program that allowed Mexican agricultural workers to work legally in the United States on a conditional and seasonal basis, known as the **Bracero Program**, came to an end. Within a year of the program's end and with unemployment rising, the Mexican government started the Border Industrialization Program, also known as the Maquiladora Program (Ferrante, 2007). Quickly, U.S.-owned firms flocked to Mexico because of the availability of inexpensive labor, the power of the dollar in comparison with the Mexican peso, and more lenient business laws. The **North American Free Trade Agreement**, implemented in 1994, allowed *maquiladoras* to grow and expand throughout the interior of Mexico as well. Currently, there are around 3,000 *maquilas* across northern Mexico's border states (Bolterstein, n.d.; Lederman & Oliver, 2013).

Carlo, a contributing author and frequent visitor to a small town 3 hours south of the U.S. and Mexican border where his grandma, aunts and uncles, cousins and friends live, will never forget childhood memories of seeing his family members picked up by the *maquiladora* buses early in the morning and waiting anxiously for them to return at the end of the day. The foreign-owned *maquiladoras* are as much a part of the fabric of that small Mexican agricultural town as the local town square, church, and main street. With his coauthor, Hsin-I, using an in-depth interview method, they seek to explore what working at *maquiladoras* means in relation to the bigger picture of cultures and economies. This essay will first present intercultural communication research on *maquiladoras* and present three themes: (1) conscious assimilation, (2) future orientation, and (3) identity struggles.

INTERCULTURAL COMMUNICATION, *MAQUILA*, AND GLOBALIZATION

Lindsley (1999a, 1999b) examined situations with communication that highlight U.S. Americans' and Mexicans' perceptions of problems and issues regarding intercultural interaction in *maquiladoras* within Mexico. Among others, five areas of cultural significance were identified in Mexico: (a) strong belief in hierarchy; (b) *palanca*—literally meaning "lever" and referring to a personal connection that serves as a tool to help the worker achieve her or his stated objective, such as attaining a certain job, service, or authorization; (c) emphasis on interpersonal relationships; (d) high value on trust and stability; and (e) present orientation (Albert, 1996; Archer & Fitch, 1994; Gannon, 2001; Lindsley, 1999a; Lindsley & Braithwaite, 1996, 2003). With these cultural patterns in mind, Lindsley emphasized the importance of sociohistorical backgrounds in addressing intercultural conflicts. In an organization in which people come from different cultural backgrounds that are interdependent but unequal, the negotiation of identity and meaning can be challenging.

In addition to U.S.-owned *maquilas*, Paik and Sohn (1998) gave warranted attention to the South Korean companies that have expanded globally and into the Mexican *maquiladora* system. Their research points out that South Korea has often been considered the "Second Japan," with similar cultural and social attributes. They found that there are similarities between South Koreans and Mexicans, such as group harmony, top-down decision making, and paternalism. But in spite of some cultural similarities, there is a large cultural distance between South Korea and Mexico. While designing intercultural workshops for a group of Mexican and Taiwanese managers, Cheng (2010) learned that similar cultural values such as work ethics are often expressed differently due to larger geopolitical, cultural, and socioeconomic structures. These findings suggest that specific cultural contexts exist within larger power structures.

Sorrells (2013) defined globalization as a "web of economic, political and technological forces that have brought people, cultures, cultural products and markets, as well as beliefs, practices and ideologies into increasingly greater proximity to and con/disjunction with one another within inequitable relations of power" (p. 171). Under the influence of globalization, dynamic social conditions such as what Beck (2009) terms "institutional individualization" (as cited in Elliott & Lemert, 2009, p. 49) occur. That is, to survive, individuals reinvent and negotiate their identities depending on conflicting family, career, and social demands. Globalization is a multifaceted mix of forces that produces complexities in which one becomes a kind of "DIY survival specialist" (p. 49). Within the practices of globalization, structures of individuals' subjectivities and societal relationships are changed. All spheres of human relations are turned into calculated exchanges based on market rationality. Political entities, aligned with financial agencies, launched projects of **neoliberalism** whereby "*homo economicus* is normatively understood as an entrepreneur, an entrepreneur of himself [*sic*] . . . being for himself his own capital . . . [and] producer" (Tadiar, 2013, p. 20). A byproduct of such global rearrangement is what Fairclough (2000) refers to as "a discourse of insecurity," in which individuals are expected to absorb structural problems caused by corporations and governmental policies, problems such as job loss due to relocations of multinational companies for cheaper labor (p. 148). Under such unequal power relations, workers in *maquiladoras* are faced with multiple demands while feeling perpetual insecurity and a need for self-investment in more "flexibility" (Ong, 1999) by accumulating maximum levels of economic and material security.

Building on the previous research on *maquiladoras*, which promotes understanding of a time period that saw a boom of *maquiladoras* sprouting across the border and interior of Mexico (Lindsley, 1999a, 1999b), the current study explores Mexican workers' perspectives on managing challenges as *maquiladora* employees almost half a century after their establishment as one of many neoliberal projects. How do *maquiladora* employees negotiate their cultural identities, practices, and norms? What are the communicative strategies Mexican workers perform in making sense of their lives?

METHOD

To address how Mexican *maquiladora* employees negotiate their various identities, we interviewed individuals who are Mexican nationals and have worked within a *maquiladora* for at least 2 years. Through snowballing, six phone or Skype interviews were conducted between June and August 2013. Each lasted from 1 1/2 to 2 hours. There are three male and three female interviewees aged 24 to 49 years. The majority of participants currently work for a U.S.-owned *maquiladora*; Osvaldo works at a South Korean–owned *maquila* and Gaby at a Japanese-owned one. Some participants—such as Osvaldo, who has worked at six *maquiladoras* just in Ciudad Juarez—have experience working in various *maquiladoras*. Important questions such as those asking for descriptions of a typical day and the work environment were used to start the interviews. More personal questions, such as those about work identity and relationship between work and family environment, were included to further the interviews.

All respondents graduated from high school, and most have earned a bachelor's degree from a Mexican university. Most respondents—Raul, Patty, Osvaldo, and Miguel—have an educational background in industrial engineering, and two are in the process of continuing their education—Tania in ecological engineering and Gaby outside of engineering. Respondents' *maquiladora* experience ranges from Miguel, who graduated in 2012 and is working at his first *maquiladora,* to Tania, who has worked 26 uninterrupted years, and Osvaldo, who accumulated his experience across six *maquiladoras*. Duties and responsibilities of our respondents include administrative tasks such as assisting superiors and responding to client complaints, and quality control and development of new engineering projects.

One of the researchers, Carlo, conducted interviews in Spanish and later translated and transcribed them in English. Following Owen's (1984) guidelines, both authors coded transcripts separately and collectively for "recurrence, repetition, and forcefulness" to interpret significant concepts used by the participants to make sense of their identities as workers in *maquiladoras*.

FINDINGS

Conscious Assimilation

> *"Working in a maquiladora in whatever form offers you the opportunity to learn many things you can use at any point in your life."*

One of the themes that occurred frequently was that of conscious assimilation to become an efficient worker. Through both verbal and nonverbal cues, workers are expected to manage their time efficiently to great extents. Long working hours are necessary to prove commitment to the *maquiladora* and to gain trust not just from managers and supervisors but also from their working peers. Each interviewee mentioned that a worker is expected to keep harmony, demonstrate commitment with long work hours, gain trust slowly, and learn to rely on her or his own self. The participants perform the ideal worker in the way they embody time. Contrary to how Mexican culture has been viewed as polychromatic in terms of the use, experience, and understanding of time (Hall, 1976; Hofstede, 2001), all participants frequently referred to not "losing time" and to managing time efficiently when working at the *maquiladora*.

Gaby, who works at a Japanese-owned *maquiladora*, explained: "I never leave an activity without completing it and I comply with the dates that are given to me." Osvaldo, in a South Korean/American *maquiladora*, worries about "making the company lose money [by] not being as productive as they expect you to be [due to the lack of training]." These statements illustrate that, for these Mexican workers, how they are perceived within the time and space of their workplace is important. Many shared their linear daily schedule. Osvaldo said:

> [I] get up at 5 am to make lunch, go at 6:30 to the bus to take me to my workplace; I arrive and check in normally before 7:30. I put on my work computer and start my work activities. At 1 or 2 in the afternoon is the time to eat; it's half an hour. I eat my food and exchange comments with fellow coworkers. I enter again and do my work. Before my departure time, they notify me if there will be extra work; if there is, it can be up to two hours more. I would leave at 6 pm and I take the shuttle back to my house. I take public transportation, two routes.

Other participants shared similar routines and mentioned starting their day by checking the daily agendas. The monochromic way time is compartmentalized and consumed with careful calculations for utmost productivity at the lowest monetary cost is an adjustment these participants shared. Some shared the necessity to acquire skills due to globalization. One interviewee, Gaby, illustrated the complex nature of a globalized and intertwined world as she discussed the challenge of working in a multinational company, headquartered in Japan, producing parts for an English-speaking market. She explained, "In this *maquiladora*, TOYOTA harnesses are made. We must develop . . . reports entirely in English and include many technical words which must be known to perfection so that it can be understood by our client." Seeing her role in the globalized world, Gaby struggled to learn these technical terms in English to fulfill the job requirement.

Stephens and Greer (1995) noted that foreign managers usually have their own views on how efficiency can and should be attained, and they often consider the local culture as a barrier to the organization's progress. Researchers such as Lindsley (1999a) and Paik and Sohn (1998) have found that cultural differences may create communication problems in a foreign-owned *maquiladora*. Yet participants in this study revealed efforts to assimilate into a foreign management culture, especially as it relates to time management and productivity. The participants, through assimilation, strategically maximize their learned abilities—such as English skills—in a globalized setting. Days are scheduled, and productive and capable workers are used and incentivized with upcoming rewards and the recognition of their multinational workplace—a global player in a globalized economy.

Isolated, Self-Reliant, Future-Oriented Workers

> *"I do this for a salary and am viewed as 'a person who covers a post during a predetermined time.'"*

A strong sense of powerlessness and fear for one's position in relation to the global economy prevailed in these interviews. All shared a recurring concern about the uncertain future beyond their control. Within this concern, recognition of lack of resources and individually based future pursuits emerged amidst feelings of isolation within their position, company, and industry.

Raul noted that the *maquiladora* is resistant to change and new projects often fail to take off because budgets are constantly too tight and fall too short. Patty, who works at an American company, was quick to point out that "lack of resources" is one of her principal concerns at work. She also said that staff cutbacks have created problems in completing work projects on time. Osvaldo shared that low pay, lack of training, and little opportunity for professional growth negatively affect not only his sense of worth but also the company.

> When you don't have the necessary experience, you never arrive at [the supervisors'] goals. And you may even make the company lose money because you cannot be as productive as they expect you to be. The secret would be to place people with the right experience or help those of us to get that capacity in the areas of their requests.

These statements indicate that the workers understand the company's priority is essentially profit. The sense of *padrinazgo* that has historically existed in the *patrón* (owner of the workers) system seemed absent from the participants' responses. In a *patrón* system, the owners would take a personal interest in the welfare of the workers and their families by helping the workers achieve individual objectives, and the workers would return the favor by providing their subservient labor (Archer & Fitch, 1994). In our interviews, participants expressed feeling disconnected and lacking identification with their employers; the participants depicted themselves as powerless *maquiladora* workers who are sometimes ineffective in a modern, complex, transnational factory setting. The traditional *padrinazgo* element appears to be absent. While such a workplace element phases itself out, an ideal system has not necessarily replaced it, as participants now turn to themselves to keep pace with employer demands.

Many participants demonstrated self-reliance by using their own free time to better their career development, taking English courses or learning to become proficient with computers. Yet a sense of powerlessness in a precarious global economy remains. Gaby suggested, "Because of the world economy we are always expecting that the company has to reduce production and even close temporarily and you can lose your job. In this moment it is very hard to maintain a job." Tania described this feeling:

> At a time when there was an economic crisis in the *maquila*, most people were forced into being given days off, receiving half of our pay. During this crisis, there were many rumors of closure in the company, and it is exhausting for someone like me who has worked so hard to be on a technical level to think that my work is finished.

With the sense of lack of control over the global economy, future-oriented ambitions such as pursuing professional training bring a feeling of empowerment and greater influence over their lives. Given the large Catholic population in Mexico (Gannon, 2001), the absence of any reference to seeking consolation through religion during such fear-laden crises deserves some attention. Each participant mentioned individual desires and plans to start his or her own business, confident that this would bring prosperity and a more stable future for his or her family. Disillusioned by the global system in which they exist—as Osvaldo lamented, "I do this for a salary and am viewed as 'a person who covers a post during a predetermined time'"—the Mexican *maquila* workers interviewed gradually become better survivors within an unstable, difficult environment.

Out of this fear, all participants shared the desire to start and operate their own business. Raul explained:

> In a future time I visualize myself climbing the upcoming positions; that is to say, I see myself with steady work, and if for some reason my work in the *maquiladora* is finished, I am ready to start my own business.

Patty stated, "In the future I see myself administering my . . . ," and after a pause she went on to state clearly, "my own company." And Miguel said, "I see myself as an owner of my own business. Completing a graduate degree in industrial management, I'll form my own company."

The Mexican *maquiladora* workers—such as Tania, who was at the operational line level and has since become a manager—narrated their toil to gain every opportunity to climb to a higher position in the *maquiladora* system. Miguel, feeling the pressures of becoming proficient in English, concludes his long day of work, which starts at 7:30 in the morning, by taking an English course in the evening. His dedication to acquire English skills resonates with what Piller and Cho (2013) found in South Korea, where the learning and implementation of English in the workplace is a professional, social, and personal requisite for advancing. The participants negotiate between a precarious reality and a dream for a more promising future sustained by their individual efforts. Surrounded by "a discourse of insecurity" under neoliberalism (Fairclough, 2000), these participants learned to absorb the structural problems and resort to themselves for security. Owning a business is a shared vision of greater security over their futures. By workers investing in themselves, the project of producing global workers who calculate daily actions in the logic of the market is completed. In the process of these struggles, these workers eventually become fitting **neoliberal subjects**.

Identity Struggles

> *"My kids cannot count on their mother 100% of the time like they should be able to."*

The final theme shared across our participants was the union of their work lives and family lives. Repetitively, each interviewee demonstrated how there is a struggle to attend to these two worlds because work requires so much time and effort. For the most part, each interviewee talked about the importance of keeping each world separate, admitting that sometimes there is not enough time in the day to go around. They shared examples of tough decisions and difficult emotions in the effort to keep both worlds harmonious.

Miguel expressed,

> It is a little difficult to maintain a good relationship. Well sometimes at work they demand a lot of time and you hardly can spend time with the family . . . and when you have free time you have to use it to rest and with the family to the side.

Gaby said she tries to be patient and cordial in both settings, never taking her work home and never bringing her life at home to work. She sums up this internal struggle in one of her primary concerns:

> My kids cannot count on their mother 100% of the time like they should be able to. Well they are growing up, not alone, but they don't do it with me like *the correct way* it should be, so that I can guide them in any moment they *need* it.

Raul expressed similar difficulties:

> The sacrifices you have to make are very diverse and there is collateral damage. For example, one of my sacrifices is not being in a family celebration to fulfill a commitment to work or the contrary, I'm not at work to meet a family

commitment. One has to decide which the more important event is considering that you should maintain balanced relations in work and home.

Raul further acknowledged that he is able to achieve balance between work and home with the support of his wife, as she stays home and attends to their four children. Tania, who in addition to working at the *maquiladora* is also working toward another educational degree, said that these are not difficulties, rather propositions that require sacrifices. She stated that one of her principal concerns is

> not being able to attend to my children as I would like to, take them to school daily and be there when they get out. These are the sacrifices that working parents have and that I have to rely on third parties for these duties to my children.

One of the challenges many *maquiladoras* face is high employee turnover, often due to employees' family needs (Lindsley & Braithwaite, 1996). Miguel, Gaby, and Raul all recognized their unmet cultural roles and obligations, where their family needs are at times sacrificed due to work demands. Unlike the traditions of family-oriented organizational structure in Mexico (Lindsley, 1999b), these participants come to view work and family as two separate domains competing for their limited resource—time. In weighing their priorities, most made the difficult decision to choose the company's demands over their familial ones. They developed strategies to meet these needs to the best of their ability by relying on other people to fulfill their roles, such as through children's day care. The *maquiladora* workers develop and negotiate their identity as Mexican workers by demarcating clear boundaries between their family and work. Knowing that the traditional practice is no longer possible, they manage to juggle multiple responsibilities as "working parents." The lack of active resistance may also suggest their recognition of their own "disposability" as global workers who are employees first and parents second.

At the same time, some participants explained how tending to work does not necessarily equate with sacrifice. Tania shared how she wants more professional development for better-paid jobs and positions to support and provide for her children's future. Patty mentioned that the sacrifice of family time is worthwhile for personal knowledge and growth in exchange for a more stable future for the next generation. Gaby said that even though she is unable to raise her children "the correct way," her sacrifice provides them better career opportunities. In expressing how gratifying it is to be a part of a workforce, they reasoned that their inability to meet the cultural role is a tradeoff for personal growth, career development, and learning for the betterment of their children. Conscious of the competing roles, the participants wrestled with the inability to abide by what they viewed as "the correct way" to engage in family relationships. Their struggle in making sense of various demands reveals multiple forces implicated in negotiating who they are in a system dominated by *maquiladoras* and global economic structure. The neoliberal economic rationale becomes the narrative frame that these participants accept as the path to accumulate more flexibility (Ong, 1999) and capital (Bourdieu, 1998) for the next generation. As individualized survivors, they constantly reinvent and negotiate these conflicting identities in the realms of family, work, and society.

CONCLUSION

Lucas (2011) argues that in the United States, a paradoxical conflict exists between the American Dream, which indicates social mobility, and the Working-Class Promise, which calls for maintenance of one's identity as a worker through generations. In our research, we saw the dream that the participants are constructing. Their dream is inclusive of many of the same elements that make up the American Dream: individual effort that includes sacrifices for a better tomorrow and results in more mobility. Such mobility is evaluated by greater economic power. The participants described their assimilation to foreign management styles, self-sufficiency and learning English, adherence to work schedules, and ideas of productivity and maximized profit. All the sacrifices they make in achieving their dreams are based on priorities in a neoliberal ethos; life means labor in which time is used to produce future monetary gains. The participants are aware of the global context of their work and recognize the value their work experience and educational background have, but, ultimately, their identity as *maquiladora* workers is sustained while they express hopes of using their skills elsewhere. In the interim, they try to traverse between the boundaries of several realities.

The findings outlined above illustrate conscious negotiations by Mexican workers to satisfy a multitude of competing needs. As *maquila* employees, they constantly struggle between conflicting cultural and workplace identities in hopes of bringing prosperity for themselves and future generations. In their efforts to separate their work and family, it seems that values and practices in the work environment, such as productivity and self-reliance, inevitably seep into their everyday lives. Their experiences and outlooks shed light on the global landscape where ideologies and relationships are intertwined and heavily influenced by economic and sociopolitical structures (Bourdieu, 1998; Harvey, 2005; Larner, 2006). With increasing global competition for cheap labor and the economic crisis in 2008, there have been massive layoffs in *maquiladoras,* as reported by the Center for Labor Research and Studies at Florida International University (see also Hall, 2002). With the slow recovery of the *maquilas* (Archibold, 2011), the participants in the current study continue adapting to global and local changes.

The participants learn to become identified as global workers whose lifestyles, ambitions, cultural values, and communication mannerisms are changing within a global dance of capitalism. This essay is an initial exploration of Mexican workers' perspectives toward themselves as *maquila* employees. We do not wish to generalize these six participants' experiences to all *maquiladora* workers in Mexico, since all our participants are either already college graduates or working toward becoming college graduates and therefore occupy a particular social location. However, their lived struggles and compromises provide a window to view how identities are accomplished through daily interactions and activities in a society largely permeated and shaped by neoliberal practices and policies such as the North American Free Trade Agreement.

From Mississippi to Hong Kong: The Power of Intercultural Communication in the Workplace

Donna M. Stringer

Cross-Cultural Consultant, Seattle, WA

Andy Reynolds

Cross-Cultural Consultant, Seattle, WA

OUR BEGINNINGS, OUR LEARNING, OUR APPROACH

We are a biracial couple who have worked individually and together on diversity and inclusion issues for more than three decades.

Donna: I am a second-generation Irish American who grew up in the Pacific Northwest in an extremely isolated rural community. My family was lower socioeconomic class both in terms of financial resources and education. The men in my family were either loggers or construction workers. The women were "homemakers." Neither the men nor the women were educated. I am the first person in my extended family to graduate from high school and the first woman to have a profession. Diversity was not part of my experience growing up—we had no TV or newspapers, we listened to the radio for stories, and the first, and only, political discussion I remember was an argument about whether Castro was communist. I was 17 years old when I first saw a person of color. I went to a very small, 30-student, country school, and my teacher saw my potential: She challenged me and made me a voracious reader and a dreamer. What she gave me was an unwavering passion for learning. What my family gave me was deeply abiding values about a community taking care of one another and about fairness. These values have been at the core of my life and work. While I began my career in gender studies, I quickly migrated to broader diversity issues as I saw the connections to equity across demographic groups. My social class upbringing has also impacted my approach to diversity in a number of ways: I care deeply about economic equity issues and am very comfortable working in blue-collar settings, but I still struggle with imposter feelings when working with executive or higher-education teams.

Andy: In many ways, Donna and I could not be more different. I am an African American who was raised in the segregated South by educated parents who worked as teachers and educational administrators. Both were first-generation college graduates in their families. While I was aware of racial differences, my community protected me from personal experiences of racism until I was in my late teens, when I became heavily involved in the civil rights movement. I was present on the first day of student sit-ins in Greensboro, North Carolina, where both physical and verbal abuse underscored individual and institutional racism. I became passionate about the social, economic, and legal inequities I saw and assumed a leadership role in CORE (Congress of Racial Equality). I learned the values of fairness and community from my African American culture and my family. My work in civil rights taught me the importance of changing both individual behaviors and institutional racism.

While Donna and I grew up very differently—in different geographical regions, different socioeconomic groups, and different ethnicities, to name a few—in the 1960s each of us became involved in antiracism workshops. We both began to feel that this approach—typically involving whites "admitting" their racism and blacks sharing how they had been damaged by racism—was not working. The end result did not seem to bring much change, either in individual or institutional/structural racism. White participants often left feeling guilty and/or angry and defensive; blacks typically left feeling as though they were victims who had been heard only temporarily and nothing had changed. We both began searching for other approaches that could have a deeper, more permanent impact.

We met in 1980 at the same time as many workplaces began initiating "diversity" initiatives. We started a consulting business to work with organizations on "diversity issues." The intercultural approach captured our attention and led to the development of our approaches with organizations. Our work involves two prongs: (1) examining organizational structures and (2) examining individual attitudes and behaviors. To work only on individual behaviors without providing organizational structures that support those behaviors is a setup for failure; likewise, to change organizational structures without helping individuals develop effective intercultural skills does not result in change. Both are needed.

Our approach to intercultural skill development is to begin by exploring cultural values, behaviors, communication styles, and nonverbal behaviors. We ask individuals to identify their own values, styles, and behaviors, and to examine how those affect the way they perceive and evaluate others who may behave differently. For example, if I believe that using direct eye contact is a way to show respect, what do I think about a person who does not use direct eye contact? What if that person learned that avoiding eye contact was a way to show respect? What do they think about me with my direct eye contact? Taking this very simple example through an entire array of personal behaviors and perceptions typically results in deep levels of "aha" understanding; it allows people to reexamine their assumptions about others. Once people begin reexamining those assumptions, they also become more open to exploring questions about racism, sexism, homophobia, and other assumptions we make about others.

In other words, our experience has been that if you begin with the conversation about racism, it can result in defensiveness and separation; approaching these questions from an intercultural perspective first allows people to talk about racism from a foundation of cultural understandings and tends to open the door to discussion.

In our work since the early 1980s, we have seen some shifts. The initial work was called "diversity" and was typically a "cover" for affirmative action hiring and legal concerns. Defensiveness and resistance came in the form of demanding "proof that it works" and discussions about how to measure the success of such programs (e.g., "Show me the data"). By the end of the 1980s, evidence that diverse work teams and workplaces could be more effective (and profitable) than homogeneous teams was readily available. There was also a growing awareness that simply hiring "diverse candidates" (which was virtually always code language for people of color and women) was not enough for organizations to be effective; turnover was often high, and complaints or lawsuits were abundant. The shift was toward "diversity *and inclusion,*" with a focus on how to create a work environment that allowed women and people of color to thrive once they were hired. And most recently, the shift has been toward understanding that diversity is far more than visible characteristics. Three major trends have shifted the field from diverse to *intercultural*: Global migration patterns are resulting in international workforces and customer bases, technology changes are resulting in many international and virtual teams, and business and education are more frequently engaging globally with international offices and international education programs.

Current trends are moving toward looking at international or global issues, which create even greater complexity when people do not understand the historical context of conflicts or tensions between national groups. Attending to global issues created by migration patterns, international business, and technical capabilities is important. At the same time, however, it is important not to allow the "sexiness" of global politics to result in ignoring the domestic issues created by U.S. historical racial politics. For example, pointing to foreign national employees or students as evidence of "diversity" rather than recruiting U.S. populations of color simply extends economic inequities and institutional racism.

INTERCULTURAL COMMUNICATION IN WORK ENVIRONMENTS

National cultures strongly influence the communication styles of individual citizens as well as those used in corporate cultures. The United States, for example, is a culture that values individualism, competition, and achievement; these values encourage and support communication styles that are direct, fast-paced, and informal. The United States is also a country where **power distance** is quite low (Bennett, 1998, p. 24); that is, employees or students don't hesitate to talk directly to their bosses or teachers, and might even address them by first name rather than by title.

Contrast this, for example, with Japan, a country that values a high power distance and a reflective, collectivist or group orientation, resulting in communication that is more formal, indirect, and slow-paced. Even accounting for individual differences within cultural groups, a visitor to businesses in the United States and Japan can pretty readily identify these communication style differences. The potential for misperception across these differences is enormous.

Japanese may perceive U.S. citizens as aggressive and/or rude based on their direct, fast-paced communication style; U.S. employees, on the other hand, may see the Japanese as shy or without personal opinions when they communicate more indirectly and at a slower pace. When Japanese observe U.S. employees addressing the boss directly, and using his or her first name, they are often astonished at what they perceive as inappropriate behavior based on their cultural value of high power distance; meanwhile, U.S. employees wonder how Japanese employees can get anything accomplished when they insist on "going through channels" instead of talking directly to the boss.

Identifying the communication norms of any two cultural groups will allow the observer to make predictions about where and how intercultural communication challenges or conflicts are likely to occur.

D. Thomas (as cited in Sorrells, 2013, p. 187) says that the cultural composition of work groups impacts group effectiveness based on (1) cultural norms about how work groups function and how they are structured; (2) cultural diversity, or the number of different cultures in the group; and (3) relative cultural distance, or the degree to which the cultures in the group differ from each other. Additionally, cultural communication styles and cultural values related to **individualism** versus **collectivism** and cultural power distance will impact how group members perceive one another and how effectively they manage their differences. Young Yun Kim (as cited in Samovar & Porter, 2003, p. 192) reminds us that intercultural communication competence is not the same as being competent to communicate within a single culture, because it requires the ability to think about, identify, and adapt one's communication style to different cultural situations.

Beyond cultural values and communication styles, it is important to have an understanding of the historical relationships between cultural groups to fully comprehend intercultural communication. For example, while both European Americans and African Americans tend to communicate using a direct style, the historical legacy of slavery in the United States will often result in African Americans becoming less direct with those who have role power in an organization—that is, exercising a higher power distance because it has been "unsafe" historically for blacks to be "too familiar" or to establish trust with whites (Kochman, 1981). Whites may exercise the same high power distance between themselves and blacks, but for a different reason: Historically, they simply have not had to acknowledge blacks, and could treat them as an "invisible" element of their environment. This difference is affected by generational culture as well as individual differences, but to fully understand what one observes, the historical context is important (Markus & Moya, 2010).

Here are two examples of how these issues can impact the intercultural perceptions, communication, and effectiveness of a group.

The Mississippi Experience: Black and White Conflict

Our first example contains two cultural groups: European Americans (white) and African Americans (black). While only two cultures were represented in this example, the cultural distance between them was significant. Both groups have strong values related to individualism and competition, but the history of the United States creates different orientations to power distance for whites and blacks—and while this is true throughout the United States, it is currently more apparent in the southern part of the country. White employees have lower power distance and therefore can more easily challenge management, while black employees tend to have a higher power distance with management and therefore are more reluctant to openly challenge management decisions. Further, in this organization, there was a clear institutional pattern of blacks being reprimanded or disciplined when they did challenge management.

This example took place in a manufacturing plant that ran 24 hours a day, 7 days a week, using four teams of 16 people each. Each team was nearly evenly divided between black and white employees. Tensions had risen between the two racial groups, to the point that employees were bringing guns to the workplace—they were left in vehicles in the parking lot, but many were clearly visible. Upon investigation, it became clear that the history of race relations in the United States, power distance, communication styles, cultural value differences, and implicit bias all played significant roles in creating this tension.

Management of the organization was entirely white men who were Southerners, born and raised. Their own racial backgrounds had led to an unconscious bias in which they assumed blacks were causing the problems and were less competent than the white employees. The result of this bias was an institutional pattern of favoring white employees in hiring decisions, promotional decisions, and decisions in mediated conflicts. These patterns, along with the detached (impersonal, showing little emotion) communication styles of management, had resulted in the African American employees feeling angry, perceiving management as not caring about them, and believing that they were being discriminated against intentionally. When the overall patterns of these decisions were reviewed with management and they were introduced to the concepts of intercultural communication styles and unconscious bias, they began to reluctantly concede that they had been misperceiving the behaviors of their black employees.

While both management and employees used direct communication styles, the African Americans communicated in a much more attached style (personal, showing passion or emotion), and the European American employees and management used a style that was far more detached (impersonal, showing little emotion). This difference alone created misperceptions: When blacks used an attached style (louder, more gestures, more passionate) they were perceived by their white counterparts as threatening or dangerous. When the whites used a detached style (calmer, quieter, more dispassionate), their black counterparts perceived them as not caring about their feelings or experiences.

Historical relationships between blacks and whites also created a cultural context in which the African Americans felt that they had no power to change the organizational structure or decision-making process. Their reaction to this sense of helplessness was to escalate their anger, which then escalated the engagement of their communication style, which in turn escalated the sense of threat and fear on the part of management. Because management held the power, their response to this perceived threat was to become more rigid in their decisions and less willing to listen to the black employees.

First management and then employees were introduced to the concept of culture and guided through identification of their cultures: the community culture, the organization's culture, the culture of their own workgroup, and their personal culture. This exploration focused on identifying core value systems, the behaviors used to support those values, and the historical reasons for the behavior differences. Fairly quickly, they identified that they shared many values but that the behaviors used to exhibit those values were different. For example, while everyone indicated that respect was an important value, the African American employees were more likely to show respect by disagreeing openly and directly; the European American employees were more likely to show respect by not disagreeing openly. This difference alone caused considerable interest and discussion. Black and white employees engaged in exploratory conversations could be heard marveling at how different their behaviors were when they were sharing the same values.

Communication styles were explored, with a focus on direct/indirect and detached/ attached styles. As with values, the differences were profound. While all these men were direct communicators, in the face of conflict the African American men became more attached in style while the European Americans became more detached in style. The black employees were then labeled "emotional and potentially out of control" by their white counterparts, while black employees felt that their white coworkers were "cold and didn't really care—they were calculating in order to get management's support."

As the group explored the roles that history played in developing different behavioral and communication patterns, they became fascinated as they learned other invisible cultural issues about each other (e.g., nonverbal behaviors, conflict styles, etc.). At one point toward the end of the training sessions, the chief protagonists of each group spontaneously met in the middle of the room and hugged each other. The white man was heard saying, "I'm sorry, man . . . I just didn't know." These men discussed the fact that their relationships had been transformed by understanding the cultural value systems, behaviors, and styles of the other group and that social change had been achieved through that understanding, which had been a significant place for them to begin. And while race and racism were clearly a backdrop to the conflicts they had experienced, beginning with a discussion of racism would not have led to the openness or understanding that the intercultural approach allowed.

A month following these sessions, the members of the group reported that they enjoyed working with one another and had continued their exploration of historical and style differences.

Hong Kong: The Distance Between the United States and Asia

Our second example took place in a class on intercultural communication. The class was offered by a U.S. corporation that hires employees and serves customers globally, and was designed to provide its employees general information in the areas of cultural values, behaviors, and communication styles. Specifically, participants learned how to identify and understand the behaviors and communication styles of their customers for greater effectiveness.

Participants in this class came from seven different Asian countries and demonstrated values of collectivism and high power distance; they communicated in indirect, formal styles using high-context language. The facilitators were European Americans whose values were individualism and low power distance. They communicated directly, informally, and with low-context language. While there are significant differences among and within Asian cultures, only minor differences were evident among the Asian participants during this short workshop. There were, however, significant differences between the participants and the facilitators.

The corporation, cultural informants, and training facilitators worked diligently to identify Asia-specific examples and to ensure that the course content and materials were free of U.S.-specific idioms and ·stories that could confuse the Asian employees. At the insistence of the corporation's training office, the focus was on the content of the course, with very little attention to the process to be used in the classroom. They insisted that these employees were accustomed to U.S. classroom-style teaching. The processes included self-assessments, brief lectures, small-group discussions, and role plays of customer service situations.

Because English fluency is a requirement for employment with this organization, classes were conducted in English. The first few sessions were confusing to the facilitators: While participants appeared engaged, they asked no questions and the role-playing was stilted and accompanied by embarrassed laughter or silent withdrawal.

Most confusing, however, was the behavior of small groups of Korean women. At several points during the day, one of these women would quietly leave the room and soon be followed by the others. There was concern about whether a food or drink problem was sending these women en masse to the restroom. Several days later, however, one of the facilitators happened to be in the women's room when the group of Korean women congregated there. This allowed the facilitator to open a different conversation with these women. Using a more indirect communication style, the facilitator noted that they seemed to be learning from one another. After lengthy exchanges, including discussion of how people learned in different countries and how language fluency made a difference in classroom process, it became apparent that the issue was their English language skill, as well as their cultural values and communication styles—not the food or drink they were being offered. They wanted to learn the class information but were getting lost in the language and the pace of the class. Their cultural power distance would not allow them to ask the facilitator to slow down and/or clarify things they didn't understand—that would have felt like challenging authority and would have risked loss of face for both themselves and the facilitator. Consequently, when one of them felt lost, she would quietly go to the bathroom, which was a signal for the others to follow. Collectively, they would discuss what each of them had heard/understood and help one another until they felt they had a grasp on the material, at which point they would return to the classroom. This created a second problem, of course: They were missing entire blocks of information while they were out of the room.

The solution was fairly simple: The facilitators slowed the pace of the class and changed the class process so that, at the end of each hour-long module, participants were asked to get into language-specific groups to discuss the information from the module, using whatever language they preferred. This allowed the Korean group to learn in their own way without violating their power-distance comfort or causing any loss of face.

This seems like a "simple" issue: changing the classroom process. It is important, however, to understand the complexity at work here. Because of the power distance (the facilitators were the "teachers"; the participants were the "learners"; the facilitators were "from headquarters"; the participants were "workers"), the problem was uncovered only after considerable exploration and, frankly, the "accident" of a facilitator being in the bathroom at the same time as these women. The fact that the facilitators had earlier "vetted" the workshop content and processes with Asian focus groups might also have prevented them from looking at workshop processes to explain the confusing behaviors of this group of participants. And, finally, communication styles contributed when the facilitators were asking direct questions about the behaviors and getting indirect responses they could not decode.

In each of these examples we can see how differential power (between employees in the first case and between training participants and facilitators in the second case) in cultural communication styles and cultural values regarding individualism versus collectivism and power distance affected perceptions across cultural groups as well as group effectiveness. Group effectiveness was improved in each case once participants understood how these cultural differences and dynamics of power operate—both in terms of role power and historical relationships of power—and were willing to modify reactions to others' behaviors. As work environments become more global, with greater numbers of cultural groups in work teams and greater differences among those cultural groups, the ability to identify, understand, and accommodate different communication styles and how these combine with relationships of power will be imperative for intercultural communication effectiveness.

CONTENT AND PROCESS IN GLOBAL VIRTUAL COMMUNICATION

Because virtual communication is becoming common in global work environments, we want to offer a couple of brief examples of virtual misunderstandings. Someone once said that the United States and Canada are two countries separated by a common language. Here are a couple of examples of how miscommunication can occur in virtual exchanges, even when both parties are using English.

In the first case, Donna was working with a Costa Rican to teach a class in Mexico and they were making preparations via e-mail to meet at the airport in Mexico City.

- *Donna:* Arrive at 7:15 p.m. on Thurs.; will wait for you at UAL baggage claim. D

- *Miguel:* My dearest Donna. I was happy to receive your note about when to expect your arrival. I am looking forward to meeting you and hope that you will have a relaxing flight. Our work will be so much fun and I am eager to spend time with you after the session so we can get to know each other better. Please travel safely. With warmest regards, Miguel.

- *What he thought*: Doesn't she like me? Her note is so cold, and she doesn't even sign her full name.

- *What she thought*: Can't he just say "OK"? Why such a long e-mail that has no real content in it?

While they were in Mexico, they were talking about communication style differences, which led to a discussion of this e-mail exchange. They were able to understand how the task orientation of Donna's style and the relationship orientation of Miguel's style were related to their cultural backgrounds as well as to the way each perceived the other. This understanding has been critical to the effectiveness of their ongoing professional relationship and personal friendship. While each of them can now modify his or her e-mails (Donna adds some "frills"; Miguel becomes a bit briefer), what is most important is that by understanding the styles, each of them can understand the other without negative judgment and impact, even if the style is not modified.

In a second e-mail exchange, Andy was working with an individual from Denmark to arrange a meeting between their two offices. The Dane consistently used the word *demand* in his e-mails. For example, "I demand that our meeting be held in a facility that has a restaurant onsite." Andy was confused—and a bit put off—about the use of the word *demand*. He could not understand why such language was necessary since they were peers and it didn't seem as though either of them had the right or was in a power position to demand anything. He chose to ignore the use of the word and proceed in good faith that they could reach appropriate agreements. The planning proceeded successfully, and the meeting was conducted effectively. During the meeting, these two developed a respectful working relationship. At one point in their discussions, Andy asked the Dane why he used the word *demand* in his e-mails. The Dane was surprised at the question and indicated that the word was simply used to indicate that what he was asking/suggesting was important and he would really like to have it if possible. He was astounded to learn that the word *demand* to someone from the United States typically means that the individual using it is insisting on having his or her way.

The resolution of differences in both of these cases occurred because (a) the individuals involved elected to stay open and continue to develop an understanding of the other before rushing to a negative judgment, and (b) they openly discussed the differences when they had the opportunity to do so in a face-to-face meeting. While not all virtual relationships will allow for resolution in a face-to-face setting, when it is possible to do so, it will generally facilitate quicker resolution and understanding of these differences.

As we explore intercultural communication, whether within the same country or across global borders, whether face-to-face or virtually, it is important to consistently attend to cultural histories, communication styles, power distance, and perception if we are to build intercultural communication competency and work effectively in global environments.

KEY TERMS

Bracero Program   168

collectivism   180

individualism   180

maquiladoras   168

neoliberal subjects   174

neoliberalism   169

North American Free Trade Agreement   168

power distance   179

DISCUSSION QUESTIONS

1. In Ammatuna and Cheng's case study, what do they mean by *neoliberal subjects*, and how do *maquiladora* workers become neoliberal subjects?

2. In the current economic climate, how is the American Dream shaped and informed by neoliberal ideologies? How do neoliberal ideologies shape the way you use time, envision the future, and approach work?

3. In their personal narrative, Stringer and Reynolds share two examples of workplace conflicts caused by cultural differences. Can you share examples of workplace conflicts you observed or experienced? Given Stringer and Reynolds's insights, how would you address challenges faced in the culturally diverse work environment?

4. Stringer and Reynolds share examples of misunderstanding caused by different styles of expression in business e-mail exchanges. What would you do to mitigate these situations? What strategies can be used to address these misunderstandings?

Border Crossing and Intercultural Adaptation

Akey contribution of intercultural communication scholarship focuses on sojourner and migrant adaption, integration, and/or assimilation into new cultural environments. At its core, cultural adaptation is a communicative process where cultural differences become highly visible and often problematic. After "coming out" as an undocumented immigrant in a *New York Times* essay, journalist Jose Antonio Vargas founded a public campaign called "Define American" to address immigration reform for undocumented residents of the United States. Questions of who/what qualifies one as an American—citizenship status, the pledge of allegiance, or the level of cultural adaptation—are central. Is patriotism a prerequisite for **migrants** to be seen as citizens? Is it possible, as the metaphor of "melting pot" implies, for everyone to simply melt into American culture? At what cost and benefit do migrants assimilate into the dominant culture? These questions inform the entries in this chapter.

In the following two entries, the authors offer particular experiences and perspectives of those who enter into the United States as migrants. The case study by Zornitsa D. Keremidchieva is a phenomenological analysis of how migrants narrate and come to make sense of themselves as migrants. Approaching migrancy as a distinct form of social belonging, she explores shared experiences of cultural enactments and embodied struggles by migrants from various parts of the world. In the personal narrative, Sachiko Tankei-Aminian chronicles aspects of her childhood in Japan, her sojourn to the United States as an international student, her professional experience as a minority faculty member, her intercultural marriage to a man of Iranian descent, and raising biracial/bicultural children in the United States. She reflects on how her cultural adaptation took place within the context of a racialized society that positions Asian women in a particular way, and how the challenges of adaptation shifted through her major rites of passage as a student, professor, and parent. Both entries illuminate the centrality of cultural experience in the process of adaptation, and how the sense of self is fundamentally challenged and transformed through the process of crossing cultural and national borders.

The Migrant Self: Intercultural Adaptation as Narrative Struggle

Zornitsa D. Keremidchieva

Macalester College

The study of **intercultural adaptation** has made important strides since Young Yun Kim and William B. Gudykunst (1988) put together the first collection of essays that focused on the communicative processes underwriting individuals' **acculturation**. There is now growing recognition that intercultural adaptation may be a nonlinear process (Smith, 2002) that produces more than neonatives, instead triggering personal and collective transformation that brings along new feelings, behaviors, and interpretations that in themselves might be empowering (Kim, 2002). Furthermore, critical perspectives have complicated the traditional socioscientific models that have long approached migrants' adjustment without much attention to the political and sociocultural contexts of their arrival (Curtin, 2010). Critical scholars have also challenged the mainstream political discourses that pathologize migrants' difference as deviance (Chávez, 2009), and they have drawn attention to the need to theorize the power dynamics and communication processes that link local and global discourses and practices of belonging (Sorrells, 2010).

The purpose of this study is to explore more deeply and more critically the experiential and meaning-making dynamics of intercultural adaptation. As Melissa L. Curtin (2010) points out, no single theoretical framework can fully capture the complex interactions that shape cultural adjustment, and I share her wish to disarticulate intercultural communication studies from "current folk and professional theorizations of assimilation and acculturation that often pathologize newcomers" (p. 282). An important step toward that goal, I would add, is acknowledging how positionality drives the desire for theorizing intercultural adaptation. As a migrant myself, I would often look to the intercultural communication literature to help me understand what I was experiencing. In the face of the scientific models, be they linear, bell curved, or spiraling, my experience seemed messy, contradictory, disorderly. In the faces of fellow migrants, in contrast, I would find compassion, understanding, acceptance, and commonality, but also struggle and ambivalence. Hence, with this project, I aim to allow the terms and tropes of adaptation to be derived *by* and *for* fellow migrants, all the while recognizing that language is never private or power neutral.

This phenomenological study addresses both substantive and critical questions related to the embodied, lived experience of migration and intercultural adaptation. Phenomenology is the study of lived experience that takes seriously the intersubjective processes behind all that is knowable, including our own selves. The focus of this particular study, then, is discovering the communicative mechanisms through which a migrant becomes a subject *as-a-migrant*. To talk about migrancy as a subject position is to mark a moment of recognition and negotiation when a self gathers its image from a range of identity positions within discourse. From a phenomenological perspective, the process of becoming a subject is simultaneously embodied, reflective, reflexive, and situational. The self-identity of the subject, as Calvin O. Schrag (1986) notes, is anchored "neither in a hovering universal form nor in an undergirding stable particular" (p. 149). Instead, the subject is inevitably decentered, marked by multiplicity, temporality, and performative embodiment; "as event and acquisition, the decentered subject emerges from and sustains itself within these performances" (p. 150). From this perspective an inquiry into how migrants make sense of their experiences is also a way of unpacking the limits and possibilities delineated by available discourses of cultural difference and identity.

Methodologically, the essay relies on narratives collected through phenomenological interviews with individuals who moved to the United States from countries such as Iran, Gambia, South Africa, Bulgaria, Brazil, Mexico, and Azerbaijan. Two of the interviewees had already lived in a country other than their birthplace prior to their arrival in the United States. At the time of the interviews, the duration of the participants' U.S. stays spanned from about 2 years to 17 years. Due to a level of risk associated with the undetermined legal status of some of the interviewees, individual speakers are not identified by name in the analysis of their narratives. Also, since intercultural adaptation is a dynamic process of identity formation that calls for negotiating diverse discourses of difference and belonging, I did not prelabel the participants with racial or ethnic categories common to U.S. mainstream culture. Instead, the interviews were open-ended, inviting the speakers to reconstruct their experiences in frames and utterances that felt most authentic and meaningful to them in the course of their dialogue with me, a researcher whom they also knew as a fellow migrant. The lived experience of migrancy was isolated in groups and themes of meaning through the phenomenological procedures of description (of the sign), reduction (of the signifier), and interpretation (of the signified) as outlined by Van Manen (1990), Moustakas (1994), and Ihde (1986). The interpretation of the migrants' statements was also informed by Peterson and Langellier's (1997) insight that (1) personal narrative necessarily requires bodily participation; (2) personal narrative is contingent on the conditions, relations, and consequences of its telling; and (3) personal narrative enacts and embodies larger relations of power. Similarly, I approached the migrants' narratives as situated performances, social events, and personal experiences.

The narrative material gathered from the interviews produced three broad themes that organize the sections of this paper. The first section focuses on the embodied experience of adaptation. It explores how migrants "do" or "show" who they are. The second theme examines how the practice of narration helps migrants construct and enact their sense of selfhood. It traces how migrants "say" or "tell" who they are. I conclude by reassessing how migrants challenge, revise, and enrich our assumptions about the experience, politics, and meaning of intercultural adaptation. Together, the themes reveal how the interaction among corporeal experience, meaning/utterance, and (global) discourse shapes the migrant's lived experience of self, and they point to the intense and intimate connections between the micropractices of individuals' narratives on the one hand and the meso and macro structures of discourse about identity and belonging on the other hand. In the end, I argue, the struggle of intercultural adaptation is also a struggle for creating a more affirming, open-ended, and cosmopolitan narrative about migrancy and cultural transformation.

ENACTMENT AND EMBODIMENT, OR
HOW TO "PUT ON" A NEW IDENTITY

That migration is a whole-body experience is the first big theme emerging from the interviews. The speakers would constantly refer to practices involving the body—seeing, listening, eating, doing, acting, reading, writing, working. The senses, the ability to see, hear, taste, feel, are all mobilized and recalibrated to capture and understand the new environment and figure one's place in it. Sight is particularly emphasized as the speakers constantly describe seeing themselves, seeing others, seeing others see them, and even seeing themselves see. For instance, a speaker describes learning the new culture as a process of seeing the new culture: "When I came . . . I *noticed* . . . it made me more *observant*. . . . I tried to *observe* and *see* the norms here." Another speaker testifies to the effort it takes to translate perception into action: "I tried to *see* that in my mind. . . . I tried just to *listen* to those things . . . and that's how I could *do* it." Thus, the participants describe their experience as a process of recalibrating the senses, of opening themselves up to the new environment.

The migrant becomes an astute audience analyst and a devoted reader of the host culture who approaches the problem of adaptation the way an actor might approach the development of a new role. One participant, for instance, describes how she learned what expressions of emotion are considered appropriate:

Sometimes you talk, you tell a joke and people don't like. . . . Sometimes you come and you want to hug because it is your birthday. . . . People are so scared, you can't even kiss their face you know, so with time you kind of learn that you can't act the same way as you act at home because people see it in the wrong way.

Audience adaptation, however, involves a certain level of self-risk and evidence of the sensibility that Kim and Gudykunst (1988) have described, as migrants' **"existential alertness"** punctuates the narratives. As one speaker points out, "you are never sure how they are understanding anything you are saying. That's why you are very cautious and you are scared when talking to these people." Another speaker captures the physical, embodied signs of alertness:

If you are constantly aware, if you are constantly reading signs, whether they are little signs, like signs on the wall which I constantly read, I read all the signs, I never used to do that. But I have become very . . . analytical. I think I always was, but now I am even more so. Very aware of body language and tuned to all sorts of signals, probably signs that are even not there but become a habit after all.

And yet another speaker confirms, "I started being more self-conscious . . . it made me more observant." Thus, the experience of migrancy unfolds as a rite of passage from a state of being in which one assumes possession of one's self-image to a regime of the body that renders this right of ownership quite problematic. It is an experience of dislocation in which one's body is no longer secured for one's self but becomes a site of uncertainty and struggle for recognition and interpretation.

The interviewees make particularly vivid the dynamic interplay between a position of "seeing" and of "being seen" as they negotiate their sense of presence and agency. This interior distance is further described as a sense of fragmentation, doubling, parceling, even double vision that allows migrants to shift between positions of seeing and seeing themselves see, between acting and witnessing themselves act, between speaking and hearing themselves speak. One participant even switches to the more impersonal "you" to describe her sense of dislocation. She explains, "You don't feel like yourself, you are not yourself, this is not your body, these are not your thoughts, you don't know what are your reactions . . . you don't react in your normal way." The "I" and the "me" are left out in this description, and by their very absence they illustrate the sense of detachment marking the migrant's experience.

In the intersubjective context of the interviews, the use of "you" might be seen as hailing me, the researcher, as a fellow migrant. But it also implicates an audience that may not be necessarily outside of the self. For **phenomenology**, the performative potential of the body lies in its hermeneutical self-implicature, in the body's possibility to contemplate itself, to write and read its own story. As Merleau-Ponty (1964) reminds us, however, the embodied self is inevitably intersubjective:

> Associated bodies must be brought forward along with my body—the "others," not merely as my congeners . . . but others who haunt me and whom I haunt; "others" along with whom I haunt a single, present, and actual Being as no animal ever haunted those beings of his own species, locale, or habitat. . . . The enigma is that my body simultaneously sees and is seen. (pp. 161, 162)

In this sense, the demands of audience adaptation come to act on the migrant's body not only when she or he is subjected to the gaze of others but also in reaction to an imagined gaze of others. The migrants engage in forms of self-monitoring and self-disciplining that distill their sense of where the boundaries of cultural belonging and difference lie. As one participant explains, "you know, I am never relaxed . . . very worried about what people are going to think, what people are going to say. . . . If there isn't anything, I invent something." Another participant's similar fear of judgment also expresses a need for external validation: "You do these things automatically without being certain that you do these things in the right way. You are never certain that you do them in the right way." The task of adaptation then becomes a process of negotiating, of drawing and redrawing, of playing and replaying invisible cultural norms. This reiterative, performative process can be characterized as a form of **mimicry** that is motivated by "the desire for a reformed recognizable Other, as a subject of a difference that is almost the same, but not quite" (Bhabha, 1994, p. 86). However, as much as a theatrical gesture is a stylized movement crafted for a particular effect on the audience, so is a migrant's enactment of acculturation invariably syncretic and generative. A migrant's mimicry would "continually produce its slippage, its excess, its difference" (p. 86). For example, the image of the polite migrant, the migrant who tries and works hard—a trope that many of the interviewees held dear— is, in fact, a hyperbolic exaggeration of a cultural norm. It is perhaps this very extraordinary effort to adapt and "normalize" one's body that marks the migrant as a foreigner.

The migrants construct the body as "a site of possibilities" (Butler, 1993), a tool for "trying on" and possibly creating alternative forms of social being. The migrant develops what Pico Iyer has described as "a wardrobe of selves from which to choose" (as cited in Kumar, 2000, p. 93). Kristeva (1991) has interpreted such multiplicity as a form of surrender:

> Settled within himself, the foreigner has no self. Barely an empty confidence, valueless, which focuses his possibilities of being constantly other, according to others' wishes and to circumstances. I do what *they* want *me* to, but it is not "me"—"me" is elsewhere, "me" belongs to no one, "me" does not belong to "me," . . . does "me" exist? (p. 8)

Such ability to exist in a state of perpetual performativity arguably makes the migrant the most cultural of us all. When migrants capture, reassemble, reembody, and reperform the norms of cultural life, they may not destabilize the visual ideologies of ethnic, racial, and national identity. But they do bring to light the dynamic, iterative, and interactive character of dominant cultural script making.

Despite the constant search for a proper new identity, the narrative evidence from this study also suggests that the embodied experience of doubling, of constantly shifting between a subject and an object position, does not diminish the migrant's embodied sense of self. On the contrary, it strengthens it. A powerful, hyperembodied "I" emerges from the migrants' utterances; it is an "I" that is able to contemplate itself as an other. The migrant's very existence is contingent on the survival instincts of an "I" that finds itself deprived of the comforts of a stable "we" or "you" or "they." When all other claims fail, the migrant turns to the "I" as an existential anchor. The migrant's "I," a dynamic assemblage of perceptions, sensations, and interpretations, becomes simultaneously a subject and an object, a terrain and a cartographer, granting the migrant a right to exist: "As much as I don't feel that in the eyes of everybody else I belong here, in my own, you know, perceptions, I feel like I belong *here*."

ENABLING VIOLATIONS, OR HOW TO "TELL" A NEW IDENTITY

While the first group of statements from this study pointed to the migrants' acute attunement to the embodied experience of migration, the second theme focused on the challenges of communicating those experiences. A migrant act is never silent; the body speaks and is read within a grammar of identity. As Langellier (1998) notes,

> the hallmark of personal narrative is to be radically contextualized—not just in identity's body but also in dialogue with empirically present listeners and other "ghostly" audiences; and not just within locally occasioned talk (conversation, ritual, interview) but also within the forces of discourse that shape language, experience, and identity. (p. 208)

Unfortunately, despite the long history of immigration in the United States, there are few tropes and scripts in the mainstream culture that migrants can tap into as means of expressing their condition. The participants confess to an overwhelming sense of frustration when they find themselves unable to affirm their presence: "You try to communicate but you cannot . . . because the very way you are trying isn't sufficient." There isn't a shortage of will but of words: "I see that they try to sympathize, but you know that they can never understand what you mean . . . because you cannot explain." Furthermore, a speaker shares how exhausting it is to constantly search for words to better express her experience:

> There were situations when you were worse. . . . [There is] something that you want to express but you cannot express in any way. . . . You get to a point when you feel you are tired of that and you going not to speak English any more. You can't do anything because of that.

There simply isn't a vocabulary to help the migrants identify themselves meaningfully: "I am . . . I'm . . . oh god, OK . . . I am going to try to avoid clichés . . . not much is left."

Short on words that can capture their experience, the migrants recoil from using the terms that permeate the U.S. vocabulary of identity. They quickly discover that race fundamentally constructs the difference between native and foreign in the United States, but they are also cognizant of and resistant to the peculiarities of American notions of race. One participant confesses,

> Something that most of my American friends can't seem to understand is that a racial factor is not a factor. . . . For the most part I could not understand why I was different. . . . I was caught to make a choice, but I didn't fit in any of the choices.

Another participant echoes a similar struggle with the demand to categorize himself by race:

> I never really know exactly what race to put exactly because I don't consider myself Hispanic, but I don't consider myself white and I don't think I am black. . . . I don't know, to tell you the truth . . . because they say you are supposed to say your original race . . . but I don't like to say . . . because I don't think I really am.

Both of these speakers recognize the arbitrary, but also menacing, function of racial identification.

The discomfort the speakers express in relation to the identity frames they are asked to occupy is reminiscent of Spivak's (1994) observation that when the **subaltern**—the people who exist outside of the hegemonic power structure—produce language, they partake in a self-destructive effort to perform a markable, tangible, unself-identity. As one participant puts it, "and so you just got to kind of go along with it, and say yeah, it would be great. And live in that fantasy world sometimes. But it's . . . [shakes his head and sighs]." Another speaker adds, "I'd always answer questions in a defensive way, you know." Defensiveness becomes a form of distancing oneself from the act of responding when being called.

At the same time, there is keen awareness that the migrants' very survival hinges on the "enabling violation" (Spivak, 1994, p. 277) of their narrative complicity with the tropes and identity themes of the mainstream culture. Using the host culture's tropes of identity, no matter how flawed, appears to be the only way the migrants can claim their existence. Yet there is an overriding awareness expressed in the interviews that for migrants the use of categories such as nationality, race, and ethnicity is not only inevitable but also strategic. Migrants may retreat to these labels, but they also attempt to revise the scripts of the dominant discourse. For instance, one of the speakers bemoans the public image of her country as derived from pictures of tourist oases and Third World faces of poverty. At the same time, she finds herself inversing the politics of tourism to supplant a different narrative to the images. She says,

> I mean, it's a good thing that they know about the bad things because that's what I even tell tourists: Don't just go. . . . I mean you have to be careful, it's dangerous, it's a violent country, but the people there are violent because they are hungry, not because they are crazy, you know.

The speaker seizes the opportunity to rewrite the dominant story about her group identity, but does this allow her to rewrite her own story? Hardly so.

The sensibility that Kumar (2000) identifies as "the shame of coming" is acutely shared by most of the interviewees. The migrant becomes the symptom bearer of global inequalities. One speaker explains,

> Humiliation is something that is the easiest to get used to . . . the idea that you don't just come to see something different, but that you have to become a part of it, that you have to stay because you don't have the opportunity in [your country] to do it. That is horrible.

Furthermore, the migrants react to the dominant cultural frames that divide the world into the (developed) West and the (underdeveloped) Rest. One participant bemoans the position that she feels she has to occupy. She feels she is being viewed with,

> I wouldn't say indignation, but like a person who, they think, sees, finds in America the paradise of the world or something like a super-rich country and you are happy that you are here. They accept that you are satisfied to be here, and you are happy simply because you can have hot water at 2 a.m.

They also squirm at discovering their entanglement within the globalized narratives of (Western) opportunity: "For some stupid reason I thought that there would be no bad things here at all. Well, there are. So I was expecting . . . utopia probably, but probably, I insist that [is] the shocking thing for me."

Migrants sense that lines of global power inequalities are drawn right on their bodies, organizing who sees and who is watched, who acts and who is seen as acting, who speaks and who is heard. The participants attribute the asymmetries of their cross-cultural encounters to a difference in investment, in motivation, in modes of survival:

> While an American doesn't need to get close to the [migrant], to go inside their mentality, because that is going to be a part of his mentality in the years ahead, a [migrant] needs to do that. The difficulty is enormous. Because he is trying to do it. While the American doesn't. He doesn't have this need.

Such asymmetrical encounters, one participant shares, "make you feel like no person." Finally, the cost of migration becomes not only the loss of links to family and friends back home but also of one's own sense of integrity and authenticity. Migrants feel bound to the very myths that marginalize them. As one participant testifies, perhaps shying away from his own complicity in the practices he describes,

> people, a lot of people . . . write home or call home and talk and really blow up things, make things bigger than they are and, oh yeah, I am driving a Jaguar here and I came here and within 6 months I made it. . . . They just lie because they are embarrassed to say that, yes, I am here, I am working, doing carpentry to make a living, you know. They are embarrassed to do that. . . . You know, you can't just come here and count that hard work and luck will help you get by. You've got to live modestly . . . I mean living here . . . and going through hell. At the same time, you write home and you don't . . . want them to be worried about you.

And so the migrants become the trusted storytellers who disseminate the very myths of immigrant America that disenfranchise them. Their quest for a sense of agency tragically falters at a nexus of global imaginations about the good life, success, and empowerment:

> This is what all of us are slaves to here. . . . I want to give up because I feel I cannot adapt to it, but then I was proud and didn't want to just go back home. . . . I didn't want to come back and [they] say, "Oh, you are a loser." So I said I am going to do this! So I suffered a lot.

RECONSIDERING THE NARRATIVE POLITICS OF INTERCULTURAL ADAPTATION

> In the end, a migrant exists as-a-migrant through the practice of telling the experience of cultural transformation. Migrants try to put on identities only to find that none fit. As one speaker eloquently explains,

> when you learn to question, when you learn not to believe what you see, you learn not to believe what you are told. It's not something that you can switch on and off. It isn't. You end up questioning everything . . . which makes me a foreigner.

Thus, the sense of closure that the concept of intercultural adaptation implies proves quite elusive. Instead, the interviews suggest that the migrant condition pushes the frontiers of our imagination about what it means to be somebody in a globalized, yet inequitable world:

> You split into two in such a way that you neither get a new identity of a person from U.S., an American, nor can you go back . . . but you live your whole life split into two and you can't find any reconciliation.

Migrancy becomes a path of no return:

> What is scary is that we are losing connection with everything else, everything that was before and after you. And you may never go back. The loss is the most scary thing. . . . You know that this is another society, or one of many societies, which is something very subjective and . . . it doesn't satisfy you.

Thus, migrancy produces a restless, nomadic consciousness. It produces also a social and political awareness in which, as Bhabha (1994) notes,

> social differences are not simply given to experience through an already authenticated cultural tradition; they are the signs of the emergence of community envisaged as project—at once a vision and a construction—that takes you "beyond" yourself in order to return, in a spirit of revision and reconstruction, to the political *conditions* of the present. (p. 3)

Paradoxically, the migrants' loss of identity also gives them a strong sense of self. As much as they resist being folded into dominant discourses of race, ethnicity, and nationality, the speakers nonetheless seek out a place from which to speak. It is a space rooted in experience and a sense of common struggle: "You cannot talk about that to the Americans, or people who haven't yet been through it." Migrants can find themselves only among other migrants. Migrancy becomes its own trope of social belonging.

Such forms of identification should not necessarily be interpreted as a rejection of the mandate of adaptation. Instead they signal a quest for adaptation, but of a different kind—an adaptation to the story of migration itself, as migrants get to tell it. As one participant explains,

> I feel like certain people who have been in my situation can do that. . . . And I feel comfortable with them. I really don't feel uncomfortable with the U.S. citizens, you know people who have grown up here . . . but in general my friends, my close friends, tend to be those types of people who [are] similar to me. Take for instance my friend . . . I like to see that the kinds of things he went through, I would probably go through, in a different way but still.

There is much power in such small acts of sharing. So for me and the fellow migrants I spoke to, the possibility of political emancipation starts with our ability to distance ourselves from the lure of the grand narratives of national identity and cultural belonging. It starts with appreciating the small and random encounters that let us cocreate our stories—our hybrid, ever-evolving scripts of (other) selfhood, solidarity, and experience. With this perspective in mind, we can appreciate the humor, the tragedy, and mostly the hope and sense of possibility contained in the migrant's pride in being nobody and everybody at the same time:

> So this guy from Ireland came up to me . . . and said, "Oh, you are from [Country Y]! . . . I never associated you with being from anywhere!" And that was kind of a compliment for me.

On Becoming *Japersican*: A Personal Narrative of Cultural Adaptation, Intercultural Identity, and Transnationalism

Sachiko Tankei-Aminian
Florida Gulf Coast University

This personal narrative attempts to capture my cultural adaptation process, formation of a new cultural identity, and maintenance of transnational practices. As a **sojourner** from Japan who has lived in the United States since 1999, I have turned to these themes as an academic pursuit as well as a personal quest. This essay illustrates how my experiences of cultural adaptation were shaped by the various stages of my life: my childhood in Japan, becoming an international student, getting married, working as a faculty member, and raising children. As a nonwhite, nonnative–English-speaking sojourner, I specifically examine how societal systems of privilege and oppression interplay with my cultural adaptation process, intercultural identity formation, and transnationalism.

MY CHILDHOOD IN JAPAN: YEARNING FOR THE WEST

Most studies on cultural adaptation focus on migrants' experiences as they leave their familiar culture for a new and unfamiliar one. Young Yun Kim (2001) explains that the cultural adaptation process includes acculturation, **deculturation**, and transformation into a new cultural identity. Acculturation refers to the process by which individuals acquire the cultural patterns and practices of a new host culture (pp. 50–51). However, retrospectively, my adaptation to U.S.-American culture started long before my journey to the United States, while I was growing up in Japan and had no clear plan about coming to the United States.

I was born in 1972 and grew up in Japan, where there was (and still is) a deeply rooted idea that "West" means progress, after "the intense import of Western concepts" (Darling-Wolf, 2004, p. 329) in both the Meiji and postwar eras. Western, particularly U.S.-American, cultural products have penetrated everyday Japanese scenes, through stories, music, films, TV programs, magazines, animated cartoons, theme parks, and dietary products. As I consumed those cultural products and learned English as a foreign language, I was subconsciously breathing Western hegemony and idolizing "the essentialized notion of the West" (p. 325), U.S.-American culture in particular.

By the end of my undergraduate study, I had already developed a tremendous yearning for acquiring English fluency and immersing myself in the U.S.-American culture. It was no coincidence that later I decided to pursue a doctoral degree in the United States. The seed of my cultural adaptation to the United States had been cultivated for years before I came to this country for the first time.

BECOMING AN INTERNATIONAL STUDENT IN THE UNITED STATES

When I finally enrolled in a graduate program in speech communication in the U.S. Midwest in 1999, I was quite happy about the fact that I was immersing myself in English and the U.S. cultural environment. Naturally, I faced the limitations of my linguistic and cultural knowledge and experienced homesickness, but I was still able to tell myself that these were all part of the cultural adaptation process and that I would be fine. "If I improve my English, get rid of an accent, and get accustomed to U.S.-American ways of living, I will be fine. I will get used to it. I will be OK." Or so I kept telling myself back then.

In graduate school, quite intensive exposure to academic discourses in English on a daily basis helped me acquire high-level English fluency. Eventually, I started thinking in English, rather than thinking in Japanese first and then translating my thoughts into English. As I advanced my English fluency, it seemed as though I was developing different filters in my head, in addition to my original ones. Through such new filters, I started seeing and perceiving certain realities in a new light. In this sense, I gained not only a linguistic duality but also an epistemological one. The linguistic and epistemological duality I acquired has had a huge impact on my approach, mental outlook, and kinesthetic understanding of reality.

For example, the concept of *ganbaru* or persistence has significant meaning in Japanese education and society (Singleton, 1990). The verb *ganbaru* means "to persist, hang on, or do one's best." We use its imperative form *ganbare* to encourage someone to succeed. In English we often use expressions such as "Good luck" or "Take it easy," by which we mean to wish others luck or a more relaxed approach to challenges.

When I face challenging moments, I still hear my inner voice telling me, "*Ganbare.*" Consequently, I feel some pressure in my mind and tension in my body. Yet now I can switch my mind-set and try to see the same reality from a new perspective by tuning to the English expressions, "Take it easy" and "Good luck." I realize that my relaxed attitude may bring a more successful outcome. Switching languages is not a mere linguistic code-switching but also a switch of my mind-set and kinesthetic understanding of reality.

However, what I think I developed is not simply the sum of bilinguistic spheres. Not only have I learned to speak and write in two languages, but I have also learned to feel, think, speak, and write in between. This experience echoes what Yoko Tawada (2004), a Japanese writer who writes in both Japanese and German, calls *exophony*—the general state in which one is out of her or his own native tongue. She stresses the importance of the space between the languages. Tawada declares, "I don't want to be an author who writes either in language A or language B. I want to find that poetical ravine that divides the two and tumble into it" (Japanese Literature Publishing and Promotion Center, 2014). This echoes my new epistemology and linguistic identity, which illustrates the "nonsummative" nature of cultural identity (Yep, 2004, p. 71).

CHALLENGES IN GRADUATE SCHOOL AS A CULTURAL OTHER

During the first few years of my stay in the United States, I hoped that things would get better, that I would not be treated as "a new kid on the block" any longer once I improved my English fluency and gained certain cultural knowledge. Therefore, I was devastated when I realized that I would never be free from being marked as the cultural "other"— either as a foreigner, second-language speaker, Asian, or Japanese—even after I made progress in my cultural adaptation process.

I noticed that I tended to receive benevolent and/or patronizing comments in the United States. "Your English has a nice ethnic accent. It is not too thick. It is easy to understand." "Don't worry about your renewal of a student visa. You will be fine. You are not one of those crazy Middle Eastern guys. You are not a dangerous one." "Asian girls are cute and sexy." Such comments are often well-intended and seemingly inclusive, yet problematic. Raka Shome (1999), a scholar and immigrant from India, writes,

> While the desired aim of such comments is to make me "feel good," they are nonetheless problematic and pernicious because the implicit rhetoric in such comments suggests that my body is still up for examination and scrutiny in relation to some preconceived, media-fed American image of an Indian woman that I may or may not fit and that to be Asian/Indian is a negative thing. (p. 124)

Such statements tend to be cast toward our becoming white, U.S. American.

While my identity included significant elements from both Japanese and U.S. cultures, I realized that I would never quite become "U.S. American" in a white-dominated society, no matter how long I stayed in the United States, or even if I became a U.S. citizen. Simultaneously, I am no longer merely "Japanese," since I have transformed culturally while living in the United States. I started calling my newly emerging cultural identity *Japerican* (Tankei, 2004; Tankei-Aminian, 2013). I have become irreversibly *Japerican*.

INTERCULTURAL MARRIAGE

I met Farshad in 2005 and married him in 2006. He is an immigrant from Iran who came to the United States in 1997 and has been a naturalized U.S. citizen since 2001. Farshad and I have placed great importance on maintaining our own cultural backgrounds in spite of potential negative social consequences in the United States. We try to maintain a mix of Japanese, Persian, and U.S.-American cultural elements in our ways of living and our own identities, which we like to call *Japersican*. We attempt to resist total assimilation and maintain our original culture in the midst of powerful dominant cultural forces (Sorrells, 2013, p. 46).

Japersican is a hybrid (Hegde, 1998) and "the third kind" (Kim, 2001), as well as a transnational (Orbe & Harris, 2008; Sánchez & Kasun, 2012) cultural identity. We consciously have incorporated each other's language and cultural ways of living, along with our English speech and acquired U.S.-American ways of living. We frequently travel to Japan and Iran. We keep close ties with our family members, relatives, and friends, as well as keep up with cultural, societal, and political events in our original cultures.

I deepened my understanding of cultural otherness by hearing and witnessing firsthand what Farshad goes through in the current context of anti-Islamic sentiments in the United States. As a Middle Eastern male and Muslim, Farshad tends to be scrutinized and is often assumed to be a potential terrorist. At airport security checkpoints, Farshad and even his 70-something-year-old mother used to be—8 or 9 times out of 10—selected for a more thorough search. Their boarding passes almost always had either the printed or handwritten code "SSSS"—the "quadruple S"—which stands for "secondary security screening selection." Even when Farshad and I purchased airline tickets together and I put the charge for both tickets on my credit card, his boarding pass got the "quadruple S," but mine did not.

Later, we learned that the "quadruple S" meant he was on a "watch list." Naomi Wolf (2007) explains how "President Bush had the intelligence agencies and the FBI create a 'watch list' of people thought to have terrorist intentions or contacts; and these agencies gave the list to the TSA [Transportation Security Administration] and the commercial airlines" (p. 96). The list contains not only sojourners and immigrants but also American citizens who "do not fit a terrorist profile [and] range from journalists and academics who have criticized the White House to activists and even political leaders who have also spoken out" (p. 94). Recently, Hamid Dabashi (2013), a professor of Iranian studies and comparative literature at Columbia University and a human rights activist, discussed this phenomenon as "traveling while Muslim" (para. 5).

Through our intercultural relationship and marriage, I have certainly gained a deep awareness of discrimination and institutional racism in the United States. Farshad and I have become "**intercultural allies**" (Sorrells, 2013, p. 167), have shared our struggles as cultural others, and have continuously educated ourselves regarding various social inequalities—not only in the U.S. context but also in the global one—while bridging our own cultural and linguistic knowledge. It is also important that Farshad and I not forget we are "immigrant elites" (Sánchez & Kasun, 2012, p. 76). We are voluntary migrants who have educational, occupational, and socioeconomic privileges. Even with such privileges, we still face racism and xenophobia in our cultural adaptation processes. We often discuss what migrants who do not possess the same privileges face during their cultural adaptation.

WORKING AS A MINORITY FACULTY MEMBER

Farshad and I started teaching as university faculty in 2007. We both teach at the same predominantly white institution. Although we both love our teaching and working at the university, our challenges as minority faculty members mirror those of faculty and students of color in academia that are addressed in many scholarly works, as well as in recent news reports.

One challenge Farshad and I face is that our knowledge and credibility can be belittled, dismissed, and/or challenged. One of my students wrote in the course evaluation: "This course was not effective in teaching the required material. I could not understand what the professor was saying most of the time and she could not pronounce half of the English language." Donald Rubin (1998) addresses the realities of NNSMNAE (nonnative speakers of mainstream North American English) instructors, which affirms what we experience:

> Here we have students judging their teachers rather than the other way around, teachers who are "others" vis-à-vis the dominant culture, and a curious power dynamic wherein teachers would surely possess high authority were it not for the compromising impact of their ethnolinguistic identities. (p. 154)

Through our classes, both Farshad and I directly or indirectly handle issues of diversity, humanity, and social justice while engaging in critical inquiry of Western hegemony, racism, sexism, and militarism. We both acknowledge that engaging in critical inquiry, or pedagogy of discomfort, "can incur feelings of anger, grief, disappointment, and resistance" (Boler & Zambylas, 2003, p. 111); yet such processes offer students new ways to examine reality. Without such processes, which force us out of our comfort zones, we cannot truly learn how to engage our humanity to create justice and peace in society.

When the course subject is on race and racism, especially at predominantly white institutions, students' resistance is enormous. Race and racism are subjects that most people, especially the racially privileged, do not want to discuss in the context of prevailing rhetoric of colorblindness (Bonilla-Silva, 2014; Johnson, 2006; Orbe & Harris, 2008; Tatum, 2003; Wise, 2011). When someone such as me, a faculty member of color, teaches race and racism, it is "mentally, emotionally, and psychologically draining" (Orbe & Harris, 2008, p. 251). I deal with racism in my own life, and "to compound those experiences with classroom instruction can be quite exhausting" (p. 251).

When Farshad and I express to our colleagues various obstacles we encounter as NNSMNAE instructors or challenges in teaching race and racism, many of them give us genuine sympathy. However, simultaneously, we sometimes feel that the specificities of our experiences as faculty of color are not completely acknowledged. Sometimes the discussion is dismissively switched to a general matter—"Oh, I am sorry. It'll get better. You'll be OK"; "Every teacher gets a trouble student once in a while"; "Have you tried different teaching style/content/assignment?"

Regardless of our colleagues' good intentions, their lack of awareness around these issues increases the risk in expressing our obstacles and frustration. There is the danger that "powerful others . . . won't like it and will retaliate with the epithets 'unprofessional,' 'malcontent,' 'maladjusted,' 'whiner,' 'too emotional,' 'bitch,' or 'out of control,' etc." (Johnson, 2006, p. 58). These interpretations and fears are not just in our imagination. Recently, a black female professor at Minneapolis Community and Technical College was "formally reprimanded by school officials after three of her white male students were upset by a lesson she taught on structural racism" (McDonough, 2013, para. 1).

These obstacles may have less to do with outright bigotry and more to do with ignorance and lack of awareness conferred through positions of privilege and dominant-group membership. More often than not, our students and colleagues are very nice folks—what Victor Lewis, an African American participant in the film *The Color of Fear,* described as "moral, fair-minded people who believe that they are lovers of justice, church-goers; people experience themselves as the decent human being" (Mun Wah, 1995). Yet we need to recognize, as Johnson (2006) articulates, how "good people with good intentions make systems happen in ways that produce all kinds of injustices and suffering for people in culturally devalued and excluded groups" (pp. 86–87).

RAISING CHILDREN

Our daughter, Mina, and our son, Kian, were born in the United States in 2009 and 2013, respectively. We are trying to raise our children in a *Japersican* style, engaging transnational practices and connecting to our family members in multiple countries "through ever-changing media applications" (Sánchez & Kasun, 2012, p. 72). We speak Japanese, Persian, and English in our household. It is challenging for us to maintain our trilingual context for our children in the United States, since we do not have our family members nearby or live in a community where we can hang around on a daily basis with folks who speak Japanese or Persian. Yet, even before our children were born, we started singing them Japanese lullabies and playing them Shahram Nazeri, a master Kurdish Iranian singer. We show many Japanese educational programs and anime TV shows to our children on a daily basis. We

Courtesy of Sachiko Tankei-Aminian

Photo 10.1 A family portrait

talk with my mother, who lives in Japan, via video chat almost every day. We took Mina to Japan three times and to Iran once. She code-switches back and forth among Japanese, English, and Persian, depending on the context or her feeling at the moment.

We are quite aware of tendencies in the United States in general and schools in particular to "try to assimilate immigrant students by subtracting the non-U.S. parts of their identity," placing "insurmountable pressure to speak only English and consequently lose their heritage languages" (Sánchez & Kasun, 2012, p. 82). For example, a sign was posted on the information board at International Students and Scholars at Southern Illinois University, where I attended graduate school: "Speak English at all times—even with your friends from home—if you hope to be successful at SIUC!" On another occasion, during a visit to the pediatrician with then-2-year-old Mina, we were asked if she goes to day care. When we answered "yes," the doctor smiled and said, "Good. Then she can pick up English no problem."

Our diet is also a mixture of Japanese, Persian, and U.S.-American food. Although I am happy to share a *Japersican* dietary style with Mina (and hopefully with Kian soon), I wonder what our children and others, such as their teachers and friends, will think about their dietary style in the future. I recall a story I heard from a Japanese sojourner who works in the U.S. Midwest. Shortly after his arrival in the United States with his family members, he enrolled his 7-year-old boy in a local elementary school. One day, his son was told not to bring *onigiri* (rice ball) for lunch any longer, because it "stinks." I wonder what it was like for his son to have one more thing to worry about, during his cultural adaptation living in

Courtesy of Sachiko Tankei-Aminian

Photo 10.2 Mina video-chatting with her grandmother

a new culture, going to a new school, learning a new school system, learning English as a foreign language, and making new friends.

I cannot help but wonder if our children will encounter such attitudes someday and how it will affect them. African American scholar Beverly Tatum (2003) wrote that she "felt it was important to make sure [her young son] saw himself reflected positively in as many ways as possible," since they lived in predominantly white communities (p. 34). Farshad and I feel that we will have to be proactive in providing our children with positive views of their identities, since they are less likely to receive these messages while living in predominantly white communities.

CULTIVATING A *JAPERSICAN* STANDPOINT

Although Farshad and I attempt to maintain our own cultural identities and share them with our children through language and daily rituals, we are also highly aware that we are becoming the other in our own cultural environments. With our cultural transformation and growth in the United States, as well as by living together, we have changed some of our cultural beliefs and values and acquired certain new perspectives. We are becoming "intercultural," or irreversibly *Japersican*.

I find Imahori (2000) best articulates our experience of becoming "intercultural." Farshad and I are able to see not only U.S.-American culture but also our own original cultures from the outside. In the United States, we are cultural others because of our race, and we are becoming others in our own cultures because of our cultural transformation while living in the United States. Consequently, we can uniquely explain and take on "minority" as well as "majority" perspectives in both cultural contexts (p. 75).

In this sense, we have developed the epistemological position of the "outsider within." Julia Wood (2004) describes "outsiders within" as those "who can understand the logic of a group from both that group's perspective and a perspective removed from the group. This enables double-consciousness, which standpoint theorists think is more accurate than any single consciousness" (p. 217). I do not suggest here that all transnational migrants will develop such a standpoint. Just as racial standpoint is not a birthright and needs to be earned, hybrid intercultural identity standpoint needs to be cultivated.

CONCLUSION

Becoming *Japersican* is about seeking new possibilities of hybridity and expanding our own frameworks. It is about processes of transformation and resistance. In the context of transnationalism, cultural identity can no longer be conceptualized as "self-contained, fixed, and stable" (Hegde, 1998, p. 37), and "ontologically given and essential" (Conquergood, 1991, p. 184). But, rather, cultural identity is "fluid" (Yep, 2004, p. 71), "constructed and relational" (Conquergood, 1991, p. 184), and "constituted and reproduced within the process of communication and everyday interaction" (Hegde, 1998, p. 37).

Cultural identity has a complex nature; it is "political, nonsummative, and paradoxical" (Yep, 2004, p. 71).

Cultural adaptation is a personally transformative process. As a result of the adaptation process and being positioned differently in a new culture, individuals often experience ethnocentrism, racism, and systems of inequity. Given these experiences, individuals can develop heightened awareness as well as resistive actions that challenge and change the society within which they are adapting. Thus, cultural adaptation can be transformative not only for the individual but for the "host" culture.

Farshad and I do not know at this moment if we will always stay in the United States or if we will eventually go to one of our "homes." We do not know what we will come to know and how we will see ourselves through our journey of cultural adaptation in 5, 10, or 20 years. Our belonging, understanding, and identity will continuously shift and reshape, depending on our experiences and new locations.

KEY TERMS

acculturation   188

deculturation   197

existential alertness   190

intercultural
   adaptation   188

intercultural allies   200

migrants   187

mimicry   191

phenomenology   191

subaltern   193

sojourner   197

DISCUSSION QUESTIONS

1. In her case study, Keremidchieva approaches "migrancy" as a particular condition of existence and a mode of experience that emerges through self-narratives. In what ways does this approach challenge the traditional view of cultural identity defined primarily by race, gender, and class? What are the strengths and limitations of this approach? What does her approach tell us about cultural identity beyond the intersections of race/gender/class/sexuality?

2. Using examples from both Keremidchieva and Tankei-Aminian's articles, discuss how migrants encounter cultural differences through bodily and kinesthetic experiences. How do these examples help you understand how migrants and sojourners go through intercultural adaptation? How do migrants embody their culturally transformed identities?

3. Based on your reading of the personal narrative by Tankei-Aminian, discuss how her "*Japersican*" standpoint is different from the "melting pot" metaphor of cultural assimilation.

Popular Culture, Media, and Globalization

Globalization, propelled by advances in communication and transportation technology, the integration of global markets, and the privatization and deregulation of media outlets in much of the world, has intensified the role of media and **popular culture** in shaping our communication with and understanding of cultures different from our own. While TV programs, celebrities, and music videos are often perceived as simply innocent and fun entertainment, these and other forms of popular culture are powerful transmitters of cultural norms, values, and expectations. While the United States continues to dominate production and dissemination of popular culture globally, numerous media circuits today originate from India, Latin America, Nigeria, and China; thus, a central dynamic of intercultural communication is how global media and distribution of popular culture alternately promote strong desires for inclusion in global culture and also mobilize intense resistance to cultural imperialism.

Media and popular culture serve as primary channels through which we learn about groups who are different from ourselves and make sense of who we are. As the authors in this chapter assert, the stories we are exposed to shape who we are, how we live in the world, and what we dream is possible. Just as limited and negative representations produced through media and pop culture promote and reinforce stereotypes impacting perceptions of others and ourselves, diasporic and migrant communities reconnect and remember home through popular culture as they resist full assimilation and otherness.

In Sheena Malhotra's longitudinal study of the impact of media and neoliberalism on youth in India, she asks how global and intercultural fluency gained through exposure to Western media impacts youth's worldviews. Her case study explores the shifts and changes in Indian youth's dreams, goals, and imaginations, particularly in relation to gender, nation, and culture, as the current generation is increasingly exposed to new consumer and media landscapes. In her personal narrative, Chigozirim Ifedapo Utah shares what she calls "migrant moments" to investigate the intercultural tensions, ruptures, visions, and possibilities of living in **pop-culture nation**. Combining stories and theory from her hybrid transnational experiences, she invites us to engage with the struggles of others, have honest conversations, and honor the humanity in one another.

Reimagining a Nation: Neoliberalism and Media's Impact on Youth's Imaginaries in India

Sheena Malhotra

California State University, Northridge

India witnessed great economic and cultural changes post-1991. This case study provides a longitudinal understanding of how notions of gender, nation, and culture have changed since India's economic "liberalization" and neoliberal policies took effect in the 1990s. Globalization not only entails increased flows of media and technology but also movement of capital, changes in national and global policies to accommodate that capital, and the accompanying changes in cultural practices. Based on a longitudinal comparison between focus-group interviews conducted in 1993 and 2011, this essay outlines shifts in the imaginaries amongst urban youth in India.

BACKGROUND AND CONTEXT

India gained her independence from British colonial rule in 1947. Given that the region consisted of hundreds of small independent kingdoms precolonization, discussions about what it meant to be an independent nation-state—focusing on uniting a people with close to 30 distinct languages, hundreds of dialects, and several religions—were ongoing. India's film industry (often referred to as "Bollywood") evolved its own genre to appeal across different language groups, using simple storylines with "over-the-top" acting, songs, and dances that could be followed and appreciated without knowing the language. Hindi-language films of the 1950s and 1960s often had nation building as their theme, defining Indian culture through their narratives as a newly independent and self-sufficient nation, valorizing values of self-sacrifice for the good of the community, celebrating farmers and the working poor as true heroes, and emphasizing values of social justice and caring for one another over materialism and wealth.

The influence of Mahatma Gandhi and other national leaders during the struggle for Indian independence resulted in efforts to form a more equitable society, loosely based on socialist principles. From 1947 to 1991 (44 years), India developed a protected economy, where the government owned and operated many industries (airlines, hospitals, schools, television networks, telephones, etc.). Eventually, only Indian nationals could own and operate businesses in India, an approach designed to encourage entrepreneurship in a young nation. However, the economy struggled, and India underwent a balance-of-payment crisis. To address the crisis, India borrowed capital from global bodies of governance such as the International Monetary Fund and World Bank. These loans came with conditions to adopt neoliberal economic policies.

In 1991, India's economy was "liberalized," which means the nation moved from a protected, socialist-leaning approach to an "open" economy divested of government holdings in various industries. The grand shift in the economy created a sea change in the Indian landscape, nowhere more apparent than in the urban centers. The sudden influx of Western corporations into India rapidly changed India's commercial districts from primarily locally owned stores to large multinationals such as Nike, Apple, Coach, and other name brands that tried to grab a foothold in India's large and quickly growing middle-class market. It was a poignant moment in Indian history, wherein a former colonial state renegotiated its cultural and national identities in the context of neocolonial/ neoliberal forces represented by multinational media corporations and framed by global bodies of governance.

Perhaps one of the most far-reaching changes of the 1990s was the shift in the television landscape in the nation. Television in India prior to the neoliberal shift consisted of one state-run, public network, popularly known as DD (or Doordarshan), with an educational and public service mission. In the afternoons, DD broadcast "educational" programs on topics from basic math to farming and civic engagement. Evenings had "entertainment programming," but even these programs were designed with a "social message" (e.g., the evils of dowry, national unity, or religious tolerance).

In the 1990s, within a span of just a few years, the landscape changed drastically when a plethora of private and public commercial television channels with both Indian and Western content were introduced. MTV, NBC, CNN, and many other Western networks began broadcasting in India. But often even more popular were the homegrown, private networks such as ZEE, SONY, STAR, and COLOURS that adopted the glossy styles of the West but kept the storyline and content Indian. The main goal of the private channels was to increase viewership, a goal that resulted in sensationalist news and reality shows, as well as sexualized and entertainment-oriented soap operas and drama series. These rapidly changing "**mediascapes**," in Appadurai's (1996) terms, and fears of U.S. hegemony have profound implications for questions of gender, nation, and culture in India. **Cultural hegemony** refers to a dominant and potentially oppressive cultural order adopted by a majority of people due to the ubiquitous nature of the mass media and advanced capitalism. An example would be the media ideal of the feminine body. A model's figure is unachievable for 97% of the population, and yet it is held up as the ideal for all women to strive for and be judged against. While the cultural hegemony of U.S. media is evident in the shifting narratives of many films in the 1990s and post-2000 (see Malhotra & Alagh, 2004), Hindi- and regional-language films continue to be a powerful media force in India.

Media representation is critical in the construction of gender, nation, and culture. The stories a culture generates are one of the primary ways we come to think about gender roles, belonging, patriotism, and how we learn our cultural realities. India has long struggled with reconciling different identities. Partha Chatterjee's (1989) study of the independence movement in India revealed contradictory impulses for freedom fighters who were often caught between narratives of modernization and progress advocated by the British and the more traditional cultural norms or rituals often equated with nationalist and patriotic identities. This contradiction was often resolved by equating women with the "home" and "inner" spiritual spheres, making them the keepers of tradition and culture and thereby allowing men to adopt "modern" and Westernized forms in the "outer" and public sphere, which were deemed necessary for the progress of the nation. These sorts of conflicting narratives (progress vs. conservation; modern vs. traditional) are often present in periods of rapid cultural change. In the case of India, they have found particular expression in the divide between Western/colonial/modernization and Indian/indigenous/cultural traditions.

Currently, a whole generation of urban Indian teenagers and college-age students have never known anything but a world populated by the connected global mediascapes of MTV-India, the simultaneous release of Hollywood films in the United States and India, and a level of comfort with Facebook that other generations had with the telephone. This is a generation as conversant with the latest happenings on *Gossip Girl* as they are with the newest Bollywood film release. How does this global and intercultural fluency impact their worldview? Homi Bhabha (1994/2003) coined the term **hybridity** in his analysis of the colonizer/colonized relations to note the creation of "transcultural forms" within colonial histories and relationships (Ashcroft, Griffiths, & Tiffin, 1998). According to Bhabha, cultural identity and cultural systems are constructed in the "Third Space of enunciation" (p. 37), wherein the **ambivalence** and interdependence of the colonizer and colonized construct **hybrid cultural identities** (Ashcroft et al., 1998, p. 118). Are youth in India developing hybrid subjectivities, in Bhabha's terms? In particular, how will this exposure transform young people's imaginaries regarding gender norms and their understanding of culture and nation?

METHODOLOGY

In 1993, I conducted four focus groups in Bangalore to explore the impact the privatization of television in India had on notions of gender, nation, and culture.[1] Acknowledging that gender roles are often in flux, culture is never static, and the nation is not monolithic, it was still important to capture the changes as viewers were being exposed to new stories. The focus groups I conducted consisted of 3 to 10 participants, ranging in age from 16 to 22. Two focus groups were women only, and two focus groups were mixed.

Based on the 1993 focus groups I conducted, along with interviews with television executives and content analysis of programming, my coauthor and I found that there was an appropriation of Western culture by many of the networks (see Malhotra & Crabtree, 2002). We highlighted the *ambivalence* (Bhabha, 1994)—defined as a love/hate relationship between the colonized subject and colonizer—generated among television audiences by such appropriations. We also found a degree of cultural hegemony being articulated by the executives (celebrating consumerism, in their notions of "progress," etc.) who produced the programming, as well as in the audiences consuming it. However, our most compelling insight from the studies conducted in the early 1990s was the contradictory construction of gender roles for Indian women; they were expected to be both superwoman (Westernized, working, good consumers) and submissive housewife (upholding traditional Indian culture). This phenomenon was indicative of the competing ideologies of Western consumerism and Indian nationalism that emerged in India at the time (Malhotra & Crabtree, 2002).

In 2011, I returned to India to conduct focus-group interviews with students in Bangalore. I conducted six focus-group interviews, the first of which consisted of high school students. The other five focus groups were at the same two colleges I had visited in 1993 (St. Joseph's and Mount Carmel College).[2] In essence, I was accessing a similar student population but

18 years and a full generation later. All names have been changed to protect the identities of the participants in the 1993 and 2011 focus groups. There were 30 participants in the 2011 round overall, ranging in age from 16 to 22. The focus groups at St. Joseph's consisted only of men, and the ones at Mount Carmel consisted only of women.

The questions driving my research in the second round of focus groups centered on changing norms in terms of gender, culture, and nation for participants who are growing up in a globally connected media landscape. I asked urban youth who their heroes were and what cultural values guide the new urban Indian identity. How did their fluency with Western programming and their highly mediated upbringing impact the gender and cultural worldviews of today's college-age generation? Are there any anxieties or disconnections emerging, or are they able to synthesize the changing mediascapes with ease, folding them into their own understandings of gender, nation, and culture?

Urban/Rural and Linguistic Divides

It is key to emphasize that the population I spoke to is not representative of large portions of India. I interviewed urban students who were in English-medium educational institutions. These students were from Bangalore, which is a large city with a population roughly equivalent to that of Los Angeles. Most of these students were considered middle or upper-middle economic class. Obviously, the experiences of students who grow up in rural India or its villages or are economically disadvantaged will differ vastly. Yet, given my focus on the impact of English-language programming on Indian youth, an urban, English-speaking population provided a good starting point for study. Students from these spaces are often the opinion leaders of tomorrow's urban India and are positioned well to become prominent players in Indian industry. Therefore, gaining insight into their notions of gender, nation, and culture at this juncture advances an understanding of an influential segment within the broad diversity of Indian youth.

FINDINGS AND DISCUSSION

India is coming of age in the post-2000 era. The country went through a metaphoric "drunk adolescence" in the 1990s, where the nation suddenly opened up to the world and made tremendous cultural shifts overnight, often binge-drinking Western consumerism and other Western values. It was a time when anything seemed possible, and anything that could go did! In the post-2000 era, a maturing is occurring as the country works to absorb the onslaught of neoliberal economic policies, Western corporate influences, and Western media into its mediascapes and econoscapes, resulting in new articulations of cultural identities in different strata of Indian society. In the intervening years since the interviews conducted in 1993, I find there is a significant and new acceptance of how notions of gender, nation, and culture are shifting. Dreams and realities of transnational mobility permeate and contend with local, bounded notions of national identity; Indian youth accept and embrace hybridized cultural identities, and expanded, less rigid gender roles are viewed as normal.

Shifting Heroes, Shifting Stories

We learn so much about our world and how to make sense of it from the stories our culture tells. There are often multiple narratives within any cultural tradition. Those narratives compete for dominance, and the meanings are contested by power structures that amplify or diminish their reach. These competing stories and narratives reflect, constitute, and transform our lived cultural experiences. Yet how are we—and particularly youth—impacted when our stories are no longer generated from within the culture to which we belong, or when we no longer pay attention to the stories our culture produces?

I asked the focus-group participants in 2011 the percentage of English-language versus Hindi- or local-language television programming they watched. The majority (about 60–65%) of participants reported that as much as 80% to 100% of the programming they watched was in English. This revelation was significant. Only 10% to 15% of participants said they watched more Hindi- and local-language programming than English programming (see Table 11.1). These findings show that students in the focus groups watched a preponderance of Western programming, even though the most popular shows in India as per ratings were still Hindi-language shows, produced by Indian networks. This may illuminate a degree of disconnection between English-speaking youth in middle-class homes and the rest of the country. It was obvious that they overwhelmingly preferred Western programming and were conversant in the latest happenings on those shows, which informed their ideas about gender and culture considerably.

Given the kinds of programs focus-group participants watched, it was no surprise that when they were asked to name their favorite star, the names Johnny Depp, Brad Pitt, Tom Cruise, and Robert Pattinson emerged. When coaxed to name favorite female stars, once again, names such as Angelina Jolie and Sandra Bullock were offered first. Names of Bollywood stars such as Shah Rukh Khan, Aamir Khan, and Kajol were mentioned, but those came up later and often only in response to a specific question about Bollywood stars. Only when naming sports stars did they mention Indian cricketers before Western sports stars. If our heroes often become our role models, this idolization of Western stars and English programming will likely lead, over time, to role models and worldviews that are more Western than Indian within this population.

Table 11.1   Percentage of English- Versus Hindi- or Local-Language Programming Watched

Kind of Programming Watched	Percentage of Focus-Group Participants
Mostly English (80–100%)	60%
50/50 mix	25%
Mostly Hindi/regional (60–90%)	15%

The first focus group I conducted in 2011 consisted of 16-year-old high school students. The group had a high level of energy, and their answers seemed earnest as they reflected on media's impact on their lives and culture. They all said they watched 99% or 100% English television programming, and maybe 1% Hindi. That proportion shifted to 60% and 40% when it came to Hollywood and Bollywood films, so there was still a young audience for Bollywood films. The participants in this group spoke effortlessly about streaming the latest Western television programs and discussed the pros and cons of Facebook and Instagram, and every single one of them said they wanted to study or live "abroad." Samara was emphatic when asked where she wanted to be in 10 years: "Somewhere *not* in India, doing something that's *not* an everyday job. I have no idea what I want to do. But I don't want to wake up every day and go to a 9-to-5 job" (Focus Group 1, 2011). The traditional emphasis of middle-class Indian families on their children becoming doctors, engineers, or IT professionals in the quest for well-paying jobs appeared to be sidelined here. Samara definitely imagined a nonnormative future for herself, a future she hoped was somewhere outside of India.

In another focus group, one young woman directly pointed to her television viewing preferences as the source of her new aspirations. Sonam told me that previously she wanted to go to the United States to teach differently-abled students because there was "a lot of scope there" for special education teachers. However, she had a new ambition. She said,

> Thanks to *Bones* and *CSI*, I want to become a criminal psychologist now. There's also the CBI . . . no, the FBI. I really want to work for the FBI. So I think I'm going to work there. (Focus Group 6, 2011)

Sonam's slip from CBI to FBI is revealing. CBI is the Central Bureau of Investigation, which is the premiere law enforcement agency in India, akin to the FBI in the United States. Influenced by U.S. programming, Sonam seemed to discard the Indian agency for its U.S. counterpart. I asked her if the FBI allows non–U.S. citizens to join. She replied that she could "if I become a U.S. citizen. My uncle is a U.S. citizen." Her friend Tara asked twice if she wanted to become a U.S. citizen. Sonam replied, "But I think it allows noncitizens too. I don't want to become a U.S. citizen, but I want to work there. It gives you good work experience" (Focus Group 6, 2011). Sonam's shifting imaginary about what she wanted to do with her life was directly connected to whom she idolized and the stories she absorbed. She was driven by an idea of the work she wanted to do, and although she didn't want to become a U.S. citizen necessarily, she was willing to do it if that path would allow her to work in the job she wanted. Both she and Samara represented one segment of the 2011 participants who manifested transnational mobility, at least in their imaginaries. It was a mobility built around neoliberal subjectivity—autonomous, individualized, independent, and flexible to meet workforce demands—produced by the desires the programming evoked. They imagined themselves as global citizens who could work where they wanted, shifting nationalities and allegiances, in service of living the life they wanted most. Just as the programming they watched 99% of the time crossed borders effortlessly, they, too, imagined for themselves a life unbounded by borders and nation.

Yet, when long-term living plans were considered, the majority of the participants actually articulated a desire to return to and settle down in India. A hint of nationalistic pride and a resistance to leaving "for good" was expressed across most of the focus groups. The attitude was characterized by one participant, Sanjana, who said she would like to study abroad but was very firm about returning to India. "But settling [there] is a bad idea. I would want to come back, open a firm here, and help my country grow, rather than helping *their* economic growth" (Focus Group 5, 2011).

She was clear about what she wanted to do, the sequence (study abroad, return to India to set up a firm), and the value of her contribution (helping the Indian economy grow). She also articulated a deliberate choice about helping her own country rather than helping the economic growth of the United States, indicating a strong sense of belonging to India's future. This sentiment was echoed over and over again by a vast majority of the participants. Most wanted to work or study abroad, but most also wanted to return to India in the long term. Through media, youth's **transnational identities** and neoliberal subjectivities are constructed, challenging and reshaping notions of national identity.

Changing Cultural and Generational Shifts

In the 1993 focus groups, a great deal of anxiety was expressed about the changes that Western programming and liberalization were bringing. One of the respondents remarked, "It's very alien to us. Especially all this sexual openness on MTV" (Kamini, Focus Group 3, 1993). Another respondent fretted about whether Indian culture was ready for it, while yet another remarked how she did not like watching Western programs with her parents because it was "a real culture shock" (Roma, Focus Group 4, 1993). These respondents were grappling with exposure to Western television and culture at an entirely new level. And they were worried about implications for their world.

Eighteen years later, a change in the level of anxiety was evident. While some participants spoke about not wanting to watch with their parents any content that had sexuality in it, there were many who said that they were comfortable as long as their parents liked the same shows.

Vidya: My mother used to be all weird before. But now that we're getting exposed to different cultures, my mother is OK with me watching . . . perverted stuff and all.

Sheena: Perverted stuff?

Vidya: She sends me "sick" messages on the phone and all. We share a bond like this because we don't have anything to hide. Before, if I got some sick joke, I had to be like, "Oh shit, my mom's here." Now I can just forward the message to her. (Focus Group 6, 2011)

Vidya's newly developing comfort with her mother allowed her to increase her exposure to content. "Sick" is a colloquial, euphemistic term used to denote sexual content. "Sick joke," for example, is often used as a way for women to refer to a sexual joke. Jokes, texts, and programming that include anything sexual (e.g., kissing or other PG-13–type content) used to be taboo. Now, apparently, it is more and more accepted and shared amongst urban Indians and even across generations. Bollywood, too, has lifted its 70-year-old avoidance of any kissing or physical contact and is becoming bolder in its portrayals of sexuality. Another focus-group exchange reflects the same changing reality between the young adults of the 1990s and those of today.

Rahul: They've grown with us. [Rahul is referencing his parents here.]

Arjun: In the beginning they never accepted all that. But now they're changing toward that. What's happening in the world. There's a change, so they're ready to accept that. (Focus Group 3, 2011)

The anxiety about cultural shifts and generational divides in 1993 morphed over the intervening 18 years to an acceptance of what is seen as an inevitable Western influence in Indian society. Tara told me she thinks "it's helped us become more open-minded" (Focus Group 6, 2011). Her sentiment was echoed by Vidya: "It [Western programming] gives us a broader view about how the world is" (Focus Group 6, 2011). The nation's middle-class taboos are being challenged with a growing acceptance of previously taboo topics across generations.

Sometimes that acceptance is accompanied by pride that the influence is not unidirectional and that India is fast becoming a player on the global stage. Sanjana, a young woman who insisted that although she would like to study abroad she wanted to return to India to settle, noted with some nationalistic pride, "India is a growing country. They say that maybe in another 10 to 15 years, it's going to be in a top position. So yeah, people are coming from everywhere. You know, it's a golden [laughs] . . . egg" (Focus Group 5, 2011). She observed that they didn't have "all these things" just 5 years back and she thinks it's "slowly coming up." Her friend Aparna remarked, "I think it will be on par with the Americans. Because going at this rate . . . I mean people are changing, drastically changing every day. So it will be Westernized" (Focus Group 5, 2011). Aparna saw the cultural changes as "drastic" and appeared to be quite accepting of their inevitability. Her friend Sanjana continued her train of thought:

We are going on par with the Americans. And the Americans are taking in the Indian trends. So maybe there'll be a reversal. They'll go to the spiritual aspects, and yoga. And we start going to the discotheques [clubs] and the malls. (Focus Group 5, 2011)

Her friend Aparna observed that it's already happening, and both of them chuckled a bit at the changes. India's growing economy and growing middle class (a prime market for multinational goods) have put India on the global stage. In 1993, while focus-group members seemingly embraced some aspects of Western freedom, they did express concerns about the consumerist ideology that Western media and the new Indian economy were introducing. By 2011, there appeared to be an acceptance of widespread consumerism, although most participants still felt that what was more important was maintaining their values (however each person articulated those values). At the very least, though, consumerism and Westernization were no longer anxiety producing. In fact, indicative of cultural hegemony, consumer culture and Western culture were read as signs of progress and as desirable. India's ability to have "all these things" meant that it was "slowly coming up" (Sanjana, Focus Group 5, 2011). The young women's views and statements contour a transition toward neoliberal subjectivity.

Opinions varied about whether the culture was changing more rapidly than is normal, as well as about what those shifts mean for India. Yet there was also a confidence that something quintessentially Indian remains untouched by shifting mediascapes. Prerna insisted that we remain Indian even today: "I think it's just our values. In no other place will you still find children touching their grandparents' feet. And we're also friendly and open [laughter]" (Focus Group 1, 2011).

Prerna was not alone in this thought. Her point was echoed by many in various focus groups. Aparna articulated the most common position: "We need to understand that if we take in the Western culture, we don't have to forget our Indian culture also" (Focus Group 5, 2011). When I asked them to articulate what Indian culture meant to them, many participants pointed to festivals, holidays, emphasis on family, respect for elders, and a nonindividualistic orientation. Some said that it was most tangible during holidays and festivals. Others mentioned "ethnic wear" days at school as another expression of culture. Negotiating hybrid cultural identities, participants held a "both/and" approach to the question of being Indian or Westernized. They took in a great deal of what the West has to offer, and they held onto a sense of their culture and their belonging, as Indians, to the Indian nation. They were invested in claiming their Indian identity, in whatever way each of them individually articulated and imagined it, revealing neoliberal influences toward individualism and autonomy even as they avowed a collective cultural identity.

Reimagining Gender and Work

The focus groups conducted in 1993 revealed anxieties not only about culture but also about the impact of Westernization on gender roles. One participant, Kunal, fretted about it when he said, "The bra-burning attitude is coming now. . . . After 3,000 years' suppression, you cannot expect a bird to fly, OK? It needs to see the world outside, take a few faltering steps before it takes off" (Focus Group 1, 1993). Kunal expressed some of the anxieties about how women might deal with their newfound freedom, worried that women would go too far too fast. His concern was echoed in public discourse at the time. In contrast, women expressed a sentiment of hope about the example that images of working women would provide women in India. One participant said, "It makes the woman more aware, you know. The woman of India, she's now more aware about things" (Priya, Focus Group 2, 1993). However, tremendous confusion about expectations for women was evident. One participant said,

> I feel like, you know, I feel a little confused. I feel a little caught between two worlds. Because when I go back home, I have to really act a little more decent, and control my tongue a little more, control my ideas a little more . . . and then when

you come here [to the city], you're expected to behave completely different. You're supposed to dress up . . . like they do on MTV!" (Neha, Focus Group 2, 1993)

Neha's statement exemplified the competing expectations that many young Indian women, living in the larger Indian cities, were expected to satisfy. While their dress, jobs and career expectations, music preferences, and ways of thinking could change, they were still expected to maintain and uphold Indian cultural traditions that teach women to be selfless and self-sacrificing. These expectations were adamantly transmitted through repeated media images pre-1990. In their comprehensive study of gender roles on Indian television, Krishnan and Dinghe (1990) found that one of the predominant images of women on Indian television was the submissive, self-sacrificing wife and mother. Even as some Indian cultural traditions may be viewed as confining and limiting for women, most Indian women interviewed did not believe the answer lay in completely denouncing Indian culture. Neha's confusion signified a moment of rupture in the construction of traditional gender roles for Indian women. At such moments, dominant (patriarchal) interests compete most fiercely with the interests of nondominant groups to create hegemonic ideologies that serve them best. In response to the changing ideas of gender, the Bhartiya Janata Party, a political party that espouses a Hindu-focused, right-wing philosophy, and a flurry of regressive television programming, which became highly popular, called for a return to sexist traditions where women were subordinated to men, presenting it as a "reclaiming of 'our' culture" or a "return to the 'Golden Age' of Hinduism." However, at precisely such moments of rupture, when everything is in flux, gender norms and associated meanings can be renegotiated and envisioned in a different manner. The promise of that possibility was very much present when the interviews were conducted in 1993. However, by 2011, those possibilities were, for the most part, co-opted into expressions of freedom through consumerism, as was fitting for a neoliberal subject, and appropriated as overt objectification and sexualization of women, rather than nurturing more independent and truly free possibilities.

If there were worries from the men in 1993 about changing gender roles, and more mixed feelings from women, there appears to be much more awareness and acceptance amongst today's young men and women. In an all-male focus group, Rahul said, perhaps hyperbolically, "In every part of India it's changing. Women have their own rights" (Focus Group 3, 2011). His friend Ishaan corrected him: "I don't think women have equal rights yet. But it's getting there. Especially in urban areas, rather than in rural areas" (Focus Group 3, 2011). They talked about what their sisters were studying; one was planning to be an engineer, another wanted to go into an MBA program, another could "be whatever she wants to be." That short discussion, perhaps, illustrates one of the more revealing attitudinal shifts toward young girls and women in urban India. In the 1993 interviews, the idea that *perhaps* women might consider careers was a question. At best, there was a sense of hope, from the women interviewed, that women with careers would become more and more common. In present-day discussions, there is no doubt that they will. Not a single woman in any of the focus groups talked about wanting to get married and "settle down" without a career. Every single female participant assumed that she would be working, as exemplified by this brief exchange in Focus Group 1: I asked, "So you all *do* want to work?"

Almost in unison, they said, "Yeah" or "Of course" or "Yes!" Samara followed up with a bit of disbelief, and the exchange that followed was telling:

Samara: Do we have a choice?

Sheena: I don't know. Do you have a choice?

Samara: To not work? [Incredulous tone]

Sheena: Yeah.

Samara: How?

Anjana: Just marry someone.

Samara: Just marry someone? No! That's stupid!

Prerna: That's bad [laughter from all]. (Focus Group 1, 2011)

I was struck by how much the imaginary of young women had shifted within the previous 18 years. Not only did they assume that they would work and have careers in the future, but they couldn't imagine how one could possibly *not* have a career! This was a very different imaginary than just a generation prior, when the emphasis on marriage for women was imperative and pervasive and careers were considered unusual or secondary at best. This may not be the reality for many parts of India, but it was for the young women in the focus group. I believe their attitudes, which are the products of shifting cultural attitudes toward gender, as well as global hegemony of **neoliberalism**, herald a larger change than we have seen up to the present moment.

CONCLUSION

Put simply, the genie of Westernization is out of the bottle. Urban India, almost 20 years after the first round of interviews, is a transformed landscape, peppered with shopping malls, multiscreen cinemas, increasingly visible wealth, and a consumer class. Perhaps even more striking than the visual changes are the attitudinal changes, the transformation in the imaginaries of urban Indian youth. The stories they grow up with today are not the same as the stories of a generation ago. These new mediascapes have transformed their dreams, their goals, and what they imagine as possible. An increasing acceptance and normalization of Western influences creates both hybrid and transnational subjectivities, even as a sense of belonging to the nation and being Indian is held dearly. Perhaps the most striking changes over the 18 years between focus-group interviews concern imaginaries regarding gender roles and work. The discussion moved from whether women should work or not to an assumption that they will obviously work and have a career. Now, it is more a matter of what they might choose to do and where. Urban youth increasingly understand their identity as framed by consumerism and the global workforce. As discourses of women's liberation are co-opted and women are reduced to their economic value as consumers and flexible workers in a neoliberal global economy, the production of neoliberal subjects is complete. Little or no conversation about women being truly independent on their own terms or for their own sake was evident in the focus groups. The rapidly increasing consumerism and rising cost of living in Indian society has necessitated two-income households, a new phenomenon in middle-class India, contributing to the normalization of a growing neoliberal workforce.

While these transformations do not yet impact all levels of Indian society, they are striking within this particular segment and notable for that reason. We certainly cannot attribute all the transformation to changing media exposure; media are just one aspect amongst many in a changing Indian and global neoliberal culture. However, media are undeniably powerful purveyors of images, ideologies, and imaginaries in the context of neoliberal India.

ACKNOWLEDGMENTS

I am very grateful for the support I received from the College of Humanities at California State University, Northridge. My research trip to conduct the 2011 focus groups was made possible through a Faculty Fellows Grant from the Dean's Office. My gratitude to Kimberlee Perez for her careful reading and insightful editing of my work. I would also like to thank Kathryn Sorrells for her thoughtful editing and her patience with multiple drafts to refine the essay.

Migrant Diaries: Communicating in Pop-Culture Nation

Chigozirim Ifedapo Utah

University of Nebraska, Lincoln

North 27th Street, Lincoln, Nebraska, is an unexpectedly rich mélange of culture. Mexican, Ethiopian, Vietnamese, Mediterranean, and European grocery stores and restaurants speckle the roadside, and included in that mix is a Nigerian grocer that makes me feel as though I've been beamed out of Lincoln and into the old Tejuosho market in Lagos. The smell inside is reminiscent of my mother's kitchen after she prepares a pot of egusi soup. Nigerian music is playing in the background, and the latest Nollywood DVDs are displayed on a wall. I smile at the melodramatic titles such as *Clash of Destiny* and *Scent of Passion*. I can tell by the storeowner's accent that we are probably the same ethnicity.

"How are you, my sister?"

"I'm fine, uncle."

"You go to school here . . . work?"

"UNL . . . I'm getting my PhD."

I receive an approving smile. Nigerians value education highly. Later that day, overwhelmed with feelings of kinship and homesickness, I settle down on the couch with a plateful of "rice and stew" and golden-brown fried plantains, wishing I was home for Christmas. A Nollywood movie acquired from YouTube provides a cherry for the top of my nostalgic cake. Familiar scenes unfold.

"Leave my son alone!"

"Mama, I don't understand . . ."

"So you think I don't know what you and your fellow witches are planning?"

"But Mama . . ."

"SHUT UP! Who is your mother? I will kill you before you kill my son!"

It is impossible to stay sad with the quintessential cries of "I am warning you!" "God punish you!" and "What is this rubbish?" ringing in my ears. It feels good to feel a little closer to home.

The landscape of contemporary popular culture is dotted with rich points of intersection between the local and global. Coke products in glass bottles are available on the "international" aisle at Super Saver, children code-switch between English and Hindi as they play derivatives of tag in the park, and Gangnam Style has taken its place amongst wedding-reception group-dance classics such as the Electric Slide, the Cupid Shuffle, and the Wobble. I refer to this fascinating web of cultural junctures and disjunctures produced by the simultaneous global movement of people and popular culture as pop-culture nation—the fragmented space of global popular culture where people and their cultural expressions and artifacts converge and diverge in novel ways. In my undergraduate days, I remember studying with a Mexican friend in a 24-hour computer lab, hopped up on candy, energy drinks, and agonizingly strong Mexican coffee. I had been taking Spanish, watching telenovelas, and practicing dialogue, and was eager to show off. My attempt to converse in Spanish was met with laughter.

"What's so funny?"

"You!"

"What do you mean?!"

". . . Never heard a Nigerian speak Spanish before!"

In this narrative, I share many more of what I like to call "migrant moments" to highlight the dynamic relationship between intercultural communication and popular culture in the global context. I offer these stories as illustrations and as an invitation to self-reflexivity, *not* as a criticism of the United States or definitive conclusions about Nigerian or U.S. culture.

GLOBALIZATION AND (POPULAR) CULTURE

Through diverse processes, our globalized world is tremendously interconnected and interdependent (Tomlinson, 2007), characterized by increasingly liquid and multidirectional flows of people, objects, places, and information (Ritzer, 2010). This results in interesting cultural configurations such as "Chocolate City" in Guangzhou, China, where many African businessmen reside (Bodomo, 2010), and China Town in Lagos, Nigeria. About 74 million (nearly half) of the migrants from developing countries reside in other developing countries (Ratha & Shaw, 2010, p. 2), which contradicts the popular belief that *everyone* is migrating to the West. The tendency to place Americanization and Westernization at the epicenter of *every* discussion of globalization reinforces the cultural imperialism that many scholars decry. While its influence is undeniable, "the United States is no longer the puppeteer of a world system of images but is only one node in a complex transnational construction of imaginary landscapes" (Appadurai, 1996, p. 31). The study of popular culture and intercultural communication on the global scale must attend to the multiplicity of cultural linkages that exist in a networked society.

Globalization contradicts the very idea that culture is bound to specific regions (Goodman, 2007). It also challenges the idea of culture as a unified set of norms. How can one possibly identify the values and customs of more than 7 billion people? However, an analysis of global culture does not require the identification of homogeneity, shared values, or social integration; rather, it requires the identification of a set of practices that *constitute* a cultural field within which struggle and contestation occur (p. 335). Alternatively, if we view culture as shifting tensions between the shared and the unshared (Collier, Hegde, Lee, Nakayama, & Yep, 2002), we uncover dynamics such as the interplay between integration and fragmentation that characterize global relations. *Likewise, the fragmented space of pop-culture nation (i.e., global popular culture) can be understood as perpetually unfolding tensions and struggles that occur when multiple cultural systems and artifacts flow into and away from one another.* When I joined the abundant stream of Nigerians migrating for university education at the age of 17, I became more aware of my movement within this space and was often alarmed at the tensions that surfaced as I encountered different systems of knowing, seeing, and being in the world. Next, I will share these tensions in tandem with four interconnected themes that reflect some of the ways popular culture shapes intercultural communication. Popular culture is a resource in identity construction and consequently enables and constrains intercultural communication. It also disrupts cultural identities leading to resistance (Sorrells, 2013, p. 126) and forges hybrid transnational cultural identities (p. 126).

(MIGRANT) IDENTITY CONSTRUCTION: CONNECTION AND DISCONNECTION

After I left home, activities such as dancing *Azonto* at Nigerian weddings, reading lifestyle blogs such as Bella Naija, and laughing at terrible contestants on *Nigerian Idol* became a haven. For migrants, both the politics of adaptation to the new environment and the stimulus to move or return are deeply affected by a mass-mediated imaginary that frequently transcends national space (Appadurai, 1996, p. 6). Thousands of miles away from the sights and sounds that constituted my identity, Nigerian popular culture provided an alternate space for identity performance, quelling feelings of otherness. Shome and Hegde (2002) poignantly describe a similar dynamic:

The highly sentimental movie plots churned out by Bollywood (as the Bombay cinema industry is popularly termed) gain a new function in the lives of immigrants, who are thus connected through song and dance to lives left behind; watching Indian movies in the transplanted context of the U.S. is an expression of ethnic desire and identity. (p. 183)

I discovered that these cultural artifacts were not entirely my own. They were part of a global system of cultural meaning, centuries in the making, and I shared them with others through similar colonial histories and political and social experiences. This realization had a profound effect on my identity, fostering a deeper sense of belonging and connection, not just to my home country but to a broader network of people and places. *But pop culture is not a panacea.*

Born and bred in the diverse, chaotic, and exciting city of Lagos, Nigeria, I hadn't expected my migratory experience to be so discombobulating. I had been exposed to the music, cinema, literature, and cuisine of different cultures, and several family members had studied abroad. Nigeria's lingua franca is English, so I did not anticipate language barriers. My naïve confidence was shattered as soon as I got lost in Atlanta's sprawling international airport.

"Please, I am looking for this gate." My itinerary was briskly inspected.

"Go north a little ways, hang a left . . ."

I listened politely, hiding my confusion behind perfunctory nods. I didn't have the foggiest idea what she was talking about! Thankfully, after minutes of bemused wandering, I found my gate. When I reached Houston, I boarded a Greyhound bus. I sat ramrod straight, clutching my handbag, afraid that I would fall asleep and miss something important. My cultural repertoire proved to be sadly deficient; *Gone With the Wind*, Bill Cosby, and pop-locking to American Christian rap at summer camp had not prepared me for the strangeness of transplanted reality. I mentally rifled through my bag of communicative tricks and found nothing useful. Retrospectively, my romantic imagination had probably conjured some image of arriving in America, walking in time to Natasha Bedingfield's "Unwritten." I must have looked really pathetic, because a man nearby offered me a sympathetic smile and a round, red candy. I accepted, attempting to forge an expression of gratitude that would simultaneously discourage further interaction. I popped the candy into my mouth, expecting an explosion of artificial, cherry-like sweetness. Instead, the overpowering taste of cinnamon spread down my tongue, and I spat out the candy when he wasn't looking. Focusing on the road, I stilled my anxiety-ridden thoughts by counting the number of pickup trucks, a considerable task in Texas. After a horrifying 10 hours, I reached my destination and almost burst into tears when I saw my sister's smiling face through the window. My notions of my own intercultural competence and redefining myself "by myself" had been drastically altered.

INTERCULTURAL COMMUNICATION: "DO YOU REALLY KNOW?"

Popular culture functions as a resource in shared meaning making. Being able to laugh at Chuck Norris and Mr. T. jokes, and chime in on humorous banter about *Coming to America* with African American friends was like balm to my foreign soul. I noticed stylistic parallels between *makossa* and salsa, similarities between Nigerian pidgin and Jamaican patwa, and that my Indian friends also called their elders auntie and uncle out of respect. Conversations with Mexican friends clarified why the family-centered plots and intrigues in telenovelas such as *Rosa Salvaje* and *Los Ricos También Lloran* had resonated so strongly with the Nigerian audience in the '90s.

However, popular culture can constrain intercultural communication and understanding as much as it enables them. When we take popular culture to be reality rather than representation, the result is an "illusion of knowing." I recall my fledgling days with both mirth and embarrassment. I thought I was culturally "plugged in" because I had watched some movies, music videos, and documentaries, and taken special pains to be friends with an American exchange student at my secondary school. I was summarily knocked off my high horse with every awkward silence caused by my brash comments. I avoided feelings of inadequacy by retreating into schoolwork, which caused my grades to soar and my spirits to plummet. It took an embarrassingly long time to realize that the poorly formed schemas, stereotypes, assumptions, and expectations I had woven out of my encounters with American popular culture were insufficient and bordering on ridiculous. Much of what "we think we know" about people, places, and ideas is obtained and confirmed by popular culture. Invariably, this finds its way into our evaluations of others and communicative choices. Do we announce to friends and family that we are "sponsoring" an international student from a "Third-World country" when all we did was volunteer to host the student during a holiday? Do we congratulate fathers for caring for their children and judge mothers for postpartum depression? Do we jump to the conclusion that religious friends are stuffing their beliefs down our throats when all they did was make a reference to God? Do we constantly push a friend who is a stay-at-home mother to pursue a vocation, assuming that she must be repressed and unfulfilled? Encounters with others through the mass-mediated space of popular culture are helpful but not a substitute for genuine conversations, relationship building, and self-reflexivity about our positionality.

DISRUPTION OF CULTURAL IDENTITY: TO RESIST OR NOT TO RESIST

The misconceptions we adopt about others can be disruptive to their sense of self because identity encompasses not only how we see ourselves but how others see us. I have encountered many strange misconstructions of my "Africanness." One is particularly humorous.

"What were you thinking!?"

"What do you mean?" I was baffled.

"How could you tell your whole class that you have malaria?!"

My decision to speak had been motivated by my mounting frustration with the negative valence of discourse about African countries in Western popular culture. I often felt conflicted, wanting to use my voice to "sound the alarm" on social issues. Still, I felt the need to resist the dominant discourse and prove that there was more to Africa than war and suffering—that it was full of funny, intelligent, and *unique* people, not homogenous masses of nameless, faceless victims who all seemed to live in a jungle or desert. Weary of hearing Africans talked about like cultural specimens, I offered a redress. I argued that the framing of malaria in our textbook was incomplete and endeavored to explain how malaria reoccurs after periods of dormancy. I also mentioned that I had had malaria several times. I never imagined my spirited attempt to rip the veil of victimhood would incite concern about my "disease" and that my friend would hear about it from a coworker.

"You can't say things like that. People won't understand."

I was perplexed at his irritation and intrigued by how quickly my identity had become attached to malaria. I wasn't "living" with malaria, in the same way that you don't live with influenza.

I was often surprised at how little my classmates and friends knew about my country, assuming that they had grown up immersed in my culture as I had in theirs. I still remember my after-school cartoon lineup: Jim Henson's *Muppet Babies*, *Sesame Street*, *Battle of the Planets*, and *Voltron*. I rapped along to the theme music for *The Fresh Prince of Bel-Air* and laughed with my family at the shenanigans of Sheneneh on *Martin*. My heart broke when Atreyu's horse was sucked into a bog in *The Never Ending Story*, and I idolized Boyz II Men and Mariah Carey so much that I spent hours in my room trying to sing *exactly* like them. On the flip side, few Americans grow up idolizing Nigerian pop stars or watching Nigerian shows. I must admit that I was often impatient, defensive, and hurt by what I interpreted as dismissiveness. How could an educated person possibly think that Africa is a country? While our globalized world is characterized by "rapidly developing interconnections and interdependencies" (Tomlinson, 2007, p. 352), these interconnections are still quite asymmetric, reflecting contemporary and historical global power dynamics. Colonial discourses about "Third-World" backwardness still linger, drowning out the diversity of experience in various locales. Hence, people from stigmatized parts of the world sometimes find themselves caught in a double bind: Speak (and be shoved even further into a neocolonialist box) or remain silent.

HYBRID TRANSNATIONAL IDENTITIES: CONVERGE OR DIVERGE

Cultural identity transcends continental, national, and regional boundaries. In the context of globalization, it is a colorful tapestry of transnational experiences and interactions. Initially, I found this distressing, not wanting to admit that in many ways I was becoming Americanized. My accent is currently an odd mix of Lagos swag, Texas twang, and, as one of my students pointed out, "Valley girl." On a recent trip home, my accent thickened as soon as I touched down in Lagos and stayed thick for a week after my return to the United States, much to the amusement of a dear friend.

"So wott haaz beeeeen happooning?"

"Wow . . ."

"Wott?"

"You sound all . . . African! I haven't heard this Chigozirim before." She started laughing her head off at my expense.

"Wotteva," I retorted, suddenly conscious of every syllable and stressed consonant.

I tried to hold on to the accent for as long as possible, remembering times when I was just "Chigozirim-Ifedapo-Igbo-Yoruba-Nigerian-Utah." It eventually slipped away, reappearing as always in conversations with other Nigerians and in bursts of road rage. I have come to accept the strangeness of the transnational experience, and I enjoy the rich texture of contemporary popular culture. Still, I am among those who worry that the culture of my country will be swept away by the agendas of powerful culture industries. I feel complicit and ashamed because I know more Spanish than my native tongue. I often marvel at the lilting musicality of Hausa, the richness of Yoruba, and the phonetic assertiveness of Igbo, wishing I could be a part of it—wishing that the number of Nigerian children who do not speak their ethnic tongue wasn't increasing.

However, in the past decade, there has been a resurgence of national pride and identification. Nigerian pop and hip-hop are often a mix of Nigerian languages, Pidgin, and English. Nollywood movies have continued to incorporate locally relevant themes such as family life and spirituality into their plots. Nigerian fashion designers have reached back in time, celebrating and modernizing traditional vintage styles such as *oleku*. National and regional media have gained a stronger foothold, reflecting the patterns Jeremy Tunstall (2008) highlights in *The Media Were American: U.S. Mass Media in Decline*. It has been wonderful to hear more Nigerian artists on Nigerian radio, and there is an increased acceptance of the arts as a legitimate career path.

The hybridization of Nigerian popular culture holds many possibilities for achieving shared meaning on the global scale and provides a sense of comfort that all is not lost. In this sense, hybridization can be interpreted not as a sullying of cultural purity but as a form of resistance against complete domination (Hegde, 2002). Nevertheless, I am wary of the increased commodification of the "young, rich, and fabulous" Nigerian in lifestyle magazines, blogs, fashion, movies, hip-hop, and advertising that in many ways has fostered the growth of celebrity culture and the entertainment elite. Popular culture always reflects the interests of its producer and, as such, should not be romanticized but scrutinized.

CONCLUSION

Considering intercultural communication in the global context sensitizes us to the complex systems of meaning that impact our communication daily. In the fragmented space of global popular culture, our identities are shaped and reshaped as we communicate across difference and make decisions to resist and comply, diverge and converge. By my sophomore year, my culture shock was more or less resolved. I discovered a diverse student body, a thriving international student community, and American students who battled with similar feelings of displacement. I got involved not out of a conscious effort to be "multicultural" but from a genuine interest in the struggles of others. Defensiveness and sarcastic rejoinders gave way to a passion for educating others about my culture. As I opened my heart to others, endless novelties and surprises were an everyday reality. I also encountered distressing differences that I had to learn to navigate, not by ignoring their existence but by learning how to have honest conversations that honored the humanity of others.

I remember with fondness one of my first college instructors. She was kind and tolerant of the fact that I contributed a little too much in class. My education in Nigeria had been rather "top-down," so I became overly excited at the opportunity to engage in intellectual discourse. One day, we were asked where people go to talk about their emotional problems.

"An agony aunt."

"A what?"

"Aah-go-nee anntt."

"Can you say that again?"

"AGONY AUNT! AGONY AUNT!"

"I'm sorry, I don't understand."

Embarrassed, I gave up, and I wish I hadn't. Intercultural communication can be messy, requiring a certain measure of vulnerability and a willingness to take risks. Embrace the awkwardness! We live in exciting times where the opportunity to learn about others is limitless. Yet we are often so afraid of looking foolish that we miss opportunities to genuinely engage. This is why college campuses are paradoxically some of the most diverse *and* segregated places on earth. Never underestimate the value of trying out new cuisine or dress, attending international student showcases at your university, or reading the celebrated literature of another culture.

Culture industries are making an attempt to acknowledge a wider range of human experience, and **diversity** is the buzzword of the century. Hypocritically, I have consumed certain types of popular culture and attended certain events to prove how multicultural I am while still remaining unwilling to shatter the limits of my comfort zone. It is rather like keeping a minority friend around to prove that you aren't racist or blasting Lil' Wayne from your car stereo to show that you're "down." Is the move toward diversity and **multiculturalism** producing more openness and compassion, or are we hiding behind it? Have we conflated the consumption of certain types of popular culture with progressiveness? Do we automatically think of Lady Gaga fans as more open-minded? Would your "openness" to another person change if he or she watched only MSNBC or Fox News? Popular culture is now an undeniable part of our everyday meaning making, and being savvy about the conclusions we draw from it is a crucial part of intercultural competence in the global context.

KEY TERMS

ambivalence 209

cultural
hegemony 208

diversity 225

hybrid cultural
identities 209

hybridity 209

mediascapes 208

multiculturalism 225

pop-culture nation 206

popular culture 206

transnational
identities 213

DISCUSSION QUESTIONS

1. Malhotra's case study highlights changing gender norms, roles, and expectations, particularly for women, in India over the past 20 years as a result of consumption of Western media. Identify the changes as outlined in the case study, and compare these with changes in gender roles/expectations in the United States and at least one other country.

2. Define *cultural hegemony* in your own words. Based on Malhotra's case study and your personal experience, provide examples of cultural hegemony. What is the impact of cultural hegemony, and how can it be resisted and challenged?

3. Utah's personal narrative addresses the junctures, struggles, and contestations of global pop culture—what she calls *pop-culture nation*. Using examples from Utah and your personal experience, discuss the impact of pop-culture nation on cultural identities and intercultural communication.

4. Malhotra uses terms and phrases such *hybridity*, *hybrid cultural identities*, and *hybrid subjectivities*, and Utah echoes with *transnational hybrid identities* and *hybridization of popular culture*. Discuss common ideas represented by these terms/phrases, as well as the nuanced variations among them. How are these terms particularly indicative of the constraints and possibilities of globalization?

NOTES

1. All interviews conducted by Sheena Malhotra in Bangalore, India, June 1993.
   Focus Group 1: Mixed-sex focus-group interviews conducted at St. Joseph's College
   Focus Group 2: Women-only focus-group interviews conducted at Mount Carmel College
   Focus Group 3: Mixed-sex focus-group interviews conducted at St. Joseph's College
   Focus Group 4: Women-only focus-group interviews conducted at Mount Carmel College
2. All interviews conducted by Sheena Malhotra in Bangalore, India, January 2011.
   Focus Group 1: Women-only focus-group interviews conducted with participants invited through personal networks
   Focus Groups 2 and 3: Men-only focus-group interviews conducted at St. Joseph's College
   Focus Groups 4, 5, and 6: Women-only focus-group interviews conducted at Mount Carmel College

CHAPTER 12

New Media in the Global Context

N *ew media* is a term that broadly refers to modes of communication characterized by advanced technologies, real-time communication, and accompanying shifts in the methods of media production, distribution, and consumption. New media entail the combination of technological devices (e.g., cell phones, tablets, personal computers), virtual platforms (e.g., Google, Facebook, Twitter, YouTube), and digital content (e.g., websites, blogs, tweets, videos). The term is used in contrast to "traditional" or "old" media, such as newspapers, TV, radio, magazines, books, and landline telephones, which largely maintained divisions between media producers and consumers and were restricted by physical and temporal boundaries. The use of digital technology allows us to overcome barriers of time and space, accelerating the process of cultural, economic, and political globalization.

The ubiquitous presence of new media today—can you imagine the time before Google?—has many implications for intercultural communication in the globalized world. New media allow for greater flexibility and interactivity between groups of people beyond physical and temporal boundaries. The real-time, simultaneous communication facilitates interaction with those who are physically distant, and online communities create opportunities for more intercultural contact in virtual space. Additionally, the rise of social media—such as Facebook, Twitter, and Instagram—points to new media's democratizing potential to facilitate a global exchange of ideas and to challenge media monopolies. Those with access to cell phones and the Internet can now directly broadcast their voices to a global audience, as seen in many social movements in the Middle East and around the world. At the same time, the disclosure by Edward Snowden in 2013 of classified material on the National Security Agency's surveillance program revealed the precariousness of digital communication as a platform for free speech and democracy. Thus, it is important to carefully examine how our global network society reflects, challenges, and/or reinforces historically constituted relations of power shaped by global capitalism and Western hegemony.

The entries in this chapter focus primarily on the role of social media in mediating **popular culture** in transnational contexts. In her case study, Nickesia S. Gordon analyzes how Jamaican popular culture is consumed and commodified by global audiences via social media. In the personal narrative, Rubén Ramírez-Sánchez traces the development of the punk movement in Puerto Rico since the early days of social media on Myspace. Both Gordon and Ramírez-Sánchez raise critical questions regarding the possibilities and limitations of social change and cultural emancipation in the global network society.

Reggae 3.0: Social Media and the Consumption of Jamaican Popular Culture

Nickesia S. Gordon

Barry University, Florida

T he consumption of global popular culture has been radically influenced by the emergence of new media technology, specifically, social media platforms such as Facebook, YouTube, and Twitter, among myriad others. Over the past 2 years, social media usage has experienced a meteoric rise among our global citizenry. In the United States alone, usage of social media has increased 30% since the third quarter of 2010, and in 10 major global markets, social networks and blogs reach more than three quarters of active Internet users (Nielsen, 2012). Globally, social media websites and blogs are the top online destinations for Internet users as well. These trends are strong indicators of social media's popularity and potential role as a purveyor of global culture. How are models of communication, particularly intercultural and mass communication, responding to these developments?

Media Studies 2.0, a reference to the study of post–broadcast-era digital media, offered theoretical responses to such questions. Studies described a new, converging media environment that was multidirectional (Gross, 2009), where the audience was increasingly autonomous (Bird, 2011). Scholars emphasized the interactive nature of new media platforms and the resulting position of audience members as producers of content. Media Studies 2.0 proposed that the masses reigned supreme in the definition and articulation of popular culture. The public, as opposed to media institutions, had control over meaning making and cultural production. However, as Miller (2009) points out, there was limited scholarship on the cultural politics associated with these developments. Not only did "faith in the active audience reach cosmic proportions" (p. 6), but important issues such as labor, production, class, race, gender, sexualities, and identities across national lines were discounted.

Using an intersectional and global perspective, Miller proposes a more critical approach to address cultural production through new communication web technologies. This framework is **Media Studies 3.0**, a perspective that acknowledges the political, economic, and cultural milieu in which "new" media emerge and are shaped. A theoretical position conscious of global inequities that often accompany technological advancements, Media Studies 3.0 also takes into consideration the context of globalization in which the "historical legacy of colonization, Western domination, and U.S. hegemony . . . continues to shape intercultural relations" (Sorrells, 2013, p. 32). Media Studies 3.0 attends to the politics of subjectivities, the glocal contexts, and the growing sociopolitical and economic inequities ushered in by powerful multinational corporations and global financial institutions.

This essay investigates the social and cultural meanings attached to Jamaican popular culture as it is consumed by global audiences via social media, using the critical lens offered by Media Studies 3.0. While Jamaica represents a key area of global cultural production, from the arena of sports to music, the country's influence on global popular culture receives little academic attention in global media and intercultural studies. In this case study, I examine how new notions of citizenship, national identity, gender, and class are evolving diasporically as a result of interactive media use among global citizenry. I also explore the power dynamics that shape consumption and argue that an element of exploitation driven by free trade characterizes consumption. As Sorrells (2013) aptly points out, the current forces of globalization position culture as a commodity to be traded in the global marketplace. Social media present an ideal venue for this marketization of culture. A brief description of what Jamaican popular culture entails now ensues.

JAMAICAN POPULAR CULTURE

For the purposes of this essay, I describe Jamaican popular culture as the practices, norms, artifacts, and ways of being consumed and produced by the Jamaican masses, often as counterculture. I term these practices **counterculture** because such expressions are often oppositional to established cultural norms, which are rooted in the European aesthetics of Jamaica's former colonizer, Great Britain. Key elements or markers of Jamaican popular culture include but are not limited to Jamaican vernacular, popular musical genres of reggae and dancehall, dancehall culture, the theoretics of Rastafari, the spoken-word or oral culture, as well as popular theatre. However, given the roles of dancehall and dancehall culture as prominent markers of Jamaican popular culture (Cooper & Donnell, 2004; Hope, 2006, 2010), specific attention will be paid to these in my examination of how Jamaican popular culture is consumed via social media. Dancehall, a particular brand of popular music derived from a cross-fertilization of various other musical forms such as ska, mento, and reggae, among others, is a controversial, yet celebrated part of Jamaican popular culture. It is often characterized by "slackness," given its "sexually explicit lyrics, performances, and dance routines that outrage the middle class and the older generation" (Mordecai & Mordecai, 2001, p. 151). Subsequently, like other elements of Jamaican cultural expression, dancehall and the behaviors it spawns operate within the milieu of tensions between Jamaica's African heritage and European colonial influence. The Jamaican cultural landscape is characterized by ambivalence as a result of the two competing value systems rooted in the country's African heritage and the values of the European ex-colonizers. Racist social systems developed under plantation slavery that legitimized the subjugation of Africans brought to the colonies created a stratified social system based on the devaluation of African culture and the privileging of Europeanism (Shepherd, 1986).

This stratification remains deeply embedded in Jamaica's social relations and is a source of cultural tensions among different groups. For example, the social categories of *uptown* and *downtown* are used to describe where one "belongs" in Jamaican society. These are social status markers, *uptown* being associated with more elite, Eurocentric, and "refined" tastes, and *downtown* being connected with "ghetto," Afrocentric, and coarse aesthetics. This cultural dichotomy is expressed in popular culture in multiple ways, and the musical genre is heavily associated with low culture and vulgarity. Language or, more precisely, vernacular communication styles, both oral and nonverbal, are also deeply associated with Jamaican popular culture as well as dancehall. Many scholars recognize the "word" as a pivotal element of this culture; "word" here refers to the local language, also known as patois or patwa in Jamaican parlance. From the musical stylings of local artists to the everyday iterations among ordinary folk, this language constitutes a critical element of dancehall cultural production. It sometimes borrows from the lexicon of Rastafari, which, over time, has produced a glossary of subversive language that is now inextricably linked to local discursive practices. Nonverbal communication involves a world of gestures and bodily significations that accompany oral expressions, which together coalesce to produce highly performative and rebellious renditions of Jamaican popular culture.

These cultural practices and meanings inform the discussion and analysis of new media and consumption of Jamaican popular culture in this case study. These key markers—namely, dancehall, dancehall culture, and local language—are used to generate web searches as well as to identify and analyze relevant texts.

METHODOLOGY

The case study uses an ethnographic approach, specifically, a type of ethnographic methodology called **webnography**. Webnography is a qualitative investigative method that is a form of web-based observation or web ethnography (Puri, 2007). It allows research via online sources such as Internet sites, social media sites, blogs, or other forms of computer-mediated communication. This methodology is particularly suited to my study of how communication practices create meaning and construct identities in the consumption of Jamaican popular culture via social media. According to Puri (2007), web-based communication platforms such as social media are social forums that are living, responsive, and interactive communities filled with insights about those who dwell there.

For data gathering, I used a 3-x-3-x-3 method. I searched the top three social media sites using the phrase "Jamaica and popular culture." The emerging texts were then categorized into three groups: dancehall, reggae, and Jamaican English. These categories were created based on the available scholarly literature on Jamaican popular culture that identified them as key elements of Jamaican popular culture. At the time of this study, Facebook, Twitter, and YouTube were among the top four social media sites visited globally. They ranked first, second, and fourth respectively. LinkedIn ranked third ahead of YouTube; however, since LinkedIn is oriented toward social *networking* and not *media*, Facebook, Twitter, and YouTube were the top three social media sites used for this case study.

The top 25 texts appearing in each category on each website were selected for analysis, making the total number of texts examined 225. These texts were reviewed over the period of a month, with the researcher doing weekly searches using the identified categories. The texts that recurred with the highest frequency over the month were then selected for analysis. Two themes emerged: transnational subjectivities and hyperrealized gender performances. A discussion of these themes follows.

WHO IS JAMAICAN? TRANSNATIONAL SUBJECTIVITIES IN SOCIAL MEDIA SPACES

Transnational subjectivities refer to identity formations that transcend geographic and cultural borders, thereby disrupting the physical and social spaces within which identities are traditionally constructed and negotiated. Theoretically, the concept of **transnationalism** is characterized by migration, border crossings, and hybridities, which are traditionally associated with geographies of physical space and the mobility of people and cultures across nations. However, an era of globalization fueled by the ubiquity of new communication technologies such as social media has collapsed physical geographic boundaries and given way to new conceptualizations of transnational identities. As Sorrells (2013) asserts, media—and in this instance, social media and popular culture—forge hybrid transnational cultural identities in a global context by recollecting **diasporic identities** as well as constructing a global semiculture. Migration is no longer a given precursor to constructing transnational identities, as members of online communities do not have to cross borders to inhabit the space of the other. Subsequently, subjectivities are constructed based on access to and ability to perform the cultural practices and norms of a given locale, giving rise to hybrid cultural forms and identities.

In the case of Jamaica, social media seem to reinforce multifaceted subjectivity formations by fostering an atmosphere of belonging among users. Through a process of *relating* (to Jamaican cultural norms and practices in social media spaces) and *performing* (the expected cultural behaviors), a transnational Jamaican subjectivity can be established online as users reproduce and emulate Jamaican cultural practices in the context of globalized social media. However, social media platforms are spaces where identities are not only cultivated but also contested. Issues of authenticity arise as a strong diasporic perspective characterizes relations online. A diasporic/transnational dichotomy thus develops, as Wulfhorst and Vianna (2012) recognized in their study of the Brazilian art form capoeira as a transnational force. Subsequently, the question of who is Jamaican becomes important, as indicated by the comments below:

> [M]e wonda how many people demma preten' to be a jamaican inna de house when dey comment - like i jus' did? (YouTube post, 2011)

> like how funny is a white boy speaking jamaican english with no apparent explanation (Tweet, May 24, 2013)

The comments above point to certain transnational practices apparent among users of the social media platforms to which they belong. The first is a response to a chain of comments addressing the Jamaican-ness of the page owner, whose authenticity was questioned because of her strong British accent. The "foreign" inflections that tainted her Jamaican accent made her suspect among other proclaimed Jamaicans who visited the page. The second comment is a tweet from a Caucasian Twitter user who has a self-proclaimed Jamaican accent. The tweet expresses a certain universalism regarding the Jamaican accent—that is, that one shouldn't be surprised that just about anyone, even a "white boy," can sound and potentially be Jamaican. While his outward appearance may be at odds with what a typical Jamaican might look like, he is able to perform his Jamaican-ness through his ability to vocalize the dialect. If his performance is good, then his authenticity or cultural pureness is not questioned. A hybridized cultural self is thus produced, which is the virtual Jamaican who lives in the global context of social media communities, themselves hybridized cultural spaces because of the active creative processes that unfold as users interact with each other and, in doing so, create cultural overlaps and intersections (Straubhaar, 2008).

On the one hand, these comments reveal the possibilities that social media spaces create for individuals to claim a transnational Jamaican identity. Social media are platforms without borders that mediate intercultural communication while facilitating itinerant and transnational practices that "disrupt national and cultural identities" (Sorrells, 2013, p. 126). On the other hand, the comments also indicate the tensions that exist between the transnational and the diasporic. For the latter, belonging to the Jamaican community is predicated on heritage or origin, and anyone who seemingly violates these criteria is treated with suspicion. I argue that this tension is a microcosm of the cultural tensions that exist offline between mainstream Jamaican culture and popular culture. Popular cultural expressions often counter pro-Victorian/neocolonial aestheticism. They are defiant responses to the oppressive and marginalizing effects of formal culture. As often happens with resistance movements, one needs to be an insider to be trusted. In Jamaica, resistance movements, from the slave rebellions to more recent inner-city protests against perceived social injustices, have always been wary of the "informer" (Johnson, 2011), a person who pretends to be legitimate but is really an agent of the oppressor. Echoes of this distrust are evident in the diasporic perspective that frames some social media exchanges. There is suspicion that those who are performing their Jamaican identities may be trying to usurp and thereby disempower the group or specific social media community that sees itself as "genuinely" Jamaican.

Performance connotes the idea of cultural hybridization and of *passing*. Both processes are facilitated by language, which seems, in the case of these virtual exchanges, to "reterritorialize" (Sorrells, 2013, p. 93) what it means to be Jamaican. Language, as it is used on social media, does not seem to *sustain* one's own sense of identity and belonging but to *create* virtual selves that in turn participate in a process of consumption. There is a recurring idea across the social media sites examined that if one can *sound* Jamaican—that is, speak patwa and have a Jamaican accent—then one can make claims of *being* Jamaican. As previously stated, who is Jamaican (or not) is not established based on any physical belonging or occupancy of Jamaica the place. Instead, Jamaican-ness is assumed based on one's ability to sound, act, or otherwise appear to have any of the cultural trappings associated with Jamaican popular culture. This makes it almost impossible to discern who is physically from Jamaica the *place* and who is from Jamaica the social media *space*. The following posts from YouTube allude to this inability to distinguish between the two categories. They are responses from a chain of comments referring to the work of Jamaican folk culture icon the Honorable Louise Bennett Coverly:

- Miss Lou...you are surely missed, no one can replace you. Proud to be JAMAICAN.

- Our language is truly rich........

- YES MI DEAR

- loooooool - gwarrrrn Miss Lou

- Miss Lou tell dem ina Jamaican style. Yuh big bowt ya.

- it nuh go so... ehh jamaica DERIVE lol

- This is BE-A-U-TI-FUL!!!!!! omg NUFF RESPECT!- Appreciate Jamaican Patwa!!

- bem bem....Jamaican patois sell off...bunununu. (YouTube posts, 2011)

Given that Jamaican English is an oral language, there is no uniform way to write it. However, some words are spelled with a fair amount of consistency—for example, *dem*, which means *them*, or *mi*, which means *me* or *my*. As a result of these linguistic trends, the fourth comment from the list stands out from the others because of the word "gwarrrrn," which is meant to represent *gwaan*, a Jamaican word that translates to "go on." This variation suggests that this iteration may be the writer's attempt at *sounding* Jamaican. The iteration is therefore performative. Nonetheless, without personal knowledge of the dialect, one would not be able to detect this "inauthentic" performance. The writer therefore easily *passes* as being Jamaican on social media, an act that would be much more difficult to accomplish in a face-to-face interaction. The examples used above illustrate how language use can blur identity distinctions on social media platforms. This blurring process facilitates cultural consumption through the performance it engenders.

Acts of passing complicate notions of cultural authenticity and "ownership" of cultural productions. Inherent in this complication are questions of legitimacy as well as exploitation. Who has cultural rights over Jamaican popular expressions, and who has rights to benefit from such expressions? Can anyone really claim such rights in spaces as fluid and creatively amorphous as social media? As Toby Miller (2010) argues, in such a situation, "an account of the conditions under which culture is made, circulated, received, interpreted, and criticized" (p. 44) must be considered. The market economy constitutes the conditions under which what passes as Jamaican popular culture online is produced. It is circulated and received by those who have access to the Internet, many of whom are not the original creators or cultural actors. The producers or developers of cultural content on social media are not necessarily the ones who benefit from its consumption online. As a result, *passing,* or performing a Jamaican cultural identity online contributes to economic exploitation in that the act of passing supplants original authorship. The original creators of culture get written out of any economic exchange that may occur online, as a result of the political economy that governs the Internet.

Identity performances are also evident in posts that relate to dancehall. In these instances, gestures and bodily significations facilitate the porosity of Jamaican cultural identities as performed online. For example, a classic marker of dancehall culture is the ability to "whine," a sexual dance move that involves intense pelvic rotations and has given birth to several dancehall competitions. The Dancehall Queen competition is the most famous of these competitions. In many of the YouTube videos, the subject's ability to perform like a dancehall queen was sufficient qualification for claiming a Jamaican cultural identity and winning the coveted title. Many non-Jamaicans have emerged as winners of

Dancehall Queen competitions, much to the dissatisfaction of many from the Jamaican community:

- HOW CAN YOU WIN A DANCEHALL QUEEN TITLE and CANT WHINE?

- This was horrible! Omg! I am Jamaican and I am embarrassed. This is not dancehall.

- This is a DANCEhall queen competition......or a gymnastics competition? (YouTube post, September 2012)

While these comments question the authenticity of the performances, they are Jamaican enough to pass as the "real thing" in the larger global context in which they occur. The Dancehall Queen competition, once a uniquely local Jamaican cultural expression, is now a cultural commodity traded in the global marketplace, revealing the link between intercultural communication and capitalism. Sorrells (2013) references this connection when she states,

> Today, cultural experiences—from music, cuisine, arts, and sports to religious holidays, weddings, bar mitzvahs, and funerals, as well as cities and communities—are commodified. The **commodification of culture** refers to the ways cultural experiences—local practices, festivals, arts, rituals, and even groups—are produced and consumed for the market. (p. 189)

Dancehall Queen competitions have now become huge business endeavors that produce tremendous financial gain for the organizers and winners. Ironically, many of these events featured on YouTube are held in Europe, the United States, and Japan, not in Jamaica where the competition originated. Thus, the country of origin receives little or none of the economic benefits derived from the trading of its own cultural form, an outcome that reveals the exploitative nature of this global consumption. The fact that anyone can be anything via social media has not been lost on marketers, who use the seamlessness afforded by social media to capitalize on Jamaican cultural products for profit, thereby marking transnationalism as decidedly hegemonic in nature. Additionally, the potential economic empowerment and sociopolitical resistance that Cooper (2004) sees accruing from these cultural productions become ineffective under such conditions. In general, dancehall and its cultural accoutrements, which challenge certain hegemonic practices offline in Jamaican society, lose that power in the online market economy.

HYPERREALIZED GENDER PERFORMANCES

Hyperreality refers to the distortion of mediated experience and reality. It is associated with "the effects of mass culture reproduction, suggesting that an object, event, experience so reproduced replaces or is preferred to its original: that the copy is 'more real than real'" (Brooker, 1999, para. 1). Social media, as arenas of mass cultural production and *re*production, are perfect spaces for hyperreal experiences and events to unfold. The "real" or original gets copied (as in the case of passing discussed in the previous section), interpreted, and reinterpreted (a condition of consumption), and eventually becomes that which is taken for the actual experience or event. In other words, reproduced performances are taken for reality. Such mediated experiences of Jamaican popular culture are evident in consumption practices observed in social media spaces, especially as they relate to gender constructs.

Hyperrealism is manifest in two ways. First, Jamaican gender norms, which are grounded in neocolonial values, are challenged by the social media representations that are steeped in dancehall culture. Masculine and feminine identity constructs online focus heavily on sex and sexuality, which is in keeping with the oppositional nature of dancehall's delineation of gender relations. Masculinities pivot around "conquering" the *punany,* or female genitalia, while female identities center on having the best body (Hope, 2006). However, while these depictions offer counterculture possibilities, they remain problematic. These performances are prone to gender stereotypes that are disempowering given dancehall's heavy reliance on sexuality to establish gender identities; additionally, they tend to reinforce the idea that all sexual identities are heterosexual in nature. Men remain dominant sexual conquerors, while women are construed as the sexualized other and objects of a masculine gaze.

YouTube videos featuring scenes from local Jamaican dancehall events are readily available. In these videos, men invariably appear in dominant sexual positions, usually feigning penetration of the female body. Concurrently, comments posted about such videos, such as "wsh i could grind d ladies on latex" (YouTube post, February 2011) and other more explicit ones, tend to be voyeuristic and further objectify women. They are an extension of the gaze that metaphorically penetrates and therefore dominates the female body, as may be deduced from this other comment: "the chick with the green shorts though? I wanna hit that NOW!!!!! Lol" (YouTube post, October 2012). As such representations of gender identities are copied, interpreted, and reproduced online, these problematic performances are assumed to reflect male/female relationships, an issue addressed by the following comment: "not all black people dance like this fools just for the record" (YouTube post, February 2012). This copy or hyperreal version of masculine/feminine relations becomes the dominant representation and is often mistakenly assumed to be the way men and women typically relate to each other culturally in Jamaica—that is to say, in purely sexual ways. This takes me to the second way hyperrealism operates on these social media sites.

Performances observed in video texts, particularly those on YouTube, are often produced in response to the presence of the video camera. This is what Hope (2006) refers to as the "video light" syndrome, wherein actors within dancehall spaces perform acts deliberately for the camera. In this sense, the gender performances enacted are no longer just metaphorical in nature but are quite literal; that is, one is acting for the camera and for an audience. The video texts then become hyperreal copies of dancehall events that are mass-produced and circulated on social media sites as the "real" thing. Take this comment for example: "i love everythings am seen in d web site" (YouTube post, October 2012). This comment was made in response to a video depicting a dancehall event in Jamaica. The observer does not, and perhaps cannot, distinguish between a hyperreal act, exaggerated for the camera and for global consumption, and what constitutes actual local practices. The concern regarding this inability to distinguish between the online and offline worlds is that it potentially leads to or reinforces existing stereotypes about Jamaica, Jamaicans, and black bodies in general—for example, that such spaces, people, and bodies are naturally promiscuous, vulgar, and hypersexual (Gordon, 2012).

One may argue that social media, given the alleged democratic nature of these platforms, present sites where representations of gender are negotiated and contested. Marginalized groups can use social media platforms to create alternative or counterimages that are more empowering. YouTube comments suggest that the women from these videos do wield their sexual power in a postfeminist way:

- this is called let loose and enjoy yourself..don't hate (YouTube post, October 2012)

- how can i get that flexible????? (YouTube post, June 2013)

- Mi na tell nuh lie, but Aneika, Pattan and Sher starrrrrrr the show. Them baddddddddddd!!!!!!! [I'm not lying, but Aneika, Pattan and Sher are the stars of the show. They are awesome!] (YouTube post, April 2013)

The comments were all made by female users expressing their admiration and appreciation of or desire to be like the women they observe in the videos. They also allude to the rhetoric of choice that permeates postfeminist discourses. Postfeminism embodies the politics of individual freedom and personal choice in which women can exert their sexual power, economic independence, and consumer savvy. Accordingly, it may be read that the women from the videos, as well as the female commentators excerpted above, are *choosing* to participate in these sexual ways and are therefore empowered through this agency. For example, the Dancehall Queen contests give participants an opportunity to benefit economically from their sexuality. Cooper (1993) has long asserted that spaces of popular cultural performance such as the dancehall offer women potential economic and social empowerment. In this regard, the participation of women in the production of popular culture resonates with postfeminism.

However, while the women are producers of these cultural products, they are at the same time being voraciously consumed via social media spaces. Social media replicate the politics of consumption that govern capitalism and cultural globalization by providing platforms that encourage participants to consume and corporations to profit from this consumption. Do the women featured on these sites, especially in the videos, realize the economic benefit that is accruing to the entertainment and advertising industries at their expense? Many of the dancehall videos and texts are accompanied by paid advertisements that appear before a video begins.

Many of their comments and images are also appropriated and used as promotional material by business operators, such as the promoter of the event noted in the screenshot below, who use the event and therefore the actors in the video to promote their career and business:

CodeRed (founder of TrendSetter Tv.com – TrendSetterRadio.com & Radio Personality for Big City 101.3 FM Boston) HAS BEEN NOMINATED FOR 2 **BOSTON MOST ELITE AWARDS** "VIDEO MAN OF THE YEAR" & BEST WEEKLY RADIO STATION SHOW (The Snack Show Show Big City 101.3)" IN BOSTON & NEEDS YOUR VOTE – VOTING ENDS SOON SO PLEASE VOTE TODAY!!!

Voting Choice #25 VIDEO MAN OF THE YEAR (CodeRed)

Voting Choice #30 BEST WEEKLY RADIO STATION SHOW (The Snack Shop Show)

Performers in the text therefore become laborers in a virtual marketplace, providing the cultural goods that are traded but for which they earn no income. Consequently, their post-feminist identities are thrown into question by these exploitative practices. Does participation in the global exchange of highly sexualized representations of women constitute a postfeminist, postmodern self? Or does it contribute to what Douglas (in Lee & Wen, 2009) refers to as new sexism, which further facilitates female objectification and enables the exploitation of women "within dominant modes of production" (Kuhn, 1994, p. 4).

Another key element of this dominant mode of production is embedded in the legacy of colonialism, which originally marked black bodies for consumption—sexual and otherwise. The Caribbean has historically been depicted as a space where visitors can expect sand, sun, and sex. "Island" culture, since the era of colonialism, has been constructed as pleasure giving and accommodating (Milne, 2001), a plantation where women are there for the taking and men are virile studs waiting to perform (Gordon, 2012). In this sense, not just female bodies are objectified for consumption but male bodies as well. Caribbean bodies in general are construed as oversexualized and powerful symbols of exoticism and otherness (Sardar, 1999), and in hyperreal spaces, such representations construct misleading and inaccurate notions of truth. Further, on social media, black Caribbean masculinities are solidified and stereotyped according to hypersexual, heterosexual norms. The videos posted present Jamaican male bodies as inherently heterosexual and sometimes even naturally homophobic (Gordon, 2012). Such readings place obvious limitations, such as the preclusion of homosexual identities, on the identities of these men in the global community.

CONCLUSION

The ways Jamaican popular culture is being consumed via the social media spaces examined underscores how technologies are not neutral but are always the products of historical, political, and social relations (Clegg, Hudson, & Steele, 2010). They are inscribed by the geographies of power that shape global social and cultural relations, as well as the gendered, diasporic, and aesthetic dynamics that accompany their proliferation. Cultural globalization via new media suggests an alternative form of cultural imperialism wherein local cultures are homogenized for global consumption. Cultural globalization is at once an economic process as well as a political one, where the marketization of world cultures depends on unequal political and economic structures that reformulate and repackage cultural forms to make them amenable to trade and consumption. What is most apparent on Facebook, Twitter, and YouTube is that Jamaican popular culture is largely for sale. Many of its cultural forms, from language to music, are co-opted for commercial purposes and turned into exotic goods destined for consumption.

Puerto Rican Punks, Globalization, and New Media: A Personal Account

Rubén Ramírez-Sánchez
University of Puerto Rico, Río Piedras

In 2006, I set out to study punk cultural production in San Juan, Puerto Rico, and the early adoption of social media, in this case Myspace, as a conduit for global cultural exchange. The work had significance, since research on Puerto Rican subcultures had been largely ignored. It was also significant on a personal level: I was part of the early development of that scene, going to shows, playing in bands, and taking part in the reproduction of a movement that was both cultural and ideological. Punk culture has defined how I see myself and society. It served me as "street pedagogy" (Malott & Carroll-Miranda, 2003), a form of education grounded in socially situated knowledge and praxis. While diverse and controversial, punk culture has had a tremendous impact on my perception of social structures by exposing me early on to issues of racial inequality, class oppression, exploitation of the environment, and a flawed capitalist system. As praxis, punk culture has taught me the importance of self-determination, social organization, and activism. In effect, punk has served me more as a philosophy than as a fashion trend or musical genre. Years later, it was this personal investment that led me to consider punk culture as an enlightening object of study. Punk has been widely investigated as a complex subcultural phenomenon, and foci such as style (Hebdige, 1979), race (Ramírez-Sánchez, 2008; Traber, 2001), globalization (O'Connor, 2004), cultural significance (Moore, 2004; Taylor, 2003), and economics (Thompson, 2004) have revealed the contradictory nature of this global subcultural practice. In fact, my own study of Puerto Rican punk became much more than a historical account, since topics such as globalization, **hybridity**, digital technology, and cultural production have become crucial factors in complicating the existence and reproduction of punk.

A BASIC HISTORY OF PUNK

The origins of punk can be traced back to both England and the United States during the early '70s, among mostly white, working-class kids (Azerrad, 2001; Marcus, 1989). The music was raw, the topics were cynically critical, and the style was shocking. As Hebdige (1979) put it, "no subculture has sought with more grim determination than punks to detach itself from the taken-for-granted landscape of normalized forms, nor to bring down upon it such vehement disapproval" (p. 19). Punk quickly became the graphic description of a problematic historical time, marked by international crises, economic downturn, and the articulation of a growing neoliberal ideology.

In the 1980s, kids in U.S. cities were engendering a new punk aesthetic that would go beyond the aesthetics of shock by creating their own punk bands, writing their own fanzines, and producing their own records. Most important, they were engaging in these practices for political reasons, as a rejection of the capitalist system and a form of authenticity (Moore, 2004, p. 307). For many punks, to be "authentic" was to reject a dominant capitalist system not only through aesthetics but also through praxis. Punks were actively taking control of their culture by taking control of their own means of production. The ethics of authenticity became a driving force in the creation of a new paradigm.

However, punk culture, in spite of its oppositional nature, is not an unproblematic social formation. In fact, it would be analytically misleading to generalize a romantic view of punk simply because it represents a practice of resistance. Punk culture holds, as it maintains complex, problematic relationships with class, race, and capitalism. Examining the development of punk culture in Los Angeles in the 1980s, Traber (2001) asserted that it relied on "**self-marginalization**" as a signifier that was central to its philosophy and politics. This phenomenon is deeply problematic insofar as punks, in their symbolic and material appropriation of marginalization—poverty, indigence, abjection—necessarily reinforce a dominant conception about a marginalized other. Many punks, by rejecting suburbia, capitalism, whiteness, and the American Dream, attempt to embrace the conditions in which those most affected by a dominant system—people of color, minorities, the poor, the homeless—must live every day. The paradox is that punk culture has historically been a mostly white, middle-class social formation. Self-marginalization is an *arbitrary* condition that is self-imposed, whereas *real* marginalization is a condition imposed by the system. Self-marginalization necessarily relies on the other's real conditions of marginalization to be fulfilled. While there certainly is a political and liberating potential in punk, punks' relationship to their cultural realities must not be seen unproblematically.

PUNK CULTURE IN PUERTO RICO

Puerto Rican punk culture is both global and local, simultaneously inheriting many of the philosophical assumptions and contradictions of punk and generating its own particularities and complexities. I view globalization as a historical stage of cultural, political, and economic dimensions that is fundamentally supported and enabled by technologies of information and exchange through global networks. By effectively transcending space and time, information technologies have enabled flows of capital, information, technology, images, and symbols (Castells, 2000, p. 442). However, globalization is a context full of contradictions that has not only enabled interconnectedness and access but also wider inequality and exploitation of resources, an "articulated fractioning of the world that reorders differences and inequality, without suppressing them" (García Canclini, 2001, p. 49; translation mine).

The Puerto Rico punk scene is relatively young, emerging in the early '90s. It mostly concentrated in the capital, San Juan, and quickly evolved as a bricolage of post-punk projects, often organizing garage, pop punk, hardcore, trash, electronica, and progressive rock under the umbrella of the "scene," eschewing the level of "specialization" sometimes seen in large-city scenes. In contrast to the punk movement in the United States, which was backed by a strong cultural tradition of rock, punk music and style were never an indigenous form of cultural expression in Puerto Rico, as its sounds and artifacts were quite different from Puerto Rican folklore and traditions.

The Puerto Rico punk movement has evolved under very particular economic determinations, social rules, and geographic constraints. I have observed in the Puerto Rico scene a diversity that is analogous to the racial and class mélange that permeates Puerto Rican society at large. Afro-Caribbean, mulatto, and Hispanic white, as well as lower-, middle-, and upper-class punks were part of the early scene and still make up its cultural composition. A large portion of Puerto Rican punks are urban and technologically savvy, with access to smartphones and computers, and many come from middle- and upper-class backgrounds. Many tensions and contradictions exist, as these identifications become entangled with, and sometimes masked by, the self-marginalizing identifications of punk: anticapitalism, classlessness, and otherness.

Puerto Rican identity is traversed by multiple contradictions stemming from its troubled sociopolitical history and the overarching, complex social problems that arise from its postcolonial condition. This dimension of the Puerto Rican experience has been the object of much debate (see Pabón, 2002, for a critique) and has permeated many aspects of Puerto Rican life. Being a commonwealth of the United States, Puerto Rico showcases an interesting case for foreign capital spending, presenting a middle ground between mainland investment and a free-trade zone. Despite its extremely low per capita income and high unemployment rate, Puerto Rico is an extremely consumerist country (Ortiz-Negrón, 2007), serving as a platform for corporate capital investment that has had consequences in the social fabric. Dozens of American chains compete for retail space in Puerto Rico, spreading throughout the landscape and, in many ways, suffocating national production and innovation. Indeed, corporations and consumerism have blended well in the Puerto Rican psyche, producing a "Puerto Rican nationality" co-opted by corporate brands (see Dávila, 1997). It is against this background that Puerto Rican punks construct their own identities.

Before digital media, the island condition made it difficult for non-mainstream cultural trends such as punk to be detected and more widely assimilated. This resulted in a tightly knit group of punk "nomads," embracing diverse genres and styles and playing different venues every weekend, without a space of their own. Nevertheless, they were able to forge a punk style that represented their subcultural status and differentiated them from mainstream youth culture in the island. While punks in Spain, Mexico, and Argentina have been producing punk in Spanish for decades, Puerto Rican punks did so "against the grain," as *rock en Español* (rock in Spanish) at the time was widely considered an oxymoron by mainstream youth. Today, Puerto Rican punk bands still produce music in Spanish that mostly reflects the social, political, and economic determinations affecting life in Puerto Rico, even as the assemblage that constitutes the Puerto Rican experience is quite complex and difficult.

DIY, NEW MEDIA, AND PUNK INFRASTRUCTURES

Punk has become a movement of global scale, bearing an ideological dimension that continues to resonate with young people all over the world. While analog networks of collaboration have always been at the center of punk culture, the advent of digital technologies has enabled a new stage of production and exchange that allows not only the low-cost self-production of cultural goods but also conduits of distribution that effectively transcend space and time. In this sense, more than international, punk has become a globalized movement that is supported by networks of information, production, and distribution.

Since its early development, punk culture has relied on many tools for constructing cultural networks for the reproduction of punk cultural production and ideology. Early on, it adopted a DIY logic that "championed musical amateurism [and] professed anarchist politics," with bands releasing records on small independent labels (Taylor, 2003, p. 14). This DIY philosophy is still at the core of punk ideology, and the accessibility of new media technologies of reproduction and distribution has made possible the propagation of punk media infrastructures globally.

This is the case for Puerto Rican punks. As an early participant, I witnessed the Puerto Rican scene go from a disorganized, local, yet highly motivated endeavor to a successful global participant that has effectively created media production infrastructures previously nonexistent in the island. This is exemplified the most by Jose Ibañez, founder of the record label Discos de Hoy. His label has been able to navigate the global underground conduits of distribution and exchange, and its bands have managed to connect to the global punk scene, touring throughout Europe, Latin America, the United States, and Japan. The Internet, social media, specialized software, and self-production technologies have been at the center of this transformation.

This has been mostly possible through a jump from low-tech to high-tech. While "old" electronic technologies such as photocopiers and four-track recorders were crucial in the early development of the Puerto Rico scene, digital technologies enabled Puerto Rican punks to transcend the limits of the island and connect to a vibrant global scene. This transition from "old" to "new" media is illustrated by Taína, an early pioneer of the Puerto Rico scene, in one of the earliest Puerto Rican punk fanzines: "As you may have noted, I have a computer now. I'm finally a modern girl! Once I have a phone number, I will have e-mail. For the time being, we will continue using the human mail" (Rosa, 1998, n.p.).

If Taína helped build the foundations of the scene through fanzines and pen-palling, then Jose and Discos de Hoy took the scene to the digital age. It was the increasing adoption of digital media, and the advent of new media such as social networks, sharing media, and self-production hardware and software that enabled Discos de Hoy to build global networks of collaboration, distribution, and exchange. For Discos de Hoy, the availability of computers, DIY recording hardware and software such as AudioBox and GarageBand, and the Internet paved the way for the globalization of punk production in Puerto Rico. Talking about one of his bands, Tropiezo, Jose and the band's bassist, Wallo, recalled an era when digital communication was not a common practice:

Jose: When I started with Tropiezo, I received letters. Dude, it sucked big time. I would answer them, but it was a burden to write to someone and send it.

Wallo: Do you remember this interview for a Belgian zine? It was done by hand. The guy sent us letters. I remember answering the questions, all tired. It was like taking a test, man. Just like taking a test!

Digital technologies quickly became naturalized into the very logic of Discos de Hoy. This became a crucial reality for Jose:

> As far as technologies are concerned, the Internet is the most valuable. You know, we can communicate five times on the same day. That helps me a lot. I mean, it helps everybody. If my computer breaks down, I'm fucked. I'd need to get me a new one. No computer means I can't record, you can't do anything. Right now, the computer in the studio controls everything: recording, the Internet. . . . But that's all basic technology. It's like having a TV or something. We're not breaking new ground here. To me, this is all basic. These are technologies that everyone has, "mandatory," so to speak. It's like the computer, without one you can't do anything. I guess you could, but if you're going to have a job, get your things going, you've got to have a computer.

But the globalization of punk production goes beyond PCs and hardware. The evolution of the computer chip has led to the development of applications of technosocial interconnectivity, self-production, and data processing, which have become an integral part of our lives under the term *Web 2.0*. Social networking platforms are no longer a novelty; they have practically become a necessity in our globalized logic. In our digital era, having an online presence not only means to have a "static" presence, as with a 1990s website, but to grow a network, to interact through content, to interconnect actively and socially.

In the case of Discos de Hoy, Myspace, an early and perhaps forgotten platform of social media, was the technology that would exponentially expand the label's participation in the global punk scene. Myspace was particularly useful for bands since it served as a multimedia platform in itself, where one could display photos, music, videos, and text. Members of your network were able to post messages for anyone to see, just as on a Facebook "wall," which became a form of advertising for a band. People could visit your site, listen to your music, learn the history of your band, and connect you with other bands.

Jose told me about the role Myspace played for his band early on and his initial skepticism:

> [Myspace] has been around for about 2 years now. When we went on tour last year, we were like, "What is this crap?" you know. At first we thought it was something like Vida Cool [a Puerto Rican virtual community regarded by punks as a "yuppie" network]. But when we went on [our first U.S. tour], all the bands had Myspace. So I decided to create a profile to see what the deal was. Now I am in contact with everyone, people from other countries and all. And it's so easy.

Myspace quickly became a standard tool for bands, and in Puerto Rico it became viral. Just as the personal computer "revolutionized" zine making, Myspace "revolutionized" how bands represented and marketed themselves. In Jose's words,

> [Myspace] really works for bands. For example, you post the MP3s, four songs of your band. People go to your page, they listen to them, if they like them, they can download them. They can contact you, they can type in "bands from Puerto Rico" and your page will show up. Anyone who wants to find you will really be able to find you. There're no more excuses, as far as contacts go. Thousands and thousands and thousands of bands are in Myspace. When I want to contact a band, I go directly to Myspace.

Wallo, who played bass in the band Tropiezo, described the networking possibilities brought about by social media:

> You know, in Myspace, I enter other people's profiles, I see bands and stuff, I click on them, and if I see something I like—it could be hip-hop or whatever—I add them [to my list of friends] and when they add me, I tell them, "Hey, check these Puerto Rican bands out." And they do write back. Sometimes it's very random people, like from Wisconsin.

Social networking platforms are not only convenient; they have practically become a necessity in our globalized logic. It has even become "common sense" in our digital era that having an online presence not only means to have a "static" presence but to grow a network, to interact through content, to interconnect actively and socially. Jose quickly understood this logic at play in Myspace:

> Like, right now I don't want to maintain a Tropiezo.com website. I just create a Myspace page and I post shows, updates, our new songs. A lot of people contact us there. For contacts is just freaking awesome. It serves the basic function of what a band website should be: post music, announce shows, and have a contacts list. That's it. Why would you want to create a band website? I mean, the people who made possible our Florida tour I met through Myspace.

Just as the zine created a symbolic and material point of convergence for punk culture, Myspace created a virtual space of convergence that was more powerful than any of the technologies and artifacts that figured in the early stages of punk. Where zines would describe music through reviews, Myspace permitted its users to *experience* music firsthand. Where the scene reports would portray "exotic" punk scenes, Myspace provided the space where *entire* scenes came to life. Where punk networks were created and stimulated through zine advertisements, Myspace became the ultimate network where virtually any band was immediately accessible. Jose discovered Myspace while touring in Florida, and it quickly became a viral tool for Puerto Rican bands. It became an exponential gateway to a global underground punk network.

The story of these Puerto Rican punks has little to do with a specific platform (Myspace is only one social network among many and has lost much of its relevance) and much to do with the general role of technology and globalization in our ever-changing social landscape. They took the technological tools available to them and effectively used them to reproduce a particular subcultural practice, with a specific ideology of solidarity, collaboration, self-production, and authenticity, and from a specific geography in connection with their counterparts around the globe.

GLOBAL INFORMATIONAL CAPITALISM AND THE PARADOX OF CULTURAL RESISTANCE

In an era of networks, punks have managed to fortify and exponentially expand their own networks, and the digital conduits available within the Web 2.0 have been crucial to the sustainability of such networks. These networks of mediated relationships of production and exchange have resulted in media infrastructures that power subsystems of production that exist alongside larger corporate, political, and economic structures.

In spite of their potential for expanding our knowledge, connecting us to people around the globe, and allowing us to create and share, new media do not exist in a structural vacuum. There is a political economy surrounding new media, and many times the swift integration of these technologies into our lives, and our reliance on them for work and leisure, "erases" some of their less liberating aspects. Developed countries have been increasingly governed by **informational capitalism**, which places a premium on knowledge and information and relies on global networks of capital flow. In a way, the interconnected world becomes a socioeconomic network, with specific nodes playing specific functions. Some innovation nodes, such as the United States, pioneer technological invention, while others, such as manufacture nodes in Asia and South America, must be able to produce those innovations quickly and inexpensively. However, these global networks become rather *tenacious*, making it almost impossible for production nodes to break away from these global roles. Exploitation of labor in undeveloped countries, e-waste, corporate monopolies and oligopolies, and intrusion of privacy are only some of the structural downsides of our digital world.

Even if not apparent, new media technologies carry within them the imprint of a globalizing logic that concentrates power on a few nodes while marginalizing others. That is, even if digital technologies and the Internet have created a technocultural landscape in which networks of communication and collaboration, self-production, and exchange are possible, technologies are also constitutive of the very logic of global capitalism, through which flows of capital become exclusive to certain geographies and where peripheral nations are mere laborers and keepers of resources to be extracted. Thus, technological innovation and the digital tools that make up our "technoscape" (Appadurai, 1996) constitute what I call a **global hardware industrial complex**, whose structure depends on the extraction of resources, cheap labor, and free trade to sustain the proliferation of software and digital services in material ways.

This imprint is not always recognized by punks, who attempt to "mask" the mark of capitalism in their practices by resignifying the capitalistic significations that permeate the punk logic. This is what Thompson (2004) has called the "shame of exchangeability," punks' insistence on "detaching" their production practices from corporate conduits. Whereas the music industries turn musical products into glamorized commodities, punks make an effort to deglamorize music by taking production into their own hands; whereas capitalism prescribes a formula for success based on sales and economic growth, punks devalue their commodities and favor microproduction over expansion. And yet punk production is reliant on global informational capitalism, with its logic of flows and technological dependence, to thrive and expand.

Punks' often problematic "masking" of capitalism creates an important discursive tension, as they are unable to fully disentangle themselves from their insertion into and reliance on capitalism as a structural system. The punk discourse, codified as a vehement rejection of capitalism, is caught between the paradox of rejecting a system and fundamentally relying on it. In other words, punks are caught within a structural power-logic as they build the networks of their reproduction on the informational networks that sustain the system. How does punk culture negotiate the underlying structural determinations of new media, such as the political economy of electronics manufacture, of social networks such as Myspace and Facebook, of search engines such as Google? How do we, as mindful citizens, negotiate them?

SUBCULTURES, NEW MEDIA, AND THE RESTRUCTURING OF CULTURAL SPACE

As citizens of capitalism—with its conditions of relative autonomy and prosperity—it becomes increasingly important to recognize and understand our roles within the power structure and how privilege affects our mobility within it. But even so, progressive outcomes are not *necessarily* obscured by this recognition, as this relative autonomy also enables the erosion of the system and its conditions. More than three decades ago, Clarke, Hall, Jefferson, and Roberts (2005) asserted that subcultural practices "are not simply 'ideological' constructs. They, too, win space for the young: cultural space in the neighbourhood and institutions, real time for leisure and recreation, actual room on the street or street-corner" (p. 103). Thus, culture itself becomes the very battleground through which people enact and contest the meanings, symbols, and actions that underlie their cultural environment.

In this sense, a countercultural practice such as punk has been able to exploit for itself the potential of new media to open new ground for its own agenda. Uses of technology can also have productive effects, as the stories I present here demonstrate. In the case of Puerto Rico, information technologies enabled a group of young people to build, from scratch, a cultural space for themselves, to create on their own terms and according to their own values, and to pave the way for others to do the same.

I have witnessed how Puerto Rican punks were able to build, from the ground up, a rudimentary but nonetheless effective media infrastructure that is both growing and expanding. And they have been able to build this cultural platform by rearticulating their relationships with capitalism and producing an infrastructure that is politically different from mainstream modes of production. Puerto Rican punks' engagement with new media exemplifies an avenue of social mobility that enables new possibilities of cultural production against a context of dominant modes of production and exchange.

We can identify at least three broad implications for intercultural communication stemming from the ever-increasing role of new media in our lives. First, new media technologies enable the creation of cultural products in a way that was not possible before. For instance, in the case of Puerto Rican punks, hardware and software made possible the creation of low-cost, high-quality recordings, enabling creative control outside mainstream modes of cultural production and contributing to the reproduction of a marginal culture. Second, new media accelerate and intensify the propagation of cultural manifestations in ways that have become embedded within social practice itself. For Puerto Rican punks, social media became a natural extension of their infrastructure, making possible the dissemination of Puerto Rican punk cultural products globally. Third, new media greatly complicate the idea of culture as a localized and localizable phenomenon, displacing it through the local and the global, the material and the virtual. If culture manifests itself in real space by means of communicative practices, the locus of these practices is shifted through time and space, changing the nature and locus of such practices. Culture becomes the product of communicative practices that are synergistically enacted through both material and virtual channels. The Puerto Rican punk scene is based in Puerto Rico, but it is also located within and part of a broader global punk scene connected through digital networks of distribution and exchange. It is both in a tiny Caribbean island and around the globe.

In the end, digital technologies have been excellent tools for empowering people and opening up cultural space, but they have never driven cultural change in and by themselves. As with any technology, it is always people who are behind digital technologies, giving them meaning, enabling their potential, justifying their relevance through practice. I have been fortunate not only to witness but to experience how a desire to transform space for ourselves, to express our views, to enjoy what we like, and to be different can transform our landscape in meaningful and unexpected ways. And while there is always the risk of being co-opted or suppressed, there is always the possibility of shifting our trajectory and finding different ways of creating new opportunities. The most important lesson I learned from my fellow Puerto Rican punks is that cultural space is infinite in as much as it is something that we forge through action. It is always there waiting to be discovered and reinvented.

Many years have passed since I first began studying punk culture in Puerto Rico, and, as it is with our rapidly technological landscape, many things have changed. Today, Jose and Discos de Hoy do not rely so much on Myspace; they are now connected to Facebook, Bandcamp, and SoundCloud, and sell their stuff through Big Cartel. Genres have been shifting as well: Jose now directs a salsa orchestra whose players are none other than punks and who have become quite popular, even outside of punk circles. And they are more global than ever: I recently called Jose up to grab a cup of coffee, but he was not available anytime soon. He was just leaving with his orchestra to play a summer festival in France.

KEY TERMS

commodification of
culture   234

counterculture   229

diasporic identities   231

global hardware industrial
complex   244

hyperreality   234

informational
capitalism   244

Media Studies 2.0   228

Media Studies 3.0   228

popular culture   227

self-marginalization   239

transnationalism   231

webnography   230

DISCUSSION QUESTIONS

1. According to Gordon, what are the differences between Media Studies 2.0 and Media Studies 3.0? In what ways does Gordon's analysis of Jamaican popular culture on the Internet reflect the principles defined by Media Studies 3.0?

2. Gordon uses "webnography" as a methodology of her case study. How does webnography differ from traditional ethnography? As a researcher, what considerations or modifications do you think you have to make when conducting an ethnographic study in virtual communities?

3. Gordon argues that online communities create hybridized cultural selves in hybridized cultural spaces. Can you think of any examples of how your cultural self has been hybridized in your use of social media? How do you engage in identity performances when you communicate via social media? Do you perform different identities online and offline?

4. Ramírez-Sánchez discusses the inherent paradox of the Puerto Rican punk movement in which its anticapitalist, antiestablishment philosophy is shared through, and sustained by, the infrastructure of global network society. What are your thoughts on this paradox? How can we productively address this tension between cultural resistance and capitalist appropriation?

5. Media theorist Marshal McLuhan famously coined the phrase "the medium is the message," indicating that the mode of communication is far more influential in shaping the meaning of the message than people typically think. In what ways do social media function as a medium of communication? Based on the entries in this chapter, can social media break down traditional hierarchies of power, or do they implicitly reinforce the relations of power?

CHAPTER 13

Intercultural Conflict in the Global Age

Today, the likelihood of **intercultural conflict** intensifies as our lives, resources, and everyday experiences become increasingly interconnected with people from diverse cultures. Greater proximity, increased competition, diminishing resources, exploitative conditions, as well as escalating social and economic inequity fuel conflicts among individuals and groups from different cultural, ethnic, racial, religious, and national backgrounds. In the context of globalization, unprecedented migration, often by refugees of the global economy, increases the presence of people who are perceived as "outsiders" and "foreigners" in rural and urban locations around the world, triggering intercultural tensions over belonging, identity, ownership, and resource distribution.

Intercultural conflicts are by nature complex, contested, and often intractable. While issues at a particular moment and in a particular place may trigger intercultural conflicts, the source of the conflict is often connected to broader historical, cultural, political, and economic inequities. For example, the intercultural conflicts experienced by indigenous immigrants in the United States and Mexico today, as Antonieta Mercado describes in this chapter, are not new. Indigenous people have experienced and survived displacement, violence, discrimination, and inequality for more than 500 years. The conflicts resulting from racial and religious discrimination that Taj Suleyman narrates here are informed by the relatively recent events of 9/11 and discourses about Islam and terrorism. However, these events and discourses need to be understood within the broader, longer-term context of colonial discourses, which have systematically targeted and constructed nonwhite and non-Christian people as the "other."

In efforts to address root causes of intercultural conflicts, people are joining together around the globe in unprecedented ways to confront inequity and challenge injustice by building intercultural alliances. Mercado documents the inspiring work of indigenous immigrants who are engaging in decolonization workshops, forming transnational alliances, and reinventing indigenous forms of knowledge and practice to resist and reframe coloniality and globalization. Suleyman's personal narrative illustrates the challenges and opportunities of negotiating intercultural conflicts as a Middle Eastern, black, Muslim immigrant male in the United States.

Transnational Practices of Communication and Social Justice: Indigenous Mexican Immigrants in the United States

Antonieta Mercado
University of San Diego

In Mexico . . . indigenous people have been considered a problem, referred to as the "indio problem," and what has been the solution to the "indio problem"? De-indianization. This is the history we want to explore. How did de-indianization start? How can we turn the negative into something positive? See the long list of negative things associated to being indigenous. This is real; we are not imagining it. We have heard this, we have seen it, we have experienced this in our own flesh. Imagine living like this. It is a matter of self-esteem, of how we see ourselves and how we see the world. That is the purpose of the workshops. How can we stop seeing the world from the point of view of our oppressors and start to see it in a more positive way? . . . We do not need to say we are better than anyone, because then we would be reproducing the vision of the conquerors. We want equality . . . to be equal but to keep our identity. If we can do this as adults, then we can develop strategies to explain this to our children.

—Gaspar Rivera-Salgado (2011)

The quote above is from a **decolonization workshop**, an organized discussion about the structural and cognitive damage that centuries of domination and colonialism have caused to indigenous people of the Americas. The interesting thing about this workshop is that it was organized by a group of indigenous immigrants from Mexico who live in Los Angeles and are part of the *Frente Indígena de Organizaciones Binacionales* (FIOB), or Indigenous Front of Binational Organizations. When originally created in 1991 in California, FIOB organized indigenous Mixteco and Zapoteco immigrants from Oaxaca who worked in the agribusinesses of the Central Valley or held service jobs in Los Angeles and San Diego.

After more than two decades, the organization has expanded across borders, becoming a multisite, panethnic, transnational organization (Velasco-Ortiz, 2002) extending through the migratory networks from rural and urban California to Baja California, Mexico City, and Oaxaca, with about 5,000 members. Likewise, FIOB has come to include other indigenous immigrants from other parts of Mexico, such as Triquis, Chatinos, Náhuas, Mayans, and Purépechas, as well as mestizo (mixed-blooded) Mexicans and others who support their work to promote social justice for indigenous people.

This case study is an account of some of the transnational communicative and organizational activities that FIOB members have developed through the years to resist their condition of **double marginality**, as minorities in their country of origin and as immigrants in the United States. As the reader of this essay will see, organized indigenous migrants have been able to turn their double marginality into an opportunity to engage in transformative communication and civic practices in transnational networks. Activities practiced by FIOB, such as the use of social media and planning of discussions and workshops in cooperation with immigrant and nonimmigrant organizations, have been means to foster **social capital**. Transnational migratory networks may prove to enable more open forms of citizenship and belonging, where diverse forms of social capital are cultivated and deployed and where "modern" and "traditional" forms of human organization and knowledge collide. The transborder project of FIOB is both a function of intellectual reformulation of indigeneity and an activist project advocating for the rights of indigenous peoples in the continent through communicative and social action.

HISTORICAL AND CONTEMPORARY CONTEXT FOR ORGANIZING INDIGENOUS MIGRANTS

The latest stage of economic globalization and the pulling factors of the market have forced indigenous people from Mexico to abandon their land and offer their labor to the service of the U.S. economy, one of the most important engines of what we have come to call economic "progress." Indigenous migrants have responded to this displacement—not very different from the one they suffered during colonial times, when their lands and resources were appropriated and they were used as free labor—by engaging in sophisticated forms of organization and communication in immigrant networks, redefining relationships of belonging to a territorial political community.

The civic activities of indigenous immigrants across borders are a good place to study contemporary forms of citizenship, which are developing outside the single nation-state, the unit traditionally associated with the idea of modernity. These forms of organization are ways of creatively defying coloniality and globalization through a more **cosmopolitan citizenship** from the grassroots (Mercado, 2011), which entails the willingness to form alliances with other groups across nations and to reinvent their conception of indigeneity as associated with the land to one associated with a more respectful and sustainable relationship with the earth. This orientation is shown by their willingness to rescue indigenous forms of knowledge, such as traditions of communal organization and cooperation, which are then practiced and reinvented across borders.

Contemporary citizenship has been conceived of as a status, granted to the individual by the nation-state (Marshall, 1963/1998); however, some scholars, such as Gershon Shafir (1998), conceive citizenship not as a definition but as an intellectual and political tradition involving a range of concepts and different practices that "coexist with and constrain one another" (p. 2). Most recently, some theorists have defined citizenship as practice (Abu El-Haj, 2009; Goldring, 2001). Thinking about citizenship this way makes it easier to understand **transnational immigrant networks** where practices of citizenship and communication defy citizenship as a fixed status, prescribed from above, instead placing it as an activity built from the grassroots. These transnational networks also allow individuals to interact with several political arrangements at the same time (Miller, 2001).

Immigrant transnationalism has been defined as the back-and-forth practices that immigrants conduct between their communities of origin and settlement (Bourne, 1916;

Glick Schiller, Basch, & Szanton Blanc, 1992, as cited in Levitt, 2001). These practices need regular long-term contact across borders to be successful (Portes, Guarnizo, & Landolt, 1999). The process of moving across borders contributes to the creation of transnational immigrant networks, which are formed by direct or indirect connections of people and groups who are linked by similar ties across nations. These connections include "communication, mutual recognition and shared participation in some activity" (Tilly, 2007, p. 7).

There are about 14 million indigenous people in Mexico, and Oaxaca is the state with the second-largest number of indigenous inhabitants in the country. Indigenous Mexicans from Oaxaca are one of the fastest-growing populations in California (Kresge, 2007), currently estimated at close to half a million (see the Oaxaca government website at www .oaxaca.gob.mx), although the exact population is unknown due to census undercounting. Indigenous Mexicans have had a presence in the United States at least since the Bracero Program in the 1940s, which involved mostly circular migration, with male sojourners returning to Mexico after a period of working in the United States. After the end of the guest-worker program in 1965, U.S. policies of family reunification and strong existing immigrant networks brought a massive new wave of immigration from Mexico (Rivera-Salgado, 2002), which intensified during the economic crises of the '80s. With the advent of the North American Free Trade Agreement (NAFTA) in the mid-'90s, U.S. industries such as agriculture and construction increasingly demanded cheap labor from Mexico. At the same time, the Mexican government was cutting its subsidies to corn growers and substituting the peasant agricultural production sector with industrialization and cheap corn imports from the United States (Portes, 2006). Many indigenous Mexicans, whose daily existence was attached to agricultural production (especially corn), ended up migrating to the United States as 2.3 million jobs were lost in Mexico's agricultural sector between 1990 and 2008 (Zepeda, Wise, & Gallagher, 2009, p. 12).

Currently, there are about 90 different Oaxacan organizations in the United States, mainly organized by people who emigrated from the same hometown in Oaxaca, although some of these organizations group smaller ones into federations and fronts. Practices of reciprocity that arise from the activities of these organizations in transnational networks are a form of *social capital*, which has been defined as the "ability of actors to secure benefits by virtue of membership in social networks or other social structures" (Portes, 1998, p. 6). The premise of social capital is that social networks have value and can affect the productivity of individuals and groups (Putnam, 2000, p. 19). Robert Putnam has defined two functions of social capital: bonding, which encompasses relationships of exclusiveness within a group, and bridging, the relationships established outside the group (pp. 22–23). FIOB has been able to cultivate transnational communicative practices that foster both bridging and bonding forms of social capital (Mercado, 2013).

According to Rufino Domínguez Santos (2004), a Mixteco immigrant from Oaxaca and one of the founders of FIOB, during the 1980s indigenous immigrants organized in the United States and Mexico to counteract human and labor rights violations and to confront discrimination along racial, linguistic, and ethnic lines. The latter goal is significant because indigenous immigrants are discriminated against both by their Anglo employers, who have difficulties communicating with them because they may not speak Spanish fluently, and by nonindigenous Mexicans, who criticize them for speaking Spanish with an accent. One of the challenges has been to bring together these organizations to make them effective in protecting indigenous migrant rights (Domínguez Santos, 2004, p. 71).

Domínguez Santos gives an account of the founding of FIOB, originally as the *Frente Mixteco-Zapoteco Binacional* (Binational Front of Mixtecs and Zapotecs), which was also a response to the 1992 celebrations of the 500th anniversary of Christopher Columbus's arrival in the Americas. He explains that indigenous natives of the American continent were stripped of their rights by the conquerors. About Columbus, he states:

> People . . . see in him a grand hero who brought good things. But they never talk about the massacres or the genocide that occurred in our villages, on the whole American continent. Our people were stripped of their culture, their belief in our gods. They told us that nature wasn't worth anything, when in reality nature gives us life. That different side of the story is what we wanted to tell all the people we could find. That was the object of the Frente Mixteco Zapoteco Binacional: to dismantle the old stereotype, to march, to protest. (Domínguez Santos, as quoted in Bacon, 2002, "Countering Racism, Breaking Boundaries")

As can be seen in this discussion, FIOB is both an intellectual and an activist project for the indigenous world in the Americas. FIOB activists state that their mission as indigenous peoples is to tell their story to the world and to form a continental movement raising people's awareness about how colonial ways of thinking embedded in our contemporary economic globalization have devastated the indigenous world (Cruz, 2005), exploiting the natural environment to feed an ever-growing thirst for consumption and displacing indigenous people from their land by turning them into cheap transnational labor. FIOB has implemented a series of programs and strategies to accomplish these goals, such as the use of culture for civic action and the organization of decolonization and human rights workshops such as the one described in the quote that opened this essay. The participation of women in organization governance has also been important over the years, because women have brought to the discussions new topics previously ignored by men; for example, issues such as health care, women's leadership, and domestic violence are now included in the organization workshops.

DECOLONIZATION WORKSHOPS

In March 2009, Rivera-Salgado, then the binational coordinator of FIOB, a sociologist from the University of California, Santa Cruz, and a Mixteco immigrant from Oaxaca, sent an invitation to a series of workshops he and the UCLA Labor Center were launching. In each of these semiformal gatherings, someone from the Oaxacan community in Los Angeles shared knowledge with other attendees. Some of these gatherings were replicated at the more than a dozen sites where FIOB works in Mexico and the United States, in an effort to promote the Right to Know Program (*Programa Derecho a Saber*) to distribute cultural, community, legal, economic, and academic knowledge for the benefit of indigenous people, especially immigrants. Along with these meetings, Rivera-Salgado and other members of

FIOB initiated decolonization workshops to discuss indigenous identity in a transnational context and to address indigenous migrants' "double marginality" as minorities in Mexico and foreign immigrants in the United States.

Decolonization workshops entail in-depth reflections and discussions of the structural and mental mechanisms of oppression that indigenous people have been subjected to since the Spanish conquest, particularly through the consolidation of the ideology of modernity and the nation-state, which viewed indigenous people as "backward." The purpose of the workshops is to identify similar mechanisms in the United States and Mexico, and counteract them with daily practices of resurgence (Corntassel, 2012) and cultural reconstruction, where indigenous ways of respecting nature and community prevail over senseless exploitation of the earth (read S. Lily Mendoza's account in Chapter 3 of this volume for further information).

Influenced by the writings of Mexican anthropologist Guillermo Bonfil Batalla (1987/1996), FIOB decolonization workshops discuss the process of "de-indianization" (*desindianización*) by the Mexican state, which consisted of promoting so-called "modernization" projects implementing educational crusades to get rid of indigenous language, culture, and ways of relating with Mother Earth—a process akin to ethnocide (Bartolomé, 1997, p. 29). These crusades promoted the idea that being indigenous was a premodern, uncivilized way of being Mexican. Paradoxically, murals and art depicting a glorious indigenous past were promoted by the same government that was trying to force uniformity on a diverse existing population.

As the quote opening this case study illustrates, decolonization workshops touch on several issues at the same time, not only indigenous ethnicity and its adaptation and reinvention as social and cultural capital in migratory circuits. The workshops are a ripe terrain for discussing gender inequality, domestic violence, and the imposition of dominant models of culture, language, citizenship, history, and standards of beauty. Thus, the workshops explore diverse themes, such as the exoticizing of the supposedly "authentic" indigenous person, the consequences of structural inequality, human rights abuses, and discrimination. Discussions in these workshops are not only a matter of building personal "self-esteem" but also of understanding the structures of oppression.

In many decolonization workshops, participants show their anger toward their historical oppressors, realizing the discrimination, violence, displacement, and inequality they and their ancestors have endured for centuries. However, the lasting purpose of these workshops is to move toward self-reflection and empowerment of participants, through valuing indigenous culture and understanding centuries-old structures of colonialism and domination, the same structures that continue operating in our globalized world, where the idea of progress is the exploitation of natural resources at an even faster pace. Once they have reflected on the importance of their culture, they can demand better conditions in an economic, social, and political order that has systematically, and often violently, denied them rights, even their right to call themselves indigenous. As Rivera-Salgado stated: "Being indigenous has been associated with backwardness and inferiority. That is why when you say, 'I am indigenous and I am entitled to have equal rights,' you are making a political statement" (personal communication, November 12, 2010, La Jolla, CA).

As Etienne Wenger (1998) discussed, human learning is social, and communities talk about the "shared historical and social resources, frameworks, and perspectives that can sustain mutual engagement in action" (p. 5). FIOB workshops and the discourses deployed there are designed to enrich participants' ethnic identity with knowledge about what they can do to achieve equality, not just personal responsibility. This emphasis runs counter to neoliberal conceptions of citizenship, where more and more relationships are relegated to the market and social reciprocity is discouraged in favor of personal agency, which, under neoliberalism, is a construction of the self as a set of marketable traits that will be deployed to generate alliances with other subjects of the market (Gershon, 2011). Immigrant networks, although partially inscribed in market relations, work differently, since a shared culture may be a more important trait for community organization and solidarity than individual agency.

CULTURE AS A TOOL FOR ACTION

Indigenous Mexicans have brought not only their labor to the agricultural fields of the Central Valley in California or to service jobs in Los Angeles and Oxnard or to the poultry plants in New Jersey; they have also brought their traditions, their forms of social and political organization embedded in systems of communal work, their foods, their festivities, their saints, their dances, their respect for nature, and their experiences of double discrimination.

One of the most important experiences that migration has offered to indigenous Mexicans is the opportunity to construct their identities from what they consider to be valuable or authentic, and to question what they consider oppressive. Thus, indigenous migrants have found that through fostering activities of "cultural preservation," they have been able to construct bridges for civic action and entry into the public sphere. Paradoxically, migration is enabling indigenous culture to be globalized, placing indigenous people in new positions of power, not because the land where they arrive receives them with open arms but because moving makes them aware that experiences of discrimination may be repeated in other contexts. Thus, indigenous immigrants find themselves actively organizing around their indigenous culture to resist discrimination, fostering their own identity and cultural claims but also reaching out to other groups who may share similar objectives, creating a transcontinental movement that started with the Zapatista uprising in Mexico and has continued with the Aymara in Bolivia, the Mapuches in Chile, and the Ennui in Canada, among others. From these positions, they can question not only the colonial structures that have oppressed them for centuries but also the new economic and political structures brought about by contemporary economic globalization. These structures enable, validate, and perpetuate oppression, placing indigenous migrants in vulnerable positions as exploitable labor when they move to other states or countries.

Once FIOB consolidated itself as an organization, it started to reach out to indigenous migrants in California, with the help of organizations such as California Rural Legal Assistance (CRLA). Domínguez Santos worked as a staff person at CRLA and dedicated himself to teaching Mixteco immigrant workers in the Central Valley about labor rights, using Mixteco language (Bacon, 2002). Soon, what may have been a liability in a foreign environment became an important asset, because he could communicate with fellow Mixteco immigrants.

FIOB leaders and members have used their cultural and social capital to continue disseminating different kinds of knowledge within the organization, for example, organizing cultural activities in California and productive projects in Oaxaca and Baja California. They have also acquired other kinds of knowledge in their daily contact with human and labor rights organizations, transnational government officers, nongovernmental organizations (NGOs), and other immigrants and actors they have encountered in migratory networks. FIOB activists have used the language of cultural preservation to open spaces to negotiate issues of inequality and distribution of resources (Poole, 2007, p. 224).

For example, in Title VI of the Civil Rights Act, which stipulates that everyone subject to a court of law is entitled to an interpreter in his or her native language, activists from FIOB saw an opportunity. Domínguez Santos explained: "We used Title VI to establish our indigenous interpreter's program in 1996" (personal communication, November 29, 2010, San Diego, CA). This program has been crucial in helping indigenous immigrants who are incarcerated or hospitalized and cannot access court or health services in their native languages. It took until 2003 for the Mexican government to enact the General Law of Linguistic Rights of Indigenous People, a law designed to promote and protect the rights of linguistic minorities in a country where more than 62 indigenous languages are spoken.

Participation in immigrant networks and transnational activism have provided a gateway for accessing a transnational world where civic activities are influenced, but not necessarily determined, by a single nation-state, creating a more flexible form of citizenship from daily communicative and civic practices. For example, indigenous immigrants in the United States are involved with daily decisions in their communities of origin in Oaxaca. Even while residing abroad, they often donate time and money to communal, civic, and infrastructural projects, such as organizing town festivities or building roads, schools, and clinics in their hometowns.

IMMIGRATION AND HUMAN RIGHTS CAMPAIGNS

Workshops organized by FIOB have also helped provide protection to immigrants vulnerable in the United States. For example, Sara is an outspoken woman in her early 40s who came to the United States less than a decade ago and has two U.S.-born children. She herself was born in the Mixteca region of Oaxaca and has participated in FIOB for the past few years. When I was talking to Sara in her apartment in Vista, California, she mentioned the importance of attending workshops organized by FIOB and other organizations—such as the American Friends Service Committee (AFSC), a Quaker civil rights organization—that put them in contact with immigration lawyers to discuss their cases for free. "For me, attending the workshops has been lifesaving," said Sara, who then talked about her encounter with agents from the Immigration and Customs Enforcement (ICE) office:

A few months ago, there were two men knocking at my door. I opened it and they entered my apartment and showed me a picture of a woman they were looking for. They asked me for my husband. I told them I lived there with my children and my brother, his wife, and their kid. One of them insisted in asking me about the lady, implying that I was her sister or her mother. I denied it, and they left. A few weeks later, they came back, wearing ICE uniforms. By that time, I had spoken to people in

FIOB, and attended a human rights workshop that they organized with the American Friends. In the workshop they told me that I was not under any obligation to open the door to immigration agents unless they showed me an official order, and that we as undocumented immigrants are not completely unprotected in this country. I told the agents I could not open the door; they insisted, but they did not have any official order, so I asked for that, and since they could not produce it, I did not open the door. (Personal communication, June 17, 2010, Vista, CA)

For Sara, the knowledge she acquired in the FIOB workshop was crucial for her safety. Since her experience with the ICE agents, Sara has been very active in talking to other immigrants in North San Diego, in case they encounter immigration officers or the police: "The day they came to get me, the agents took one of my neighbors, leaving her children behind. I felt that I needed to do something," she said, holding a brochure produced by the AFSC with information about the legal rights of immigrants in case they are detained by authorities. Here we see how U.S. activists and NGO workers, as in the case of the AFSC, are part of the everyday contacts of FIOB members.

Although Sara does not speak English, her involvement in FIOB allowed her to access the knowledge being circulated in the organization to use in her everyday life. Attending FIOB workshops gave her the chance to participate in "collective learning" through social relations (Wenger, 1998) and to bring that knowledge back to her neighborhood, where immigration authorities were making impromptu appearances. "So far, the human rights workshop has been the most useful FIOB workshop I had attended," said Sara, "but I have also learned a lot in the decolonization workshops and all the talks we have at FIOB. . . . I learned that we have rights, like everybody else, and no one can just walk all over us when they please."

Disseminating information through communication campaigns and knowledge about human rights through workshops and seminars is very important in keeping FIOB a transnational organization. FIOB transmits its main ideas, narratives, and information through its internal and external communication practices, including its active engagement in creating media outlets, such as *El Tequio* magazine, to express its ideas in the public sphere; its connection to other organizations and members of different transnational communities who may support indigenous causes for human dignity and sustainability; and its own self-awareness through internal discussions such as decolonization workshops. Thus, participants are able to construct their indigenous identity in a globalized context, which, in turn, helps enable communicative and civic action.

THE ROLE OF WOMEN IN FIOB

Women who join the organization have created some spaces for social action to promote gender equity. Despite the difficulties of securing spaces in a male-dominated environment, and certain shortcomings of this participation, women are an important voice in FIOB, as in the case of Sara, who played a significant role in FIOB San Diego until she decided to return to her hometown in Oaxaca. While FIOB was initially created by male agricultural workers, economic conditions have pulled their families with them, making the presence of women more prominent in migratory networks (Hondagneu-Sotelo, 1994). Many women who belong to immigrant organizations have complained that men push them to adopt traditional roles such as cooking and serving food for the meetings, taking care of children, organizing raffles, and other activities considered proper for females, while the men discuss the organization's projects and politics.

Odilia Romero Hernández, a Zapoteco immigrant from Oaxaca who joined FIOB in 2002 and has been the binational coordinator of women's affairs, is actively working to overcome this division and has implemented leadership and reproductive justice workshops for indigenous women through a project begun in 2006 called *Mujeres Indigenas en Liderazgo* (MIEL), or Indigenous Women in Leadership. Prior to joining FIOB in 2002, Romero Hernández worked in Los Angeles in an organization of immigrants from her hometown of Zoogocho, Oaxaca, but she stopped working there. She explained,

> There was a lot of inequality, because they wanted you to cook for the patron saint celebrations. I had heard about FIOB on television, and then someone else had told me about them. . . . I was very excited because I found what I was looking for. (Romero Hernández, as quoted in Blackwell, 2009, p. 153)

Romero Hernández is one of the most influential voices in FIOB, and her opinion is well respected by male leaders. Her MIEL initiative has touched on important issues such as domestic violence, spousal abuse, reproductive justice, and women's autonomy. Yet her leadership initiative has not been without controversy; some men in the community do not want to bring their wives to MIEL meetings. Romero Hernández lamented: "They say that I will tell them things and turn them against them . . . because I will fill their heads with ideas" (personal communication, December 2010, Los Angeles, CA).

FIOB has incorporated women into important positions because their work is crucial to maintaining the organization, although male recognition of women as leaders has been difficult at times. Some women in FIOB still feel that their voices are not heard or that conditions have not been cultivated so women can thrive, citing issues related to a lack of help with domestic work and child care or the opposition of their partners to their participation because they think women do not belong in the world outside the home (Romero Hernández, Maldonado Vásquez, Domínguez Santos, Blackwell, & Velasco, 2013). Nevertheless, as the scope of their activities increases, organizations such as FIOB are reaching out to incorporate more women, and as women join migratory networks, they are also finding their way into transnational civic organizations.

Photo 13.1 Odilia Romero Hernández conducts a decolonization workshop session, with Jose González and Juan Ramón (Mission San Luis Rey, Vista, CA, May 17, 2009).

Photo courtesy of Antonieta Mercado

CONCLUSION

This account points to what immigrant organizations can accomplish, how they can organize to transfer social and cultural capital through transnational migratory networks, and the way they can convert this capital into political and social action. FIOB transnational activities are also proof that citizenship as a status may be something hard to attain—as in the case of undocumented indigenous migrants living in the United States—but that does not mean people cannot practice citizenship by engaging in communicative action, even without the formal approval of state institutions. These practices can in fact extend across multiple states, as in the case of indigenous Mexican immigrants who have engaged in communicative and civic practices involving creation and transmission of knowledge, civic association and solidarity through transnational immigrant networks, production of media, and use of social media to communicate and organize. All these practices amount to a de-facto citizenship related to everyday activities, as mundane as they may seem, and not to the state admonition requiring a formal and bureaucratic acknowledgement of the citizen to validate citizenship action.

The experience of migration has helped indigenous immigrants cultivate social capital inside and outside their own ethnic groups, fostering pluralistic values and self-awareness. Confronting their own myths and assumptions about belonging to a group or state, they develop the flexibility and understanding to adjust to new situations and think about their identity (Silverstone, 2007, as cited in Rogers, 2010). The claim, "We do not want to be more, but equal," shows an important level of self-awareness and a willingness to struggle for dignity and equality.

Photo courtesy of Antonieta Mercado

Photo 13.2 José González talks at a human and immigrant rights workshop for indigenous Mexican migrants in San Diego, with AFSC (Vista, CA, March 2011).

FIOB has acted where opportunities have opened up, sometimes invoking "traditional" or cultural forms of organization and other times pushing nontraditional agendas, such as pioneering an interpreters' program for indigenous languages in the United States or publishing a trimestral magazine. This does not demonstrate a lack of programmatic consistency but, rather, flexibility and openness. FIOB has engaged in different binational campaigns, such as the push for extensive U.S. immigration reform; development of myriad workshops, including decolonization workshops under the "Right to Know" banner; and programmatic outreach from FIOB leaders to other organizations in the world.

While the narratives and communicative practices inside and outside FIOB can be related to more flexible forms of citizenship practiced every day, FIOB members consider immigration and their own organizing to be dynamic processes. They still speak of future transformations and needs of their organization, such as the growing presence of indigenous migrants from other parts of Mexico, the incorporation of second-generation indigenous migrants, and the institutionalization of different cooperative and communicative activities through the networks. FIOB member José González summarized the endeavor when he said, "Our fight is in many fronts. We want to end discrimination of us as indigenous, but also against women and other people. We are not done yet" (personal communication, June 30, 2011, San Diego, CA).

Negotiating Intercultural Conflict: A Middle Eastern, Black, Muslim Male's Perspective in Post-9/11 United States

Taj Suleyman
University of the Pacific

This narrative uses my personal experiences to illustrate dynamics related to intercultural conflict. In this essay, I shed light on what it is like to acculturate to the United States, arriving as a young adult Muslim male who grew up in Lebanon. I was raised in downtown Beirut during the war by a black, Muslim, Sudanese father and a Saudi Arabian mother with Christian values. I grew up in a neighborhood of Muslims (both Sunni and Shia), Christians (Armenian Apostolic Orthodox, Maronite Catholics, and Greek Catholics), Jews, and Druze communities. I was encouraged to celebrate most of the religious events in the neighborhood. I would go to church on Sunday with my Christian neighbors; I would help my Jewish neighbors run errands on Saturday for Sabbath, and I'd also attend Friday prayer (*Salat*) with Muslims. This multicultural, multireligious environment was a breeding ground for conflict, but it also provided the perfect opportunity for me to develop the necessary negotiation skills to deal with the intercultural conflicts I encountered in the United States.

The following stories are told from my perspective as a black, Middle Eastern, Arab, Muslim son and brother. My diverse upbringing and my acculturation as a refugee in the United States have guided me in dealing with experiences of **Islamophobia** and racism. Throughout the essay, I discuss my experiences and strategies for handling intercultural conflict using the **intercultural praxis** model (Sorrells, 2013; Sorrells & Nakagawa, 2008).

INTERCULTURAL CONFLICTS UPON ENTERING THE UNITED STATES

My life in the United States started when I arrived in Salt Lake City, Utah, in May of 2000. I entered as a Sudanese refugee coming from Lebanon. I was 18 years old. Accompanying me were my Sudanese father, Lebanese stepmother, one younger brother, and two younger sisters. I was extremely resistant and sad to leave behind my life in Lebanon; yet underneath the grief and fear was an inkling of excitement. At that time, the only knowledge I had about the United States came from what I had heard from people in Lebanon, which was based purely on stereotypes. I was soon to find out that attaining the "American Dream" was not as simple as it had been made out to be.

My family and I were placed in an apartment complex primarily housing immigrants and refugees. The residents came from all over the world, including Bosnia, Serbia, Kosovo, Russia, Congo, Togo, South Sudan, and Mexico. As I became more familiar with the apartment complex, I started interacting with my neighbors. One of the first families to welcome us lived next-door. They came from Kosovo and introduced themselves as Muslims when they saw my stepmother wearing her **hijab**. My stepmother used the few English words she knew to talk to the mother of the family. Needless to say, the language barrier called for us to use creative ways to communicate with our neighbors. Most of our communication was done with gestures and drawings.

Not all our interactions with the people in our new home were so positive, however. Our family encountered conflict with the manager of our apartment complex over a misunderstanding. The manager was a white male who lived onsite with his wife. It was no secret that all the tenants found him to be rude and abrasive. I noticed that he had a standoffish attitude and did not interact with us—even though we always said "hello" when we saw him around the complex.

The conflict occurred because the manager had instructed my parents to pay rent with a money order and deposit it in the rent drop box. My parents, unfamiliar with the process of money orders and paying rent, knocked on his door to ask him if their money order was made out correctly. He yelled at my stepmother, "Don't come and knock at my door next time, you understand?" My father took great offense at this treatment but did not feel he could say anything, for fear that we would be kicked out of the complex. Our only retaliation was to stop greeting the manager when we saw him. This should have shown him that we were upset; however, he did not seem to get the message.

The dynamics between the manager and our family sparked my curiosity. I wanted to understand more about how white people communicated. One of the things that really annoyed us about the manager was his lack of interaction. He walked around with a forced smile on his face, and whenever we saw him, we would smile back and say "hello." Despite our greetings, he treated us as though we barely existed. This made him a source of many complaints and jokes behind closed doors. My dad used to say, "This *khawaja* (Sudanese Arabic term for 'white person') is so *masikh* ('unbearable')." Although I was annoyed by the manager's attitude, I was still intrigued. I began to observe his behavior more closely. I noticed that he greeted some people while ignoring others. Later on I realized he tended to interact much better with the Sudanese men who were more proficient in English. His body language indicated to us that he was confrontational (because he was straightforward and less verbal). He looked people straight in the eyes when he talked. *Does he do this because he's in a powerful position?* I wondered. *Or maybe this is just how white people interact.* This was the beginning of my attempt to understand differences in this new culture, rather than simply judging them.

In the above conflict, I intuitively used inquiry as a point of entry to question myself and the behavior of the apartment manager. I asked myself, *What could possibly explain the tension between the apartment manager and the residents?*

POST-9/11 AND EXPERIENCES WITH ISLAMOPHOBIA

I had lived in this country a mere 16 months before the 9/11 attacks. That morning, I was watching a local television channel when I saw the air attack. With my limited English, I was able to understand that two airplanes had crashed into two towers in New York. I heard Arabic names, saw brown-skinned people, and understood that Arab Muslims were involved in the attack.

Anger. Fear. Frustration. Those were the feelings I can recall experiencing in that moment, as I thought about what all this would mean for my family and our community. I started thinking about what might happen to my stepmother, who wears a hijab. What if my little siblings were with her? What if someone hurt them and I wasn't around? Where would we go?

That day, my family gathered in the living room after my siblings came home from school. My stepmother told everyone that she would stop wearing her hijab because she didn't feel safe walking in the city while wearing it. "No. Why? We're not part of this mess!" I said. Part of me did think it might be safer for my stepmother if she didn't wear it, but I stood by my statement. We should not have to compromise our values because of fear and ignorance. Instead, I told my stepmother that I'd take her to work every day to make sure she would be OK.

During that time, my sister Zeinab reached the age of 9—the age when girls in Islam are obligated to wear the hijab, as understood in some cultural traditions. My sister approached my stepmother about beginning to wear the hijab. Everybody in the family was happy and supportive; however, we all felt a secret fear. We'd started hearing that in other Muslim families, the females, to avoid harm and harassment, stopped wearing their hijabs. Months later, my sister would come home crying over the harassment she experienced at school and in the neighborhood. She started realizing the ugly truth about society's fear of and negativity toward what (they thought) the hijab represented. Her choice to continue wearing it caused her to lose friends at school. Other girls would tell her just to take off her hijab and that it was fine since she was in the United States now.

Zeinab was experiencing a social dilemma that was a huge topic of debate for women in Islam during that time. I remember her telling me, as I was driving her to school, that she was considering taking off her hijab. "I don't fit in, Taj," she said, as tears rolled down her cheeks. "I can't swim or dance or sing at school. I just want to be like everyone else." To be honest, I wasn't really sure what to tell her. As her older brother, I had a religious responsibility to encourage her to keep wearing it. At the same time, I understood how hard it was to be ostracized and alienated from society, especially at her young age. "Zeinab," I said, "I can't tell you that you should take the hijab off, and I can't tell you to keep it on. The only thing I can tell you is that it is your decision to make. Do not let pressure from anyone make your decision for you." I knew this advice was much easier said than done, but I wanted my sister to realize the importance of deciding what was right for her—rather than going by what other people thought was right. In a world with so many conflicting rules, we are faced with a lot of pressure to compromise our values just to survive, even though we are in a "free country." I went on to tell her, "Whether you decide to take it off or keep it on, you're my little Zeinab, and you always will be."

Hegemonic beliefs in the United States that the hijab represents the oppression of women lead to Islamic women's being perceived as "oppressed victims" (Cloud, 2004). As a result, Islamic women are positioned as victims to be rescued, particularly by the more progressive, liberated West (Steet, 2000). This "savior" mentality that the United States has aptly demonstrated throughout history ultimately victimizes Muslim girls and women who act outside of the dominant cultural norm. In the name of "liberating" the oppressed, the dominant society confronts, marginalizes, and targets Muslim girls and women. These are attempts to liberate the perceived "victims" from their oppression; yet Islamic women no longer feel safe wearing the hijab as a result.

In Islam, when girls reach puberty (generally around the age of 9), they are seen as young women and their religious responsibilities begin. They are required to start praying five times a day and are obligated in some cultural traditions to start wearing the hijab. While definitions vary for the word *hijab*, the literal Arabic meaning is "cover" or "barrier." This Islamic law is regulated differently in different countries and cultural traditions, as well as according to the beliefs of particular families. In some Islamic countries, women are required to wear the hijab; however, in some countries, such as Lebanon, women can choose to wear it or not, according to individual beliefs.

Women who choose to wear the hijab believe that modesty starts with wearing it. Muslim women say that wearing it is more convenient and results in less focus on appearance and less unwanted sexual attention. They find it empowering because it promotes the development of their personalities and intellect. They feel they can be seen for more than just their physical qualities (Diffendal, 2006; Droogsma, 2007; El Guindi, 1999; Witteborn, 2004). While people in the United States often perceive the hijab as a symbol of oppression, an alternative perspective is that women in the United States are exploited and oppressed, because there is so much pressure for women to be attractive and sexy. Women spend a great deal of time, money, and trouble on beautifying themselves to feel accepted. The level of importance placed on women's sexual attractiveness can lead them to believe that their beauty defines their value.

My family encouraged our young women to wear the hijab and live according to the values we were raised with. With that being said, we also accept that the decision to wear it or not is up to the women themselves. My father seemed to understand the plight my sisters faced. He understands that Muslim women wearing the hijab tend to have fewer social and professional opportunities. Generally speaking, U.S. society considers women wearing the hijab to be less integrated into the dominant culture and to be more likely to be isolated and to have less freedom.

As a young woman, some of the comments my sister had to endure from her peers were, "Are you covering your hair because you have bad hair?" "Are you bald?" and "Please let me see your hair!" The more well-meaning comments were, "Nice costume" or "I like your style." She continued wearing her hijab for a while, but as she grew into her teen years, she eventually took it off. I was sad when she stopped wearing it, because I felt that society had forced her to change herself. She was at a stage where she was trying to find her identity between two strong cultures, and this was an indication that the dominant U.S. culture had won. I completely believe in establishing one's own identity, including adopting the dominant culture if one chooses, but I do not agree with the dominant culture's bullying and marginalizing other cultures' values and practices.

In dealing with Islamophobia, I became more aware of my complex **positionality** as a Muslim male in the United States. Using "positioning" and "framing" from intercultural praxis, I can see how my religious identity was framed by the heightened discourse of antiterrorism. Also, my own framing of Islamophobia was slightly different from my sister's in that her struggle was shaped by both sexism and Islamophobia. As a Muslim woman, she is positioned to negotiate not only her religious identity but also her gender identity and performance that are perceived as "different" from normative Western femininity. Since I have not personally experienced sexism, I realize that I'm not in a position to speak on behalf of my sister who experienced the sexist Islamophobic attack about her choice to wear the hijab. However, in my role as her brother, I provided support as someone who could empathize and understand her struggle. This is an example of how I can use my privileged positioning as a male to seek to understand my sister's experience and work in alliance with her to challenge oppressive systems.

RACISM AND ISLAMOPHOBIA

I was a volunteer with the American Red Cross when Hurricane Katrina struck in August of 2005. To aid the victims, I was sent to one of the main American Red Cross Headquarters in Montgomery, Alabama. They originally asked me to take a caseworker position and stay at headquarters, but I asked instead to be assigned to a bulk-distribution site in Mississippi.

When I arrived in Mississippi, I drove a Budget truck and was accompanied by a white American woman, who helped me navigate. Our assignment was to take large truckloads of ready-to-eat food (MREs) and other supplies to people affected by the disaster. One day, we traveled to Jackson, Mississippi, to see what the extent of the damage was and to provide assistance to the survivors.

I remember seeing a family standing outside, attempting to pick up the pieces of their ravaged house. I saw a flag that was still standing; it reminded me of the American flag, but it was different, yet with similar colors. "That's a cool way of having the American flag designed," I said to my partner. "Stay in the truck this time. Don't get out. I'll be back," she said in a strange tone of voice. Her face showed signs of worry and fear. "Why?" I asked. "Shouldn't I come with you?" I had no idea why she wanted me to stay in the truck this time. "No. Please stay in the truck," she insisted as she climbed out. Seconds later, an older white man approached the truck. He had a long grey beard and hair and wore a head bandana in the colors of the American flag. I opened the window of the truck and smiled at him. "Where you from?" he asked me. "I'm African," I said. It was too complicated to explain that I was of Sudanese/Saudi Arabian descent but came from Lebanon. I figured my accent wouldn't help if I told him that I was a U.S. citizen living in Salt Lake City, Utah. "What are you doing in this country?" he asked, rather confrontationally. I could sense that question didn't just come from innocent curiosity. I knew that I had better find an answer he'd approve of; otherwise, I was not going to be safe. "I'm a student in this country," I explained. "I heard about what happened, so I came to help." I counted about 20 seconds of total silence. Finally, he nodded his head approvingly. "Look what happened to my Mustang, man," he said, pointing to his damaged car. "That's horrible, man," I said. "I'm glad you and your family are safe." Inside, I breathed a sigh of relief, realizing I had narrowly escaped a potentially dangerous situation. As we handed over supplies to his family, I realized I had barely averted what could have been an ugly display of racism.

Using historical framing as an entry point, I realized that my racial and cultural identity as a black male with a "non-U.S.-American accent" instigated an already established stereotype for the Mississippi gentleman. In this instance, I was aware of the history of racism and segregation in the United States and imagined that the gentleman saw me as a threat. When I'm engaged in dialogue such as this one with the gentleman in Mississippi, I have the choice either to initiate conflict or attempt to foster understanding. In the above instance, I chose to shape the conversation in a way that shifted the interaction from a confrontational and competitive argument to an opportunity for peaceful exchange.

After serving in Mississippi, I was sent to Louisiana. I worked as a transporter distributing Red Cross personnel and equipment to different areas. This allowed me to interact with more volunteers and see more cities in the South. When I arrived in Louisiana, I met with my supervisor. He was a former sergeant in the U.S. military. I introduced myself. I told him that I am half Middle Eastern and half African, and that my dream was to work for the International Federation of the Red Cross and Red Crescent Societies in Iraq—to work with prisoners of war and ensure that their rights were upheld. After my declaration, the sergeant announced, "Excuse me, ladies and gentlemen, Taj is from Africa and he's also an Arab. Right, Taj?" "Yes!" I replied with a proud smile on my face. "He's going to work for the International Federation of Red Cross and Red Crescent Societies to monitor our soldiers while they're dealing with the terrorists in the prison," the sergeant continued. The room fell silent, and everyone looked at me. As I looked around the room, I noticed it predominantly consisted of American-born white people. They all put on fake smiles and responded to this announcement with comments such as, "Interesting," "Wow," and "Really?!"

After this incident I noticed the volunteers did not want to interact with me. As I walked by groups of talking, laughing volunteers, they would fall silent when they saw me. It became obvious that I wasn't welcome. At the time, I was too busy to try to understand what it meant, so I let it roll off my back, so to speak.

These attitudes did not actually get to me until a few days later. I was attending a quick training course on how to use the GPS equipment when an older white woman commented, "My son is in the military; he uses the GPS system to find the Muslim terrorists," and she looked at me directly. These types of comments were made repeatedly. I just looked back at her and smiled at the time, but later, when I went to my room, I cried out of frustration and anger.

The following day was September 11, 2005, and a ceremony was being held to honor those who were lost during the terrorist attacks. The same woman who had made the terrorist comment in the GPS training approached me. "Taj, I'm sure you're going to attend the ceremony to honor our men and women that were killed by the Muslim terrorists on September 11th. Right?" she asked pointedly, as if she expected me to be resistant to the idea. "Of course I will," I replied, with an easy smile.

During my time working on the Hurricane Katrina project, I was subjected to many prejudiced comments and perspectives. This was a product of the fear and hate toward Islam that had spread across the country after the events of 9/11. Zouaoui (2012) reported that the Islamophobia sweeping the media was perpetuated by groups of self-proclaimed experts spreading anti-Islam propaganda through books, reports, websites, and blogs. They talked to the media and even advised Congress. As a result, many people feared and/or hated Islam. Cohen (2006) published poll results reflecting that after the events of 9/11, almost 60% of Americans believed that Islam was more likely to produce violent extremism than were other religions.

I wasn't quite sure how to process what was happening to me, but I continued to react politely and did not let it stop me from doing what I was there to do. While it was a disturbing experience, I was no stranger to prejudice, having grown up in an extremely diverse, and rather volatile, community, and I had already developed carefully honed conflict-resolution strategies. I learned from my mother how to deal with conflicting cultural values. She always did what she thought was right, no matter what others around her said. I remember she would often take a stand for what she believed in even when it was controversial. Her influence contributed largely to the restraint, patience, curiosity, and willingness to dialogue that I exercised at this early stage of my acculturation in the United States.

INTERRELIGIOUS CONFLICTS

To complete my undergraduate degree in international studies, I was required to work a certain number of hours with an organization to get international experience. I received an internship with the Desert Industries Humanitarian Center, a nonprofit organization created by the Church of Latter Day Saints (LDS). I worked with immigrants and refugees, helping with the 2-year training program designed to give trainees the necessary skills to live and work in the United States.

I was called to a meeting to discuss an issue that the administrators considered to be very important. Some of the Muslim and Buddhist trainees were refusing to participate in the mandatory Monday meetings, which were held in a church. The members of the church started the meetings with a prayer, asking for blessings, safety, and success for the center. This made the attendees uncomfortable; they feared that this might be a duplicitous way of trying to convert them. The administrators assured everyone that this wasn't their intent. They explained that the prayer was simply to support the nature of the work at Desert Industries.

As a solution, I proposed that a person from each faith say a prayer in his or her own language during these Monday meetings. This would help the trainees feel more comfortable and accepted. The administrators looked around at one another with wonder at this new idea. My friend, who was an LDS member, smiled and said, "I don't see why not." Everyone else agreed, and I could feel the energy in the room go from tense to relaxed.

I went to talk to the trainees and asked them to say small prayers on Monday because the staff would be interested in hearing and praying along. This showed the trainees with other faiths that their religions were valued and respected by the organization. An African trainee did the first prayer in Arabic. It meant, "Allah, blessings for what you've bestowed on us and keep our faith." Muslims, Buddhists, and LDS members all said "Amen" afterward, even though they may not have understood what was said. This change brought about a new feeling of unity among everyone in the organization.

In addressing the tension surrounding diverse practices of faith, I carefully reflected on my thoughts and action. Understanding my own views on religion and faith prompted me to respect and embrace other forms of faith. In the processes of self-reflection, I can assess the strengths and weaknesses of my actions to generate the necessary balance in a given situation. In every incident of intercultural conflict, the ability to reflect, observe, and remain flexible has been a valuable skill to resolve conflict.

CONCLUSION

The six steps of Sorrells' (2013) intercultural praxis model have helped me approach and analyze multiple conflicts I have experienced in the United States. The multidimensional framework of analysis for intercultural conflict allowed me to integrate multiple aspects of my identity at an interpersonal level, hold the complexities of Islamophobia and racism on an intergroup level, and consider the geopolitical realities of refugees and xenophobia on the international level. Additionally, I have found the six points of entry of the intercultural praxis model to be essential in moving toward intercultural conflict transformation. I learned not to let fear of making a mistake or being ostracized stop me from living a life true to myself. Where others were rejecting that which was different, I learned instead to see opportunities for growth and beauty. This helped me understand and embrace the differences within myself, allowing me to use and integrate my different cultural frames into my identity even when they seemed to be conflicting. I realize now that my positionality, in relation to my sister, allowed me to empathize when I witnessed my sister's intercultural conflict. Understanding my positionality and how it changes in different contexts has enabled me to serve as a bridge across cultural differences in conflict situations.

Overall, integrating the complex (and sometimes opposing) elements of my identity helped me gain a deeper understanding of intercultural conflict. I learned not to leap or take a side too quickly, and I understood well how complicated certain conflicts can be. As a result, I have adopted patience, emotional restraint, and an attitude of never underestimating the process of conflict resolution. As an adult, when dealing with the intercultural conflicts caused by ignorance and fear, I try to remain respectful and defuse potentially intense situations. I know that I cannot immediately change people's views, but I can lead by example and provide opportunities for people to see for themselves that there is more to the story than they thought.

KEY TERMS

cosmopolitan
    citizenship   250

decolonization
    workshop   249

double marginality   249

hegemonic beliefs   262

hijab   260

immigrant
    transnationalism   250

intercultural conflict   248

intercultural praxis   259

Islamophobia   259

positionality   263

social capital   250

transnational immigrant
    networks   250

DISCUSSION QUESTIONS

1. In Mercado's case study, she describes decolonization workshops sponsored by FIOB. Based on your reading of the case study, identify the similarities between the historic processes and practices of colonization and the mechanisms operating today in the United States and Mexico. What practices are fostered in the workshops to reconstruct and reclaim indigenous cultural ways? How might you personally benefit from attending decolonization workshops?

2. According to Mercado, how do the experiences of transnational migration impact indigenous migrants' understanding of their identities? How is culture a tool for action and resource in transnational organizing and alliance building? Discuss how the construction of indigenous identities in the global context is intertwined with various communication practices and media.

3. Throughout his personal narrative, Suleyman discusses how his positionality impacted his framing of situations, as well as how his positionality is framed by others. Using examples from his narrative, discuss the relationship between positionality and framing. What does Suleyman mean when he states that integrating his conflicting identities has helped him understand intercultural conflict? How might your identity/identities and positionality serve as tools or resources for addressing intercultural conflicts?

4. As illustrated in the entries in this chapter, intercultural conflict is complex and often infused with intensely felt, unresolved tension and historical trauma. Using examples from both entries in the chapter, discuss approaches, skills, and strategies for addressing the multiple and deep layers of intercultural conflict.

CHAPTER 14

Intercultural Alliances for Social Justice

$\mathbf{A}$s people from different backgrounds increasingly intersect, clash, and bond in the context of globalization, critical questions with significant implications emerge. What is the purpose and outcome of our engagements with people across cultural differences? Can we forge relationships across racial, ethnic, cultural, gender, sexual orientation, religious, and national lines to challenge hierarchies of difference entrenched through history and maintained today? Can our affiliations bridge differences to become sources of healing from past infractions and historical trauma? Drawing on our diversity as we challenge inequities past and present, can we create a more equitable and just world through our intercultural **alliances** and activism?

Throughout history, intercultural communication has played a critical role in alliances for social change. This may sound lofty and unlikely. Indeed, it is probably easier to think of examples of how intercultural communication has aided discrimination, exploitation, and genocide, as dominant ideologies, institutions, social norms, and prevailing narratives reproduce and reinforce hierarchies of difference. Yet, if we look closely at significant social movements for justice in the 20th century—the women's liberation movement, the labor movement, and the civil rights movement, for example—alliances across lines of race, class, and gender, while contested and fragile, were foundational to the strength and success of these movements.

Sara DeTurk's case study documenting the Esperanza Peace and Justice Center provides an example of a multi-issue organization committed to holistic views on social change. Esperanza effectively develops intercultural alliances for social change by emphasizing systemic approaches to oppression and justice highlighting intersectionality, relationship building, and belonging. Amer F. Ahmed shares his journey as a South Asian American Muslim man navigating racially, culturally, and religiously charged landscapes of his Midwestern hometown and high school, travels abroad, and work in higher education. His personal narrative illustrates how activism grounded in hip-hop culture validates and gives voice to marginal identities and histories, builds intercultural alliances for social change, and transforms the lives of so many around him.

"The Unrelenting Social Conscience of the City": Strategies and Challenges of a Multi-Issue Social Change Organization

Sara DeTurk
University of Texas, San Antonio

M ost **social justice** movements, as observed by Gandhi and Shah (2006), are focused on single identities such as race, gender, or sexual orientation. A notable exception is the Esperanza Peace and Justice Center in San Antonio, Texas, whose vision statement reads as follows:

> The people of Esperanza dream of a world where everyone has civil rights and economic justice, where the environment is cared for, where cultures are honored and communities are safe. The Esperanza advocates for those wounded by domination and inequality—women, people of color, queer people, the working class and poor. We believe in creating bridges between people by exchanging ideas and educating and empowering each other. We believe it is vital to share our visions of hope . . . we are esperanza.

Esperanza's activities include explicitly political work such as organizing San Antonio's International Women's Day march and lobbying the City Council to preserve historic buildings on San Antonio's historically working-class, Mexican American Westside. It also promotes the preservation of cultural memory through the collection of oral histories and *fotohistorias*. In addition, Esperanza is an important local venue for the arts, which its founders believe is central to the cultural grounding, self-validation, and political expression of marginalized communities, as well as intercultural understanding and dialogue. The diversity of Esperanza's efforts in terms of both its goals and its tactics is relatively unique among social change organizations, which more typically address single issues such as racism or sexism. This **intersectionality** is a great strength of the organization, but it also introduces particular challenges.

Esperanza's work has never been without controversy in San Antonio. It has been demonized by social conservatives for promoting homosexuality, attacked by political and economic elites, and sensationalized by the news media. Its very existence was threatened in 1997 when the city withdrew public funding for all its arts programming. Esperanza responded by mobilizing supporters, educating the community, and winning a lawsuit against the city. Esperanza continues to surprise its naysayers, winning battles that others have long written off as lost. It recently celebrated its 25th anniversary and has (according to at least one local journalist) gained credibility and influence throughout the city.

As a scholar of intercultural communication and intergroup alliances, I have watched Esperanza closely, with particular interest in how it manages its alliances with single-issue organizations. In 2011 and 2012, I conducted an ethnographic study of the organization to systematically explore its communication tactics, strategies, successes, and challenges. I sought, specifically, to understand Esperanza's approaches to social change as a **multi-issue organization**, and the particular challenges inherent in its multi-issue focus.

METHODOLOGY

From August 2011 to August 2012, I acted as a participant-observer at the Esperanza Peace and Justice Center and at events with which the organization was involved. I spent about 90 hours attending meetings, press conferences, marches, performances, art exhibits, workshops, and volunteer sessions to prepare the center's newsletter for mailing. In addition, I conducted 22 formal interviews with staff members, board members, volunteers, leaders of coalition partner organizations, and other members of the local community. Finally, I examined *La Voz de Esperanza,* the center's monthly news journal, and (with the help of three students who received independent-study credit) conducted close rhetorical analyses of several articles and images.

My approach to data collection and analysis was guided by various schools of activist research (Hale, 2006; Speed, 2006), participatory action research (Kemmis & McTaggart, 2000; Maguire, 1987), and critical ethnography (Madison, 2005). I strove, in particular, to situate the research within my commitment to political goals shared with the Esperanza Center; to frame it in ways that can contribute to community action through the application of broad, social analysis; and to share ownership of the project with Esperanza and its constituents through dialogic and collaborative analysis.

To interpret the findings, I took a grounded theory approach, which Charmaz (2011) has argued is especially suitable for studying social justice. Throughout the period of participant observation and interviewing, I periodically reviewed my field notes and transcripts to identify emergent themes. Then, upon completion of data collection, I examined the themes to identify those that were the most prevalent, forceful, and resonant. Finally, I reviewed them to identify how the various themes related to one another and to the central research questions. This last stage continued throughout the writing process as I connected themes to extant research and theory and (in consultation with other stakeholders) continually reassessed the significance of the findings.

APPROACHES TO SOCIAL CHANGE

The Esperanza Peace and Justice Center takes a holistic view of social change that reflects idealism (evident in its vision statement), optimism (reflected in its name, which means "hope"), and uncompromising rhetoric that emphasizes the systemic nature of oppression. Esperanza depends heavily on a large network of supportive individuals and works consistently in coalitions and alliances with other organizations.

Holism

The holistic nature of the Esperanza Center's efforts is twofold. First, the organization takes the long view in regard to social change. Even campaigns that might seem to an outsider like clear failures are framed by the members of Esperanza's inner circle as successes, or at least as opportunities for further activism, mobilization, and education. When Esperanza sued the city in 2008 to block an ordinance against organizing political marches without paying a fee, they lost the suit, but they frame the conflict as an ongoing opportunity to educate citizens about the importance of free speech and the right to march. Antonia Castañeda, a historian and advocate of Esperanza, observed:

> Some would say that the lawsuit was not successful. We didn't win. But I wouldn't call that not successful. The fact that we went through the process of taking it to the district court, that, to me, was success, because people are learning, and they're growing, and they're seeing, and they're engaging, and they're thinking, and they're being put in positions to observe, to assess, to analyze, to interpret. How can that not be termed an achievement?

A second reflection of Esperanza's holistic vision is its multi-issue approach to organizing. Whereas most social change organizations focus on environmental protection, advocacy for the poor, equality for women, or civil rights for people of color, Esperanza addresses all these issues and more. Indeed, when the organization's leaders describe its founding, it reflects this multidimensional understanding of identity. Graciela Sánchez, Esperanza's executive director, recalled that

> the idea was that as different groups used the center, that were talking about social justice, from police brutality to climate justice, from lesbian/gay rights to antiwar stuff, whatever it was, they would run into each other, and then that whole cross-pollinization, or synergy, could take place.

Gloria Ramírez, who was also present at the center's founding, recalls that she was "seeking to find a place for myself, particularly in expressing all of the parts of myself that I am, which is a Latina, a woman, a lesbian, an activist, an educator, and working class." For her, "it just didn't make sense to go off and be focused on a single issue, working in an isolated way, when it seemed like the roots of oppression were all from the same source, which is a systemic source." The early organizers, according to Graciela, were especially frustrated by patriarchal dynamics within the Chicano movement and were also informed by scholarship on multicultural feminist alliances (e.g., Moraga & Anzaldúa, 1983).

Marisol Cortez, a recent addition to Esperanza's staff, described the organization's aims as "to further the work of social movements that connect a broad variety of oppressions, including race, class, gender, sexuality, and disability, but also colonialism and exploitation of the earth." She observed that "so much of what we do is all about the same sort of root conditions, namely capitalist land use decisions and a colonialist relationship to the land." For her, Esperanza helped her see connections between environmental preservation of buildings (the emphasis of much of their current work), preservation of local knowledge (namely, that of San Antonio's overwhelmingly Mexican American Westside), and ethnic pride.

Esperanza's approach to social change is intersectional not only in terms of identities and issues but also in terms of strategies and activities. One of its most unique aspects is its focus on arts programming as a means to foster political empowerment. Center staff spend a large portion of their time organizing concerts, art exhibits, and other events aimed at cultural expression. They view these activities as ways to give voice to members of marginalized communities but also to foster dialogue across constituencies. Staff and volunteers alike spoke of elders who come into the center for the arts programming, despite its reputation for being run by "a bunch of communist lesbians." Once they are there, the elders' personal relationships with the staff break down cultural and political barriers. "We create these moments of community that help to break down those walls that divide us," said Graciela. "We break down those wedge issues and stereotypes, you know; we humanize each other." In terms of intersectionality, this process reflects Carrillo Rowe's (2008) insight that identity is as much about belonging as about race, class, or gender. Esperanza, according to interviewees, is a safe space for *everyone*. Many of the people who frequent the Esperanza Center for its cultural programming, moreover, are inspired by what they learn there to become politically active.

Friends and **allies** of the center express appreciation for its multi-issue approach. Maria Berriozábal, a former member of the City Council, remarked, "What's so unique and so good about Esperanza is that they address civil rights and human rights, but also the systemic issues, by which I mean energy, water, and growth." Historian Antonia Castañeda concurred: "The Esperanza is the one institution in town where it is not compartmentalized; everything is part of a whole, and so it brings all elements of our being—our social, political, cultural, artistic, aesthetic being—together. And speaks to all of that whole."

Uncompromising Rhetoric

Related to Esperanza's idealistic and holistic approach to organizing is the uncompromising nature of its rhetoric. Interviewees consistently used words such as *tireless, determined, tenacious*, and *uncompromising* to describe how Graciela Sánchez, as a person, and Esperanza, as an organization, go about their pursuit of a more just society. As one former staff member put it, "Esperanza winds up often being the voice '*sin pelos en la lengua*,' without hair on their tongue. They say the truth, and they bring up the things that other organizations are afraid to bring up." Another staff member, Marisol Cortez, reflected:

> What Esperanza does well is to refuse to not speak. Refuse to not act, even though it's painful to confront people in power who think they're doing the right thing. It presents an embodied analysis that needs to be heard within public discourse in a loud way. In a determined way. Esperanza refuses to not do that work. Like, no, we are gonna speak truth to power, and we won't ever stop, even if you hate us for it.

Santiago Garcia, an economic development specialist who worked for the city, remarked, "I think you can expect certain things from the Esperanza. You can expect a dose of conscience, and being called out, in not a spiteful way, but in a way where certain values are not gonna be forgotten." This relentless confrontation of injustice does not always win friends; one local journalist told me that she perceived Esperanza staff as having a reputation for being angry troublemakers.

It also subjects Esperanza's staff members to very high standards, and when these standards are internalized across such a broad range of ideals and principles, it can add to the already high risk of burnout. Indeed, two staff members left the organization during my 12 months of observation. Both described the difficulty of working collaboratively across multiple dimensions of identity when staff members—even those belonging to similar identity groups—understand those identities differently, and when there is never enough time for the constant processing of identity that Lichterman (1999) observed as necessary in multi-issue work. The consistency, though, with which Esperanza's core staff have both asserted and reflected their commitment to the center's ideals has earned them both admiration from allies and respect and credibility from city leaders.

Gary Houston, an activist from the city's historically African American Eastside, explained this as follows:

> They're honest. And impatient. And often angry. And those are understandable responses to some of the stuff that we minorities have all had to deal with. I think that kind of directness, and refusal to even consider compromise on certain standards, has its own integrity. One of their real strengths is that you really know where they're coming from at all times. There's an absence of guile or vanity about them. With the women of Esperanza, it's totally about the issues. With community-based organizations, sometimes certain leaders are overly concerned about the glow of the spotlight and how it burnishes their reputations and sense of importance. Not there. Their gratification is derived from outcomes and results and is unrelated in any way to inflating personal egos or even the reputation of the organization. That's pretty impressive, and unique.

Antonia Castañeda observed that Esperanza "demonstrates that you can, and must, take a position for what is right. And that you can, and should, challenge the structures of power. No matter the cost." She went on: "They began and continue to be the *unrelenting* social conscience of this city."

Alliances

A central component of Esperanza's work is its network of alliances and coalitions with other, mostly single-issue, organizations. Esperanza works closely with other civil rights, labor, environmental, and arts organizations, as well as thousands of individual supporters. These alliances have turned out to be a key element of Esperanza's greatest successes.

In terms of individual supporters, Esperanza maintains a mailing list of more than 10,000 subscribers to its newsletter, as well as databases of people who support each of the center's various types of cultural events and political efforts. With remarkable alacrity, staff can mobilize large groups of people to attend last-minute protests, press conferences, and City Council meetings. They also have a broad network of volunteers with a wide variety of skills and personal contacts. Collectively, Esperanza refers to these people as the community's "*buena gente*" (good people).

At the organizational level, Esperanza—which grew out of a network of civil rights organizations—has always worked closely with other groups, not only locally but internationally. Indeed, as Esperanza has grown and matured, it has nurtured the emergence of younger women's groups, which have, in turn, become core supporters of Esperanza. Petra Mata, cofounder and codirector of Fuerza Unida, recalls the origins of her workers' rights group when she and more than a thousand other workers were laid off by Levi-Strauss. "Esperanza was there," she said. The center offered space, financial donations, and training in grant writing and civil rights law. "We love them," said Petra. "Esperanza will be there for us." Sarwat Husain, president of the San Antonio chapter of the Council on American Islamic Relations, tells a similar story. After a series of hate crimes against Muslims in 2001, she said, Esperanza reached out to offer support. "Here we were thinking we were alone, and here's a whole community that was with us," she recalled. "Esperanza is a place you can go at any time, and they will help. They will organize a press conference, and they will gather the people." Sarwat observed that the Esperanza Center has been an important source for her training in civil rights work but also a channel through which to make the Latino community more aware of the Muslim community.

CHALLENGES OF APPLYING UNCOMPROMISING RHETORIC TO A MULTI-ISSUE APPROACH

While some of these alliances and coalitions have remained mostly trouble-free, others have been more contentious. These tensions, I argue, emerge largely from the application of Esperanza's uncompromising rhetoric to its holistic approach to social change. Its consistent confrontation of injustice, that is, often creates or exposes conflict in the context of its intersectional approach. As Antonia Castañeda observed,

> the Esperanza has been willing to speak out and to take action in situations where other people would not have, and they have been criticized for it, and not always supported for it, and sometimes that lack of support has also come from the progressive community.

Indeed, two of Esperanza's staff members observed that some of their biggest frustrations have come from tensions with coalition partners. Interviews with Esperanza staff members and coalition partners alike suggest three main sources of conflict in these relationships. The first involves differences in priorities and concerns. The second is resistance by individuals with social **privilege** based on race or gender (for example) to having that privilege challenged or confronted by women of color. The third is a desire on the part of people with social privilege to avoid risking that privilege through political confrontation.

Single-Issue Organizations Do Not Share All the Same Concerns as a Multi-Issue Organization

Because Esperanza is a multi-issue organization, not all of its allies agree with it on all issues. Graciela recalled,

> I remember in our earlier history, when a black woman would write in *La Voz* about racism in San Antonio, and all of a sudden we'd get several calls from so-called white allies, saying, "Get me off the mailing list."

She recounted, similarly, difficulties over gender politics in alliances with male-dominated gay organizations and Chicano organizations, and tensions over sexual orientation with some organizations advocating racial justice. Some tensions have stemmed from differences in priorities. Some gay rights organizations, for example, have wanted to fight for marriage equality, whereas the Esperanza staff espouse a feminism that rejects marriage altogether as a patriarchal institution. Some environmental organizations, correspondingly, have emphasized a scientific analysis of environmental threats that, according to Esperanza staff members, lack concern for racial justice. One staff member put it this way:

> In order to do single-issue organizing, you have to really simplify what's going on, and kind of block out this and that. So the environmental folks, they want to get all into the science of nuclear, and think that's what will motivate people. And they have a way of looking at how things work, like if we could only teach the City Council to understand . . . so there are some blinders to the bigger political picture of the power structure, especially in terms of poor communities of color. So we're always gonna have a different take, you know?

These experiences echo other research on social movements. In an analysis of Queer Nation in San Francisco, for example, Gray (2009) observed that the movement's white, middle-class constituency "saw no common cause" with its working-class members of color. As early as 1983, feminist scholars such as Hartsock (1983) articulated the problem that our identities position us with profoundly different standpoints from which to perceive social reality. Harding (1991), moreover, argued that members of marginalized social groups tend to have greater insights about oppression than do those of dominant groups; she termed this insight "strong objectivity."

Other feminist scholar-activists (e.g., Albrecht & Brewer, 1990; Anzaldúa, 1999; Collins, 1990; Lugones & Spelman, 1983; Moraga & Anzaldúa, 1983; Reagon, 1983) have observed that alliances, by definition, imply both common goals and differences, and that the differences must be honored. This can be especially difficult for would-be allies whose identities imbue them with social privilege and an unwillingness to engage in authentic dialogue that acknowledges that privilege. These challenges are echoed by intercultural communication research, which highlights the importance of vulnerability, trust, and resilience (Chavez, 2007); the largely paradoxical nature of collaborating across identities in the interest of social justice (DeTurk, 2011); and the reality that "there are more ideological forces, institutional policies and practices, and social norms that reinforce hierarchy and elites keeping their privileges in place than there are ideologies, policies, practices, and norms encouraging and rewarding intercultural alliances" (Collier, 2003, p. 14). Communication scholars have consistently advocated that allies in social justice activism confront and interrogate their own and each other's identity-based privilege. However, this is easier said than done.

People With Social Privilege Do Not Want It to Be Challenged

In a variety of ways, Esperanza consistently challenges its allies' positions and uses of power. Perhaps most fundamentally, its leadership largely consists of Chicana lesbians.

While these women stress that the organization is for everyone, it is typically not perceived that way. There is a widespread assumption—revealed in interviews with staff, allies, and other community members—that because it is led by Chicana lesbians, it must be *for* Chicana lesbians. Underlying this assumption seems to be a discomfort with the idea of being led by women, lesbians, and/or Chicanas. One local journalist, for example, said that when she first heard about Esperanza, she was told, "Oh, it's a gay and lesbian organization, and they're pretty far out there." Over time, though, she came to see that "it's defined by woman power, and maybe that's why people thought that; it was a way for them to dismiss their power." Noel Poyo, director of a Latino community development organization, agreed: Esperanza, he observed, faced men in the city who "can't take it" from a woman, and who were probably resentful or threatened by Esperanza's growing power.

The social power generally conferred to people who are white, male, and/or heterosexual is frequently challenged by Esperanza, not only through the dominance of lesbians of color in coalition meetings but by their uncompromising rhetoric. Esperanza's leadership is not shy about asserting its voice and challenging oppression and marginalization. One member of an environmental organization recalled some friction during a meeting with Esperanza when one of its leaders accused him and other white men of dominating the discussion. As he perceived it, the accusation lacked legitimacy because the task at hand was one of environmental protection, not social justice.

More than one interviewee observed that because Esperanza's leaders challenge the structures of power and the people in power, they are considered confrontational and unreasonable. One staff member said, "The way that we do our politics, it's really not confrontational; it's always kind of, 'Here we are, this is who we stand for, this is why we have as much place as anybody else.'" This claim, when made by Latina lesbians, is subversive and shocking enough to some people to be threatening and is thus *met* with confrontation. Ray McDonald, a regular Esperanza volunteer who is frequently the only white man in the room, described what he viewed as a common reception to Graciela Sánchez's challenges of injustice: "She was a small voice talking to this large, white, dominant, wealthy crowd. And who the hell is she, you know? She's Hispanic, and she's a woman. 'After you finish doing my housekeeping, then maybe I'll listen to you.'"

People With Privilege Want to Avoid Conflict and Confrontation

According to some of its allies and critics alike, the Esperanza Center often does thrive on confrontation. Marisol Cortez, when asked about the nature of the organization's power, said, "Esperanza's power is only the power of the people involved, as we are able to place our bodies into those spaces of power, and contest the way things are done." Many of its political efforts, therefore, have involved protests, marches, press conferences, speeches before the City Council, critical letters to city leaders, and even lawsuits. Noel Poyo observed that confrontation "gets people riled up, mobilized, and feeling their own power" and, as such, has been an effective way for the organization to encourage activism among its constituents who have otherwise felt voiceless.

Esperanza's leadership sees confrontation less as a choice than a necessity. Marisol Cortez recalled a recent transition in the city-owned utility company, when it hired an African American man as its CEO and decided to replace a coal plant with investments in solar power. Although most people in the progressive community appreciated these changes, Esperanza's response was that the changes were welcome but insufficient. Marisol felt compelled to write a public letter urging city officials to (1) acknowledge the role of activists in pushing for change, (2) challenge the idea of "clean coal," and (3) more closely examine the nature of sustainability not only from a technocentric perspective but also in terms of social justice. Despite her compulsion to write the letter, she recalled that it was quite painful to present it to the city officials. "It was awful," she said, not just because it was difficult to confront people in power but because

> you're sitting around the room, at that table were other environmental groups that you might be allied with, but who don't necessarily agree with that analysis, or think it's a strategic misstep. Other groups were wanting to be very congratulatory of [the power company], like, "Oh, you're investing all this money in clean technology." But no, we have to go further. It's not enough. It'll never be enough.

Graciela Sánchez, reflecting on Esperanza's white, middle-class environmental allies, remarked, "They want everything to go smoothly, and they want the mayor and everybody to be happy with them all the time. And, you know, for us, we've never necessarily had those folks happy with us *ever*."

Graciela's observation was supported by one of the white, middle-class environmentalists she referred to:

> Our organization has always tried to work more with the establishment and the powers-that-be, and less confrontationally. We tend not to want to go out and do the street protests and that sort of stuff. I guess I see that as related to the fact that a lot of our leaders have professional types of positions, and do you really want to be out there on TV, you know, when your conservative colleagues will see it?

As an organization representing alternative ideologies and the city's least powerful people, the Esperanza Center finds itself in near constant conflict with those in power, even those who largely share its values and want to see the organization succeed. This can be attributed largely to differences in priorities and concerns; resistance by those with privilege to having that privilege challenged or confronted, especially by women of color; and their fear of risking that privilege through political confrontation. These tensions are also aggravated by the center staff's feeling that no single advance toward social or environmental justice "will ever be enough," and their willingness to confront their allies whenever they perceive injustice. These two central attitudes—a holistic, intersectional approach to justice and an uncompromising rhetorical stance—are both reflections of Esperanza's idealism and dogged commitment to its values.

CONCLUSION

The Esperanza Peace and Justice Center is an organization that takes political action across a range of ideals that may seem disparate to others but are connected by deep structures of culture and power. The center's unabashed confrontation of many different forms of injustice is simultaneously essential to its mission and a challenge to its important relationships with allies. How does Esperanza make it work? Its combination of political organizing with arts programming, for one thing, is an approach that, while grounded in the historically Mexican cultural context of San Antonio, can serve as a model for other organizations elsewhere. Its emphasis on relationship building and belonging, in particular, responds to many of the challenges that have historically frustrated intergroup alliances. Esperanza's successes, second, can be attributed largely to the tireless efforts of its staff, as well as their idealistic commitment to, and unwavering focus on, the organization's shared values. Esperanza, finally, provides a distinctive case study not only as a successful multi-issue activist organization but also because it is led by people—primarily Latina lesbians with working-class origins—who typically lack power and credibility in mainstream society. Indeed, the political marginalization from which the organization has emerged has also served as a source of "strong objectivity" across a wide range of issues, which carries with it a special capacity to see and articulate the connections among these issues. In conclusion, the success of the Esperanza Peace and Justice Center reflects hard work, savvy communication tactics, fidelity to its values, and also changes in the broader culture (e.g., increasing acceptance of sexual minorities and expanding power of Latinos), which the center itself has helped bring about.

A South Asian American Muslim Man's Global Journey Through Hip-Hop Activism

Amer F. Ahmed

University of Michigan

I have been involved in **hip-hop activism** for most of my adult life. As a South Asian American from the Midwestern United States, many people are surprised by my engagement with hip-hop; yet hip-hop has been a critical component of the social justice work I have participated in within the Unites States and around the world. For me, as a member of the hip-hop generation, hip-hop culture has facilitated numerous intercultural interactions and encounters that have helped me develop a deeper understanding of issues, inequities, and injustices in various cultural contexts around the world.

Hip-hop culture is not perfect; no human culture is. Hip-hop has been commodified and co-opted by corporate media, which have exploited the culture by peddling misogynistic, homophobic, materialistic messages with demeaning representations of black and brown people. These issues extend far beyond hip-hop culture to a broader capitalist agenda enacted through popular culture and media that marginalize and stereotype numerous identities. However, I believe that living into the core principles and values of hip-hop can help create a better world for everyone. The current **co-optation and commodification of hip-hop** requires those of us participating in the culture to challenge ourselves to find ways to strengthen it. I remain steadfast and vigilant in my commitment to use hip-hop as a tool for empowerment. Based on the powerful experiences I've had around the world, I continue to work through this culture to enact change that I believe is important and necessary in our world today. To help you understand why hip-hop is so important to me, a little more understanding of my background is needed.

FOUNDATIONAL INTERCULTURAL EXPERIENCES

I was born and raised in Springfield, Ohio, by Indian Muslim immigrants. My family was part of a small South Asian Muslim community in a blue-collar town where the largest employer built semitrucks. Like many cities in the Midwest, Springfield was relatively segregated along racial and class lines, with most black and lower-economic groups living on the south side and most white and upper-middle-class people living on the north side. My high school was about 60% white and 38% black; I was part of the tiny percentage of students categorized as "other." Like most adolescent youth, I just wanted to fit in. This proved to be challenging since I was raised in a vastly different cultural environment than were most of my peers.

I found myself moving between different groups of white and black people with varying experiences of acceptance. Through those encounters, it became evident to me that many of the perceptions each group held about the other seemed inaccurate. I often felt like a bridge between divergent perceptions and across perspectives people had never considered about the other group. As a young person in high school, I was unaware of why such divergent perspectives and worldviews existed and the history behind them. One thing that was abundantly clear was that black folks empathized with me about being different while white folks seemed to expect me to be like them. Those differences led me to learn and understand the marginalizing experiences that were so deeply part of being black in the United States.

Meanwhile, my Islamic upbringing allowed me to meet South Asian, Arab, African, black American, and even some Malaysian Muslims. Amongst the South Asian community, there were Hindus, Sikhs, Jains, Christians, and Muslims who all had very different traditions due to religion as well as regional and linguistic diversity. As I look back on my upbringing, I realize how much code-shifting and adaptation I engaged in each day when I left my home. I became adept at shifting my communication styles in different contexts, translating into effective encounters across diverse cultural spaces. I later realized that these experiences shaped my understanding of intercultural communication.

CULTIVATING A COMMITMENT TO SOCIAL JUSTICE

Beyond my cultural experiences in the United States while I was growing up, my family also traveled back to India every 4 years. It was always so shocking for me to see poverty on a scale beyond what most in the United States could even comprehend. Each trip, I had numerous disturbing experiences involving encounters with people struggling to survive in horrific conditions that no human being should have to endure. I got sick and lost a significant amount of weight during each trip as well. When I was younger, I couldn't wait to leave India and felt embarrassed at how "backward" and "undeveloped" my culture and motherland seemed to be compared with life in the West.

Back in Springfield, I felt embarrassed about how backward my South Asian and Muslim cultures seemed compared with the broader American culture. I was often frustrated by all the aspects of my culture that made me so different from everyone else. Meanwhile, I continued to struggle to fit in and sought to use popular culture as an entry to relate and connect with other young people who typically thought my culture was strange and unusual. Popular culture and music in particular gained me entry into groups that otherwise would not have been interested in including me.

I went to high school in the mid-1990s, when rap music was entering its golden era and Dr. Dre, Snoop, Tupac, Notorious B. I. G., Wu-Tang Clan, A Tribe Called Quest, Cypress Hill, and so many others were dominating the music scene of my generation. Although grunge music and other genres were part of the mix, in my community rap music cut across most groups and was a significant part of the ethos of youth culture. Although rap music (and hip-hop culture) was important to me and a significant part of my life, it was not nearly as meaningful to me as it became during my college years.

During college, I attended a university that comprised an overwhelming majority of white, upper-middle-class Americans from Midwest suburban environments. They came from very homogenous high schools with similar demographics that lacked cultural and racial diversity. The majority of the people I met listened to bands such as Dave Matthews Band and Phish. I felt I couldn't relate to my white peers on numerous levels. Oftentimes it was strange moving between the campus environment and my friends back home in Springfield. In general, I never felt a true sense of acceptance or comfort at that university.

SOUTH AFRICA, COLONIALISM, AND GLOBAL RACISM

Out of frustration, I decided that I needed to study abroad to survive my college experience. Without fully understanding where I was visiting, I chose to study in Durban, South Africa. I was the first person in the history of my university to study abroad in South Africa. What attracted me to Durban was its racial and ethnic diversity. South Africa is a diverse country that was newly open to hosting American students following the dismantling of **apartheid** (a legalized system of racial segregation) only 4 years prior to my arrival. What I didn't realize was that Durban had the largest South Asian population outside of the subcontinent, due to British importation of labor from India for work on railroads and sugarcane plantations that began more than 100 years prior. This racial composition would impact and change the way I view and understand my positionality in society.

I was in South Africa during a historic time when former freedom fighter Nelson Mandela was serving as president and the country was wrestling with the transition of building a unified society while dealing with the trauma of racism and the atrocities that occurred under the apartheid system. The Truth Commission published its findings while

I was in South Africa; each day in the newspaper I would read about the violence and hor-rific acts that had been committed. Names of those who had perpetrated violence were released to the public. Although the perpetrators received amnesty from prosecution, jus-tice for the victims and their families came in the form of public shaming of the people responsible for these crimes under apartheid.

While in South Africa, it was fascinating for me to be in a racially divided (and only recently integrated) environment where South Asians made up a significant portion of the population. For the first time in my life, I lived somewhere I felt I had a racial place in soci-ety. I was racialized in ways that placed expectations on me to operate only amongst South Asians in South Africa. Given that I had moved among many groups my whole life, I refused to restrict myself to operating only in one group and instead chose to engage all racial and ethnic groups I encountered.

During this time, my experiences in South Africa enhanced my understanding of the global legacy of **colonialism** (Ashcroft, Griffiths, & Tiffin, 2006). I realized that not only was my motherland of India robbed of its wealth and left in horrific conditions, but my Indian brothers and sisters had also been shipped all over the world as laborers in a broader colo-nizing agenda by the British in Africa, the Caribbean, and many other places. At the same time, I began to realize the depth of the legacy of colonialism throughout Africa and spe-cifically in South Africa, where everyone I encountered experienced its historical impact.

I came to understand the effects of European colonialism on the realities people throughout the world continue to face (Winant, 2001). It was then that I realized racism is not an issue simply within the United States and South Africa but a global phenomenon that occurred differently across numerous contexts around the world (Macedo & Gounari, 2005). Furthermore, racism around the world varies depending on the history of colonial-ism in a given context. These sociocontextual dynamics vary according to the manner in which European contact occurred, the kinds of labor imported from other colonial territo-ries around the world (e.g., African slaves, Indian and Chinese laborers, indentured ser-vants, etc.), and the impact of European domination over local indigenous populations.

While spending time amongst black South Africans, I was exposed to a style of music known as *kwaito,* which dominated the music of youth culture. It combined South African musical sensibilities and language with the style and rhythms of rap music. *Kwaito* could be heard in the streets, in the clubs, and wherever young people gathered. It reminded me how global hip-hop culture had become.

While in South Africa, I traveled to Mozambique, which only recently had emerged from 30 years of war. While visiting a small town called Imhabane along the Indian Ocean, I met people who had lived in relative isolation because they had been surrounded by war, which limited travel. The only way to leave town during the war was by boat, which was how sup-plies arrived and all contact with the outside world was made. Outside my hostel were a couple of local guys wearing Wu-Tang Clan T-shirts. When I approached them and asked them about their shirts, they said they loved Wu-Tang and hip-hop. They said they identi-fied with it and wished they could travel to experience it more. In the meantime, they had to settle with whatever music arrived in their small town.

Everywhere I traveled in Africa, images of Tupac Shakur appeared next to those of Bob Marley. People often told me how they identified with Tupac's messages of resistance, struggle, and empowerment in the face of racism and oppression. In addition, hip-hop was facilitating connections across the diverse cultural contexts I was engaging in. I couldn't help but be moved by the power of hip-hop culture and, more specifically, the way rap music was providing a voice for marginalized people throughout the world. Hip-hop is a global phenomenon and a tool of empowerment used by those who continue to face the legacy of colonialism and global racism.

HIP-HOP AS INTERCULTURAL COMMUNICATION AND SOCIAL JUSTICE ACTIVISM

In my later travels and broader encounters with numerous groups (Palestinians, native/ Chicano/indigenous people, Moroccans/Algerians in France, Sri Lankans, Africans), I witnessed and experienced marginalized people identifying with the power of rap music and hip-hop culture. Furthermore, I encountered people producing expressions of hip-hop in a manner that connected to their own cultural and social realities. Facilitated by technology, I also encountered people with limited resources who were able to use whatever they had to create, share, and express themselves to empathetic audiences around the world through hip-hop culture.

Upon my return to the United States, I deepened my studies of black history and culture in the United States and across the diaspora around the world. Amiri Baraka's (1963) *Blues People* details the history of black music as a part of resistance and healing in the face of ongoing oppression. I began to realize that hip-hop music is the latest iteration of a historical legacy of Negro spirituals, ring shouts, blues, jazz, gospel, and many other musical traditions. However, what made hip-hop different from its very inception in the postindustrial and economically suppressed neighborhoods of the South Bronx in New York City was that it was a multicultural phenomenon. Many groups, including Latinos and Jews, were part of the culture from the beginning, which has created space for nonblack participation in the culture as long as there is a respect for its roots, heritage, and inherited legacy (Chang, 2005; Kitwana, 2006).

In addition to its diversity, the foundations of hip-hop culture provide principles, definitions, and examples that motivate and inspire hip-hop activists around the world. One individual who was critical in this development was a DJ from the South Bronx known as Afrika Bambaataa, founder of the Universal Zulu Nation (a name inspired by his experiences and travels to South Africa as a witness to anti-apartheid movements) and the individual credited with defining the core elements of hip-hop culture. Viewed as the "godfather" of hip-hop culture, he defined the elements of hip-hop as DJing, MCing, graffiti, b-boy/b-girling (widely known as breakdancing), and knowledge (because knowledge is essential to be effective in your craft and participate in hip-hop culture).

Bambaataa believed that the values of hip-hop were based on "Peace, Unity, Love and Having Fun." In addition, much of the activity of the Universal Zulu Nation occurred in youth community centers, to bring young people away from drug and gang culture and provide them safe and positive spaces to express themselves. *Hip-hop activism* means using the foundational principles, definitions, values, and environments where the culture originally emerged and is being re-created as inspiration that motivates and grounds our work to challenge injustice, empower through education and creativity, and use the culture as a facilitator of social change. In addition, given that hip-hop culture is often engaged by marginalized youth all over the world, it provides a vehicle to communicate, create, and organize activism (Chang, 2005).

Photo 14.1 Ahmed hosting the Annual Hip Hop Congress Midwest Summit at University of Michigan–Ann Arbor. The event featured performances, element workshops (MCing, DJing, graffiti, breakdancing), and panels with artists, activists, educators, organizers, youth, and students.

Photo courtesy of Amer F. Ahmed.

Hip-hop culture provided me a space to express my ideas, feelings, and emotions, particularly my anger and frustration about the racism and oppression happening all over the world. This became an even more acute feeling following more direct experiences of racism after the attacks of September 11, 2001. It was a time when people who looked like me were widely cast as the enemy by a society that knew little about Islam, world history, and the legacy of colonialism. I began to write poetry at a moment when the spoken-word poetry scene was emerging in the United States.

I Stand Poisoned

I stand poisoned by religion and decisions of sin,

As television spins the lies of White men.

I see no friends, as the media sends,

the myth of the truth to fear my Brown skin.

So let me begin with my fallen kin,

When the panic of the frantic killed Americans.

Now eyes of despise are surrounding the lies,

As bombs terminate the end of human lives.

While the husbands and wives in suburban lives,

lock all the doors and remain terrorized.

So I must comply, to the FBI,

I'm a suspect who is subject to my ethnic ties.

Though American born, my heart remains torn,

to my people who are equal all around the world.

Cause the hors of war, are beating the drum,

Hidden in the sins and lies for freedom.

So stand up son, cause we have no time,

An eye for an eye makes the world go blind.

—Amer F. Ahmed (aka Dawah),

Reprinted with permission by Amer F. Ahmed.

After performing at an open mic poetry night, I was invited to perform at a local hip-hop festival organized by a chapter of Hip Hop Congress, a grassroots nonprofit organization committed to using hip-hop culture to empower people and communities. As I began to learn more about the organization, I realized that its work engaging social justice movements was exactly what I wanted to be involved in.

As a member of Hip Hop Congress, I began organizing hip-hop festivals that highlighted all the elements of hip-hop culture and featured positive and talented artists who could show people what hip-hop was all about. I would get resources as a student by arguing and proving that hip-hop created more racially diverse social spaces than could be found anywhere else on campus. Later, I was hired by various colleges and universities to promote diversity and social justice efforts. At each institution, I used my programming budgets to pull together regional hip-hop summits that brought students, artists, educators, and activists into one place to participate in the culture, engage issues, and discuss how people could work together to use hip-hop as a change agent for social justice in the world.

For the events I organized, I would access a vast network of artists, activists, educators, and organizers in Hip Hop Congress and beyond to bring together diverse constituencies committed to using hip-hop culture as a tool for creating social change. In each city where I lived, I reached out to people working with youth, particularly from the most marginalized populations in the area. For example, in Minnesota, I brought Native American hip-hop artists to perform and conduct workshops for Native American youth from the region. In the workshops, I consistently saw how excited young people were to see role models who used hip-hop in a positive way. The youth were inspired, motivated, and energized by their experience, which instilled a sense of positivity and possibility.

Young people walked away from these summits more confident, more expressive, and more interested in education. It was a rare opportunity for them to be on a college campus with students of similar backgrounds who also shared their interest in hip-hop. They also got to meet numerous people of other diverse backgrounds in a fun and safe environment. Suddenly, the gulf between their lives and higher education did not seem as wide. Many youth realized that they, too, could potentially be college students and participate in programs they found interesting and relevant. In addition, youth also saw their own local mentors and teachers encouraging their participation. They did not feel ashamed of expressing themselves through hip-hop, which is a major barrier in the lives of many young people who are frequently told that hip-hop is not positive.

While working at various institutions, I realized that my approach could not focus simply on racism. Instead, I realized my work needed to expand to address all forms of power, inequity, and unearned privilege resulting from historical injustices that remain and continue to impact our modern world. I began to learn about the importance of linking these social justice principles with intercultural communication to deepen understanding of difference and inequities at the same time. Hip-hop is a powerful tool for enacting intercultural praxis, as the core principles of the culture encourage inquiry, framing, positioning, dialogue, reflection, and action (Sorrells, 2013). Hip-hop can be used to explore new ideas (inquiry), challenge dominant narratives (framing) and oppression (positioning), facilitate communication across diverse experiences (dialogue), deepen understanding (reflection), and motivate individuals and groups to enact informed and impactful change in the world (action).

Sorrells (2013) used hip-hop as a case study to illustrate how each of the dimensions is critical and necessary to enter intercultural praxis. Intercultural praxis as a model emphasizes the importance of integrating an awareness of cultural differences, as identified in the study of intercultural communication, with an analysis of power dynamics to address, engage, and seek to change inequities and **systemic hierarchies** in our globalizing world. This model helped synthesize my approach and validate my experience and understanding of my work.

Beyond my work on campuses, I remain committed to helping build hip-hop activist networks around the country and the world. I helped support people who were interested in starting chapters of Hip Hop Congress and tried to ensure that people could navigate the vast network of hip-hop activists, educators, and artists. I also worked in concert with my fellow members of Hip Hop Congress to ensure that we were always committed to working collaboratively with other organizations and never put self-interests ahead of our broader goals to strengthen hip-hop culture and social justice movements.

Hip-hop activism and culture have opened up so many opportunities in my life that I otherwise never would have thought possible. Over the years, I have met amazing people from all over the world who have talents and gifts that continue to astound me. I have seen our work transform, connect, motivate, and inspire people in real ways that have transformed lives and fundamentally altered people's life trajectories for the better. I have also seen how the culture facilitates understanding across distant and vastly diverse cultural contexts around the world.

I believe we need more people to commit themselves to arts activism work to inspire and transform the lives of individuals and communities around the world that continue to face forces of oppression. In addition, we need to work together through networks and by sharing resources to create more opportunities for self-determination. Art has the power to inspire a sense of possibility and communicate impactful messages to people with all sorts of backgrounds and experiences. Regardless of whether someone is an educator, artist, journalist, or anyone else who seeks to inspire new possibilities for social change, arts activism creates the potential for unique impact.

THE PATH FORWARD

As a South Asian Muslim man, hip-hop activism has provided me with a global community where I am accepted and find a purpose dedicated to developing intercultural understanding and challenging injustices. I no longer experience the internalized negativity of my own cultural background that I carried in my younger years, because I believe I have space to bring all my identities to the table. I now realize that the embarrassment I once felt was due to an internalization of colonization. I feel empowered to use my identity/identities as unique contributions that I bring to the movement to challenge racism and other forms of inequity that continue to communicate to marginalized people that they are unequal and/or inferior.

At the same time, I also know that my contribution is as unique as that of each and every other member of the community and that everyone has something to offer that can benefit social justice movements. As we all engage in our own process of validating our identities, we can join together in a common purpose. That is the beauty of hip-hop; there is room for anyone and everyone to contribute and participate. The key is for us all to recognize the core principles at the heart of the culture to enact change in the world and make it a better place for everyone.

KEY TERMS

alliances   268

allies   272

apartheid   280

colonialism   281

co-optation and commodification of hip-hop   279

hip-hop activism   278

intersectionality   269

multi-issue organization   269

privilege   274

social justice   269

systemic hierarchies   285

DISCUSSION QUESTIONS

1. The Esperanza Peace and Justice Center is a multi-issue social justice organization in San Antonio, Texas. DeTurk points out how the organization's commitment to intersectionality of issues and methods is a great strength and also presents challenges. Based on the case study, discuss why this intersectionality is both a strength and a challenge.

2. DeTurk notes the importance of allies' confronting and interrogating their own and each other's identity-based privilege to be effective in social justice activism. Discuss why this is central to social justice work. Based on the case study and your personal experience, identify obstacles that often emerge when discussing identity-based privilege. What attitudes, skills, and strategies assist when collaborating across identities in the interest of social justice?

3. Based on your reading of Ahmed's personal narrative, discuss what hip-hop activism means and provide examples to support your response. In what ways is hip-hop culture uniquely equipped to address social inequities and advance social justice?

4. What does hip-hop culture have to do with intercultural communication? In what ways can/ does hip-hop facilitate intercultural understanding? How can/does hip-hop contest and reframe the legacy of colonialism and global racism?

References

INTRODUCTION

Appadurai, A. (1996). *Modernity at large: Cultural dimensions of globalization*. Minneapolis: University of Minnesota Press.

Giddens, A. (1990). *The consequences of modernity*. Stanford, CA: Stanford University Press.

Held, D., McGrew, A., Goldblatt, D., & Perraton, J. (1999). *Global transformations: Politics, economics and culture*. Stanford, CA: Stanford University Press.

Jones, A. (2010). *Globalization: Key thinkers*. Malden, MA: Polity Press.

Sekimoto, S. (2014). Transnational Asia: Dis/orienting identity in the globalized world. *Communication Quarterly, 62*(4), 381–398. doi:10.1080/01463373.2014.922485

Shome, R., & Hegde, R. (2002). Culture, communication, and the challenge of globalization. *Critical Studies in Media Communication, 19*(2), 172–189.

Sorrells, K. (2013). Intercultural communication: Globalization and social justice. Thousand Oaks: CA: Sage.

Sorrells, K., & Nakagawa, G. (2008). Intercultural communication praxis and the struggle for social responsibility and social justice. In O. Swartz (Ed.), *Transformative communication studies: Culture, hierarchy, and the human condition* (pp. 23–61). Leicester, UK: Troubador.

Winant, H. (2001). The world is a ghetto: Race and democracy since World War II. New York: Basic Books.

CHAPTER 1

Aiello, G., Bakshi, S., Bilge, S., Hall, L. K., Johnston, L., Pérez, K., & Chávez, K. (2013). Here, and not yet here: A dialogue at the intersection of queer, trans, and culture. *Journal of International & Intercultural Communication, 6*(2), 96–117. doi:10.1080/17513057.2013.778155

Alexander, B., Arasaratnam, L. A., Avant-Mier, R., Durham, A., Flores, L., Leeds-Hurwitz, W., Mendoza, S. L., . . . Yin, J. (2014). Our role as intercultural scholars, practitioners, activists, and teachers in addressing these key intercultural urgencies, issues and challenges. *Journal of International and Intercultural Communication, 7*(1), 68–99.

Allen, B. J., Broome, B. J., Jones, T. S., Chen, V., & Collier, M. J. (2002). Intercultural alliances: A cyber-dialogue among scholar-practitioners. In M. J. Collier (Ed.), *Intercultural alliances: Critical transformations* (Vol. 25, pp. 279–319). Thousand Oaks, CA: Sage.

Asante, M. K. (1998). *The Afrocentric idea* (Rev. ed.). Philadelphia, PA: Temple University.

Bacevich, A. J. (2008). The limits of power: The end of American exceptionalism. New York: Henry Holt.

Bardhan, N., & Orbe, M. (Eds.). (2012). Identity research and communication: Intercultural reflections and future directions. Lanham, MD: Lexington Books.

Blum, W. (2008). Killing hope: U.S. military and C.I.A. interventions since World War II (Updated ed.). Monroe, ME: Common Courage Press.

Broome, B., Carey, C., De la Garza, S. A., Martin, J., & Morris, R. (2005). "In the thick of things": A dialogue about the activist turn in intercultural communication. *International and Intercultural Communication Annual, 28*, 145–175.

Carbaugh, D. (1999). "Just listen": "Listening" and landscape among the Blackfeet. *Western Journal of Communication, 63*(3), 250–270.

Carrillo Rowe, A. (2010). Entering the inter: Power lines in intercultural communication. In T. K. Nakayama & R. T. Halualani (Eds.), *A companion to critical intercultural communication studies* (pp. 216–226). Hoboken, NJ: Blackwell.

Chawla, D., & Rodriguez, A. (2011). Postcoloniality and the speaking body: Revisioning the English oral competency curriculum. *Cultural Studies/Critical Methodologies, 11*(1), 76–91. doi:10.1177/1532708610386923

Chen, T. (2005). Double agency: Acts of impersonation in Asian American literature and culture. Stanford, CA: Stanford University Press.

Cheong, P. H., Martin, J. N., & Macfadyen, L. P. (Eds.). (2012). *New media and intercultural communication: Identity, community and politics*. New York: Peter Lang.

Chude-Sokei, L. (2005). The last "darky": Bert Williams, black-on-black minstrelsy, and the African diaspora. Durham, NC: Duke University Press.

Cole, C. M., & Davis, T. D. (Eds.). (2013). Routes of blackface [Special issue]. *TDR: The Drama Review, 57*(2).

Collier, M. J. (1998). Researching cultural identity: Reconciling interpretive and postcolonial perspectives. In A. Gonzalez & D. V. Tanno (Eds.), *Communication and identity: International and intercultural communication annual* (pp. 112–147). Thousand Oaks, CA: Sage.

Collier, M. J. (2009). Contextual negotiation of cultural identifications and relationships: Interview discourse with Palestinian, Israeli and Palestinian/Israeli young women in a U.S. peace-building program. *Journal of International and Intercultural Communication, 2*(4), 344–368.

Collier, M. J., Hegde, R. S., Lee, W. S., Nakayama, T. K., & Yep, G. A. (2001). Dialogue on the edges: Ferment in communication and culture. In M. J. Collier (Ed.), *Transforming communication about culture: Critical new directions* (pp. 219–280). Thousand Oaks, CA: Sage.

Cooks, L. (2003). Pedagogy, performance, and positionality: Teaching about whiteness in interracial communication. *Communication Education, 52*(3–4), 245–257. doi:10.1080/0363452032000156226

Curtin, M. L. (2010). Coculturation: Toward a critical theoretical framework of cultural adjustment. In T. K. Nakayama & R. T. Halualani (Eds.), *The handbook of critical intercultural communication* (pp. 270–285). Malden, MA: Blackwell.

Daniels, J. (2013). What's up with racism and Halloween? *Racism Review.* Retrieved from http://www.racismreview.com/blog/2013/10/31/whats-up-with-racism-and-halloween/

Deardorff, D. K. (2009). *The SAGE handbook of intercultural competence*. Thousand Oaks, CA: Sage.

Dempsey, S. E., Dutta, M., Frey, L. M., Goodall, H. L., Madison, D. S., Mercieca, J., Nakayama, T., & Miller, K. (2011). What is the role of the communication discipline in social justice, community engagement, and public scholarship? A visit to the CM Café. *Communication Monographs, 78*, 256–271.

Elisseeff, V. (2000). *The Silk Road: Highways of culture and commerce*. New York: Berghahn Books.

Feagin, J. R. (2010). The white racial frame: Centuries of racial framing and counter-framing. New York: Routledge.

Food and Agriculture Organization of the United Nations. (2012). *The state of food insecurity in the world*. Rome, Italy: Author.

Frazier, K. (2005). *People of Chaco: A canyon and its people*. New York: W. W. Norton.

Gonzalez, A., Houston, M., & Chen, V. (Eds.). (2011). *Our voices: Essays in culture, ethnicity and communication*. New York: Oxford University Press.

Gudykunst, W. B., & Nishida, T. (1994). *Bridging Japanese/North American differences*. Thousand Oaks, CA: Sage.

Hall, E. T. (1959). *The silent language*. New York: Anchor Books.

Hall, E. T. (1966). *The hidden dimension*. Garden City: NY: Doubleday.

Halualani, R. T., Mendoza, S. L., & Drzewiecka, J. A. (2009). "Critical" junctures in intercultural communication studies: A Review. *Review of Communication, 9*(1), 17–35.

Hofstede, G. (1983). Culture's consequences: International differences in work-related values. Beverly Hills, CA: Sage.

Hofstede, G. (1991). Cultures and organizations: Software of the mind. London: McGraw-Hill.

Holman Jones, S., Adams, T. E., & Ellis, C. (Eds.). (2013). *The handbook of autoethnography*. San Francisco, CA: Left Coast Press.

Jameson, F. (1971). Marxism and form: Twentieth century dialectical theories of literature. Princeton, NJ: Princeton University Press.

Johnson, C. (2010). The sorrows of empire: Militarism, secrecy and the end of the republic. New York: Henry Holt.

Kinefuchi, E. (2010). Finding home in migration: Montagnard refugees and post-migration identity. *Journal of International & Intercultural Communication, 3*(3), 228–248. doi:10.1080/17513057.20 10.487220

Leeds-Hurwitz, W. (1990). Notes in the history of intercultural communication: The foreign service institute and the mandate for intercultural training. *Quarterly Journal of Speech, 76*(3), 262–281.

Lorde, A. (1984). Age, race, class and sex: Women redefining difference. In *Sister outsider: Essays and speeches* (pp. 114–123). Trumansburg, NY: Crossing Press.

Lott, E. (1993). Love and theft: Blackface minstrelsy and the American working class. New York: Oxford University Press.

Martin, J. N., & Nakayama, T. K. (1999). Thinking dialectically about communication and culture. *Communication Theory, 9*, 1–25.

Mendoza, S. L. (2013). Savage representations in the discourse of modernity: Liberal ideology and the impossibility of nativist longing. *Decolonization, Indigeneity, Education & Society, 2*(1), 1–19.

Miike, Y. (2007). An Asiacentric reflection on Eurocentric bias in communication theory. *Communication Monographs, 74*(2), 272–278.

Mitchell, W. J. T. (2005). *What pictures want: The lives and loves of images*. Chicago, IL: University of Chicago Press.

Moon, D. G. (1996). Concepts of 'culture': Implications for intercultural communication research. *Communication Quarterly, 44*, 70–84.

Nakayama, T. K., & Halualani, R. T. (2010). *The handbook of critical intercultural communication*. Malden, MA: Blackwell.

Nakayama, T. K., & Krizek, R. L. (1995). Whiteness: A strategic rhetoric. *Quarterly Journal of Speech, 81*, 291–309.

Oetzel, J. G., & Ting-Toomey, S. (2003). Face concerns in interpersonal conflict: A cross-cultural empirical test of the face negotiation theory. *Communication Research, 30*(6), 599–624. doi:10.1177/0093650203257841

Oh, D. C. (2012). Black-yellow fences: Multicultural boundaries and whiteness in the *Rush Hour* franchise. *Critical Studies in Media Communication, 29*(5), 349–366. doi:10.1080/15295036.2012.697634

Okihiro, G. Y. (1994). *Margins and mainstreams: Asians in American history and culture*. Seattle: University of Washington Press.

Ono, K. A. (1998). Problematizing "nation" in intercultural communication research. In D. V. Tanno & A. Gonzalez (Eds.), *Communication and identity across cultures* (pp. 34–55). Thousand Oaks, CA: Sage.

Rogers, E. M. (1999). Georg Simmel's concept of the stranger and intercultural communication research. *Communication Theory, 9*(1), 58–74.

Rogers, E. M., Hart, W. B., & Miike, Y. (2002). Edward T. Hall and the history of intercultural communication: The United States and Japan. *Keio Communication Review, 24*, 3–26.

Rogin, M. (1996). Blackface, white noise: Jewish immigrants in the Hollywood melting pot. Berkeley: University of California Press.

Shome, R., & Hegde, R. (2002). Postcolonial approaches to communication: Charting the terrain, engaging the intersections. *Communication Theory, 12*(3), 249–270.

Shotwell, A. (2011). *Knowing otherwise: Race, gender, and implicit understanding*. University Park: Pennsylvania University Press.

Shuter, R. (2011). Introduction: New media across cultures—prospect and promise. *Journal of International and Intercultural Communication, 4*(4), 241–245.

Shuter, R. (2012). Research and pedagogy in intercultural new media studies. *China Media Research, 8*(4), 1–5.

Starosta, W. J., & Chen, G. M. (Eds.). (2003). *Ferment in the intercultural field: Axiology/value/praxis*. Thousand Oaks, CA: Sage.

Smith, A. (2005). Conquest: Sexual violence and American Indian genocide. Cambridge, MA: South End Press.

Sorrells, K. (2010). Re-imagining intercultural communication in the context of globalization. In T. K. Nakayama & R. T. Halualani (Eds.), *The handbook of critical intercultural communication* (pp. 171–189). Malden, MA: Blackwell.

Sorrells, K. (2013). Intercultural communication: Globalization and social justice. Thousand Oaks, CA: Sage.

Sorrells, K., & Nakagawa, G. (2008). Intercultural communication praxis and the struggle for social responsibility and social justice. In O. Swartz (Ed.), *Transformative communication studies: Culture, hierarchy, and the human condition* (pp. 23–61). Leicester, UK: Troubador.

Stiglitz, J. E. (2002). *Globalization and its discontents*. New York: W. W. Norton.

Takaki, R. (2008). *A different mirror: A multicultural history of America* (Rev. ed.). Boston, MA: Little, Brown.

Ting-Toomey, S. (1999). *Communicating across cultures*. New York: Guilford Press.

Todorov, T. (1984). The conquest of the Americas: The question of the other. New York: Harper Row.

Warren, J. T. (2001). Doing whiteness: On the performative dimensions of race in the classroom. *Communication Education, 50*(2), 91–108.

Winant, H. (2001). The world is a ghetto: Race and democracy since WWII. New York: Basic Books.

Winn, M. (2008). Closing the food gap: Resetting the table in the land of plenty. Boston, MA: Beacon Press.

Yep, G. A. (2008). The dialectics of intervention: Toward a reconceptualization of the theory/activism divide in communication scholarship and beyond. In O. Swartz (Ed.), *Transformative communication studies: Culture, hierarchy and the human condition* (pp. 191–207). Leicester, UK: Troubador.

CHAPTER 2

Allen, B. J. (1998). Black womanhood and feminist standpoints. *Management Communication Quarterly, 11*, 575–586.

Bell, K., Orbe, M., Drummond, D., & Camara, S. K. (2000). Accepting the challenge of centralizing without essentializing: Black feminist thought and African American women's communicative experiences. *Women's Studies in Communication, 23*(1), 41–62.

Boylorn, R., & Orbe, M. (Eds.). (2013). *Critical autoethnography: Intersecting cultural identities in everyday life*. Walnut Creek, CA: Left Coast Press.

Cohen, J., & Balz, D. (2013, July 22). Race shapes Zimmerman verdict reaction. *Washington Post*. Retrieved from http://www.washingtonpost.com/politics/race-shapes-zimmerman-verdict-reaction/2013/07/22/3569662c-f2fc-11e2-8505-bf6f231e77b4_story.html

Collins, P. H. (1986). Learning from the outsider within: The sociological significance of black feminist thought. *Social Problems, 33*(6), S14–S23.

Cooke-Jackson, A. F., Orbe, M., Crosby, R. A., & Ricks, J. (2013). Relational, pleasure, and fear-associated aspects of condom use for disease prevention: A qualitative study of high risk African American men. *Qualitative Research Reports in Communication, 14*(1), 62–68.

Crenshaw, K. (1991). Mapping the margins: Intersectionality, identity politics and violence against women of color. *Stanford Law Review, 43*, 1241–1299.

Davies-Popelka, W., & Wood, J. T. (1997, November). *Where do we stand on standpoints? A response*. Paper presented at the annual meeting of the National Communication Association, Chicago, IL.

DeTurk, S. (2011). Allies in action: The communicative experiences of people who challenge social injustice on behalf of others. *Communication Quarterly, 59*(5), 569–590.

Harding, S. (1991). *Whose science? Whose knowledge? Thinking from women's lives*. Ithaca, NY: Cornwell University Press.

Hartsock, N. C. M. (1983). The feminist standpoint: Developing the ground for a specifically feminist historical materialism. In S. Harding & M. D. Hintikka (Eds.), *Discovering reality: Feminist perspectives on epistemology, metaphysics, methodology, and philosophy of science* (pp. 283–310). Boston, MA: D. Reidel.

Ifill, G. (2009). The breakthrough: Politics and race in the age of Obama. New York: Doubleday.

Madison, D. S. (2005). Critical ethnography: Methods, ethics, and performance. Thousand Oaks, CA: Sage.

Martin, J. N., & Nakayama, T. (1999). Thinking dialectically about culture and communication. *Communication Theory, 9*(1), 1–25.

Miller, A. N., & Harris, T. M. (2005). Communicating to develop white racial identity in an interracial communication class. *Communication Education, 54*(3), 223–242.

O'Brien Hallstein, D. L. (2000). Where standpoint stands now: An introduction and commentary. *Women's Studies in Communication, 23*(1), 1–15.

Ono, K. A. (2010). Postracism: A theory of the "post-" as political strategy. *Journal of Communication Inquiry, 34*(3), 227–233.

Orbe, M. (2011). Communication realities in a "post-racial" society: What the U.S. public really thinks about Barack Obama. Lanham, MD: Lexington Books.

Orbe, M., & Harris, T. M. (2008). *Interracial communication: Theory into practice*. Thousand Oaks, CA: Sage.

Patton, M. Q. (2002). *Qualitative evaluation methods*. London: Sage.

Richardson, B. K., & Taylor, J. (2009). Sexual harassment at the intersection of race and gender: A theoretical model of the sexual harassment experiences of women of color. *Western Journal of Communication, 73*(3), 248–272.

Rowe, A. C., & Malhotra, S. (2006). (Un)hinging whiteness. In M. Orbe, B. J. Allen, & L. A. Flores (Eds.), *The same and different: Acknowledging the diversity within and between cultural groups* (pp. 166–192). Washington, DC: National Communication Association.

Sorrells, K. (2013). Intercultural communication: Globalization and social justice. Thousand Oaks, CA: Sage.

Staley, C. C. (1990). Focus group research: The communication practitioner as marketing specialist. In D. O'Hair & G. Kreps (Eds.), *Applied communication theory and research* (pp. 185–202). Hillsdale, NJ: Lawrence Erlbaum.

Todd, C., & Gawiser, S. (2009). How Barack Obama won: A state-by-state guide to the historic 2008 presidential election. New York: Vintage Books.

Vavus, M. D. (2010). Unhitching from the "post" (of postfeminism). *Journal of Communication Inquiry, 34*(3), 222–227.

Warren, K. T., Orbe, M. P., & Greer-Williams, N. (2003). Perceiving conflict: Similarities and differences between and among Latino/as, African Americans, and European Americans. In D. I. Rios & A. N. Mohamed (Eds.), *Brown and black communication: Latino and African American conflict and convergence in mass media* (pp. 13–26). Westport, CT: Praeger.

Wertz, F. J. (2005). Phenomenological research methods for counseling psychology. *Journal of Counseling Psychology, 52,* 167–177.

Wood, J. T. (2005). Feminist standpoint theory and muted group theory: Commonalities and divergences. *Women and Language, 28*(2), 61–64.

CHAPTER 3

Anzaldúa, G. (2002). (Un)natural bridges, (un)safe spaces. In G. Anzaldúa & A. Keating (Eds.), *This bridge we call home: Radical visions for transformation* (pp. 1–5). New York: Routledge.

Bardhan, N. (2012). Postcolonial migrant identities and the case for strategic hybridity: Toward "inter"cultural bridgework. In N. Bardhan & M. P. Orbe (Eds.), *Identity research in intercultural communication: Reflections and future directions* (pp. 149–164). Lanham, MD: Lexington Books.

Bhabha, H. (1994). *The location of culture.* New York: Routledge.

Brennan, T. (2004). *The transmission of affect.* Ithaca, NY: Cornell University Press.

Carrillo Rowe, A. (2005). Be longing: Toward a feminist politics of relation. *NWSA Journal, 17*(2), 15–46.

Carrillo Rowe, A. (2010). Entering the inter: Power lines in intercultural communication. In T. K. Nakayama & R. T. Halualani (Eds.), *The handbook of critical intercultural communication* (pp. 216–226). Malden, MA: Wiley-Blackwell.

Chawla, D., & Rodriguez, A. (2011). *Liminal traces: Performing, storying, and embodying postcoloniality.* Boston, MA: Sense Publishers.

Clifford, J. (1992). Traveling cultures. In L. Grossberg, C. Nelson, & P. Treichler (Eds.), *Cultural studies* (pp. 96–116). New York: Routledge.

Clifford, J. (1994). Diasporas. *Cultural Anthropology, 9*(3), 302–338.

Clough, P. T., & Hailey, J. (Eds.). (2007). *The affective turn: Theorizing the social.* Durham, NC: Duke University Press.

Diamond, S. (1974). *In search of the primitive: A critique of civilization.* New Brunswick, NJ: Transaction Books.

Diamond, J. (1999). Guns, germs, and steel: The fates of human societies. New York: W. W. Norton.

Gregg, M., & Seigworth, G. J. (Eds.).(2010). *The affect theory reader.* Durham, NC: Duke University Press.

Hall, S. (1990). Cultural identity and diaspora. In J. Rutherford (Ed.), *Identity: Community, culture and difference* (pp. 222–237). London: Lawrence & Wishart.

Hoffman, E. (1998). Life in a new language. In M. Zournazi (Ed.), *Foreign dialogues* (pp. 17–26). Annandale, New South Wales: Pluto Press.

hooks, b. (1989). *Talking back: Thinking feminist, thinking black.* Boston, MA: South End Press.

Jensen, D. (2001). Saving the indigenous soul: An interview with Martin Prechtel. *The Sun.* Retrieved from http://thesunmagazine.org/issues/304/saving_the_indigenous_soul

Loomba, A. (2005). *Colonialism/postcolonialism* (2nd ed.). London: Routledge.

Lorde, A. (2007). *Sister outsider: Essays and speeches by Audre Lorde*. Berkeley, CA: Crossing Press. (Original work published in 1984)

Malhotra, S., & Pérez, K. (2005). Belonging, bridges, and bodies. *NWSA Journal, 17*(2), 47–68.

Martin, J. N., & Nakayama, T. K. (1999). Thinking dialectically about culture and communication. *Communication Theory, 9*(1), 1–25.

Mendoza, S. L. (2006). Tears in the archive: Creating memory to survive and contest empire. In R. Lustig & J. Koester (Eds.), *Among US: Essays on identity, belonging, and intercultural competence* (2nd ed., pp. 233–245). Boston, MA: Pearson.

Mendoza, S. L. (2013a). B(e)aring the *babaylan*: Body memory, colonial wounding, and return to indigenous wildness. In S. L. Mendoza & L. Strobel (Eds.), *Back from the crocodile's belly: Philippine babaylan studies and the struggle for indigenous memory* (pp. 243–255). Santa Rosa, CA: Center for Babaylan Studies.

Mendoza, S. L. (2013b). Savage representations in the discourse of modernity: Liberal ideology and the impossibility of nativist longing. *Decolonization, Indigeneity, Education & Society, 2*(1), 1–19.

Negri, A. (1999). Dossier: Scattered speculations on value—Value and affect. *Boundary 2, 26*(2), 77–100.

Prechtel, M. (2004). *Long life, honey in the heart: A story of initiation and eloquence from the shores of a Mayan Lake*. Berkeley, CA: North Atlantic Books.

Prechtel, M. (2011). *The unlikely peace at Cuchumaquic: The parallel lives of people as plants: Keeping the seeds alive*. Berkeley, CA: North Atlantic Books.

Quinn, D. (1996). *The story of B*. New York: Bantam Books.

Robertson, R. (1992). *Globalization: Social theory and global culture*. London: Sage.

Rushdie, S. (1982, July 3). The empire writes back with a vengeance. *Times* (London), p. 8.

Said, E. (1978). *Orientalism*. London & Henley: Routledge & Kegan Paul.

Sandoval, C. (2000). *Methodology of the oppressed*. Minneapolis: University of Minnesota Press.

Shome, R. (2003). Space matters: The power and practice of space. *Communication Theory, 13*, 39–56.

Shome, R., & Hegde, R. S. (2002). Postcolonial approaches to communication: Charting the terrain, engaging the intersections. *Communication Theory, 12*(3), 249–270.

Sobré-Denton, M., & Bardhan, N. (2013). Cultivating cosmopolitanism for intercultural communication: Communicating as global citizens. New York: Routledge.

Sorrells, K. (2013). Intercultural communication: Globalization and social justice. Los Angeles, CA: Sage.

Spivak, G. C. (1987). *The postcolonial critic: Interviews, strategies, dialogues* (S. Harasym, Ed.). New York: Routledge.

Stannard, D. (1992). *American holocaust: The conquest of the new world*. New York: Oxford University Press.

Warren, J. T. (2008). Performing difference: Repetition in context. *Journal of International and Intercultural Communication, 1*(4), 290–308.

Weedon, C. (2004). Identity and culture: Narratives of difference and belonging. Berkshire, UK: Open University Press.

Young, R. (1990). White mythologies: Writing history and the West. London: Routledge.

CHAPTER 4

Alexander, B. K. (2005). Performance ethnography: The reenacting and inciting culture. In N. K. Denzin & Y. S. Lincoln (Eds.), *The SAGE handbook of qualitative research* (3rd ed., pp. 411–442). Thousand Oaks, CA: Sage.

Alexander, B. K. (2012). The performative sustainability of race: Reflections on black culture and the politics of identity. New York: Peter Lang.

Bacigalupe, G., & Cámara, M. (2012). Transnational families and social technologies: Reassessing immigration psychology. *Journal of Ethnic and Migration Studies, 38*(9), 1425–1438. doi:10.1080 /1369183x.2012.698211

Benítez, J. L. (2012). Salvadoran transnational families: ICT and communication practices in the network society. *Journal of Ethnic and Migration Studies, 38*(9), 1439–1449. doi:10.1080/13691 83x.2012.698214

Bernhard, J. K., Landolt, P., & Goldring, L. (2009). Transnationalizing families: Canadian immigration policy and the spatial fragmentation of care-giving among Latin American newcomers. *International Migration, 47*(2), 3–31. doi:10.1111/j.1468-2435.2008.00479.x

Calafell, B. M., & Moreman, S. T. (2010). Iterative hesitancies and Latinidad: The reverberances of raciality. In T. K. Nakayama & R. T. Halualani (Eds.), *The handbook of critical intercultural communication* (pp. 400–416). West Sussex, UK: Wiley-Blackwell.

Chávez, K. R. (2013). Pushing boundaries: Queer intercultural communication. *Journal of International and Intercultural Communication, 6*(2), 83–95.

Chen, V. (2010). Authenticity and identity in the portable homeland. In T. K. Nakayama & R. T. Halualani (Eds.), *The handbook of critical intercultural communication* (pp. 483–494). West Sussex, UK: Wiley-Blackwell.

Delgado, R., & Stefancic, J. (2012). *Critical race theory: An introduction* (2nd ed.). New York: New York University Press.

Eguchi, S. (2011a). Cross-national identity transformation: Becoming a gay "Asian American" man. *Sexuality & Culture, 15*(1), 19–40.

Eguchi, S. (2011b). Negotiating sissyphobia: A critical/interpretive analysis of one "femme" gay Asian body in the heteronormative world. *Journal of Men's Studies, 19*(1), 37–56.

Fung, R. (2005). Looking for my penis: The eroticized Asian in gay video porn. In R. Guins & O. Z. Cruz (Eds.), *Popular culture: A reader* (pp. 338–348). London: Sage.

García Canclini, N. (1995). *Hybrid cultures: Strategies for entering and leaving modernity* (C. L. Chiappari & S. L. Lopez, Trans.). Minneapolis: University of Minnesota.

González Gutiérrez, C. (1999). Fostering identities: Mexico's relations with its diaspora. *Journal of American History, 86*(2), 545–567. doi:10.2307/2567045

Goodman, R. (2012). From pitiful to privilege? The fifty-year story of the changing perception and status of Japan's returnee children (Kikokushijo). In R. Goodman, Y. Imoto, & T. Toivonen (Eds.), *A sociology of Japanese youth* (pp. 30–52). New York: Routledge.

Hamamoto, D. (1994). Monitored peril: Asian Americans and the politics of TV representation. Minneapolis: University of Minnesota Press.

Hamera, J. (2011). Performance ethnography. In N. K. Denzin & Y. S. Lincoln (Eds.), *The SAGE handbook of qualitative research* (4th ed., pp. 317–330). Thousand Oaks, CA: Sage.

Han, C.-S. (2006). Geisha of a different kind: Gay Asian men and the gendering of sexual identity. *Sexuality & Culture, 10*(3), 3–28.

Han, C.-S. (2008). No fats, femmes, or Asians: The utility of critical race theory in examining the role of gay stock stories in the marginalization of gay Asian men. *Contemporary Justice Review, 11*(1), 11–22.

Han, C.-S. (2009). Asian girls are prettier: Gendered presentations as stigma management among gay Asian men. *Symbolic Interaction, 32*(2), 106–122.

Han, C.-S. (2010). One gay Asian body: A personal narrative for examining human behavior in the social environment. *Journal of Human Behavior in the Social Environment, 20*(1), 74–87.

Haritaworn, J., Tauqir, T., & Erdem, E. (2008). Gay imperialism: Gender and sexuality discourse in the "War on Terror." In A. Kuntsman & E. Miyake (Eds.), *Out of place: Interrogating silences in queerness/raciality* (pp. 71–95). York, UK: Raw Nerve Books.

Hiller, H. H., & Franz, T. M. (2004). New ties, old ties and lost ties: The use of the Internet in diaspora. *New Media and Society, 6*(6), 731–752. doi:10.1177/146144804044327

INEGI. (2011). *Sistema de Cuentas Nacionales de México: Producto Interno Bruto por entidad federativa 2005-2009; Año base 2003*. Retrieved from http://www.inegi.org.mx/prod_serv/contenidos/espanol/bvinegi/productos/derivada/regionales/pib/2005_2009_seg/PIBE2009.pdf

INEGI. (2014, May 13). *Resultados de la Encuesta Nacional de Ocupación y Empleo*. Retrieved from http://www.inegi.org.mx/inegi/contenidos/espanol/prensa/comunicados/estrucbol.pdf

INEGI. (n.d.). Aguascalientes. *México en Cifras: Información Nacional, por Entidad Federativa y Municipios*. Retrieved from http://www3.inegi.org.mx/sistemas/mexicocifras/default.aspx?e = 1

Jackson, R. L., & Moshin, J. (2010). Identity and difference: Race and the necessity of the discriminating subject. In T. K. Nakayama & R. T. Halualani (Eds.), *The handbook of critical intercultural communication* (pp. 348–363). West Sussex, UK: Wiley-Blackwell.

Johnson, E. P. (1995). SNAP! culture: A different kind of "reading." *Text and Performance Quarterly, 15*(2), 122–142.

Lomnitz, C. (2001). *Deep Mexico, silent Mexico: An anthropology of nationalism*. Minneapolis: University of Minnesota.

Madison, D. S. (2012). *Critical ethnography: Method, ethics, performance* (2nd ed.). Thousand Oaks, CA: Sage.

Martin, J. N., & Nakayama, T. K. (2008). Intercultural communication and dialectics revisited. In T. K. Nakayama & R. T. Halualani (Eds.), *The handbook of critical intercultural communication* (pp. 59–83). West Sussex, UK: Wiley-Blackwell.

Morley, D. (2000). *Home territories: Media, mobility, and identity*. London: Routledge.

Muñoz, J. E. (1999). Disidentifications: Queers of color and the performance of politics. Minneapolis: University of Minnesota Press.

Nakayama, T. K. (2002). Framing Asian Americans. In C. R. Mann & M. S. Zatz (Eds.), *Images of color: Images of crime* (pp. 92–99). Los Angeles, CA: Roxbury.

Nguyen, V. T. (2002). Race and resistance: Literature and politics in Asian America. New York: Oxford University Press.

Okihiro, G. Y. (1994). *Margins and mainstreams: Asians in American history and culture*. Seattle: University of Washington Press.

Paz, O. (1985). *The labyrinth of solitude and other writings*. New York: Grove Press.

Phinney, J. S., Ong, A., & Madden, T. (2000). Cultural values and intergenerational value discrepancies in immigrant and non-immigrant families. *Child Development, 71*(2), 528–539. doi:10.1111/1467-8624.00162

Phua, V. C. (2002). Sex and sexuality in men's personal advertisements. *Men and Masculinities, 7*, 178–191.

Phua, V. C. (2007). Contesting and maintaining hegemonic masculinities: Gay Asian American men. *Sex Roles, 57*, 909–918.

Poon, M. K.-L. (2006). The discourse of oppression in contemporary gay Asian diasporal literature: liberation or limitation? *Sexuality & Culture, 10*(3), 29–58.

Poon, M. K.-L., & Ho, P. T.-T. (2008). Negotiating social stigma among gay Asian men. *Sexualities, 11*(1–2), 245–268.

Said, E. W. (1979). *Orientalism*. New York: Vintage Books.

Sekimoto, S. (2012). A multimodal approach to identity: Theorizing the self through embodiment, spatiality, and temporality. *Journal of International and Intercultural Communication, 5*(3), 226–243.

Shain, Y. (1999). The Mexican-American diaspora's impact on Mexico. *Political Science Quarterly, 114*(4), 661–691. doi:10.2307/2657788

Sorrells, K. (2010). Re-imagining intercultural communication in context of globalization. In T. K. Nakayama & R. T. Halualani (Eds.), *The handbook of critical intercultural communication* (pp. 171–189). West Sussex, UK: Wiley-Blackwell.

Sun, W., & Starosta, W. J. (2006). Perceptions of minority invisibility among Asian American professionals. *Howard Journal of Communications, 17*(2), 119–142.

Vargas, L. (2008). Ambiguous loss and the media practices of transnational Latina teens: A qualitative study. *Popular Communication, 6*(1), 37–52. doi:0.1080/15405700701697587

Wilding, R. (2006). 'Virtual' intimacies? Families communicating across transnational contexts. *Global Networks, 6*(2), 125–142. doi:10.1111/j.1471-0374.2006.00137.x

CHAPTER 5

Adams, T. E., & Jones, S. H. (2013). Performing identity, critical reflexivity, and community: The hopeful work of studying ourselves and others. *Liminalities: A Journal of Performance Studies, 9*(2), 1–5.

Alvarez, W. (2013). Finding "home" in/through Latinidad ethnography: Experiencing community in the field with "my people." *Liminalities: A Journal of Performance Studies, 9*(2), 49–58.

Anderson, B. (1991). Imagined communities: Reflections on the origin and spread of nationalism. London: Verso.

Anthias, F. (2005). Social stratification and social inequality: Models of intersectionality and identity. In F. Devine, M. Savage, J. Scott, & R. Crompton (Eds.), *Rethinking class: Culture, identities and lifestyles* (pp. 24–45). New York: Palgrave-Macmillan.

Brah, A., & Phoenix, A. (2004). Ain't I a woman? Revisiting intersectionality. *Journal of International Women's Studies, 5*(3), 75–86.

Catungal, J. (2011). Circulating Western notions: Implicating myself in the transnational traffic of 'progress' and commodities. In N. Wane, A. Kempf, & M. Simmonds (Eds.), *The politics of cultural knowledge* (pp. 23–36). Boston, MA: Sense.

Chávez, K. R. (2009). Embodied translation: Dominant discourse and communication with migrant bodies-as-text. *Howard Journal of Communications, 20*(1), 18–36.

Chávez, K. R. (2010). Spatializing gender performativity: Ecstasy and possibilities for livable life in the tragic case of Victoria Arellano. *Women's Studies in Communication, 33*(1), 1–15.

Collins, P. H. (1986). Learning from the outsider within: The sociological significance of black feminist thought. *Social Problems, 33*(6), S14–S32.

Combahee River Collective. (2003). The Combahee River Collective statement. In T. P. McCarthy & J. McMillian (Eds.), *The radical reader: A documentary history of the American radical tradition* (pp. 449–452). New York: New Press. (Original work published in 1977)

Deutsch, B. (2010). The male privilege checklist. In M. S. Kimmel & M. A. Messner (Eds.), *Men's lives* (8th ed., pp. 14–16). Boston, MA: Allyn & Bacon.

Elia, J. P., & Yep, G. A. (2012). Introduction: Sexualities and genders in an age of neoterrorism. *Journal of Homosexuality, 59*, 879–889.

Fisher, D. (2003). Immigrant closets: Tactical-micro-practices-in-the-hyphen. In G. A. Yep, K. E. Lovaas, & J. P. Elia (Eds.), *Queer theory and communication: From disciplining queers to queering the discipline(s)* (pp. 171–192). Binghamton, NY: Harrington Park Press.

Geertz, C. (1973). *The interpretation of cultures.* New York: Basic Books.

Gyekye, K. (1996). *African cultural values: An introduction.* Philadelphia, PA: Sankofa.

hooks, b. (1989). *Talking back: Thinking feminist, thinking black.* Boston, MA: South End Press.

Houston, M. (2012). Foreword: Difficult dialogues; Intersectionality as lived experience. In K. R. Chávez & C. L. Griffin (Eds.), *Standing in the intersection: Feminist voices, feminist practices in communication studies* (pp. ix–xii). Albany: State University of New York Press.

Johnson, E. P. (2001). 'Quare' studies, or (almost) everything I know about queer studies I learned from my grandmother. *Text and Performance Quarterly, 21*(1), 1–25.

Johnson, J. R. (2013). Cisgender privilege, intersectionality, and the criminalization of CeCe McDonald: Why (critical) intercultural communication needs trans-analysis and transgender studies. *Journal of International and Intercultural Communication, 6*(2), 135–144.

Jones, R. G., & Calafell, B. M. (2012). Contesting neoliberalism through critical pedagogy, intersectional reflexivity, and personal narrative: Queer tales of academia. *Journal of Homosexuality, 59*(7), 957–981.

Kim, Y. Y. (2015). Intercultural personhood: An integration of Eastern and Western perspectives. In L. A. Samovar, R. E. Porter, E. R. McDaniel, & C. S. Roy (Eds.), *Intercultural communication: A reader* (14th ed., pp. 405–416). Boston, MA: Cengage Learning.

Lee, W. (2003). Kauering queer theory: My autocritography and a race-conscious, womanist, transnational turn. In G. A. Yep, K. E. Lovaas, & J. P. Elia (Eds.), *Queer theory and communication: From disciplining queers to queering the discipline(s)* (pp. 147–170). Binghamton, NY: Harrington Park Press.

Levine-Rasky, C. (2011). Intersectionality theory applied to whiteness and middle-classness. *Social Identities, 17*(2), 239–253.

Magat, J. G. (2013). *Spectacular embodiments: Filipina trans women and the biopolitics of performance.* Unpublished master's thesis, San Francisco State University, San Francisco, CA.

Manalansan, M. F. (2003). *Global divas: Filipino gay men in the diaspora.* Durham, NC: Duke University Press.

McCall, L. (2005). The complexity of intersectionality. *Signs: Journal of Women in Culture and Society, 30*(3), 1771–1800.

Mohanty, C. T. (2003). Feminism without borders: Decolonizing theory, practicing solidarity. Durham, NC: Duke University Press.

Muñoz, J. E. (1999). Disidentifications: Queers of color and the performance of politics. Minneapolis: University of Minnesota Press.

Mutua, E. (2012, Fall). You were not born here. *Women & Language, 35*, 91–94.

Mutua, K., & Swadener, B. (Eds.). (2004). *Decolonizing research in cross-cultural contexts: Critical personal narratives.* Albany: State University of New York Press.

Nyamnjoh, F. (2007). From bounded to flexible citizenship: Lessons from Africa. *Citizenship Studies, 11*(1), 73–82.

Outerbridge, D. (2011). What might we learn if we silence the colonial voice? Finding our own keys. In N. Wane, A. Kempf, & M. Simmonds (Eds.), *The politics of cultural knowledge* (pp. 111–120). Boston, MA: Sense.

Rodney, W. (1984). *How Europe underdeveloped Africa* (4th ed.). Washington, DC: Howard University Press.

Rodriguez, A., & Chawla, D. (2010). *Intercultural communication: An ecological approach.* Dubuque, IA: Kendall Hunt.

Sekimoto, S. (2012). A multimodal approach to identity: Theorizing the self through embodiment, spatiality, and temporality. *Journal of International and Intercultural Communication, 5*(3), 226–243.

Shome, R. (2003). Space matters: The power and practice of space. *Communication Theory, 13*(1), 39–56.

Shome, R. (2010). Internationalizing critical race communication studies: Transnationality, space, and affect. In T. K. Nakayama & R. T. Halualani (Eds.), *The handbook of critical intercultural communication* (pp. 149–170). Malden, MA: Blackwell.

Shome, R. (2012). Mapping the limits of multiculturalism in the context of globalization. *International Journal of Communication, 6,* 144–165.

Shome, R., & Hegde, R. (2002). Postcolonial approaches to communication: Charting the terrain, engaging the intersections. *Communication Theory, 12*(3), 249–270.

Smith, L. (1999). *Decolonizing methodologies: Research and indigenous people.* New York: Zed Books.

Sorrells, K. (2013). *Intercultural communication: Globalization and social justice.* Thousand Oaks, CA: Sage.

wa Thiong'o, N. (1993). *Moving the centre: The struggle for cultural freedoms.* Oxford, UK: James Currey.

wa Thiongo, N. (1994). *Decolonising the mind: The politics of language in African literature.* Nairobi, Kenya: East African Publishers.

Wane, N., Kempf, A., & Simmonds, M. (Eds.). (2011). *The politics of cultural knowledge.* Boston, MA: Sense.

Woods, J. (2013). The black male privileges checklist. In M. S. Kimmel & M. A. Messner (Eds.), *Men's lives* (9th ed., pp. 26–31). Boston, MA: Pearson.

Yep, G. A. (2002). My three cultures: Navigating the multicultural identity landscape. In J. N. Martin, T. K. Nakayama, & L. A. Flores (Eds.), *Readings in intercultural communication: Experiences and contexts* (2nd ed., pp. 60–66). Boston, MA: McGraw-Hill.

Yep, G. A. (2010). Toward the de-subjugation of racially marked knowledges in communication. *Southern Communication Journal, 75*(2), 171–175.

Yep, G. A. (2013a). Privilege and culture. In A. Kurylo (Ed.), *Inter/cultural communication: Representation and construction of culture* (pp. 163–184). Thousand Oaks, CA: Sage.

Yep, G. A. (2013b). Queering/quaring/kauering/crippin'/transing "other bodies" in intercultural communication. *Journal of International and Intercultural Communication, 6*(2), 118–126.

Yep, G. A., Olzman, M., & Conkle, A. (2012). Seven stories from the "It Gets Better" Project: Progress narratives, politics of affect, and the question of queer world-making. In R. A. Lind (Ed.), *Producing theory in a digital world: The intersection of audiences and production in contemporary theory* (pp. 123–141). New York: Peter Lang.

CHAPTER 6

Ahearn, L. (2012). *Living language: An introduction to linguistic anthropology.* Malden, MA: Wiley-Blackwell.

Ammon, U. (2010). World languages: Trends and futures. In N. Coupland (Ed.), *The handbook of language and globalization* (pp. 101–122). Oxford, UK: Wiley-Blackwell.

Bailey, B. (2000). The language of multiple identities among Dominican Americans. *Journal of Linguistic Anthropology, 10*(2), 190–223.

Battistella, E. L. (2009). Bad language—Bad citizens. In S. D. Blum (Ed.), *Making sense of language: Readings in culture and communication* (pp. 125–136). Oxford, UK: Oxford University Press.

Bilefsky, D. (2011, August 1). In neighborhood that's diverse, a push for signs to be less so. *New York Times.* Retrieved from http://www.nytimes.com/2011/08/02/nyregion/queens-councilman-wants-english-to-dominate-store-signs.html?_r = 0

Blommaert, J., & Rampton, B. (2011). Language and superdiversity. *Diversities, 13*(2), 1–21.

Crawford, J. (2000). *At war with diversity: U.S. language policy in an age of anxiety.* Clevedon, UK: Multilingual Matters.

Curtin, M. L. (2009). Indexical signs, identities and the linguistic landscape. In E. Shohamy & D. Gorter (Eds.), *Linguistic landscape: Expanding the scenery* (pp. 221–237). New York: LEA/Routledge Press.

Curtin, M. L. (2014). Mapping cosmopolitanisms in the linguistic landscape of Taipei: Toward a theorization of cosmopolitanism in linguistic landscape research. *International Journal of the Sociology of Language, 2014*(228), 153–177.

Executive Yuan Office of Information Services. (2013). *Republic of China yearbook 2013: Taiwan.* Taipei, Taiwan: Author. Retrieved from http://yearbook.multimedia.ey.gov.tw/enebook/web/index.html

The French Canadians in New-England [Editorial]. (1892, June 6). *New York Times*, p. 4.

Griffin, H. J. (1961). *Black like me.* New York: Signet.

Hill, J. H. (2008). *The everyday language of white racism.* Malden, MA: Blackwell.

hooks, b. (1989). *Talking back: Thinking feminist, thinking black.* Cambridge, MA: South End Press.

Kelly, S. R. (2013, July 23). Bonjour, America! *New York Times.* Retrieved from http://www.nytimes.com/2013/07/24/opinion/bonjour-america.html?_r = 0

Ko, E. (2009, January 9). Government to seek UNESCO listing for traditional Chinese. *Taiwan Today.* Retrieved from http://www.taiwantoday.tw/fp.asp?xItem = 47488&CtNode = 427

Leeman, J. (2004). Racializing language: A history of linguistic ideologies in the U.S. Census. *Journal of Language and Politics, 3*(3), 507–534.

Leeman, J. (2012). Investigating language ideologies in Spanish as a heritage language. In S. Beaudrie & M. Fairclough (Eds.), *Spanish as a heritage language in the US: State of the field* (pp. 43–59). Washington, DC: Georgetown University Press.

Lin, M. (2002, July 13). Linguists back *tongyong* as symbol of independence. *Taipei Times*, p. 3.

Lovett, K. (2007, August 1). Spanish sign in New Hampshire sparks controversy. *The Telegraph.*

Lovett, K. (2008, April 19). Town council approves rule limiting use of Wasserman Pond. *The Telegraph.*

Mar-Molinero, C. (2010). The spread of global Spanish: From Cervantes to *reggaetón.* In N. Coupland (Ed.), *The handbook of language and globalization* (pp. 162–181). Oxford, UK: Wiley-Blackwell.

Mithun, M. (1999). *The languages of native North America.* Cambridge, UK: Cambridge University Press.

MLA Language Map Data Center. (2010). Retrieved from http://www.mla.org/map_data

Parrillo, V. N. (2009). *Diversity in America* (3rd ed.). Thousand Oaks, CA: Sage.

Pavlenko, A. (2002). 'We have room for but one language here': Language and national identity in the U.S. at the turn of the 20th century. *Multilingua, 21*, 163–196.

Pew Research Center. (2013, January 29). *A nation of immigrants: A portrait of the 40 million.* Washington, DC: Author.

Piller, I., & Takahashi, K. (2011). Linguistic diversity and social inclusion. *International Journal of Bilingual Education and Bilingualism, 14*(4), 371–381.

Record number travel between Chinese mainland, Taiwan. (2014, January 15). *China Daily Europe.* Retrieved from http://europe.chinadaily.com.cn/business/2014-01/15/content_17237732.htm

Romaine, S. (2001). Multilingualism. In M. Aronoff & J. Rees-Miller (Eds.), *The handbook of linguistics* (pp. 512–532). Oxford, UK: Blackwell.

Seng, G. Y., & Lai, L. S. (2010). Global Mandarin. In V. Vaish (Ed.), *Globalization of language and culture in Asia: The impact of globalization processes on language* (pp. 14–33). London: Continuum International.

Simpson, A. A. (2007). Taiwan. In A. A. Simpson (Ed.), *Language and national identity in Asia* (pp. 235–259). Oxford, UK: Oxford University Press.

Sorrells, K. (2013). *Intercultural communication: Globalization and social justice.* Los Angeles, CA: Sage.

Sui, C. (2011, June 16). Taiwan deletes simplified Chinese from official sites. *BBC News Taipei.* Retrieved from http://www.bbc.co.uk/news/world-asia-pacific-13795301?print = true

Touré. (2011). *Who's afraid of post-blackness: What it means to be black now.* New York: Free Press.

Traditional characters embody beauty of Chinese culture. (2014, January 1). *Focus Taiwan News Channel.* Retrieved from http://focustaiwan.tw/news/aedu/201401010030.aspx

U.S. Census Bureau. (2013, August 6). New Census Bureau interactive map shows languages spoken in America [Press release]. Retrieved from http://www.census.gov/newsroom/releases/archives/education/cb13-143.html

Woolard, K. A. (2004). Codeswitching. In A. Duranti (Ed.), *A companion to linguistic anthropology* (pp. 73–94). Oxford, UK: Blackwell.

CHAPTER 7

Antoine, T. J. (2007). Making heaven out of hell: New urbanism and the refutation of suburban spaces. *Southern Communication Journal, 72*(2), 127–144. doi:10.1080/10417940701316351

Campbell, H. (2005). A tale of two families: The mutual construction of 'Anglo' and Mexican ethnicities along the US–Mexico border. *Bulletin of Latin American Research, 24*(1), 23–43. doi:10.1111/j.0261-3050.2005.00123.x

Carrillo Rowe, A., & Malhotra, S. (2006). (Un)hinging whiteness. In M. P. Orbe, B. J. Allen, & L. A. Flores (Eds.), *International and intercultural communication annual* (Vol. XXIX, pp. 166–192). Washington, DC: National Communication Association.

Chang, G. H. (Ed.). (2001). *Asian Americans and politics: Perspectives, experiences, prospects.* Washington, DC: Woodrow Wilson Center Press.

Cleaveland, C., & Kelly, L. (2009). Shared social space and strategies to find work: An exploratory study of Mexican day laborers in Freehold, NJ. *Social Justice, 35*(4), 51–65.

Collins, P. H. (1990). Black feminist thought: Knowledge, consciousness, and the politics of empowerment. New York: Routledge.

Crenshaw, C. (1997). Resisting whiteness' rhetorical silence. *Western Journal of Communication, 61*(3), 253–279.

Davis, S. G. (2003). Space jam: Media conglomerates build the entertainment city. In G. Dines & J. M. Humez (Eds.), *Gender, race, and class in media: A text-reader* (2nd ed., pp. 159–170). Thousand Oaks, CA: Sage.

Dickinson, G. (1997). Memories for sale: Nostalgia and the construction of identity in Old Pasadena. *Quarterly Journal of Speech, 83*(1), 1–27.

Dickinson, G. (2006). The *Pleasantville* effect: Nostalgia and the visual framing of (white) suburbia. *Western Journal of Communication, 70*(3), 212–233. doi:10.1080/10570310600843504

Durrheim, K., & Dixon, J. (2001). The role of place and metaphor in racial exclusion: South Africa's beaches as sites of shifting racialization. *Ethnic and Racial Studies, 24*(3), 433–450. doi:10.1080/01419870020036738

Foucault, M. (1986). Of other spaces. *Diacritics, 16,* 22–26.

Frankenberg, R. (1993). *White women, race matters.* Minneapolis: University of Minnesota.

Giddens, A. (1984). *Constitution of society.* Berkeley: University of California Press.

Harvey, D. (1972). *Society, the city and the space-economy of urbanism.* Washington, DC: Association of American Geographers.

Harvey, D. (1990). Between space and time: Reflections on the geographical imagination. *Annals of the Association of American Geographers, 80,* 418–434.

Harvey, D. (1996). Justice, nature and the geography of difference. Malden, MA: Blackwell.

Hetherington, K. (1998). *Expressions of identity: Space, performance, politics.* Thousand Oaks, CA: Sage.

Hise, G. (2004). Border city: Race and social distance in Los Angeles. *American Quarterly, 56*(3), 545–558.

Hytten, K., & Warren, J. T. (2003). Engaging whiteness: How racial power gets reified in education. *Qualitative Studies in Education, 16*, 65–89. doi:10.1080/0951839032000033509

Johnson, J. R., Rich, M., & Cargile, A. C. (2008). "Why are you shoving this stuff down our throats?": Preparing intercultural educators to challenge performances of white racism. *Journal of International and Intercultural Communication, 1*(2), 113–135. doi:10.1080/17513050801891952

Johnson, P. C. (1999). Reflections on critical white(ness) studies. In T. K. Nakayama & J. N. Martin (Eds.), *Whiteness: The communication of social identity* (pp. 1–12). Thousand Oaks, CA: Sage.

Johnson, R., Chambers, D., Raghuram, P., & Tincknell, E. (2004). *The practice of cultural studies.* Thousand Oaks, CA: Sage.

Jully, S. (Producer & Director). (1997). *bell hooks: Cultural criticism and transformation* [Documentary film]. Northampton, MA: Media Education Foundation.

Krause, K. (2008). Spiritual places in post-industrial places: Transnational churches in North East London. In M. P. Smith & J. Eade (Eds.), *Transnational ties: Cities, migrations, and identities* (pp. 109–130). New Brunswick, NJ: Transaction.

Kruse, K. M. (2005). *White flight: Atlanta and the making of modern conservatism.* Princeton, NJ: Princeton University.

Lefebvre, H. (1991). *The production of space* (D. Nicholson-Smith, Trans.). Oxford, UK: Basil Blackwell.

Lemanski, C., & Saff, G. (2010). The value(s) of space: The discourses and strategies of residential exclusion in Cape Town and Long Island. *Urban Affairs Review, 45*(4), 507–543. doi:10.1177/1078087 409349026

Madison, K. J. (1999). Legitimation crisis and containment: The "anti-racist-white-hero" film. *Critical Studies in Mass Communication, 16*, 399–416. doi:10.1080/15295039909367108

Maldonado, M. M. (2009). 'It is in their nature to do menial labour': The racialization of 'Latino/a workers' by agricultural employers. *Ethnic and Racial Studies, 32*(6), 1017–1036. doi:10.1080/01419870 902802254

Mapes, L. V. (2000, June 19). Farmworkers arriving from Mexico don't plan to stay, but they do. *Seattle Times.* Retrieved from http://seattletimes.nwsource.com/special/mexico/stories/mex3b.html

Martin, J. N., & Nakayama, T. K. (2004). *Intercultural communication in contexts.* Boston, MA: McGraw-Hill.

Massey, D. (2005). *For space.* Thousand Oaks, CA: Sage.

McIntosh, P. (2010). White privilege: Unpacking the invisible knapsack. In M. L. Andersen & P. H. Collins (Eds.), *Race, class, and gender: An anthology* (7th ed., pp. 99–104). Belmont, CA: Wadsworth.

Molnar, J. J., & Wu, L. S. (1989). Agrarianism, family farming, and support for state intervention in agriculture. *Rural Sociology, 54*(2), 227–245.

Moon, D. (1999). White enculturation and bourgeois ideology: The discursive production of "good (white) girls." In T. K. Nakayama & J. N. Martin (Eds.), *Whiteness: The communication of social identity* (pp. 177–197). Thousand Oaks, CA: Sage.

Murray, K. (2010). *Quincy Valley.* Charleston, SC: Arcadia.

Nakayama, T. K. (1994). Show/down time: "Race," gender, sexuality, and popular culture. *Critical Studies in Mass Communication, 11*, 162–179. doi:10.1080/15295039409366893

Nakayama, T. K., & Krizek, R. L. (1995). Whiteness: A strategic rhetoric. *Quarterly Journal of Speech, 81*, 291–309. doi:10.1080/00335639509384117

Patton, T. O. (2004). In the guise of civility: The complicitous maintenance of inferential forms of sexism and racism in higher education. *Women's Studies in Communication, 27*, 60–87. doi:10.1080 /07491409.2004.10162466

Relph, E. (1976). *Place and placelessness.* London: Pion.

Shome, R. (1999). Whiteness and the politics of location: Postcolonial reflections. In T. K. Nakayama & J. N. Martin (Eds.), *Whiteness: The communication of social identity* (pp. 107–128). Thousand Oaks, CA: Sage.

Shome, R. (2003). Space matters: The power and practice of space. *Communication Theory, 13*(1), 39–56. doi:10.1111/j.1468-2885.2003.tb00281.x

Sorrells, K. (2013). *Intercultural communication: Globalization and social justice.* Thousand Oaks, CA: Sage.

Tuan, Y. F. (1977). *Space and place: The perspective of experience.* Minneapolis: University of Minnesota.

U.S. Census Bureau. (2010). *American factfinder.* Retrieved from http://factfinder2.census.gov/faces/nav/jsf/pages/index.xhtml

Van Maanen, J., & Barley, S. R. (1985). Cultural organization: Fragments of a theory. In P. J. Frost, L. F. Moore, M. R. Louis, C. C. Lundberg, & J. Martin (Eds.), *Organizational culture* (pp. 31–53). Beverley Hills, CA: Sage.

Warren, J. T. (2001). Doing whiteness: On the performative dimensions of race in the classroom. *Communication Education, 50,* 91–108. doi:10.1080/03634520109379237

CHAPTER 8

Bonilla-Silva, E. (1996). Rethinking racism: Toward a structural interpretation. *American Sociological Review, 62,* 465–480.

Bonilla-Silva, E. (2006). Racism without racists: Color-blind racism and the persistence of racial inequity in the United States (2nd ed.). Lanham, MD: Rowman & Littlefield.

Childs, E. C. (2005). Navigating interracial borders: Black–white couples and their social worlds. New Brunswick, NJ: Rutgers University Press.

Chuang, R. (2003). A postmodern critique of cross-cultural and intercultural communication research: Contesting essentialism, positivist dualism, and Eurocentricity. In W. J. Starosta & G. M. Chen (Eds.), *Ferment in the intercultural field: Axiology/value/praxis* (pp. 24–35). Thousand Oaks, CA: Sage.

Collier, M. J. (2002). Negotiating intercultural alliance relationships: Toward transformation. In M. J. Collier (Ed.), *Intercultural alliances: Critical transformations* (pp. 1–15). Thousand Oaks, CA: Sage.

Collier, M. J. (2005). Theorizing cultural identifications: Critical updates and continuing evolution. In W. B. Gudykunst (Ed.), *Theorizing about intercultural communication* (pp. 235–256). Thousand Oaks, CA: Sage.

Collier, M. J. (2009). Contextual negotiation of cultural identifications and relationships: Interview discourse with Palestinian, Israeli, and Palestinian/Israeli young women in a U.S. peace-building program. *Journal of International and Intercultural Communication, 2*(4), 344–368.

Frankenburg, R. (1993). *White women, race matters: The social construction of whiteness.* Minneapolis: University of Minnesota Press.

Jordan, M. (2012, February 17). More marriages cross race, ethnicity lines. *Wall Street Journal.* Retrieved from http://online.wsj.com/article/SB10001424052970204880404577226981780914906.html

Killian, K. D. (2002). Dominant and marginalized discourses in interracial couples' narratives: Implications for family therapists. *Family Process, 41*(4), 603–618.

LeBaron, M. (2003). *Bridging cultural conflicts: A new approach for a changing world.* San Francisco, CA: Jossey-Bass.

Nieto-Phillips, J. M. (2004). *The language of blood: The making of Spanish-American identity in New Mexico, 1880s–1930s.* Albuquerque: University of New Mexico Press.

Omi, M., & Winant, H. (1994). Racial formation in the United States: From the 1960s to the 1990s (2nd ed.). New York: Routledge.

Qian, Z., & Lichter, D. T. (2011). Changing patterns of interracial marriage in a multiracial society. *Journal of Marriage and Family, 73*, 1065–1084.

Ringera, K., & Collier, M. J. (2014). Beyond development to grassroots dances: International peace initiatives in Kenya. In M. J. Collier (Ed.), *Community engagement and intercultural praxis: Dancing with difference in diverse contexts* (pp. 112–136). New York: Peter Lang.

Sorrells, K. (2013). *Intercultural communication: Globalization and social justice.* Thousand Oaks, CA: Sage.

Thompson, J., & Collier, M. J. (2006). Toward contingent understandings of intersecting identifications among selected U.S. interracial couples: Integrating interpretive and critical views. *Communication Quarterly, 54*(4), 487–506.

Troy, A. B., Lewis-Smith, J., & Laurenceau, J. P. (2006). Interracial and intraracial romantic relationships: The search for differences in satisfaction, conflict, and attachment style. *Journal of Social and Personal Relationships, 23*(1), 65–80.

U.S. Census Bureau. (2012, April). *Households and families: 2010.* Retrieved from http://www.census.gov/prod/cen2010/briefs/c2010br-14.pdf

Wang, W. (2012). *The rise of intermarriage: Rates, characteristics vary by race and gender.* Washington, DC: Pew Research Center. Retrieved from http://www.pewsocialtrends.org/files/2012/02/SDT-Intermarriage-II.pdf

CHAPTER 9

Albert, R. D. (1996). A framework and model for understanding Latin American and Latino/Hispanic cultural patterns. In D. Landis & R. S. Bhagat (Eds.), *Handbook of intercultural training* (2nd ed., pp. 327–348). Thousand Oaks, CA: Sage.

Archer, L., & Fitch, K. (1994). Communication in Latin American multinational organizations. In R. L. Wiseman & R. Shuter (Eds.), *Communicating in multinational organizations* (pp. 75–93). Thousand Oaks, CA: Sage.

Archibold, R. C. (2011, July 10). Despite violence, U.S. firms expand in Mexico. *New York Times.* Retrieved from http://www.relooney.info/0_New_10416.pdf

Bennett, M. J. (Ed.). (1998). *Basic concepts of intercultural communication.* Yarmouth, ME: Intercultural Press.

Bolterstein, E. (n.d.). *Environmental justice case study: Maquiladora workers and border issues.* Retrieved from http://www.umich.edu/ ~ snre492/Jones/maquiladora.htm

Bourdieu, P. (1998). *Practical reason.* Stanford, CA: Stanford University Press.

Center for Labor Research & Studies, Florida International University. (2009-2010). *Annual Report: Boundary of the United States of America.* Retrieved February 21, 2014, from http://labor.fiu.edu/publications/annual-reports/annual-report-2010.pdf

Cheng, H.-I. (2010). A critical reflection on an intercultural communication workshop: Mexicans and Taiwanese working on the U.S.–Mexico border. In R. Halualani & T. Nakayama (Eds.), *Blackwell handbook of critical intercultural communication* (pp. 549–564). Malden, MA: Wiley-Blackwell.

Elliott, A., & Lemert, C. (2009). *The new individualism: The emotional costs of globalization* (Rev. ed.). London: Routledge.

Fairclough, N. (2000). Language and neoliberalism. *Discourse & Society, 11*, 147–148.

Ferrante, J. (2007). *Sociology: A global perspective.* Belmont, CA: Wadsworth.

Gannon, M. (2001). Understanding global cultures: Metaphorical journeys through 23 nations (2nd ed.). Thousand Oaks, CA: Sage.

Guarnizo, L. E. & Michael P. S. (1999). "The locations of transnationalism." In M. Smith & L. Guarnizo (Eds.), *Transnationalism from below* (pp. 3-34). New Brunswick: Transaction Publishers.

Hall, E. T. (1976). *Beyond culture*. Garden City, NY: Anchor Press.

Hall, K. G. (2002, April 25). Mexico loses factory jobs to China, Central America. *Knight Ridder/Tribune Business News*. Retrieved from http://www.highbeam.com/doc/1G1-85053550.html

Harvey, D. (2005). *A brief history of neoliberalism*. New York: Oxford University Press.

Hickel, J. (2012, April 09). *A short history of neoliberalism (and how we can fix it)*. Retrieved from http://www.newleftproject.org/index.php/site/article_comments/a_short_history_of_neoliberalism_and_how_we_can_fix_it

Hofstede, G. (2001). Culture's consequences: Comparing values, behaviors, institutions, and organizations across nations. Thousand Oaks, CA: Sage.

Hofstede, G. (1980). *Culture's consequences: International differences in work-related values*. Beverly Hills, CA: Sage.

Larner, W. (2006). Neoliberalism: Policy, ideology, and governmentality. In A. D. Goede (Ed.), *International political economy and poststructural politics* (pp. 199–218). New York: Palgrave.

Kochman, T. (1981). *Black and white styles in conflict*. Chicago, IL: University of Chicago Press.

Lederman, D., & Oliver, J. (2013, April 22). The lessons of Mexico's maquiladoras: Where free trade and labor rights compete. *America Economia*. Retrieved from http://www.worldcrunch.com/business-finance/the-lessons-of-mexico-039-s-maquiladoras-where-free-trade-and-labor-rights-compete/nafta-low-skilled-workers-globalization/c2s11434/

Lindsley, S. L. (1999a). Communication and "The Mexican Way": Stability and trust as core symbols in maquiladoras. *Western Journal of Communication, 63*, 1–31.

Lindsley, S. L. (1999b). A layered model of problematic intercultural communication in U.S.-owned maquiladoras in Mexico. *Communication Monographs, 66*, 143–167.

Lindsley, S. L., & Braithwaite, C. A. (1996). "You should 'wear a mask'": Facework norms in cultural and intercultural conflict in maquiladoras. *International Journal of Intercultural Relations, 20*, 199–225.

Lindsley, S. L., & Braithwaite, C. A. (2003). U.S. Americans and Mexicans working together: Five core Mexican concepts for enhancing effectiveness. In L. A. Samovar & R. E. Porter (Eds.), *Intercultural communication: A reader* (pp. 293–299). Belmont, CA: Wadsworth/Thomson Learning.

Lucas, K. (2011). The working class promise: A communicative account of mobility-based ambivalences. *Communication Monographs, 78*, 347–369.

Markus, H. R., & Moya, P. M. L. (2010). *Doing race: 21 essays for the 21st century*. New York: W. W. Norton.

Ong, A. (1999). Flexible citizenship: The cultural logics of transnationality. Durham, NC: Duke University Press.

Owen, W. (1984). Interpretive themes in relational communication, *Quarterly Journal of Speech, 70*, 274–287.

Paik, Y., & Sohn, J. H. D. (1998). Confucius in Mexico: Korean MNCs and the maquiladoras. *Business Horizons, 41*(6), 25–33.

Piller, I., & Cho, J. (2013). Neoliberalism as language policy. *Language in Society, 42*, 23–44.

Samovar, L. A., & Porter, R. E. (2003). *Intercultural communication: A reader* (10th ed.). Belmont, CA: Thompson.

Sorrells, K. (2013). *Intercultural communication: Globalization and social justice*. Thousand Oaks, CA: Sage.

Stephens, G. K., & Greer, C. R. (1995). Doing business in Mexico: Understanding cultural differences. *Organizational Dynamics, 24*, 39–55.

Tadiar, N. X. M. (2013). Life-times of disposability within global neoliberalism. *Social Text, 31*, 19–48.

CHAPTER 10

Bhabha, H. K. (1994). *The location of culture*. New York: Routledge.

Bonilla-Silva, E. (2014). *Racism without racists: Color-blind racism and the persistence of racial inequality in America*. Lanham, MD: Rowman & Littlefield.

Boler, M., & Zembylas, M. (2003). Discomforting truths: The emotional terrain of understanding difference. In P. P. Trifonas (Ed.), *Pedagogies of difference: Rethinking education for social change* (pp. 110–136). New York: RoutledgeFalmer.

Butler, J. (1993). *Bodies that matter: On the discursive limits of sex*. New York: Routledge.

Chávez, K. (2009). Exploring the defeat of Arizona's marriage amendment and the specter of the immigrant as queer. *Southern Communication Journal, 74,* 314–324.

Conquergood, D. (1991). Rethinking ethnography: Towards a critical cultural politics. *Communication Monographs, 58,* 179–194.

Curtin, M. L. (2010). Coculturation: Toward a critical theoretical framework of cultural adjustment. In T. K. Nakayama & R. T. Halualani (Eds.), *The handbook of critical intercultural communication* (pp. 270–285). Malden, VA: Blackwell.

Dabashi, H. (2013, November 19). Consenting Muslims in America. *Al Jazeera*. Retrieved from http://www.aljazeera.com/indepth/opinion/2013/11/consenting-muslims-america-2013111744019446852.html

Darling-Wolf, F. (2004). Sites of attractiveness: Japanese women and Westernized representations of feminine beauty. *Critical Studies in Media Communication, 21,* 325–345.

Hegde, R. S. (1998). Swinging the trapeze: The negotiation of identity among Asian Indian immigrant women in the United States. In D. V. Tanno & A. González (Eds.), *Communication and identity across cultures* (pp. 34–55). Thousand Oaks, CA: Sage.

Ihde, D. (1986). *Experimental phenomenology*. Albany: State University of New York Press.

Imahori, T. T. (2000). On becoming 'American.' In M. W. Lustig & J. Koester (Eds.), *Among us: Essays on identity, belonging, and intercultural competence* (pp. 68–77). New York: Longman.

Japanese Literature Publishing and Promotion Center. (2014). Yoko Tawada. *J-Lit: Books From Japan*. Retrieved from http://www.booksfromjapan.jp/authors/authors/item/759-yoko-tawada

Johnson, A. G. (2006). *Privilege, power, and difference*. Boston, MA: McGraw-Hill.

Kim, Y. Y., & Gudykunst, W. B. (1988). *Cross-cultural adaptation: Current approaches*. Newbury Park, CA: Sage.

Kim, Y. Y. (2001). Becoming intercultural: An integrative theory of communication and cross-cultural adaptation. Thousand Oaks, CA: Sage.

Kim, Y. Y. (2002). Cross-cultural adaptation: An integrative theory. In J. N. Martin, T. K. Nakayama, & L.A. Flores (Eds.), *Readings in intercultural communication: Experiences and contexts* (2nd ed., pp. 237–245). Boston, MA: McGraw-Hill.

Kristeva, J. (1991). *Strangers to ourselves* (L. S. Roudiez, Trans.). New York: Columbia University Press.

Kumar, A. (2000). *Passport photos*. Berkeley: University of California Press.

Langellier, K. M. (1998). Voiceless bodies, bodiless voices: The future of personal narrative performance. In S. J. Dailey (Ed.), *The future of performance studies: Visions and revisions* (pp. 207–213). Annandale, VA: National Communication Association.

McDonough, K. (2013, December 2). Three white college students file racial discrimination complaint against professor over lesson on structural racism. *Salon*. Retrieved from http://www.salon.com/2013/12/02/three_white_college_students_file_racial_discrimination_complaint_against_professor_over_lesson_on_structural_racism/

Merleau-Ponty, M. (1964). *The primacy of perception*. Evanston, IL: Northwestern University Press.

Moustakas, C. (1994). *Phenomenological research methods.* Thousand Oaks, CA: Sage.

Mun Wah, L. (Director). (1995). *The color of fear* [DVD]. United States: StirFry Seminars and Counseling.

Orbe, M. P., & Harris, T. M. (2008). *Interracial communication: Theory into practice.* Los Angeles, CA: Sage.

Peterson, E. E., & Langellier, K. M. (1997). The politics of personal narrative methodology. *Text and Performance Quarterly, 17,* 135–152.

Rubin, D. L. (1998). Help! My professor (or doctor or boss) doesn't talk English! In J. N. Martin, T. K. Nakayama, & L. A. Flores (Eds.), *Readings in cultural contexts* (pp. 149–160). Mountain View, CA: Mayfield.

Sánchez, P., & Kasun, G. S. (2012). Connecting transnationalism to the classroom and to theories of immigrant student adaptation. *Berkeley Review of Education, 3*(1), 71–93.

Schrag, C. O. (1986). *Communicative praxis and the space of subjectivity.* Bloomington: Indiana University Press.

Shome, R. (1999). Whiteness and the politics of location: Postcolonial reflections. In T. K. Nakayama & J. N. Martin (Eds.), *Whiteness: The communication of social identity* (pp. 107–128). Thousand Oaks, CA: Sage.

Singleton, J. (1990). Gambaru: A Japanese cultural theory of learning. In J. J. Shields, Jr. (Ed.), *Japanese schooling: Patterns of socialization, equality, and political control* (pp. 8–15). University Park, PA: Pennsylvania State University Press.

Smith, S. L. (2002). The cycle of cross-cultural adaptation and reentry. In J. N. Martin, T. K. Nakayama, & L. A. Flores (Eds.), *Readings in intercultural communication: Experiences and contexts* (2nd ed., pp. 246–259). Boston, MA: McGraw-Hill.

Sorrells, K. (2010). Reimagining intercultural communication in the context of globalization. In T. K. Nakayama & R. T. Halualani (Eds.), *The handbook of critical intercultural communication* (pp. 171–189). Malden, VA: Blackwell.

Sorrells, K. (2013). *Intercultural communication: Globalization and social justice.* Thousand Oaks, CA: Sage.

Spivak, G. (1994). Bonding in difference. In A. Arteaga (Ed.), *An other tongue: Nation and ethnicity in the linguistic borderlands* (pp. 273–285). Durham, NC: Duke University Press.

Tankei, S. (Performer, Writer, & Codirector). (2004). *On becoming Japerican* (S. Howell & A. McDonald, Codirectors; H. Arima, Y. Kakinuma, M. Sato, K. Watanabe, & N. Watanabe, Performers). The Kleinau Theatre, Southern Illinois University–Carbondale, IL.

Tankei-Aminian, S. (2013). On becoming Japerican [Video]. *Liminalities: A Journal of Performance Studies, 9*(3). Retrieved from http://liminalities.net/9-3/japerican.html

Tatum. B. D. (2003). *"Why are all the black kids sitting together in the cafeteria?" and other conversations about race.* New York: Basic Books.

Tawada, Y. (2004). *Ekusofoni: Bogo no soto e deru tabi* [Exophony: A journey to get outside of mother tongue]. Tokyo, Japan: Iwanami.

Van Manen, M. (1990). *Researching lived experience: Human science for an action sensitive pedagogy.* Albany: State University of New York Press.

Wise, T. (2011). *White like me: Reflections on race from a privileged son.* Berkeley, CA: Soft Skull Press.

Wolf, N. (2007). *The end of America: Letter of warning to a young patriot.* White River Junction, VT: Chelsea Green.

Wood, J. T. (2004). *Communication theories in action: An introduction.* Boston, MA: Wadsworth.

Yep, G. A. (2004). Approaches to cultural identity: Personal notes from an autoethnographical journey. In M. Fong & R. Chuang (Eds.), *Communicating ethnic and cultural identity* (pp. 69–81). Lanham, MD: Rowman & Littlefield.

CHAPTER 11

Appadurai, A. (1996). *Modernity at large: Cultural dimensions of globalization*. Minneapolis: University of Minnesota Press.

Ashcroft, B., Griffiths, G., & Tiffin, H. (1998). *Key concepts in post-colonial studies*. London: Routledge.

Bhabha, H. K. (2003). *The location of culture*. New York: Routledge. (Original work published in 1994)

Bodomo, A. (2010). The African trading community in Guangzhou: An emerging bridge for Africa–China relations. *China Quarterly, 203*, 693–707.

Chatterjee, P. (1989). The nationalist resolution of the women's question. In K. Sangari & S. Vaid (Eds.), *Recasting women: Essays in colonial history* (pp. 233–253). New Delhi, India: Kali for Women.

Collier, M. J., Hegde, R. S., Lee, W., Nakayama, T. K., & Yep, G. A. (2002). Dialogue on the edges: Ferment in communication and culture. In M. J. Collier (Ed.), *Transforming communication about culture: Critical new directions* (pp. 219–280). Thousand Oaks, CA: Sage.

Goodman, D. (2007). Globalization and consumer culture. In G. Ritzer (Ed.), *The Blackwell companion to globalization* (pp. 330–351). Malden, MA: Blackwell.

Hegde, R. (2002). Translated enactments: The relational configurations of the Asian Indian immigrant experience. In J. N. Martin, T. K. Nakayama, & L. A. Flores (Eds.), *Readings in intercultural communication: Experiences and contexts* (2nd ed., pp. 259–266). New York: McGraw-Hill.

Krishnan, P., & Dinghe, A. (1990). *Affirmation and denial: Construction of femininity on Indian television*. New Delhi, India: Sage.

Malhotra, S., & Alagh, T. (2004). Dreaming the nation: Domestic dramas in Hindi films post-1990. *South Asian Popular Culture, 2*(1), 19–37.

Malhotra, S., & Crabtree, R. D. (2002). Gender, inter(nation)alization, and culture: Implications of the privatization of television in India. In M. J. Collier (Ed.), *Transforming communication about culture: Critical new directions* (pp. 60–85). Thousand Oaks, CA: Sage.

Ratha, D., & Shaw, W. (2010). *South-South migration and remittance* (World Bank Working Paper No. 102). Washington, DC: World Bank. Retrieved from http://siteresources.worldbank.org/INTPROSPECTS/Resources/334934-1110315015165/SouthSouthMigrationandRemittances.pdf

Ritzer, G. (2010). *Globalization*. West Sussex, UK: Wiley-Blackwell.

Shome, R., & Hegde, R. (2002). Culture, communication and the challenge of globalization. *Critical Studies in Media Communication, 19*(2), 172–189.

Sorrells, K. (2013). *Intercultural communication: Globalization and social justice*. Thousand Oaks, CA: Sage.

Tomlinson, J. (2007). Cultural globalization. In G. Ritzer (Ed.), *The Blackwell companion to globalization* (pp. 352–366). Malden, MA: Blackwell.

Tunstall, J. (2008). *The media were American: U.S. mass media in decline*. New York: Oxford University Press.

CHAPTER 12

Appadurai, A. (1996). *Modernity at large: Cultural dimensions of globalization*. Minneapolis: University of Minnesota Press.

Azerrad, M. (2001). *Our band could be your life: Scenes from the American underground 1981–1991*. New York: Back Bay/Little, Brown.

Bird, S. (2011). Are we all producers now? *Cultural Studies, 25*(4–5), 502–516.

Brooker, W. (1999). Hyperreality. Retrieved from http://faculty.washington.edu/cbehler/glossary/hyperrea.htm

Castells, M. (2000). *The rise of the network society* (2nd ed.). Oxford, UK: Blackwell.

Clarke, J., Hall, S., Jefferson, T., & Roberts, B. (2005). Subcultures, cultures and class. In K. Gelder (Ed.), *The subcultures reader* (pp. 100–111). London: Routledge.

Clegg, S., Hudson, A., & Steele, J. (2010). The emperor's new clothes: Globalisation and e-learning in higher education. *British Journal of Sociology of Education, 24*(1), 39–53.

Cooper, C. (1993). *Noises in the blood: Orality, gender and the "vulgar" body of Jamaican popular culture.* London: McMillan Press.

Cooper, C. (2004). *Sound clash: Jamaican dancehall culture at large.* New York: Palgrave McMillan.

Cooper, C., & Donnell, A. (2004). Jamaican popular culture. *Interventions: The International Journal of Postcolonial Studies, 6*(1), 1–17.

Dávila, A. (1997). Contending nationalisms: Culture, politics, and corporate sponsorship in Puerto Rico. In F. Negrón-Muntaner & R. Grosfoguel (Eds.), *Puerto Rican jam: Rethinking colonialism and nationalism* (pp. 231–242). Minneapolis: University of Minnesota Press.

García Canclini, N. (2001). *La globalización imaginada.* Mexico City: Paidós.

Gordon, N. (2012). Virile bodies, docile subjects: The representation of Caribbean masculinities in international women's magazines. In K. A. Gentles-Peart & M. L. Hall (Eds.), *Re-constructing place and space: Media, power, and identity in the constitution of a Caribbean diaspora* (pp. 15–32). Newcastle upon Tyne, UK: Cambridge Scholars.

Gross, L. (2009). My media studies: Cultivation to participation. *Television and New Media, 10*(1), 66–68.

Hebdige, D. (1979). *Subculture: The meaning of style.* London: Methuen.

Hope, D. (2006). *Passa passa*: Interrogating cultural hybridities in Jamaican dancehall. *Small Axe: A Caribbean Journal of Criticism, 21*, 119–133.

Hope, D. (2010). *Man vibes: Masculinities in Jamaican dancehalls.* Kingston, Jamaica: Ian Randle.

Johnson, H. N. (2011). *Challenges to civil society: Popular protest and governance in Jamaica.* London: Cambria Press.

Kuhn, A. (1994). *Women's pictures: Feminism and cinema* (2nd ed.). New York: Verso.

Lee, J. L., & Wen, H. (2009). Where the girls are in the age of new sexism: An interview with Susan Douglas. *Journal of Communication Inquiry, 33*, 93–103.

Malott, C., & Carroll-Miranda, J. (2003). Punkore scenes as revolutionary street pedagogy. *Journal for Critical Education Policy Studies, 1*(2), 80–108.

Marcus, G. (1989). *Lipstick traces: A secret history of the twentieth century.* Cambridge, MA: Harvard University Press.

Miller, T. (2009). Media studies 3.0. *Television and New Media, 10*(1), 5–6.

Miller, T. (2010). A future for media studies: Cultural labor, cultural relations, cultural politics. In B. Beaty, D. Briton, G. Filax, & R. Sullivan (Eds.), *How Canadians communicate III: Contexts of Canadian popular culture* (pp. 35–53). Alberta, Canada: Athabasca University Press.

Milne, L. (2001). Sex, gender and the right to write: Patrick Chamoiseau and the erotics of colonialism. *Paragraph, 24*(3), 59–75.

Moore, R. (2004). Postmodernism and punk subculture: Cultures of authenticity and deconstruction. *Communication Review, 7*, 305–327.

Mordecai, M., & Mordecai, P. (2001). *Culture and customs of Jamaica.* Westport, CT: Greenwood Press.

Nielsen. (2012, December 4). *State of the media: The social media report 2012.* Retrieved from http://blog.nielsen.com/nielsenwire/social/2012/

O'Connor, A. (2004). Punk and globalization: Spain and Mexico. *International Journal of Cultural Studies, 7*(2), 175–195.

Ortiz-Negrón, L. T. (2007). Space out of place: Consumer culture in Puerto Rico. In F. Negrón-Muntaner (Ed.), *None of the above: Puerto Ricans in the global era* (pp. 39–50). New York: Palgrave Macmillan.

Pabón, C. (2002). *Nación postmortem: Ensayos sobre los tiempos de insoportable ambigüedad* [Postmortem nation: Essays on the time of unbearable ambiguity]. San Juan, Puerto Rico: Ediciones Callejón.

Puri, A. (2007). The web of insights: The art and practice of webnography. *International Journal of Market Research, 49*(3), 387–408.

Ramírez-Sánchez, R. (2008). Marginalization from within: Expanding co-cultural theory through the experience of the *Afro Punk. Howard Journal of Communications, 19*(2), 89–104.

Rosa, T. (Ed.). (1998, April). *Zine Vergüenza* #8 [Zine]. Carolina, Puerto Rico: Author.

Sardar, Z. (1999). *Orientalism*. Buckingham, UK: Open University Press.

Shepherd, V. (1986). The dynamics of Afro-Jamaican–East Indian relations in Jamaica, 1845–1945: A preliminary analysis. *Caribbean Quarterly, 32*(3–4), 14–26.

Sorrells, K. (2013). *Intercultural communication: Globalization and social justice*. Thousand Oaks, CA: Sage.

Straubhaar, J. D. (2008, November 25). Global, hybrid or multiple? Cultural identities in the age of satellite TV and the Internet. *Nordicom Review, 29*(2), 11–30. Retrieved from http://www.nordicom.gu.se/sites/default/files/kapitel-pdf/270_straubhaar.pdf

Taylor, S. (2003). *False prophet: Field notes from the punk underground*. Middletown, CT: Wesleyan University Press.

Thompson, S. (2004). *Punk productions: Unfinished business*. Albany: State University of New York Press.

Traber, D. S. (2001). L.A.'s "white minority": Punk and the contradictions of self-marginalization. *Cultural Critique, 48*, 30–63.

Wulfhorst, C., & Vianna, E. (2012). Communicating new forms of belonging in the transnational space of capoeira. In D. Cogo, M. ElHajji, & A. Huertas (Eds.), *Diaspora, migration, communication technologies and transnational identities* (pp. 85–104). Bellaterra: Institut de la Comunicació, Universitat Autònoma de Barcelona. Retrieved from http://incom.uab.cat/diasporas/download/diaporas_migraciones_tic_identidades_04.pdf

CHAPTER 13

Abu El-Haj, T. R. (2009). Becoming citizens in an era of globalization and transnational migration: Re-imagining citizenship as critical practice. *Theory Into Practice, 48*(4), 274–282.

Bacon, D. (2002, August 21). *Binational Oaxacan indigenous migrant organizers face new century*. Silver City, NM: Americas Program, Interhemispheric Resource Center. Retrieved from http://www.hartford-hwp.com/archives/41/255.html

Bartolomé, M. A. (1997). *Gente de costumbre y gente de razón: Las identidades étnicas en México* [People of reason and people of tradition: Ethnic identities in Mexico]. México, DF: Siglo XXI Editores.

Blackwell, M. (2009, September–December). Mujer rebelde: Testimonio de Odilia Romero Hernández [Rebellious woman. A testimony by Odilia Romero Hernández]. *Desacatos, 31*, 147–156.

Bonfil Batalla, G. (1996). *México profundo: Reclaiming a civilization* (P. A. Denis, Trans.). Austin: University of Texas Press. (Original work published in 1987)

Bourne, R. (1916, July). Transnational America. *Atlantic Monthly, 118*, 86–97.

Cloud, D. (2004). "To veil the threat of terror": Afghan women and the < clash of civilizations > in the imagery of the U.S. war on terrorism. *Quarterly Journal of Speech, 90*, 285–306.

Cohen, J. (2006, March 8). Poll: Americans skeptical of Islam and Arabs. *ABC News*. Retrieved from http://abcnews.go.com/US/story?id = 1700599

Corntassel, J. (2012). Re-envisioning resurgence: Indigenous pathways to decolonization and sustainable self-determination. *Decolonization, Indigeneity, Education & Society, 1*(1), 86–101.

Cruz, Y. (2005). *Sueños binacionales* [Binational dreams] [Documentary]. Oaxaca, Mexico: Petate Productions.

Diffendal, C. (2006). The modern hijab: Tool of agency, tool of oppression. *Chrestomathy, 5*, 129–136.

Domínguez Santos, R. (2004). *The FIOB experience*. In J. Fox & G. Rivera-Salgado (Eds.), *Indigenous Mexican migrants in the United States* (pp. 69–79). La Jolla: Center for U.S.-Mexican Studies, University of California, San Diego.

Droogsma, R. A. (2007). Redefining hijab: American Muslim women's standpoints on veiling. *Journal of Applied Communication Research, 35*(3), 294–319.

El Guindi, F. (1999). *Veil: Modesty, privacy, and resistance*. New York: Berg.

Gershon, I. (2011). Neoliberal agency. *Current Anthropology, 52*(4), 537–555.

Goldring, L. (2001). Disaggregating transnational social spaces: Gender, place and citizenship in Mexico–US transnational spaces. In L. Pries (Ed.), *New transnational social spaces: International migration and transnational companies in the early twenty-first century* (pp. 59–76). London: Routledge.

Hondagneu-Sotelo, P. (1994). *Gendered transitions: Mexican experiences of immigration*. Berkeley: University of California Press.

Kresge, L. (2007). *Indigenous Oaxacan communities in California: An overview*. Buda, TX: National Center for Farmworker Health. Retrieved from http://www.ncfh.org/?plugin = ecomm&content = item&sku = 7340

Levitt, P. (2001). *Transnational villagers*. Berkeley: University of California Press.

Marshall, T. H. (1998). Citizenship and social class. In G. Shafir (Ed.), *The citizenship debates* (pp. 93–111). Minneapolis: University of Minnesota Press. (Original work published in 1963)

Mercado, A. (2011). *Grassroots cosmopolitanism: Transnational communication and citizenship practices among indigenous Mexican immigrants in the United States*. Unpublished doctoral dissertation, University of California, San Diego.

Mercado, A. (2013). *El Tequio*: Social capital, civic advocacy journalism and the construction of a transnational public sphere by Mexican indigenous migrants in the US. *Journalism: Theory, Practice and Criticism*. doi:10.1177/1464884913509782

Miller, T. (2001). Introducing . . . cultural citizenship. *Social Text, 19*(4), 1–5.

Poole, D. (2007). Mestizaje, distinción y presencia cultural: La visión desde Oaxaca. In M. De la Cadena (Ed.), *Formaciones de indianidad: Articulaciones raciales, mestizaje y nación en América Latina* (pp. 197–232). Bogotá-Lima: Editorial Envión.

Portes, A. (1998). Social capital: Its origins and applications in modern sociology. *Annual Review of Sociology, 24*, 1–25.

Portes, A. (2006, July 31). NAFTA and Mexican immigration. *Border Battles: The U.S. Immigration Debates*. Brooklyn, NY: Social Science Research Council. Retrieved from http://borderbattles.ssrc.org/Portes/

Portes, A., Guarnizo, L. E., & Landolt, P. (1999, March). The study of transnationalism: Pitfalls and promise of an emergent research. *Ethnic and Racial Studies, 22*, 217–237.

Putnam, R. D. (2000). *Bowling alone: The collapse and revival of American community*. New York: Simon & Schuster.

Rivera-Salgado, G. (2002). Cross-border grassroots organizations and the indigenous migrant experience. In D. Brooks & J. Fox (Eds.), *Cross-border learning: Lessons from Mexico-US social movement coalitions*. La Jolla: Center for U.S.-Mexican Studies, University of California, San Diego.

Rivera-Salgado, G. (2011, January). Decolonization workshop. Los Angeles, CA: Frente Indígena de Organizaciones Binacionales.

Rogers, A. (2010, August). *Mediated cosmopolitanism? The other's mediated dialogical space on BBC World's* Hardtalk. Unpublished doctoral dissertation, London School of Economics and Political Science.

Romero Hernández, O., Maldonado Vásquez, C., Domínguez Santos, R., Blackwell, M., & Velasco, L. (2013). Género, generación y equidad: Los retos del liderazgo indígena binacional entre México y Estados Unidos en la experiencia del FIOB. In C. Hale & L. Stephen (Eds.), *Otros saberes: Investigaciones colaborativas de los pueblos afro-descendientes e indígenas en América Latina* (pp. 75–100). Santa Fe, NM: School of Advanced Research Press.

Shafir, G. (1998). Introduction. In G. Shafir (Ed.), *The citizenship debates* (pp. 1–28). Minneapolis: University of Minnesota Press.

Sorrells, K. (2013). *Intercultural communication: Globalization and social justice.* Thousand Oaks, CA: Sage.

Sorrells, K., & Nakagawa, G. (2008). Intercultural communication praxis and the struggle for social responsibility and social justice. In O. Swartz (Ed.), *Transformative communication studies: Culture, hierarchy, and the human condition* (pp. 23–61). Leicester, UK: Troubador.

Steet, L. (2000). *Veils and daggers: A century of* National Geographic's *representation of the Arab world.* Philadelphia, PA: Temple.

Tilly, C. (2007). Trust networks in transnational migration. *Sociological Forum, 22*(1), 3–25.

Velasco-Ortiz, L. (2002, May–August). Agentes étnicos transnacionales: Las organizaciones de indígenas migrantes en la frontera México-Estados Unidos. *Estudios Sociológicos, 20,* 335–369. México City: El Colegio de México.

Wenger, E. (1998). *Communities of practice: Learning, meaning, and identity.* Cambridge, UK: Cambridge University Press.

Witteborn, S. (2004). Of "being an Arab woman" before and after September 11: The enactment of communal identities in talk. *Howard Journal of Communication, 15,* 83–99.

Zepeda, E., Wise, T., & Gallagher, K. (2009). *Rethinking trade policy for development: Lessons from Mexico under NAFTA.* Washington, DC: Carnegie Endowment for International Peace. Retrieved from http://ase.tufts.edu/gdae/Pubs/rp/CarnegieNAFTADec09.pdf

Zouaoui, N. (2012, September 12). Fear, anger and politics. *Al Jazeera.* Retrieved from http://www.aljazeera.com/programmes/aljazeeraworld/2012/08/2012829125952344368.html

CHAPTER 14

Albrecht, A., & Brewer, R. M. (1990). *Bridges of power: Women's multicultural alliances.* Philadelphia, PA: New Society.

Anzaldúa, G. (1999). *Borderlands/La Frontera: The new mestiza* (2nd ed.). San Francisco, CA: Aunt Lute Books.

Ashcroft, B., Griffiths, G., & Tiffin, H. (Eds.). (2006). *The postcolonial studies reader* (2nd ed.). New York: Routledge.

Baraka, I. A. (1963). *Blues people: Negro music in white America.* New York: W. Morrow.

Carrillo Rowe, A. (2008). *Power lines: On the subject of feminist alliances.* Durham, NC: Duke University Press.

Chang, J. (2005). *Can't stop won't stop: A history of the hip-hop generation.* New York: Picador.

Charmaz, K. (2011). Grounded theory methods in social justice research. In N. K. Denzin & Y. S. Lincoln (Eds.), *The SAGE handbook of qualitative research* (4th ed., pp. 359–380). Thousand Oaks, CA: Sage.

Chavez, K. R. (2007). *Coalitional politics and confronting the constructions of queers and migrants in the state of Arizona.* Unpublished doctoral dissertation, Arizona State University, Tempe.

Collier, M. J. (Ed.). (2003). *Intercultural alliances: Critical transformation.* Thousand Oaks, CA: Sage.

Collins, P. H. (1990). *Black feminist thought: Knowledge, consciousness, and the politics of empowerment.* Winchester, MA: Unwin Hyman.

DeTurk, S. (2011). Allies in action: The communicative experiences of people who challenge social injustice on behalf of others. *Communication Quarterly, 59*(5), 1–21.

Gandhi, N., & Shah, N. (2006). Inter movement dialogues: Breaking barriers, building bridges. *Development, 49,* 72–76.

Gray, M. L. (2009). "Queer Nation is dead/long live Queer Nation": The politics and poetics of social movement and media representation. *Critical Studies in Media Communication, 26*(3), 212–236. doi:10.1080/15295030903015062

Hale, C. R. (2006). Activist research v. cultural critique: Indigenous land rights and the contradictions of politically engaged anthropology. *Cultural Anthropology, 21,* 96–120.

Harding, S. (1991). *Whose science/whose knowledge?* Milton Keynes, UK: Open University Press.

Hartsock, N. C. M. (1983). The feminist standpoint: Developing the ground for a specifically feminist historical materialism. In S. Harding & M. B. Hintikka (Eds.), *Discovering reality: Feminist perspectives on epistemology, metaphysics, methodology, and philosophy of science* (283–310). Boston, MA: D. Reidel.

Kemmis, S., & McTaggart, R. (2000). Participatory action research. In N. K. Denzin & Y. S. Lincoln (Eds.), *The SAGE handbook of qualitative research* (2nd ed., pp. 567–605). Thousand Oaks, CA: Sage.

Kitwana, B. (2006). *Why white kids love hip-hop: Wankstas, wiggers, wannabes and the new reality of race in America.* New York: Basic Civitas Books.

Lichterman, P. (1999). Talking identity in the public sphere: Broad visions and small spaces in sexual identity politics. *Theory and Society, 28*(1), 101–104.

Lugones, M. C., & Spelman, E. V. (1983). Have we got a theory for you! Feminist theory, cultural imperialism and the demand for "the woman's voice." *Women's Studies International Forum, 6,* 573–581.

Macedo, D., & Gounari, P. (2005). *The globalization of racism.* Boston, MA: University of Massachusetts Press.

Madison, D. S. (2005). *Critical ethnography.* Thousand Oaks, CA: Sage.

Maguire, P. (1987). *Doing participatory research: A feminist approach.* Amherst: Center for International Education, School of Education, University of Massachusetts.

Moraga, C., & Anzaldúa, G. (1983). *This bridge called my back: Writings by radical women of color.* New York: Kitchen Table/Women of Color Press.

Reagon, B. J. (1983). Coalition politics: Turning the century. In B. Smith (Ed.), *Home girls: A black feminist anthology.* New York: Kitchen Table/Women of Color Press.

Sorrells, K. (2013). *Intercultural communication: Globalization and social justice.* Thousand Oaks, CA: Sage.

Speed, S. (2006). At the crossroads of human rights and anthropology: Toward a critically engaged activist research. *American Anthropologist, 108,* 66–76.

Winant, H. (2001). *The world is a ghetto: Race and democracy since World War II.* New York: Basic Books.

Index

Note: Page numbers in *italics* indicate figures and tables.

About the Editors

Kathryn Sorrells (PhD, University of New Mexico, 1999) is professor of communication studies at California State University, Northridge, and currently serving as department chair. Kathryn's diverse research interests include globalization and intercultural communication, the commodification of culture, intercultural conflict, social justice, and global movements for justice and peace. Kathryn is author of the book *Intercultural Communication: Globalization and Social Justice* (2nd edition, SAGE Publications, 2016), which retheorizes intercultural communication in the context of globalization, highlighting the significance of history, power, and global institutions on intercultural communication. Kathryn has published numerous articles and book chapters on globalization and social justice, the commodification of culture, intercultural praxis, and intercultural training in the global context in journals and volumes such as *The Handbook of Critical Intercultural Communication* and *The Routledge Handbook of Intercultural Communication*.

Kathryn is cofounder of Civil Discourse & Social Change at California State University, Northridge, an initiative that seeks to engender critical consciousness, academic engagement, and advocacy to create a more equitable and socially just campus, community, and world. She has received numerous awards for founding and directing the Communicating Common Ground Project, an innovative community action research project that guided students in developing creative alternatives to intercultural and interethnic conflict. Kathryn has a passion for researching and teaching about culture, gender, race, and social justice with people of all ages and in a variety of educational settings. She combines critical, cultural studies and postcolonial perspectives in her research and teaching, balancing both political and aesthetic dimensions.

Sachi Sekimoto (PhD, University of New Mexico, 2011) is assistant professor of communication studies at Minnesota State University, Mankato. Her research focuses on theorizing and critiquing the materiality of culture, identity, ideology, and power through critical and phenomenological perspectives. Her scholarly work has appeared in *Journal of International and Intercultural Communication* and *Communication Quarterly*, in which she developed alternative ways of theorizing identity by focusing on the phenomenological significance of spatial, temporal, and embodied experiences in intercultural and transnational contexts. She is currently writing about and researching the cultural politics of the senses, examining the social and embodied construction of sensory experiences as a source of meaning, knowledge, and production/reproduction of power. She teaches undergraduate and graduate courses in intercultural communication, gender and communication, communication theory, critical pedagogy, and courses related to cultural studies and globalization.

About the Contributors

Amer F. Ahmed (ABD doctoral candidate in adult and higher education, University of South Dakota, 2014) serves as dean of the sophomore class and director of the Intercultural Center at Swarthmore College, associate faculty at the Summer Institute for Intercultural Communication, and a member of SpeakOut: Institute for Democratic Leadership and Culture. An individual with eclectic personal and professional experience, he is a hip-hop activist, spoken-word poet, diversity consultant, and college administrator, channeling his diverse experiences into facilitating effective intercultural development. Amer's education in anthropology and black studies, professional experience in higher education, and extensive global experience support his efforts to address issues of social justice that continue to challenge traditionally marginalized communities. He is also engaged in the field of intercultural communication, with a focus on a developmental approach to intercultural competency. Such approaches have been useful in his work in organizational assessment and development, inclusive human resource management, workshop facilitation, public speaking, leadership development, and student support.

Bryant Keith Alexander (PhD, Southern Illinois University–Carbondale, 1998) is professor of communication and performance studies, and serves as dean of the College of Communication and Fine Arts at Loyola Marymount University. He is the coeditor of *Performance Theories in Education: Power, Pedagogy, and the Politics of Identity* (Erlbaum Press, 2005), with education scholars Gary L. Anderson and Bernardo P. Gallegos. He is the author of *Performing Black Masculinity: Race, Culture, and Queer Identity* (Alta Mira, 2006), *The Performative Sustainability of Race: Reflections on Black Culture and the Politics of Identity* (Peter Lang, 2012), and the forthcoming *Storying the Educational Self: Autocritography, Critical Film Pedagogy, and the Imagined Classroom* (Peter Lang Press). His work appears in such volumes as the *Handbook of Performance Studies*, *Handbook of Critical and Indigenous Methodologies*, *Handbook of Communication and Instruction*, *Handbook of Critical Intercultural Communication*, and *Handbook of Autoethnography*.

Carlo Ammatuna (BA, Santa Clara University, 2010) was a nominee for the Santa Clara University Department of Communication Prize based on the quality of his coursework, commitment to communication ethics, and service to others. As a first-generation American whose worldview was shaped on both sides of the border between the United States and Mexico, Carlo was drawn to study and research intercultural communication, globalization, and transnational economics. His studies led him to explore these areas as they applied to a small region in the Mexican border state of Chihuahua, where his family is from. He is currently applying his passion for communication in a new setting, contributing to social change with a marketing team at a leading Sacramento advertising agency.

Nilanjana R. Bardhan (PhD, Ohio University, 1998) is professor in the Department of Communication Studies at Southern Illinois University–Carbondale. She is the coauthor of *Cultivating Cosmopolitanism for Intercultural Communication* (Routledge, 2013) and coeditor of *Identity Research and Communication* (Lexington Books, 2012) and *Public Relations in Global Cultural Contexts* (Routledge, 2011). She has published several book chapters, and articles in journals such as the *Journal of International and Intercultural Communication, Journal of Public Relations Research, Journal of Communication Management, Mass Communication and Society, Communication Education, International Journal of Strategic Communication,* and *Journal of Health Communication.* Her research spans two areas: intercultural communication and public relations. Her current work focuses on critical cosmopolitanism and issues of identity, culture, and communication, specifically within the conditions of postcolonial globality.

Christopher Brown (PhD, University of New Mexico, 2009) is an assistant professor and director of Graduate Studies in the Department of Communication Studies at Minnesota State University, Mankato. His scholarly research exploring the discourses of white supremacist groups and white male elites' constructions of race transcendence on President Barack Obama appeared in the *Howard Journal of Communications* and *Communication Monographs,* respectively.

Yea-Wen Chen (PhD, University of New Mexico, 2010) is assistant professor in the School of Communication Studies at Ohio University. Her research examines how partners communicate about, relate across, and negotiate intersecting identity positions in ways that hinder and/or facilitate intercultural interactions. She is currently working on a grant-funded project in partnership with a pan-Asian nonprofit organization to focus on identity, storytelling, and community organizing. She has received numerous Top (Four) Paper Awards at international, national, and regional communication conferences. Her work appears in such journals as *Communication Monographs, Journal of International and Intercultural Communication, Journal of Intercultural Communication Research,* and *Howard Journal of Communications,* and she has also contributed invited chapters and online publications.

Hsin-I Cheng (PhD, Bowling Green State University, 2006) is associate professor in the Department of Communication at Santa Clara University. Her research focuses on everyday identity productions and reproductions in the context of global migrations. She is the author of *Culturing Interface: Identity, Communication, and Chinese Transnationalism* (Peter Lang, 2008), and her work has been published in *Journal of Intercultural Communication, Journal of International and Intercultural Communication, Language and Intercultural Communication,* and *Women and Language.*

Mary Jane Collier (PhD, University of Southern California, 1982) is professor of communication at the University of New Mexico. Professor Collier has been a visiting fellow/scholar at the University of Cape Town, South Africa; Birkbeck College, the University of London; and Corrymeela Centre for Reconciliation, Ballycastle, Northern Ireland. Her latest book is *Community Engagement and Intercultural Praxis: Dancing With Difference in Diverse Contexts* (Peter Lang, 2014). Her work appears in the *Journal of International and Intercultural Communication, Negotiation and Conflict Management Research, International Journal of Intercultural Relations, Communication Monographs, Communication Quarterly,* and *Western Journal of Communication,* as well as in various edited books. She has received the

Distinguished Scholarship Award in the International and Intercultural Communication Division of the National Communication Association, Feminist Scholar Award in the Organization for Research on Women and Communication, and a Spotlight Scholar Award in International and Intercultural Communication, Western States Communication Association. She is a founding board member of International Peace Initiatives.

Melissa L. Curtin (PhD, University of New Mexico, 2007) holds an interdisciplinary appointment at the University of California, Santa Barbara, where she is researcher and coordinator of special projects in language, culture, and communication, and adjunct assistant professor of linguistics, with affiliations to the Department of Communication and the Department of Global Studies. Her research focuses on "identity politics and belonging," investigating ways that language and other social semiotic processes are used (1) in processes of identification and differentiation, (2) in the social construction of place, and (3) in positioning sociocultural groups within frames of "differential belonging." Integrating theorizations of language, identity, globalization, and intercultural communication, her critical ethnographic research is published in several edited volumes, such as *The Handbook of Critical Intercultural Communication*; *Seeking Identity: Language in Society*; *Linguistic Landscape: Expanding the Scenery*; and *Conflict, Exclusion, and Dissent in the Linguistic Landscape*. Her work also appears in peer-reviewed journals such as *International Journal of Sociology of Language* and *Social Semiotics*.

Sara DeTurk (PhD, Arizona State University, 2004) is associate professor in the Department of Communication at the University of Texas at San Antonio. Having worked in training, group facilitation, and community development in a wide variety of cultural and intercultural contexts, her research primarily addresses social justice activism, intergroup alliances, and the role of dialogue in shaping ideologies about identity and difference. Her work has been published in books and journals such as *Communication Quarterly, Communication Education, Howard Journal of Communications,* and *Journal of Intergroup Relations*. Her most recent project is a book titled *Activism, Alliance Building, and the Esperanza Peace and Justice Center* (Lexington Books, 2014).

Shinsuke Eguchi (PhD, Howard University, 2011) is an assistant professor of intercultural communication in the Department of Communication and Journalism at the University of New Mexico. His research interests focus on critical intercultural communication, GLBTQ (gay, lesbian, bisexual, transgender, queer) communication studies, Asian/Asian American communication studies, and performance studies. His work on cultural and gender issues of identity, performance, and representation appear in *Communication, Culture, and Critique*; *Cultural Studies* ↔ *Critical Methodologies; Howard Journal of Communication*; *Qualitative Research Reports in Communication*; *Journal of Intercultural Communication Research*; and multiple other venues.

Nickesia S. Gordon (PhD, Howard University, 2007) is associate professor of communication at Barry University, Florida. While her research primarily focuses on media, globalization, and culture, particularly in the Jamaican context, she has also published multiple articles and book chapters in the areas of mass media and popular culture, new/social media, and development communication. She is coeditor of *Still Searching for Our Mother's*

Gardens: Experiences of New, Tenure-Track Women of Color at 'Majority' Institutions (University Press of America, 2011) with Marnel N. Niles and author of *Media and the Politics of Culture: The Case of Television Privatization and Media Globalization in Jamaica 1990–2007* (Universal Publishers, 2008). In 2012, she received the National Communication Association, African American Communication and Culture Division's Outstanding Book Chapter Award.

Richie Neil Hao (PhD, Southern Illinois University–Carbondale, 2009) is associate director of academic affairs at Columbia College Hollywood. At the time of his contribution to this reader, he was assistant professor of communication studies at the University of Denver. His research interests are in the areas of critical intercultural communication, communication pedagogy, and performance studies. More specifically, he is interested in representations and performances of Asian Pacific Americans, diasporic hybridity, and whiteness in popular culture, education, and other everyday contexts. He has recently published in *Cultural Studies ↔ Critical Methodologies*, *Review of Communication*, and *Text and Performance Quarterly*.

Joshua F. Hoops (PhD, Washington State University, 2012) is assistant professor in the Department of Communication and Theatre at William Jewell College. His research focuses on intersections of space and race, with particular emphasis on discourses of whiteness. He received the Outstanding Dissertation Award in 2013 from the International and Intercultural Communication Division of the National Communication Association for his project *The Spatialization of Whiteness in Migrant Farm Communities*. His research has appeared in *Journal of International and Intercultural Communication*, *Journal of Intercultural Communication Research*, and *Critical Studies in Media Communication*.

Zornitsa D. Keremidchieva (PhD, University of Minnesota, 2007) is a senior lecturer in the Political Science Department and affiliated faculty in women's, gender, and sexuality studies at Macalester College. Her research investigates the rhetorical dimensions of citizenship and politics in national and international contexts, and appears in such journals as the *Quarterly Journal of Speech*, *Argumentation and Advocacy*, *Women and Language*, and *Journal of Argumentation in Context*, as well as in edited collections such as the *SAGE Handbook of Rhetorical Studies* and *SAGE Handbook of Gender and Communication*. She is the recipient of research and teaching awards from the National Communication Association, the International Communication Association, and the University of Minnesota.

Sheena Malhotra (PhD, University of New Mexico, 1999) is professor of gender and women's studies and director for the MA in Humanities Program at California State University, Northridge. She has coauthored a book on call centers in India with Aimee Carrillo Rowe and Kimberlee Perez titled *Answer the Call: Virtual Migrations in Indian Call Centers* (University of Minnesota Press, 2013). Dr. Malhotra has also coedited an anthology on feminism and silence with Dr. Carrillo Rowe. The anthology, titled *Silence and Power: Feminist Reflections at the Edges of Sound* (Palgrave MacMillan, 2013), interrogates the often unexamined assumption that silence is oppressive, to consider the multiple possibilities silence enables.

S. Lily Mendoza (PhD, Arizona State University, 2000) is associate professor of culture and communication in the Communication and Journalism Department at Oakland University. She is the author of *Between the Homeland and the Diaspora: The Politics of Theorizing Filipino and Filipino American Identities* (Routledge, 2002; revised Philippine edition, 2006) and the lead editor of *Back From the Crocodile's Belly: Philippine Babaylan Studies and the Struggle for Indigenous Memory* (Center for Babaylan Studies, 2013). She has published widely on questions of identity and subjectivity; indigenization studies; cultural politics in national, postnational, and transnational contexts; bridge building across traditions of scholarship; and, more recently, deep ecology, indigenous wisdom, and what it means to be human.

Antonieta Mercado (PhD, University of California, San Diego, 2011) is currently an assistant professor of communication and social justice in the Department of Communication Studies at the University of San Diego. She teaches classes on media and conflict, international communication, diversity, and social action. Her areas of study are cosmopolitan citizenship, advocacy journalism, media and conflict resolution, communication and social justice, immigrant media, transnational indigenous movements, decolonization, and indigeneity. Her work has been published in *Journalism: Theory, Practice and Criticism*; *Journal of Border Studies*; *Comunicación y Sociedad*; and other interdisciplinary outlets dedicated to communication, citizenship, and social justice research. She is a native of Mexico.

Eddah M. Mutua (PhD, University of Wales, Aberystywth, United Kingdom, 2000) is associate professor in the Department of Communication Studies at St. Cloud State University, Minnesota. She teaches in the area of intercultural communication. Her research focuses on peace communication in postconflict societies in East Africa, with a special interest in the role of women in peace building. She is known for her research on women and community-driven peace-building initiatives in postgenocide Rwanda. In the United States, her scholarship focuses on East African refugee and host communities' interactions in Central Minnesota, critical service learning as a pedagogical practice in peace education, and African and African American relations. Her publications appear in *Qualitative Inquiry*, *Africa Media Review*, *African Yearbook of Rhetoric*, *Women and Language,* and several edited books. Dr. Mutua has received numerous awards for her nationally recognized service-learning project on intercultural and interracial relations in Central Minnesota.

Gordon Nakagawa (PhD, Southern Illinois University–Carbondale, 1987) is Emeritus Professor of the Departments of Communication Studies and Asian American Studies at California State University, Northridge (CSUN). His research has examined contemporary discourses on difference, diversity, and marginalization, including studies of Japanese American incarceration narratives. He is the founding chair of the Asian Pacific American Caucus and the Asian Pacific American Communication Studies Division of the National Communication Association (NCA). The NCA recognized his work in a 2003 Spotlight Panel on Scholarship, citing his career of "outstanding research, service, mentorship, and teaching contributions to Equal Opportunity, Asian American Studies, and the field of Communication." He has also served as the director of Equity and Diversity at CSUN and as the director of Diversity Integration at Hamline University. He is currently a consultant on diversity and equity in higher education.

Mark P. Orbe (PhD, Ohio University, 1993) is professor of communication and diversity in the School of Communication at Western Michigan University, where he also holds a joint appointment in gender and women's studies. His research and teaching focuses on the inextricable relationship between culture, power, and communication as manifested in a variety of contexts. Professor Orbe has published more than 100 books, articles, and book chapters, and received numerous awards for his teaching, research, and service.

Rubén Ramírez-Sánchez (PhD, University of New Mexico, 2007) is associate professor at the School of Communication of the University of Puerto Rico, Río Piedras. His research interests revolve around the political economy of emergent media and the network society, resistance to capitalism from a digital context, visual culture, and software studies. His recent work includes punk media networks, the political economy of crowdsourcing, and the semiotics of metadata. He is also a musician and digital designer.

Andy Reynolds (Columbia Graduate School of Journalism, 1970) has more than four decades of successful experience consulting, teaching, and training in race and gender relations, workplace diversity, and customer service. Andy is on the faculty of the Summer Institute for Intercultural Communication, which attracts a prestigious global faculty and student body. He is past president of SIETAR-USA (Society for Intercultural Educators, Trainers and Researchers). Andy's commitment and involvement in the business and education communities has resulted in his receiving a number of local and national leadership awards.

Karambu Ringera (PhD, University of Denver, 2008) earned an MA in media studies from the University of Natal; an MA in theology, peace, and justice at the Iliff School of Theology; and a PhD in intercultural communication at the University of Denver. She is the founder and president of International Peace Initiatives, based in Meru, Kenya. The international nonprofit, nongovernmental organization conducts programs of peace building, reconciliation, and women's grassroots organizing throughout Africa, and the design and successful implementation of a working model of Amani homes of peace for orphans and vulnerable children in Kenya. Her published work appears in *World Pulse* and many books on international community engagement and conflict transformation. In 2012 she was a recipient of the African International Achievers Award.

Donna M. Stringer (PhD, University of California, Davis, 1981) is a cross-cultural consultant. She was founder and president for 27 years of a successful organization development company specializing in cross-cultural issues, located in Seattle. A social psychologist with more than 40 years' experience as a manager, teacher, researcher, and writer, Donna specializes in cross-cultural instructional design, cultural values, team building, and culture change strategies for organizations in the United States, Asia, Latin America, and Europe. She has coauthored three books, *52 Activities for Exploring Values Differences* (Intercultural Press, 2003), *52 Activities for Improving Cross-Cultural Communication* (Intercultural Press, 2009), and *52 Activities for Successful International Transitions* (Intercultural Press, 2014), and has written many articles and book chapters on leadership, diversity, gender, and generations. She was recognized as a "Diversity Legend" by the International Society for Diversity and Inclusion Professionals in 2012.

Taj Suleyman (MA, University of the Pacific, 2014) holds an MA in intercultural relations, which was completed in conjunction with the Intercultural Communication Institute in Portland, Oregon. Taj is an associate facilitator in personal leadership methodology, focusing on intercultural and social justice theoretical frameworks to better understand intercultural negotiation processes. In diversity training sessions with local government agencies, he supports facilitators in improving training models to meet the needs of various communities. Throughout his 10-year career working with humanitarian organizations, he has assisted and empowered the integration of refugees and immigrants into U.S. society. In his most recent position as project manager with the Center for Intercultural Organizing, he developed and managed committees that served the needs of immigrant and refugee communities. As a liaison between different groups, he established systems that enable communities to empower themselves and contribute to society as a whole.

Sachiko Tankei-Aminian (PhD, Southern Illinois University–Carbondale, 2009) is assistant professor in the Department of Communication and Philosophy at Florida Gulf Coast University. She teaches and studies intercultural, interracial communication and Japanese pop culture from interpretive and critical perspectives. Her current areas of research include cultural adaptation, intercultural identity, and the concept of privilege in relation to racism. She uses various methods in her scholarly work, such as personal narrative, autoethnography, performance, and filmmaking. She created an autoethnographic performance called "On Becoming Japerican," which was originally performed at Southern Illinois University–Carbondale in 2004. From 2004 to 2007, she performed at universities and in conferences. The video version of "On Becoming Japerican" appears in *Liminalities: A Journal of Performance Studies.* Her article regarding crosscultural adaptation appears in *A Forum on Language and Communication.* She also cocreated a number of films with Farshad Aminian-Tankei, including *What Would You Like to Become? Iranian Children's Voices.*

Chie Torigoe (PhD, University of New Mexico, 2011) is an associate professor in the Department of Literature at Seinan Gakuin University in Fukuoka, Japan, where she teaches intercultural communication and communication theories to Japanese undergraduate and graduate students. Her research interests include discourse on race and identity, and racism in Japan. She is currently involved in two research projects funded by the Ministry of Education, Culture, Sports, Science, and Technology in Japan. One explores multiculturalism and intersecting identities in Japan, and the other focuses on critical intercultural communication pedagogy.

Chigozirim Ifedapo Utah (MA, Wichita State University, 2010) is a doctoral candidate at University of Nebraska, Lincoln. Her research centers on how "African problems" are discursively constructed by social actors in the context of globalization, and how these constructions help and hinder social change organizing. Her pedagogical work focuses on developing learner-centered models of teaching in higher education.

Gerardo Villalobos-Romo (MBA, Tecnológico de Monterrey, Guadalajara, Mexico, 1995) is a doctoral candidate at the Institute of Communication Research at the University of Illinois. He was professor and director of the Department of Communication and Humanities at the Tecnológico de Monterrey, Guadalajara Campus, México. He has participated in numerous national and international congresses, and has conducted research in the fields of education and communication. His current research focuses on media, migration, and communication technology in a transnational context. He has received multiple recognitions as a scholar and teacher.

Gust A. Yep (PhD, University of Southern California, 1990) is professor of communication studies, core graduate faculty of sexuality studies, and faculty in the EdD program in educational leadership at San Francisco State University. His research focuses on communication at the intersections of culture, gender, sexuality, and health. In addition to three books, he has published more than 70 articles in (inter)disciplinary journals and anthologies. He is the recipient of a number of research, teaching, mentoring, and community service awards, including the 2006 National Communication Association Randy Majors Memorial Award for Outstanding Lesbian, Gay, Bisexual, and Transgender Scholarship in Communication, and the 2011 San Francisco State University Distinguished Faculty Award for Professional Achievement (Researcher of the Year).

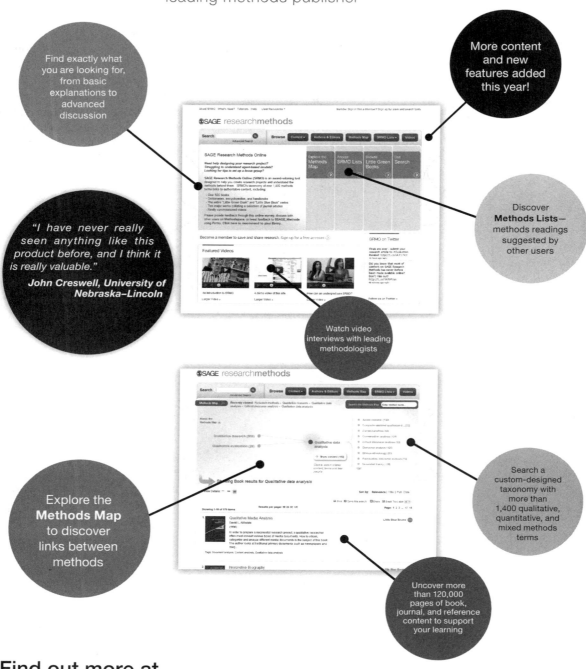

⑤SAGE research**methods**

The essential online tool for researchers from the world's leading methods publisher

Find exactly what you are looking for, from basic explanations to advanced discussion

More content and new features added this year!

"I have never really seen anything like this product before, and I think it is really valuable."

John Creswell, University of Nebraska–Lincoln

Discover **Methods Lists**— methods readings suggested by other users

Watch video interviews with leading methodologists

Explore the **Methods Map** to discover links between methods

Search a custom-designed taxonomy with more than 1,400 qualitative, quantitative, and mixed methods terms

Uncover more than 120,000 pages of book, journal, and reference content to support your learning

Find out more at
www.sageresearchmethods.com